PHP

DEVELOPER'S DICTIONARY

SAMS 201 West 103rd Street, Indianapolis, Indiana 46290

PHP Developer's Dictionary

Copyright © 2001 by Sams Publishing

International Standard Book Number: 0-672-32029-0

Library of Congress Catalog Card Number: 00-105843

First Printing: December 2000

02   01   00   4   3   2   1

Trademarks

Warning and Disclaimer

Acquisitions Editor
Shelley Johnston

Development Editor
Scott D. Meyers

Managing Editor
Charlotte Clapp

Project Editor
Dawn Pearson

Copy Editor
Mike Henry

Indexer
Johnna Dinse

Proofreader
Juli Cook

Technical Editor
Dallas Releford

Team Coordinator
Amy Patton

Interior Design
Gary Adair

Cover Design
Alan Clements

Contents at a Glance

Table of Contents

Contents

About the Authors

R. Allen Wyke

R. Allen Wyke, of Durham, North Carolina, is a Director of Product Technology at Engage's Software division—a profile-driven, online marketing solutions company. At Engage, he works with product managers, product marketing, and engineering to ensure that products have the proper vision and direction in both the online and offline worlds. He is constantly working with XML, JavaScript, Perl, PHP, and various other Internet technologies in implementing the online marketing software and services that Engage has to offer.

He co-authored *JavaScript Unleashed, 3rd Edition*; *Pure JavaScript*; *The Perl 5 Programmer's Reference*; and *The Official Netscape Navigator 4 Book*. He also contributed to two other titles on the topics of Web development: *HTML Publishing on the Internet, 2nd Edition* and *The HTML 4 Programmer's Reference*. In addition, he used to write a weekly column about Windows and UNIX integration for ITworld.com and wrote the monthly "Webmaster" column for SunWorld.

Michael J. Walker

Michael J. Walker, of Knightdale, North Carolina is a Senior Systems Engineer for Engage, Inc. At Engage, he currently serves as a technical resource for the field pre-sales engineers. His previous work with Engage included heading the consulting and custom development teams as well as being a developer of custom Web applications using C/C++, HTML, JavaScript, and ODBC.

While at Engage, he has also provided consultation to many of the top-tier Web sites in the U.S. and throughout the world. He has more than ten years of computer industry experience in various roles, including data processing operations, Internet software implementation, and client/server development. He has developed software on many platforms ranging from micro-controllers to mainframes, using Assembly language, C/C++, SQL, Visual Basic, PowerBuilder, and Java. He holds Bachelor of Science degrees in Theoretical Computer Science and Electrical Engineering from Northern Illinois University.

Robert Cox

Robert Cox, originally from Winslow, Arizona and now residing in Raleigh, North Carolina, is the Manager of Technical Support at Engage Technologies. He is a graduate of Brigham Young University with a Bachelor of Science degree in Electronics Engineering Technology. He has a love of computers that dates back to 1980 when he continually snuck out of his high school American History class to work on programs in the local college computer lab.

He has designed many Web pages, the bulk of them using PHP and ColdFusion to generate content dynamically. Much of his formal development experience was gained on the job working for Developer Support at Novell, Inc. There he was able to learn the intricacies of the C and C++ programming languages as well as to gain valuable networking experience.

Dedications

R. Allen Wyke

For Bryant, Emily, Alex, and Jaclyn (the newest edition) - you all make me happy and proud to be an uncle.

Michael J. Walker

To Hien Do, who taught me what it means to work hard, and what rewards come with it.

Robert Cox

To Kaitlin and Austin, the best things that could happen to a daddy. I love you both.

Acknowledgments

R. Allen Wyke

First, I would like to thank Bob Kern of TIPS Technical Publishing—yet another project complete, my friend! I would also like to thank my co-authors, Mike and Rob, who helped push me hard to make this the best possible reference out there on PHP. I would also like to thank Shelley Johnston, who has been one of the most wonderful Acquisition Editors I have ever worked with, and Scott Meyers, who is one of the hardest-working Development Editors I have seen. In addition, I would like to thank the rest of the Sams team for making this book a success.

Finally, I would like to thank the woman in my life, J, who puts up with my crazy schedule and personality when working on these projects. She has truly been a gift and the most wonderful thing that has ever happened to me.

Michael J. Walker

I would also like to thank all the people Allen mentioned earlier who helped this book come together and become an invaluable desktop reference. In addition, I thank all my Engage co-workers for the assistance, respect, and camaraderie they have given me.

Finally, to my wife Kendra, I thank you for your endless support in all my career and personal endeavors. I could not ask for more.

Robert Cox

Thanks to Allen, Mike, Bob Kern, and the Sams publishing team for this opportunity to write a book on a subject that I am excited about and find fascinating. Thanks to my beautiful wife and friend, Sheila, for her support. Honey, you put up with a lot. I love you. You're the best! Finally, thanks to my parents for the vision to always push to accomplish goals. You taught me to reach stretch and work to be my best.

I have many friends, co-workers, teachers, and mentors who have, by proxy, contributed to this book. It might not be through the printed word or through direct contribution, but your inspiration, dedication, and enthusiasm have molded me into what I am and have given me a vision of what I want to become. Thanks to you all, and God bless.

Tell Us What You Think!

As the reader of this book, *you* are our most important critic and commentator. We value your opinion and want to know what we're doing right, what we could do better, what areas you'd like to see us publish in, and any other words of wisdom you're willing to pass our way.

You can email or write me directly to let me know what you did or didn't like about this book—as well as what we can do to make our books stronger.

Please note that I cannot help you with technical problems related to the topic of this book, and that due to the high volume of mail I receive, I might not be able to reply to every message.

When you write, please be sure to include this book's title and author as well as your name and phone or fax number. I will carefully review your comments and share them with the author and editors who worked on the book.

Fax: 317-581-4770
E-mail: webdev_sams@mcp.com
Mail: Mark Taber
         Associate Publisher
         Sams Publishing
         201 West 103rd Street
         Indianapolis, IN 46290 USA

INTRODUCTION

Welcome to the *PHP Developer's Dictionary*. We hope that you will find this book the most useful PHP reference available today. This is truly the type of book that should be open next to your workstation, except for those of you who have obtained expert PHP programming status. Even the best of us need to double-check code syntax every once in awhile.

Within the pages of this book you will find a quick introduction to the language and a complete reference to the PHP4 language. As a developer, you might often find yourself scrambling for the correct syntax for a function or maybe some clarification on how something works, and this book intends to fill that void.

Who Should Buy This Book?

Because this is a developer's dictionary, you will not find an in-depth tutorial on the PHP language or complete project code for an application. What you will find is a starter introduction to the language and a complete reference. Because of this, the book is targeted to current PHP developers—developers who need a complete reference of the newest version of the PHP language to keep with them as they program.

Organization of the Chapters

The book is broken into two primary sections. The first, Chapters 1–3, is a brief introduction to the language, and the remaining ten chapters act as a reference.

For those of you who have been programming in PHP for only a short while, you will find that the first section gives you a good understanding of what can be accomplished with PHP and how you might go about it. The rest of you will find an introduction to many topics that you might not have known fall within the PHP domain. This portion of the book will get your mind thinking about how you can exploit these powerful concepts in today's applications.

The second section of the book is pure reference. We have tried to group all the PHP functions and language elements in an easy-to-understand and easy-to-access way, for you, the developer. Because the PHP language is always growing and adding new functions, we also tried to organize it in a manner similar to the official documentation so that you can quickly check online for any new additions, comments, or bug reports.

Writing Conventions

Like all books, we have used a few writing conventions. These are items that you will see throughout the book, and understanding what they mean will better help you use the book. These conventions are as follows:

- **Inline Syntax**—Because this is a book about a programming language, there will be times that we reference language elements or functions in the body of a paragraph. We have used a special monospaced font to signify that these are part of the PHP language. Here is an example:

  "You can use the `phpinfo()` function to…"

- **Italics**—Within a programming book, there are also instances where we need to specify parameters or variables. These are not language elements, but placeholders for where you will plug in the appropriate values. For this, we will put the placeholder in an italic monospaced font. For instance, we might say

  "The `header()` function takes a *header_directive* as its only argument, which…"

- **Notes, Tips, Warnings**—There are many times that we need to give you more information or advice on a topic, but it doesn't really warrant an entire paragraph. So, you will find Notes, Tips, and Warnings interlaced within the chapters to give you a heads up on problem areas, or maybe a URL for an online resource.

In addition to these structural elements of the book, you will see other conventions used in the reference section. Primarily based around the organization of the entries, and to help ensure that you get what you need out of the reference, the entries will have the following:

- **Entry Name**—Each entry in the book will begin with the entry's name. These are organized by topic, subtopic, and then alphabetical. Because the PHP programming language is so rich, there are instances of sub-subtopics, but this should be fairly self-explanatory.

- **Syntax**—After the entry's name you will see a brief syntax definition. This will include the actual syntax that should be used when calling the function, as well as the return type of the function. If there are any parameters passed, the definition will point out the data types of the parameters.

- **Description**—The final element in each entry is a description of what it does. Within this area we will provide more information about the parameters, let you know if the element is new to version 4 of PHP, and provide short code examples when needed.

And that is all we are going to say. Like yourself, we are developers and small talk does nothing but consume time. We appreciate that you took the time to read the Introduction, and now we will return the favor by wishing you well on your use of the *PHP Developer's Dictionary*.

R. Allen Wyke
Michael J. Walker
Robert Cox

PART I
Concept Reference

CHAPTER

CHAPTER 1

Basic PHP

Background and History

In 1994, Rasmus Lerdorf created the predecessor to what has evolved into one of the fastest-growing server-side scripting languages. PHP started as a set of tools that Rasmus used to track users on his personal Web page. In the spring of 1995, Personal Home Page Tools version 1 was introduced. It contained limited server-side–parsed macros and simple utilities such as a guest book and a hit counter. Later that same year, the parser engine was completely rewritten and released as PHP/FI version 2. This version contained a form interpreter and native mSQL database support.

In 1997, PHP took a huge step forward. The parser was completely rewritten by a team of developers led by Zeev Suraski and Andi Gutmans. This parser formed the foundation for version 3 of PHP. The success of PHP is difficult to gauge, but it has been estimated that there are more than 1 million Web sites using PHP and that number is increasing every month. PHP user groups have sprung up all over the globe, many of them swearing allegiance to PHP and predicting the demise of Microsoft's Active Server Pages. Much of this fervor is due to the excitement of PHP's open source policy. The software and source code are available free on the Internet.

Price is not the only factor driving the popularity of PHP. Flexibility, extensibility, and performance are key elements in the success of PHP. Much of the syntax used in PHP was borrowed from C, Perl, and Java. Individuals with basic training in any these languages can pick up PHP's syntax with very little effort. This inherent familiarity also contributes to PHP's increasing popularity.

The current main PHP team includes developers from all over the world. Zeev Suraski and Andi Gutmans are in Israel, Shane Caraveo resides in Florida, Stig Bakken is from Norway, Andrei Zmievski is in Nebraska, Sascha Schumann and Thies C. Arntzen are from Germany, Jim Winstead is from Los Angeles, and the father of PHP, Rasmus Lerdorf, resides in North Carolina. Because of PHP's open source, many developers and hobbyists contribute to the PHP's code. The contributions from this unpaid group of experts add to PHP's popularity and its spectacular feature set.

PHP version 4 is currently in beta and includes many optimizations and feature improvements. These improvements include a compiler, enabling code to run significantly faster. There is support for caching compiled code, a code optimizer, and a formal debugger. PHP 4 also includes better object-oriented syntax, self-contained extensions, and a thread-safe core.

Advantages of PHP 4

PHP has two main competitors: Microsoft's Active Server Pages and Allaire's ColdFusion. PHP has many advantages over these commercial packages. As mentioned previously, one of the main advantages PHP has over ASP and ColdFusion is its price. PHP is completely free and is available for download at hundreds of mirror sites all over the globe. For many, this advantage is the deciding factor; however, there are many more technical reasons to use PHP. PHP has the capability to run on NT and UNIX. It is just as easy to build complex Web sites that run on either platform. This cross-platform compatibility makes the transition from NT to UNIX an easy proposition. Before PHP, converting Web code meant that changing a server operating system was an extremely painful task. Operating-system independence isn't the only advantage PHP has over ASP and ColdFusion. PHP boasts a simple and elegant syntax, object support, and excellent documentation. PHP is also tailored to the Web developer. Other scripting languages require cumbersome coding and expert knowledge to perform tasks that can be done in PHP with just a few function calls. In fact, PHP code can be inserted alongside HTML code with very little performance impact or extra coding.

PHP is also very fast. Any ASP developer can tell you that IIS tends to slow down when parsing an ASP page. Given a moderately powered Web server, PHP rarely, if ever, bogs down under heavy loads. As discussed earlier, PHP 4 will further separate itself from its competitors with the capability to compile and optimize PHP source and cache the compiled source in memory.

In short, the advantages of PHP are

- Speed—Function for function, PHP is faster than ASP.

- Functionality—PHP offers greater functionality for Web developers with the ability to imbed PHP code directly in the HTML source.

- Price—At no cost, PHP is available for download at hundreds of locations all over the Internet.

- Ease of use—PHP has a familiar syntax for those who know popular programming languages.

- Cross-platform support—Developers can use the same code on both NT and UNIX operating systems.

Installation

For the purposes of this book, we will discuss the installation procedure and options at a high level. This discussion covers an overview of the process for the two main operating systems that PHP supports. This chapter is more specific about the installation of PHP with Apache on Linux, but we also discuss the installation process on a Windows NT and IIS4 system.

PHP Installation General Overview

The installation of the PHP module on any Web server assumes that you have a working Web server. In this case, we assume that Apache has been successfully installed on your UNIX machine, or that you have IIS installed on your Windows NT Server and you are able to serve regular HTML pages to a Web browser. Installation procedures and binaries for the Apache Web server are available at the Apache Web site (http://www.apache.org). Installation procedures for IIS are available at Microsoft's site (http://www.microsoft.com). If PHP is to be used on a UNIX system, the source must be compiled using a standard ANSI compiler such as gcc or g++. These compilers are packaged with most Linux distributions, but the compilers are freely available at GNU's site (http://www.gnu.org/gnulist/production).

UNIX Environment with the Apache Web Server

This detailed installation procedure steps through the process of installing PHP as a Dynamically Shared Object (DSO). The alternative to the DSO method is to compile PHP into the Apache Web Server as a static module. The static method is sometimes preferred because of the performance overhead of the DSO. But because of the simplicity of the dynamic method and the ease with which modules can be changed, we describe the DSO method here.

After the Apache Web server is up and running, note the location of the apxs directory of the Apache installation. This should be something like /usr/local/apache_1.3.12/bin/apxs. If you will be installing support for a database, also note the home directory for the database. For MySQL, your home directory might be something like /usr/local/mysql.

You need to obtain the current PHP source from the PHP Web site (http://www.php.net). You will find a file named something like php-4.0.1pl2.tar.gz available for download. Place this file on your system where you have other applications installed. This will likely be /usr/local or /opt.

Uncompress the gzipped file by typing something similar to the following line:

```
gzip php-4.0.1pl2.tar.gz
```

This line reflects the current version of PHP and will vary accordingly.

This will create a .tar file in the current directory. Untar the file by typing

```
tar -xvf php-4.0.1pl2.tar
```

This creates a php-4.0.0 directory and places all the PHP source files inside. Change directories to the php-4.0.0 directory and type

```
./configure --with-mysql=/[path to mysql] --with-apxs=/[path to apxs]
```

where *[path to mysql]* is the path to your MySQL installation and *[path to apxs]* is the path to the Apache apxs directory. Please see the "Configuration Options" section for more details about compiling options into PHP.

This configures your environment and creates the make script. After the configure script is complete, type

```
make
```

This compiles the PHP source into the binary DSO file. If make encounters any errors, it halts execution of the script and displays the error. You must correct the error before compiling again. When the script has completed successfully, type

```
make install
```

This places the DSO module in the appropriate place in the Apache directory structure and makes a few modifications to the httpd.conf file.

The final modification is to edit the httpd.conf file and look for the following lines:

```
# And for PHP 4.x, use:
#
#AddType application/x-httpd-php .php
#AddType application/x-httpd-php-source .phps
```

Delete the #s from the two AddType lines and save the file. This instructs Apache to use the PHP DSO to parse all files ending with the .php extension. If the file is a PHP source file (.phps), special formatting parameters are used to display the code properly. If you would rather name the PHP files with the .php4 extension, this is the place to do so.

You are now ready to test the PHP module. Start the Apache Web server. Create a file called test.php in the Apache server's document root directory. The contents of this file should be

```
<? phpinfo(); ?>
```

Save the file and then call it from your Web browser. The location line should look something like this:

```
http://[hostname]/test.php
```

You should receive a PHP information page that displays the state of some of the PHP variables, CGI variables, session variables, and a host of other information. If you do not see this page, something is wrong and you must repeat the process to verify that all the steps were completed properly.

Windows Environment with Internet Information Server (IIS)

The configuration of PHP on Windows NT and IIS4 is much simpler than the compilation and configuration of PHP on Linux and Apache. You must realize that this simpler install comes with a price, and that price is functionality. PHP was designed from the outset to work in a UNIX environment. PHP's commands are UNIX-based, and you will notice as you read this book that many of the commands and functions are not supported or are not fully functional in a Windows/IIS environment.

This section assumes that you have IIS4 and Windows NT already installed and configured on your server. You must first download the PHP for Windows installation from the PHP Web site (http://www.php.net). Find the Downloads section and download the Win32 binaries. At the time of this writing, the filename is php-4.0.2-Win32.zip.

The first thing you need to do is unzip the PHP package and copy all the .dll files from the distribution to the Windows system directory. This is usually C:\WINNT\SYSTEM32 for Windows NT. Under a normal installation, all the dlls are not usually necessary, but this setup makes it easier to add modules and extensions in the future.

You now need to copy the php.ini-optimized file to the C:\WINNT directory and rename it to php.ini.

Next, start the Microsoft Internet Service Manager. This is usually under the Windows NT 4.0 Option Pack section of the Start menu. Right-click on Default Web Site and choose Properties. Choose the ISAPI Filters tab and select Add. Enter PHP4, or similar descriptive text, as the filter name and then type in the path to the php4isapi.dll filter. This should be C:\WINNT\system32\php4isapi.dll. Apply the changes and then click the Home Directory tab in the Management Console. Click the Configuration button and add a new entry to the application mappings. Enter the path to the php4isapi.dll as the executable. Again, this path should be C:\WINNT\system32\php4isapi.dll. Enter .php as the extension, and make sure that method exclusions are not checked and the script engine checkbox is selected. Click Apply and then click OK.

You must now restart the IIS server by stopping and restarting the NT services. These services are the World Wide Web Publishing service and the IIS Admin service. The IIS Admin service might ask you if it is okay to stop other services; select OK. After these services are stopped, you can restart them in no particular order.

Go back into the Management Console and select the properties of the Default Web Server. Choose the ISAPI Filters tab. If the name of your PHP filter is in the Filters box with a green up arrow, the filter is installed correctly.

You are now ready to test the PHP module. Create a file called test.php in the IIS server's document root directory. The contents of this file should be

```
<? phpinfo(); ?>
```

Save the file and then call it from your Web browser. The location line should look something like this:

```
http://[hostname]/test.php
```

You should receive a PHP information page that displays the state of some of the PHP variables, CGI variables, session variables, and a host of other information. If you do not see this page, something is wrong and you must repeat the process to verify that all the steps were completed properly.

Configuration Options

There are many ways to configure PHP with specific options and behavior. Some options are configured when PHP is compiled; other options are available through the use of the php.ini configuration file. This section describes the different options available in PHP and where and how to configure those options.

Compile-Time Configuration Options

The PHP module has a multitude of configuration options. Many of these can be controlled through the php.ini file (usually located in the /usr/local/lib directory) providing the option is compiled into the PHP module. To view the options available, go to the PHP installation directory and type

```
./configure -help | more
```

This lists all the options and a short description of each. Chapter 12, "PHP Compilation Options," details the options that are available when using the configure script.

An example of a configure command line that includes support for Apache APXS, support for PostgreSQL, and support for MySQL is as follows:

```
./configure -with-apxs=/www/bin/apxs -with-pgsql=/usr/include/pgsql
-with-mysql=/usr/include/mysql
```

Consider only the options that are needed when using this command. If unnecessary options are compiled into PHP, a degradation in performance is likely.

Configuration File Options

Some options in PHP must be compiled into PHP to work, but others are controlled through configuration settings in the .ini file. When settings in the .ini file are used, PHP reads the configuration options from the php.ini only on startup. For the server module versions of PHP, this happens only once when the Web server is started. For the CGI version, it happens every time the PHP CGI is called.

Three different types of configuration options can be made in the .ini file. These are detailed in the following discussion.

php_config_name *string*

This option sets the configuration variable to the specified string value.

Example:

```
include_path = /usr/include/php   ; UNIX: "/path1:/path2"  Win: "\path1;\path2"
doc_root = /www/htdocs            ; the root of the php pages
```

php_config flag_name *on|off*

This option sets the configuration variable on or off. This is a Boolean configuration option with only two valid options.

Example:

```
short_open_tag    = On     ; allow the <? tag.  otherwise, only <?php and
                           ; <script> tags are recognized.
asp_tags = Off     ; allow ASP-style <% %> tags
```

php_config name *integer*

This option sets the configuration variable to the specified integer value.

Example:

```
max_execution_time = 30 ; Maximum execution time of each script, in seconds
memory_limit = 8388608  ; Maximum amount of memory a script may consume (8MB)
```

All the configuration file options are described in Chapter 13, "PHP Directives."

Types, Variables, and Constants

This section describes PHP's use of arrays, strings, type conversions, variables, and constants. No programming language would be complete without these necessary items. If you are familiar with other programming languages, these should be very intuitive. The syntax for most of these items is similar to the C programming language and their functionality is as you would expect. The following sections are not intended to be an exhaustive review of arrays, variables, and type conversions, but rather a basic review.

Arrays

As with every programming language, PHP would be incomplete if it did not include the capability to define and manipulate arrays. PHP supports arrays that are indexed by number and associative arrays. PHP also supports multidimensional arrays.

Arrays are variables that contain multiple elements indexed by numbers or names. This means that a variable called FirstName[1] could contain the value Kaitlin, whereas another variable called FirstName[2] could contain the value Austin. The variable name is FirstName, and the index is the [1] or [2].

The array() function in PHP is used to define an array and assign values to it. This function would be used like this:

```
$CustomerName = array ("Jean", "Loren", "Ted", "Gladys" );
```

The elements in the $CustomerName array can now be accessed by using the variable name and the index in the following way:

```
print "$CustomerName[3]";
```

This would print the name Gladys, which is actually the fourth item in the array. Remember that array indexes begin at 0.

Associative arrays are indexed with strings instead of numbers. This is useful when describing the contents of the element using the index.

To define an associative array, we use the array() function and we must define both the key and value for each element. In the following example, we create an associative array called $Contacts with three elements: FirstName, Phone, and Email.

```
$Contacts = array(Name=>"Eric", Phone=>"289-9272",Email=>"eric@winslow.com");
```

We can now access any of the fields of `$Contacts` like this:

```
print $Contacts[Email];
```

This would print the value `eric@winslow.com`.

PHP also supports multidimensional arrays. A multidimensional array can be thought of as an array of arrays. In other words, we could define the `$Contacts` array to contain multiple entries for different contacts. That definition would look like this:

```
$Contacts[1] = array(Name=>"Eric",Phone=>"289-9272",Email=>"eric@winslow.com");
$Contacts[2] = array(Name=>"Ryan",Phone=>"289-9446",Email=>"ryan@winslow.com");
```

Now, if we want to retrieve Ryan's email address, the code looks like this:

```
print $Contacts[2][Email];
```

PHP also has many functions that enable the programmer to manipulate, sort, and return information about the array. These functions make it easy to access your array information quickly and easily. Details about these functions are described in Chapter 5, "PHP Language Extensions."

Strings

PHP has many functions that enable you to manipulate and format strings. These functions provide methods of determining the length of a string, finding a substring in a string, removing white space from a string, replacing substrings, and changing the case of a string. This section does not discuss all these cases, but it does provide a general overview of these functions.

If you are familiar with the C programming language, you recognize the `printf()` function. This function enables you to output a string and variables in a multitude of different ways. Consider the following example:

```
printf("This is a formatted number: %d\n", 1957 );
```

This prints out the number, 1957, as a decimal value, which is defined by the `%d` specifier. There are other specifiers available to the `printf()` function. These include specifiers that will print the value as a hexadecimal, ASCII, octal, binary, or floating-point number. Chapter 5 discusses this function in detail and describes all the available options.

The strlen() function returns the length of the string. This function is useful for error checking and formatting. The following is an example of how to use this function and what information is returned:

```
$Test = "This is a test string";
print strlen($Test);  // prints out 21
```

The strstr() function returns part of the entire string. The portion of the string that is returned is defined by an integer number. This integer number defines the number of characters to return. A positive number starts counting characters from the front of the string; a negative number counts from the end of the string. An example of this function follows:

```
$date = "03-October-1957";
$Test = substr( $date, 10 )
print $Test; // Prints out the string "03-October";
```

The trim() function is useful when a variable that is to be used has white space or padding that needs to be removed. This function removes the spaces from the beginning and the end of the string. An example of this is

```
$Test = "   A String with leading and trailing spaces   ";
$Test = trim($Test);
print $Test;  // prints out the string without the spaces
```

The strtoupper() and the strtolower() functions convert the specified string to all uppercase or all lowercase, respectively. Often when you are doing string comparisons, it is a problem to test all possible cases. These functions convert the string to one case, and thus make it easier to evaluate comparisons. The following is an example of the strtoupper() and strtolower() functions in use:

```
$Test = "ThIs Is A mIxEd Up StRiNg";
$Upper = strtoupper( $Test );
print $Upper; // prints out the string "THIS IS A MIXED UP STRING"
$Lower = strtolower( $Test );
print $Lower; // prints out the string "this is a mixed up string"
```

This is by no means the entire list of string functions that are available in PHP. The entire list of functions, along with their complete descriptions, is in Chapter 5.

Type Conversion

In many programming languages, it is necessary to declare the variable as some type. Different types of variables are handled in different ways and take different amounts of memory. PHP does not require you to declare a variable's type when the variable is initialized. PHP calculates the variable's type based on what value the variable has. For instance, if a variable has the value of 3, the variable is typed as integer. If the variable has a value of 3.1415927, the variable is typed as a double. Data types in PHP can be integer, double, string, boolean, object, or array.

PHP has some functions to enable you to detect what a variable's type is. The function gettype()returns a variable's type based on the value that is passed into the function. PHP also gives you the ability to set an integer's type by using the settype() function.

Type casting is also supported in PHP. To cast a variable as a certain type, you place the name of the data type in parentheses in front of the variable. For example, to cast a copy of the variable named $pi to a double, the code is

```
$pi = 3.1415927
$copyofpi = (double)$pi;
print $copyofpi;
```

This example prints out the value 3.1415927. If the same variable were cast to an integer, the code would be

```
$pi = 3.1415927
$copyofpi = (integer)$pi;
print $copyofpi;
```

The output of this example would be 3 because the variable would contain no decimal point.

Variables

Variables in PHP come in many forms, but they are always preceded with a dollar sign ($). Variables can contain letters, numbers, and the underscore (_) character. Variables must contain only alphanumeric characters and must not contain any spaces.

PHP also enables you to use something known as *dynamic variables*. A dynamic variable is one in which the variable name can be stored in a variable. This can be quite confusing, but quite useful at the same time. Please consider the following example:

```
$FirstName = "Kaitlin";
```

This variable declaration is the same as

```
$Variable="FirstName";
$$Variable = "Kaitlin";
```

The $Variable variable contains the string "FirstName". You can think of the variable $$Variable as a single $ followed by the value of $Variable or "FirstName".

Constants

Constants are values that are defined in your PHP script and that do not change. Constants are defined by using the define() function. After the constant is defined, it cannot be changed. Constants are accessed by using the name of the constant only. There is no dollar sign preceding the name of the constant. For example, the constant PI is defined like this:

```
define( "PI",3.1415927);
```

To access the value of PI, the code would look like this:

```
$Circumference = PI*($Radius*$Radius);
```

Note that constants are usually defined using all capital letters. PHP also has some internal constants. For instance, the constant __FILE__ returns the name of the file that PHP is currently reading. The constant __LINE__ returns the line number of the file. These constants are normally used when you are generating error messages.

Operators and Mathematical Functions

PHP, like other programming languages, provides functions for performing many types of mathematical functions. Details of these mathematical functions are described in Chapter 5. This section gives you an overview of the mathematical operators and functions that are available in PHP and examples of how to use them.

Expressions and Operators

Mathematical expressions consist of operators and operands. Usually, two operands are connected by an operator to create the expression. Consider this example:

```
6=2+4
```

The numbers 2 and 4 are operands, the operator is the plus (+) sign, and the result is 6. This entire example is referred to as an *expression*.

PHP has four different types of operators: assignment operators, mathematical operators, comparison operators, and logical operators. Assignment operators assign a specific value to a variable. Assignment operators are described in Table 1.1.

Table 1.1   *Assignment Operators*

Operator	Example	Description
=	$x = 2	Assign the number 2 to $x
+=	$x += 2	Assign the value of $x + 2 to $x
-=	$x -= 2	Assign the value of $x - 2 to $x
/=	$x /= 2	Assign the value of $x divided by 2 to $x
*=	$x *= 2	Assign the value of $x multiplied by 2 to $x
%=	$x %= 2	Assign the value of $x to the modulus 2 of $x
.=	$x .= " value"	Assign the value of $x to the value of $x concatenated with " value"

The mathematical operators in PHP do exactly what you would expect. They include the basic addition, subtraction, division, and multiplication operators. PHP also uses the modulus operator. This operator divides the left operand by the right operand, and returns the remainder. Table 1.2 lists the mathematical operators available in PHP.

Table 1.2   *Mathematical Operators*

Operator	Description
+	Addition
-	Subtraction
/	Division
*	Multiplication
%	Modulus

Comparison operators compare the left and right operands and return either a Boolean true or Boolean false. The comparison operators are listed in Table 1.3.

Table 1.3   *Comparison Operators*

Operator	Description
==	Equivalent to
!=	Not equivalent to
===	Identical to
>	Greater than
>=	Greater than or equal to

Table 1.3 *(continued)*

Operator	Description
<	Less than
<=	Less than or equal to

In the PHP language, logical operators include the typical and, or, xor, and not operators. The syntax of these operators is detailed in Table 1.4.

Table 1.4 *Logical Operators*

Operator	Description
||	Or
or	Or
xor	Xor
&&	And
and	And
!	Not

When an equation is evaluated, the entire expression is considered to determine operator precedence. This precedence determines the order in which the operators are executed. Table 1.5 details PHP's operator precedence.

Table 1.5 *Operator Precedence*

Operators	
++, --	(Highest Precedence)
/, *, %	
+, -	
<, <=, =>, >	
==, ===, !=	
&&	
||	
=, +=, -=, /=, *=, %=, .=	
and	
xor	
or	(Lowest Precedence)

Remember that parentheses can be used to arrange expressions into groups to circumvent the operator precedence. It is always a good idea to use parentheses to be sure that the expression is properly evaluated.

Control Structures

Control structures determine the way that code is executed and the decisions that are made depending on variables. These control structures enable you to reuse code, evaluate expressions, and determine the code path. This control comes in the form of four basic statements: `if` statements, `switch` statements, `while` loops, and `for` loops.

The `if` statement has three different constructs. The first is the basic `if` statement, which evaluates the expression and then executes the code in the braces if the expression is true. The pseudo code looks like this:

```
if(expression)
{
    /* This code is executed if the expression evaluates to true */
}
```

The second way of working with the `if` statement is to provide an alternative if the expression doesn't resolve to true. This is known as the `if-else` statement and the pseudo code looks like this:

```
if(expression)
{
    /* This code is executed if the expression evaluates to true */
}
else
{
    /* This code is executed if the expression evaluates to false */
}
```

The last type of `if` statement is known as the `if-elseif` statement. This statement evaluates multiple expressions and executes the appropriate code depending on which expressions evaluate to true. The pseudo code looks like this:

```
if(expression one)
{
    /* This code is executed if expression one evaluates to true */
}
elseif(expression two)
{
```

```
    /* This code is executed if expression two evaluates to true */
}
else
{
    /* This code is executed if the both expressions evaluate to false */
}
```

Another way of determining program flow is through the use of the `switch` statement. This statement evaluates one expression and then executes the appropriate code. This statement is useful when the expression can evaluate to multiple results. An example of the `switch` statement follows:

```
switch(expression)
{
    case item_one:
        /* This code is executed if expression evaluates item_one */
        break;
    case item_two:
        /* This code is executed if expression evaluates item_two */
        break;
    default:
        /* This code is executed if expression doesn't evaluate */
        /* to item_one or item_two */
}
```

Just as there are multiple versions of the `if` statement, there are two different types of the `while` loop. The first is the basic `while` statement. This statement evaluates the expression and then executes the code if the expression evaluates to true. The code in the braces continues to execute until the expression evaluates to false. An example of this follows:

```
while(expression)
{
    /* This code is executed if expression evaluates to true */
}
```

Sometimes you want to execute the code in the braces before evaluating the expression. This is done with the `do-while` statement. An example of this follows:

```
do{
    /* This code is executed FIRST and then the expression is evaluated */
    /* This code continues to execute if expression evaluates to true */
}
while(expression);
```

Mathematical Functions

PHP provides more than 30 functions that perform some type of mathematical evaluation. These functions are used to perform advanced mathematical functions. These functions include trigonometric functions such as sine, cosine, tangent, arc sine, arc cosine, and arc tangent. Other functions calculate the square root, natural logarithms, base-10 logarithms, and exponential expressions.

These functions, although useful, will probably not be used in your day-to-day programming. However, there are functions included in this section that you will use more often. These include functions that allow numbers to be converted from decimal to hexadecimal, octal, or binary and from hexadecimal, octal, and binary back to decimal. There are three functions that generate random numbers, a function that returns an absolute value, and functions that return the maximum or minimum values in a list.

Chapter 5 details the mathematical functions that are available in PHP. There you will find the functions defined with their input parameters along with their return values.

Functions, Classes, and Objects

Functions in PHP come in two basic forms: internal functions and user-defined functions. Internal functions are those that are built into PHP and are available to all users. User-defined functions are those that you define that can be called and reused. PHP also provides object-oriented support and enables you to define classes and objects. This section describes how to create and use functions, classes, and objects.

Functions

This section describes how to define a function, pass variables to the function, and return information from the function.

When information is passed to a function, the pieces of information are often referred to as arguments. The following example shows how to define a function that expects an argument to be passed:

```
function MyFunction($MyArgument,$YourArgument)
{
    print "MyArgument is: ".$MyArgument."<BR>";
    print "YourArgument is: ".$YourArgument."<BR>";
}
```

The `MyFunction()` function is called like this:

```
MyFunction("Mine","Yours");
```

The output of this function looks like this:

```
MyArgument is: Mine
YourArgument is: Yours
```

After you have defined a function and are able to pass information into it, there is one step remaining: returning values from a function. Let's consider the following example:

```
function ReturnSomthing($First,$Second)
{
    print "First is: ".$First."<BR>";
    print "Second is: ".$Second."<BR>";
    $result = $First + $Second;
    return $result;
}
```

The `ReturnSomething()` function is called like this:

```
$Value = ReturnSomething(5,2);
print $Value;
```

This example returns and prints out the value 7.

Classes and Objects

PHP provides the ability to define classes and work with the methods and objects associated with those classes. A *class* is a group of functions, or methods, and variables, or properties that perform a specific task.

By definition, an *object* is an instance of a class that exists in memory. In other words, a class defines the functionality that exists when an object is instantiated or initialized. All the properties and methods of a class are available for use when the object is instantiated.

This object-oriented functionality is very useful. It allows code to be reused and provides a very clean interface to functions and variables. We now examine how to define a class and use objects in PHP. The following code shows how to define a class:

```
class myclass
{
    function HelloWorld()
    {
```

```
        print "Hello World";
    }
}
```

This is a very simple example. To access the `HelloWorld` method, you must first instantiate the object like this:

```
$myobj = new myclass();
```

Then you can access the `HelloWorld()` method like this:

```
$myobj->HelloWorld();
```

This simple example prints out `"Hello World"` to the screen.

PHP also has some built-in classes that provide object-oriented functionality. One of these functions is the `dir()` function. After the directory is opened like this

```
$mydir = dir("/etc/passwd");
```

the properties of the directory can be read by using object-oriented syntax. To read the directory handle, you access the property like this:

```
echo "The directory handle is: ".$mydir->handle;
```

This example returns the directory handle. The path property can be accessed like this:

```
echo "The path property is: ".$mydir->path;
```

This produces `"/etc"` as the output.

CHAPTER 2

Generating HTML

As Web sites become more and more user friendly, Web publishers want the content to be more attractive and tailored to the tastes of each user. Visit any of the top-tier Web sites today and each of them will offer some type of customization based on your preferences. This customization might be in the form of personalized weather, stock quotes, or news. Each of these preferences is read from a database based on your login ID or a cookie value that is passed in from your browser.

This section describes some of the methods for generating dynamic content by using PHP. We discuss the use of variables in generating content and how to use the environment, dates, and times to affect what the user sees. We also discuss sending email from within PHP and using PHP to authenticate to a Web site.

Generating Dynamic Content

This section defines dynamic content and then discusses practical ways to generate content. The dynamic contents discussed in this section are limited to using request variables and the environment to generate content. Other methods, namely using databases to generate content, will be discussed in the next chapter.

Defining Dynamic Content

Let's first define dynamic content. *Dynamic content* is where the user's Web experience is determined by outside influences. This means that content seen on a site in the morning, without intervention from the Webmaster, will change in the afternoon, and possibly again at night.

Using Request Variables to Generate Content

PHP can use a number of variables to generate dynamic content. Table 2.1 describes the environment variables that are available to the PHP script.

Table 2.1 *PHP Variables*

Variable	Description
argv	argv is defined as an array of arguments passed to the script on the command line. This functionality gives a C-like look and feel to command-line parameters. When the PHP script is called using the GET method, argv will contain any query string information.
argc	argc is defined as the number of command-line parameters passed to the script. This adds a C-like look and feel to running the PHP scripts from the command line.
PHP_SELF	PHP_SELF is defined as the current executing PHP script. This allows the script to pass variables to itself based on input.
HTTP_COOKIE_VARS	HTTP_COOKIE_VARS is defined as an associative array of variables passed to the PHP script containing the client's cookies.
HTTP_GET_VARS	HTTP_GET_VARS is defined as an associative array of variables passed to the PHP script by a client using the HTTP GET method.
HTTP_POST_VARS	HTTP_POST_VARS is defined as an associative array of variables passed to the PHP script by a client using the HTTP POST method.

These variables are accessed through the use of PHP variables. To illustrate how different types of information can be passed from one Web page to a PHP script, consider the following example:

```
<HTML>
<HEAD>
<TITLE>Posting Variables</TITLE>
<BODY>
<CENTER>Enter the following information:
```

Generating Dynamic Content

```
<P>
<TABLE width="200"><TR><TD align="left">

<FORM ACTION="phpvaribles.php?ITEM=10" METHOD="POST">
Your name:<BR>
<INPUT TYPE="text" NAME="name" SIZE="20" MAXLENGTH="30">
<P>
Your email address:<BR>
<INPUT TYPE="text" NAME="email" SIZE="20" MAXLENGTH="30">
<P>
I prefer:
<SELECT NAME="preference">
<OPTION value = Yankees>Yankees
<OPTION value = Braves>Braves
</SELECT>
<P>
<INPUT TYPE="submit" VALUE="Post Variables">
</FORM>
</TD></TR></TABLE></CENTER>
</BODY>
</HTML>
```

This file is a regular HTML page with no special qualities other than the FORM ACTION that calls a PHP script named phpvaribles.php with a variable passed in the query string portion of the URL. The query string is any information after the question mark (?); in this case, ITEM=10.

The second part of this example is the phpvariables.php script, which prints the information gathered in the form. The script looks like this:

```
<?
echo "ITEM = $ITEM <br>";
echo "Email = $email <br>";
echo "Name = $name <br>";
echo "Preference = $preference <br>";
echo "argc = $argc <br>";
echo "argv = $argv[0] <br>";
echo "PHP_SELF = $PHP_SELF <br>";
phpinfo();
?>
```

This script reads the variables from the PHP environment and prints them out to the browser. Your results should look something like this:

```
ITEM = 10
Email = robertcox@anywhere.com
Name = Robert Cox
Preference = Braves
argc = 1
argv = ITEM=10
PHP_SELF = /phpbook/phpinfo.php
```

There should also be additional information at the bottom of this Web page generated from the phpinfo() function. This function is useful to view the variables that are available for you to use. For instance, under the Environment section of the phpinfo() output, you should see something like the information in Table 2.2. (Please note that not all the information output by phpinfo() is in this table.)

Table 2.2   *PHP Environment Variables Displayed by* phpinfo()

Variable	Value
ClassPath	D:\Program Files\Exceed.nt \hcljrcsv.jar;D:\Program Files\Exceed.nt\;
COMPUTERNAME	PHOENIX
CONTENT_TYPE	application/x-www-form-urlencoded
HTTP_ACCEPT_LANGUAGE	en-us
HTTP_HOST	phoenix
HTTP_REFERER	http://phoenix/phpbook /postvars.html
HTTP_USER_AGENT	Mozilla/4.0 (compatible; MSIE 5.01; Windows NT)
HTTP_COOKIE	AAMUILoginName; AAMUILoginPassword; AAMUILoginLocale
PATH_INFO	/phpbook/phpinfo.php
PATH_TRANSLATED	c:\InetPub\wwwroot\phpbook \phpinfo.php
QUERY_STRING	ITEM=10
REMOTE_ADDR	172.31.70.107
REMOTE_HOST	172.31.70.107
REQUEST_METHOD	POST
SCRIPT_NAME	/phpbook/phpinfo.php
SERVER_NAME	phoenix
SERVER_PORT	80

Table 2.2   *(continued)*

Variable	Value
SERVER_PORT_SECURE	0
SERVER_PROTOCOL	HTTP/1.1
SERVER_SOFTWARE	Microsoft-IIS/4.0

There is also a section that is output by the phpinfo() function that displays PHP variables. This information differs somewhat from the environment variables detailed in Table 2.2. Refer to Table 2.3 for this information.

Table 2.3   *PHP Variables Displayed by* phpinfo()

Variable	Value
PHP_SELF	/phpbook/phpinfo.php
HTTP_GET_VARS["ITEM"]	10
HTTP_POST_VARS["name"]	Robert Cox
HTTP_POST_VARS["email"]	robertcox@engage.com
HTTP_POST_VARS["preference"]	Braves
HTTP_SERVER_VARS["PHP_SELF"]	/phpbook/phpinfo.php
HTTP_SERVER_VARS["argv"]	Array
	(
	[0] => ITEM=10
	)
HTTP_SERVER_VARS["argc"]	1

Using the Environment to Generate Content

One of the ways that you can vary content to the browser is to use the environment to dictate what the user sees in the browser. For instance, the information in the request variables could be used to alter the information that PHP displays. In a similar manner, the date or time of day could be used to display greetings or other customized information to the user.

In the following example, the input on the initial page determines what the user's experience will be on the resulting page. This is a very elementary example, but it illustrates how the Web page can be modified on-the-fly to tailor content to the user.

```
<HTML>
<HEAD>
<TITLE></TITLE>
<BODY>
<CENTER>Enter the following information:
<P>
<TABLE width="200"><TR><TD align="left">

<FORM ACTION="result.php" METHOD="POST">
Please select your gender:<BR>
<SELECT NAME="gender">
<OPTION value = Male>Male
<OPTION value = Female>Female
</SELECT>
<P>
<INPUT TYPE="submit" VALUE="Submit">
</FORM>
</TD></TR></TABLE></CENTER>
</BODY>
</HTML>
```

This is the initial page where the user, through the use of a drop-down list box, chooses his/her gender. The resulting page will display a pink background if the chosen gender is female, or blue if the gender is male. The text of the page will also reflect the choice that is made. Here is the code for the result.php page:

```
<HTML>
<HEAD>
<TITLE>Result Page</TITLE>
<?
if($gender=="Male"){
$color = "Blue";
}
elseif($gender=="Female"){
$color = "Pink";
}
?>
<BODY bgcolor=<? echo $color ?>>
<center><b>
```

```
<?
if($gender=="Male"){
echo "You selected Male";
}
elseif($gender=="Female"){
echo "You selected Female";
}
?>
</b></center>
</BODY>
</HTML>
```

This same technique can be used to change the content based on other variables detailed in Table 2.2. You can determine what browser a user has and alter the content accordingly or you could read the time of the PHP server by using the date() function and modify the content based on what time the user hits the site. These are just a few examples of how to use the PHP environment to tailor content to the user. The limit to this customization is up to you and your imagination.

Working with the Filesystem

Sometimes you might find it necessary to read the host filesystem to determine rights to directories, to display files, to write to files, or any number of things. PHP provides many filesystem functions that enable the developer to read, delete, and modify any number of attributes on directories or files. Please remember that when using these functions, the Web server oftentimes runs as a specific user with limited rights. All the filesystem operations discussed will return information based on the user as which PHP (or the Web server) is running. This means that if you try to create a file and you don't have the appropriate rights, you will receive an error. Please keep this in mind as you work with files and directories.

Directory Functions

When working with directory functions such as readdir() rewinddir(), the basic idea is threefold. First, you must open a directory handle by using the opendir() function. This handle is a reference that is used in subsequent directory operations. Second, you perform operations on the directory. These could be anything from renaming the directory to changing permissions. Third, you close the directory handle by using the closedir() function. Some directory functions do not require the use of a directory handle. For functions such as is_dir(), mkdir(), and rmdir(), only the directory name is required. The following example tests for the existence of the current directory. Of course, this will always return true. You can change the $dirname variable and experiment with what happens if the is_dir() function returns false.

```html
<html>
<head>
    <title>Testing for a Directory</title>
</head>
<body>
<?
$dirname = ".";
if ( is_dir( $dirname ) )
   print $dirname." is a directory";
else
   print $dirname." is not a directory";
?>
</body>
</html>
```

With the object-oriented look and feel of some of the functions in PHP, reading a directory is as simple as using the directory object and the read() method. The following example illustrates the use of the dir() function and the associated read() and close() methods:

```html
<HEAD>
<TITLE>Reading a Directory</TITLE>
</HEAD>
<BODY>
<?
$dirname = ".";
$dh = dir($dirname );
while ($filename = $dh->read()){
   print "$filename<br>";
   }
$dh->close();
?>
</BODY>
</HTML>
```

These simple examples illustrate the use of some of the directory functions in PHP. Because of the nature of the filesystem, some of the functions that operate on directories also perform a similar operation on files. The following section discusses some of these functions.

Filesystem Functions

The method of working with directory handles described earlier holds true for filesystem functions. Some functions use file handles and others do not. Some of the functions that do not require file handles are `is_readable()`, `is_writeable()`, and `filesize()`. Examples of how to use these functions are described in the following code snippets.

The following code snippet checks the file named samplefile.doc and returns a string indicating whether the file is readable:

```
if ( is_readable( "samplefile.doc" ) )
    print "The file IS readable";
else
    print "The file IS NOT readable";
```

The following snippet of code is similar to the preceding code except that it checks whether samplefile.doc is writeable and returns the appropriate string:

```
if ( is_writeable( "samplefile.doc" ) )
    print "The file IS writeable";
else
    print "The file IS NOT writeable";
```

You can also return other information about a file. For instance, our fictional file, samplefile.doc, has certain properties that can be displayed. These properties include the last access time, the last modified time, the last changed time, and the size of the file. The following sample code illustrates how to return the information about a file:

```
<HTML>
<HEAD>
<TITLE>Returning information about a file</TITLE>
</HEAD>
<BODY>
<?
print "The size of the file is ";
print filesize( "samplefile.doc" );
print "<br>";
$atime = fileatime( "samplefile.doc" );
print "This file accessed on ";
print date("l, M d, Y g:i a", $atime);
print "<br>";
$mtime = filemtime( "samplefile.doc" );
print "This file was modified on ";
```

```
print date("l, M d, Y g:i a", $mtime);
print "<br>";
$ctime = filectime( "samplefile.doc" );
print "This file was changed on ";
print date("l, M d, Y g:i a", $ctime);
?>
</BODY>
</HTML>
```

For the next example, you will need to create a file called tenfile.txt and place this file in the same directory as the PHP script. The file's contents should be

```
01234567890123567889 0123456789
```

This example will open a file in read-only mode using the `fopen()` function and assign the returned file pointer to `$fp`. The `while` loop will first check for an End-of-File (EOF) and if an EOF is not returned, ten characters are read using the `fread()` function. These characters are stored in the `$tenchars` variable. The `$tenchars` variable is then printed with an HTML break (`<br>`) following the variable. The following is a listing of the code:

```
<HTML>
<HEAD>
<TITLE>Opening a File and Reading 10 Characters at a Time</TITLE>
</HEAD>
<BODY>
<?
$file = "tenfile.txt";
$fp = fopen( $file, "r" );
while ( ! feof( $fp ) ){
    $tenchars = fread( $fp, 10 );
    print "$tenchars<br>";
}
?>
</BODY>
</HTML>
```

The output of this example looks like this:

```
0123456789
0123567889
0123456789
```

The previous two sections are closely related and the techniques that you learned can be easily transferred between the directory and the filesystem functions.

HTTP Authentication

One of the more sophisticated features in Web development is the topic of HTTP authentication. This involves authenticating to a restricted area of a Web site, usually with a username and password. This restriction can entice visitors to your Web site to register or pay fees. It can also be a means to restrict access to sensitive information on a company's intranet.

Overview

PHP provides HTTP authentication when it is running as an Apache module. This functionality is not available when running PHP as a CGI or an IIS filter. This is because the authentication mechanism in PHP uses the Header() function to send an "authentication required" message to the browser. This causes a username and password window to pop up in the browser. After the user has filled in a username and a password, the variables $PHP_AUTH_USER, $PHP_AUTH_PW, and $PHP_AUTH_TYPE are set to the username, password, and authentication type, respectively. An example of this is

```php
<?php
  if(!isset($PHP_AUTH_USER)) {
    Header("WWW-Authenticate: Basic realm=\"Initial Realm\"");
    Header("HTTP/1.0 401 Unauthorized");
    echo "The user hit the Cancel button\n";
    exit;
  } else {
    echo "Hello $PHP_AUTH_USER.<P>";
    echo "You entered $PHP_AUTH_PW as your password.<P>";
  }
?>
```

In this example, instead of printing the $PHP_AUTH_USER and $PHP_AUTH_PW, you would probably want to check the username and password for validity, perhaps by sending a query to a database.

Limitations

In basic HTTP authentication, the password is passed over the network as uuencoded, plain text. The username and password are not encrypted in any way. Anyone capturing network traffic will not see the password as text, but the password will be easily decoded.

This method of authentication is roughly as safe as Telnet-style username and password security. In other words, if you trust your machine to be on the Internet for telnet sessions, you have no reason not to trust this method of HTTP authentication.

Other Authentication Methods

This section provides an overview of alternative authentication methods. These methods often include setting a session variable that is then used by all secure pages to validate the user. Session variables are supported by PHP 4 and are the method of passing information to subsequent Web pages. When sessions are enabled, a user to your Web page is assigned a unique session identifier. This session ID is either saved in a cookie or is passed on the URL. The following example will display the session ID for the specific user:

```
<?

session_start();
?>
<HTML>
<TITLE>Session IDs</TITLE>
<HEAD>
</HEAD>
<BODY>
<?
echo "The session ID is ".session_id()."<br>";
?>
</BODY>
</HTML>
```

After a user session is established, you can register variables as session variables and make them available to the entire Web application. The following three sample pages will take some user input, namely a username and password, and register the variables in a user session. The first part of this example is a simple HTML form that calls the second PHP script in the FORM ACTION.

```
<HTML>
<HEAD>
<TITLE>Session Variable Example</TITLE>
</HEAD>
<BODY>
```

```
<H1>Input your LoginName and Password</H1>
<FORM ACTION="page2.php" METHOD="POST">
Login Name: <input type="text" name="LoginName"><br>
Password: <input type="password" name="Password"><br>
<INPUT TYPE="submit" VALUE="Submit"><br>
</FORM>
</BODY>
</HTML>
```

These input fields are registered in the following example as session variables and then printed out in the body of the Web page:

```
<?
session_start();
?>
<HTML>
<HEAD>
<TITLE>Register the Session Variables</TITLE>
</HEAD>
<BODY>
<?
session_register( "LoginName" );
session_register( "Password" );
echo "Your LoginName and Password have been registered!<P>";
echo "<A HREF=page3.php>Check Session Variables</A><br>";

echo "LoginName: ".$LoginName."<br>";
echo "Password: ".$Password."<br>";

?>
</BODY>
</HTML>
```

To illustrate the functionality of session variables, notice that there is a hyperlink that directs you to another PHP script. This script source follows, and the only thing it does is print out $LoginName and $Password. No hidden variables are passed to this script and there is nothing in the query string to make these variables available to this script. The only way for this script to know about the $LoginName and $Password is for the values to be stored as session variables.

```
<?
session_start();
?>
```

```
<html>
<head>
    <title>Check the Session Variables</title>
</head>

<body>
<H1>These are you Registered Variables</H1>
<?
echo "LoginName: ".$LoginName."<br>";
echo "Password: ".$Password."<br>";
?>

</body>
</html>
```

Session variables are very useful and can be the means of validating permissions to Web pages. This type of validation can be as simple as an if-then conditional that checks for a valid login name and password. This check can display an error message if the check does not pass or display the content if the permissions are appropriate.

Working with Email

Email is a very useful tool and one that is easy to use as long as you understand the workings of the email system. Email can automatically notify users of important events, and provide details of user accounts or other information. Email can also be used to send dynamic bulk information to a group of users. Email, like other areas of PHP, is flexible and is limited only by your imagination.

Email Overview

This is a general overview of how email works on the Internet. Please realize that there are many varieties of email clients and email servers; this is just an overview and describes some of the mechanisms on which most every Internet email systems rely.

All standard email messages contain certain information, such as the sender's name and email address, the recipient's name and email address, a subject for the message, and some kind of message in the body of the email.

Email messages are composed of two basic parts: the headers and the body. Headers define where the email is going and any special routing information. Generally, the user does not see this information. Email clients usually format the content in a user-friendly manner and mask this information from the user.

After an email is composed, the email client or Mail User Agent (MUA) sends the information to the SMTP host or Mail Transfer Agent (MTA). SMTP stands for Simple Mail Transfer Protocol and is the foundation for virtually all Internet email messages. The SMTP host takes the message and adds additional information to aid in the routing of the email. The MTA is responsible for delivery of the email message.

After the MTA has the outgoing email, it adds information to the message. For example, it adds a unique message identifier, a time and date stamp, and other important standardizing information.

When the outgoing message is formed with all the right headers, the MTA is ready to try to deliver the message. The MTA performs what is known as an MX (Mail Transfer) record lookup in the Domain Name System (DNS) to find out to what machine the email is to be delivered. If multiple MX records are found, the one with the lowest priority is used.

The sending MTA and the receiving MTA establish a connection, negotiate protocols and special functions, and then the sending MTA delivers the email to the receiving MTA.

Email and PHP

PHP contains one function that is used to send email. This function uses the SMTP mail server to send the message. Don't let the single function fool you; it is essentially all you need to send emails. This function, which is described in detail later in this reference, accepts four parameters: the recipient's email address, the email's subject, the message body, and any additional headers. The additional header parameter is used to define the sender's email address and any other special delivery information. The following line is the description of how to format the parameters of the `mail()` function.

```
mail(to, subject, message, additional_headers);
```

The following example shows how to use the `mail()` function in the real world. This snippet of code will send an email to the user gcox@winslow.com from shiatt@mayberry.com. The subject of the message will be Rats in the Office and the body of the email details an attempt to rid an office of a rodent problem.

```
mail("To: Gladys Cox   <gcox@winslow.com>",
"Rats in the Office",
"Gladys,\n\nOn Thursday, the exterminators will arrive to deal with our
terrible rat problem. Please be advised that we are evacuating the office for
such a procedure, and you will have the day off. \n
```

```
Also, remember that Friday is jeans day! Thank you.\n
Sheila Hiatt\n
Director of Facilities",
"From: Sheila Hiatt  <shiatt@mayberry.com>");
```

You can expand the scope of this example to include a dynamic email message and a for loop that reads unique email addresses from a file or database. You will begin to see the flexibility of this function and the potential it provides.

Calendar and Date Functions

PHP has 12 calendar functions that provide the ability to convert between different calendar formats. The formats that are supported by PHP are the Julian calendar, the Gregorian calendar, the Jewish calendar, and the French Republican calendar. The 11 date and time functions in PHP provide the ability to retrieve and format the current date and time, and work with the UNIX timestamp.

Overview of Time and Date Functions

One of the most powerful features when working with date and time functions is the ability to use the UNIX timestamp. This timestamp is defined as the number of seconds since January 1, 1970, 00:00:00 GMT. PHP provides a number of functions that retrieve and use the UNIX timestamp; namely gmmktime(), microtime(), mktime(), and time().

The conversion specifiers in Table 2.4 are recognized in the format string.

Table 2.4   strftime() *Formatting Parameters*

Format	Description
%a	Abbreviated weekday name according to the current locale
%A	Full weekday name according to the current locale
%b	Abbreviated month name according to the current locale
%B	Full month name according to the current locale
%c	Preferred date and time representation for the current locale
%d	Day of the month as a decimal number (range 00 to 31)
%H	Hour as a decimal number using a 24-hour clock (range 00 to 23)
%I	Hour as a decimal number using a 12-hour clock (range 01 to 12)
%j	Day of the year as a decimal number (range 001 to 366)

Table 2.4   *(continued)*

Format	Description
%m	Month as a decimal number (range 1 to 12)
%M	Minute as a decimal number
%p	Either am or pm according to the given time value, or the corresponding strings for the current locale
%S	Second as a decimal number
%U	Week number of the current year as a decimal number, starting with the first Sunday as the first day of the first week
%W	Week number of the current year as a decimal number, starting with the first Monday as the first day of the first week
%w	Day of the week as a decimal, with Sunday being 0
%x	Preferred date representation for the current locale without the time
%X	Preferred time representation for the current locale without the date
%y	Year as a decimal number without a century (range 00 to 99)
%Y	Year as a decimal number including the century
%Z	Time zone or name or abbreviation
%%	A literal % character

```
<HTML>
<HEAD>
<TITLE></TITLE>
<BODY>
<?
$timestamp = time();
echo "The UNIX timestamp is: $timestamp<br>";

$currentdate = strftime("%a",$timestamp);
echo "strftime() with %a format string: $currentdate<br>";
$currentdate = strftime("%A",$timestamp);
echo "strftime() with %A format string: $currentdate<br>";
$currentdate = strftime("%b",$timestamp);
echo "strftime() with %b format string: $currentdate<br>";
$currentdate = strftime("%B",$timestamp);
echo "strftime() with %B format string: $currentdate<br>";
$currentdate = strftime("%c",$timestamp);
echo "strftime() with %C format string: $currentdate<br>";
$currentdate = strftime("%d",$timestamp);
echo "strftime() with %d format string: $currentdate<br>";
```

```php
$currentdate = strftime("%H",$timestamp);
echo "strftime() with %H format string: $currentdate<br>";
$currentdate = strftime("%j",$timestamp);
echo "strftime() with %j format string: $currentdate<br>";
$currentdate = strftime("%m",$timestamp);
echo "strftime() with %m format string: $currentdate<br>";
$currentdate = strftime("%M",$timestamp);
echo "strftime() with %M format string: $currentdate<br>";
$currentdate = strftime("%p",$timestamp);
echo "strftime() with %p format string: $currentdate<br>";
$currentdate = strftime("%S",$timestamp);
echo "strftime() with %S format string: $currentdate<br>";
$currentdate = strftime("%U",$timestamp);
echo "strftime() with %U format string: $currentdate<br>";
$currentdate = strftime("%W",$timestamp);
echo "strftime() with %W format string: $currentdate<br>";
$currentdate = strftime("%x",$timestamp);
echo "strftime() with %x format string: $currentdate<br>";
$currentdate = strftime("%X",$timestamp);
echo "strftime() with %X format string: $currentdate<br>";
$currentdate = strftime("%y",$timestamp);
echo "strftime() with %y format string: $currentdate<br>";
$currentdate = strftime("%Y",$timestamp);
echo "strftime() with %Y format string: $currentdate<br>";
$currentdate = strftime("%Z",$timestamp);
echo "strftime() with %Z format string: $currentdate<br>";
?>
</BODY>
</HTML>
```

Output:

```
The UNIX timestamp is: 966647810
strftime() with %a format string: Fri
strftime() with %A format string: Friday
strftime() with %b format string: Aug
strftime() with %B format string: August
strftime() with %C format string: 08/18/00 21:16:50
strftime() with %d format string: 18
strftime() with %H format string: 21
strftime() with %j format string: 231
```

```
strftime() with %m format string: 08
strftime() with %M format string: 16
strftime() with %p format string: PM
strftime() with %S format string: 50
strftime() with %U format string: 33
strftime() with %W format string: 33
strftime() with %x format string: 08/18/00
strftime() with %X format string: 21:16:50
strftime() with %y format string: 00
strftime() with %Y format string: 2000
strftime() with %Z format string: Eastern Daylight Time
```

Calendar Functions

There are four calendar formats that are supported in PHP; they are the Gregorian calendar, the Julian calendar, the Jewish calendar, and the French Republic calendar. Although the Gregorian calendar is recognized worldwide as the standard calendar format, some applications might require conversions to other formats. The Julian calendar was created in 46 B.C. and has the basic format of today's Gregorian calendar. There are officially 365.25 days in the Julian calendar, and the only difference between the Julian and the Gregorian calendars is how the leap years are handled. Compare the 365.25 days in the Julian calendar to the currently accepted 365.242199 days in the Gregorian calendar and you will soon realize that there must be compensation for this difference somewhere. The Gregorian calendar system states that centennial years are not leap years unless they are divisible by 400. This is why 2000 is a leap year, but 1900 was not, nor will be 2100.

The Jewish calendar is the format that has been in use by the Jewish people for thousands of years. This format has either 12 or 13 months with 29 or 30 days per month. The Jewish calendar has dependencies based on the religious holidays and positioning of the Sabbath during the year. These are all taken into account in the PHP calendar functions.

The French Republican calendar was very short-lived. It was used in France after the French Revolution and was to be centered on science, mathematics, and astronomy rather than religion. This calendar system was adopted in October 1793 and was abandoned a little more than 13 years later in January 1806.

PHP provides eight functions to convert between these four types of calendars. These conversion functions are detailed in Tables 2.5 and 2.6.

Table 2.5   *Calendar Conversion Functions*

Function	Description
JDToGregorian()	This function converts a Julian day count to a Gregorian date
GregorianToJD()	This function converts a Gregorian date to a Julian day count
JDToJulian()	This function converts a Julian day count to Julian calendar date
JulianToJD()	This function converts a Julian calendar date to Julian day count
JDToJewish()	This function converts a Julian day count to the Jewish calendar
JewishToJD()	This function converts a date in the Jewish calendar to Julian day count
JDToFrench()	This function converts a Julian day count to the French Republican calendar
FrenchToJD()	This function converts a date from the French Republican calendar to a Julian day count

Table 2.6   *Remaining PHP Calendar Functions*

Function	Description
JDMonthName()	This function returns the Julian month name
JDDayOfWeek()	This function returns the Julian day of the week
easter_date()	This function returns the UNIX timestamp for midnight on Easter of a given year
easter_days()	This function returns the number of days between March 21 and Easter

CHAPTER 3

Database Access

This chapter discusses setting up a database. More specifically, it discusses setting up a PostgreSQL database and using that database to store information that will be made available to Web browsers. Many open-source applications are available to Web developers. This chapter assumes that you have an Apache Web server configured to use PHP, and that your configuration of PHP is compiled to integrate with PostgreSQL. Examples of this configuration are detailed in Chapter 1, "Basic PHP."

Working with Connections and Data Sources

The standard PostgreSQL installation uses port 5432 to listen for TCP/IP connections. This is the port on which the postmaster process listens for connections. The postmaster is the process that manages the communications between the front-end clients and the back-end server. For the examples included in this book, it is assumed that the port is left at the default, 5432. In other words, the connections made to the PostgreSQL back end are assumed to be on port 5432. You will see how to make this connection using PHP later in this chapter.

Setting Up the Database

Initial installation and configuration of the PostgreSQL package is beyond the scope of this chapter. Please refer to the PostgreSQL Web site (`http://www.postgresql.org`) for installation and configuration documentation.

This section describes the initial creation of the test database that will be used in the remainder of the examples in this chapter. The first thing to do is check your PostgreSQL installation for the existence of a database named test. All the examples in this chapter refer to this test database; if this database already exists, you might want to create a database with a different name.

To check for the existence of a test database, use the following command:

```
psql -l
```

The psql application is the PostgreSQL client that is used to interact with the backend. The `-l` option lists the available databases. Your output should look similar to this:

```
[postgres@phoenix bin]$ psql -l
datname  |datdba|encoding|datpath
---------+------+--------+---------
template1|   40|       0|template1
(1 row)
```

To create a database named test, use the following command:

```
[postgres@phoenix bin]$ createdb test
```

You can now view your newly created database by using the -l option once again. The output should be similar to this:

```
[postgres@phoenix bin]$ psql -l
datname  |datdba|encoding|datpath
---------+------+--------+---------
template1|   40|       0|template1
test     |   40|       0|test
(2 rows)
```

Now that the database is created, you must create a user that will have access to the database. Remember that this user will be running with the same permissions as the Web server. In our examples, the Web server will be running as the user nobody, so the user that must be created in PostgreSQL must be named nobody.

To check for the existence of the user nobody, you can query the pg_user table using psql. The sequence of commands looks like this:

```
[postgres@phoenix bin]$ psql test
Welcome to the POSTGRESQL interactive sql monitor:
  Please read the file COPYRIGHT for copyright terms of POSTGRESQL
[PostgreSQL 6.5.3 on i586-pc-linux-gnu, compiled by gcc egcs-2.91.66]

   type \? for help on slash commands
   type \q to quit
   type \g or terminate with semicolon to execute query
 You are currently connected to the database: test


test=>
```

This will bring you to the psql command prompt. Use the following SQL select query to check for the nobody user:

```
test=> select * from pg_user;
usename |usesysid|usecreatedb|usetrace|usesuper|usecatupd|passwd   |
--------+--------+-----------+--------+--------+---------+--------+
postgres|     40|t          |t       |t       |t        |********|
 (1 row)
```

To create a database user named nobody, use the createuser utility that is included in the PostgreSQL installation. The output of the command will look something like this:

```
[postgres@phoenix bin]$ createuser
Enter name of user to add ---> nobody
Enter user's postgres ID or RETURN to use unix user ID: 99 ->
Is user "nobody" allowed to create databases (y/n) n
Is user "nobody" a superuser? (y/n) n
createuser: nobody was successfully added
Shall I create a database for "nobody" (y/n) n
don't forget to create a database for nobody
```

After the user is created, the pg_user table will look like this:

```
test=> select * from pg_user;
usename |usesysid|usecreatedb|usetrace|usesuper|usecatupd|passwd   |
--------+--------+-----------+--------+--------+---------+--------+
postgres|     40|t          |t       |t       |t        |********|
nobody  |     99|f          |t       |f       |t        |********|
 (2 rows)
```

For simplicity, we will use a single table in our examples. Create a text file named database.sql with the following contents:

```
create table contacts (
    cid             int4  DEFAULT NEXTVAL('c'),
    name            char (50),
    address         char (50),
    city            char (50),
    state           char (2),
    zip             char (10),
    phone           char (25),
    fax             char (25),
    email           char (50),
primary key (cid));

create sequence c start 101;

grant all on contacts to nobody;

grant all on c to nobody;
```

These SQL commands create a table named contacts in the test database. The script also creates a sequence that will be used to generate a unique contact ID. The last thing that this script does is grant permissions to the nobody user for the table and the sequence. From the psql command line, the output of this command will look like this:

```
test=> \i database.sql
create table contacts (
    cid             int4  DEFAULT NEXTVAL('c'),
    name            char (50),
    address         char (50),
    city            char (50),
    state           char (2),
    zip             char (10),
    phone           char (25),
    fax             char (25),
    email           char (50),
primary key (cid));
NOTICE:  CREATE TABLE/PRIMARY KEY will create implicit index 'contacts_pkey'
for table 'contacts'
CREATE
```

```
create sequence c start 101;
CREATE

grant all on contacts to nobody;
CHANGE

grant all on c to nobody;
CHANGE
EOF
test=>
```

You can now check for the existence of the table and sequence by using the \dt
(display tables) and \ds (display sequences) commands. The output of these commands
should look like this:

```
test=> \dt
Database     = test
    +-----------------+--------------------------------------+----------+
    | Owner           |                 Relation             |   Type   |
    +-----------------+--------------------------------------+----------+
    | postgres        | contacts                             | table    |
    +-----------------+--------------------------------------+----------+

test=> \ds
Database     = test
    +-----------------+--------------------------------------+----------+
    | Owner           |                 Relation             |   Type   |
    +-----------------+--------------------------------------+----------+
    | postgres        | c                                    | sequence |
    +-----------------+--------------------------------------+----------+
```

To verify that the permissions were changed, use the \z command. The output should
look something like this:

```
test=> \z
Database     = test
    +----------+---------------------------+
    | Relation | Grant/Revoke Permissions  |
    +----------+---------------------------+
    | c        | {"=","nobody=arwR"}       |
    | contacts | {"=","nobody=arwR"}       |
    +----------+---------------------------+
```

Using PostgreSQL and PHP

This section describes the integration of PHP with the PostgreSQL database. There are many instances in Web development when data must be stored and readily retrieved from a database. PHP easily integrates with popular databases such as dBASE, mSQL, MySQL, Informix, Sybase, SQL Server, and PostgreSQL. PHP provides functions to connect with these databases to execute queries, and manage connections and transactions. The examples in the following sections illustrate how to integrate PHP with the PostgreSQL database server.

PostgreSQL Overview

PostgreSQL is a very powerful open-source client/server relational database management system (RDBMS). PostgreSQL was first conceived in 1986 and was known as the Berkley Postgres Project. The project evolved and improved until 1994, when developers Andrew Yu and Jolly Chen added a Structured Query Language (SQL) interpreter to Postgres. This release was known as Postgres95 and was released to the open-source community.

In 1996, Postgres95 was overhauled again and the result was released as PostgreSQL version 6.0. This release of Postgres included increased back-end speed, SQL92 standard enhancements, and important back-end features including subselects, defaults, constraints, and triggers.

PostgreSQL is a very robust package and has many of the features available in a large, commercially available RDBMS. These features include transactions, subselects, triggers, views, foreign key referential integrity, and sophisticated locking. PostgreSQL also lacks some features that are available in commercial databases, such as user-defined types, inheritance, and rules. From a user's standpoint, just about the only major feature that PostgreSQL does not have is outer joins. Outer joins will be added in a later version.

PostgreSQL offers two operational modes. One mode guarantees that if the operating system or hardware crashes, the data has been stored to the disk. This mode is often slower than most commercially available databases because of the flushing (or syncing) method that is used. The other mode doesn't offer the data guarantees that the first mode does, but it often runs faster than commercial databases. Unfortunately, at the present time, there is no intermediate mode that offers a level of data security with increased performance. This, too, will be provided in a later version.

Connecting Postgres and PHP

The connection between PostgreSQL and PHP is made through the use of the pg_Connect() function. This function accepts five parameters: the hostname of the database server, the port on which the postmaster is listening, any connection options, the tty, and the database name. For our purposes, we assume that the PostgreSQL and PHP are installed on the same machine, and that no connection options or tty information are required. In our examples, the call to pg_Connect() looks like this:

```
$conn = pg_Connect("localhost", "5432", "", "", "test");
```

The variable $conn will contain the database connection handle if the function is successful. A sample program looks like this:

```
<html>
<head>
    <title>Making the Connection</title>
</head>
<body>
<?
$conn = pg_Connect("localhost", "5432", "", "", "test");
  if (!$conn) {echo "An database connection error occurred.\n"; exit;}
  else {echo "You have connected to the database successfully.\n";}
pg_Close($conn);
?>
</body>
</html>
```

If the output of this script looks like this:

```
You have connected to the database successfully.
```

then congratulations—you have successfully connected to the test database.

Select, Insert, Update, and Delete Queries

You will routinely perform four types of queries when using any type of database. The insert query will place items in the database, the update query will update information that is already in the database, the select query will display information in the database, and the delete query will delete items from the database. When you query databases from inside PHP, you will allocate memory when a database connection is made and when the result set is returned from your query. When your script is finished executing, all memory will be freed, but it is good programming practice to free the result by using the `pg_FreeResult()` function and to close the connection by using the `pg_Close()` function.

Insert Queries

We will use the following example to insert information into our newly created database. This example consists of two parts. The first part is a simple form that enables the user to input specific information to be added to the database. This form calls the PHP script that takes the form variables, and then creates and executes the insert query. The HTML form looks like this:

```html
<html>
<head>
<title>Insert Record</title>
</head>
<body>
    <b>Please provide us with the following:</b></font>
    <p><font size="2" face="Arial, Helvetica, sans-serif">
    <form action="insert.php" method="POST" enablecab="Yes">
      Full Name (Last, First MI):<br>
      <input type="Text" name="FullName" align="LEFT" required="Yes"
       size="59" value=""><br>
      Address:<br>
      <input type="Text" name="Address" align="LEFT" required="Yes"
       size="59" value=""><br>
      City:<br>
      <input type="Text" name="City" align="LEFT" required="Yes"
       size="29" value=""><br>
      State:<br>
      <input type="Text" name="State" align="LEFT" required="Yes"
       size="2" value=""><br>
      Zip:<br>
      <input type="Text" name="Zip" align="LEFT" required="Yes"
       size="10" value=""><br>
      Phone:<br>
      <input type="Text" name="Phone" align="LEFT" required="No"
       size="25" value=""><br>
      Fax:<br>
      <input type="Text" name="Fax" align="LEFT" required="Yes"
       size="25" value=""><br>
```

Select, Insert, Update, and Delete Queries

```
    Email:<br>
    <input type="Text" name="Email" align="LEFT" required="Yes"
     size="59" value=""><br>
    <input type="Submit" name="Submit" value="Submit" align="MIDDLE">
  </form>
</body>
</html>
```

Notice that the form variables in the example are FullName, Address, City, State, Zip, Phone, Fax, and Email. The PHP script, which is named insert.php, refers to these posted form variables as $FirstName, $Address, $City, $State, $Zip, $Phone, $Fax, and $Email. The PHP script looks like this:

```
<html>
<head>
    <title>Insert the Form Data</title>
</head>
<body>
<?
// Connect to the Postgres Database
$conn = pg_Connect("localhost", "5432", "", "", "test");
  if (!$conn) {echo "An database connection error occurred.\n"; exit;}
// Insert the form values into the database
$result = pg_Exec($conn,"INSERT INTO contacts VALUES
(NEXTVAL('c'),'$FullName','$Address','$City','$State','$Zip',
 '$Phone','$Fax','$Email');");
  if (!$result) {echo "An INSERT query error occurred.\n"; exit;}
// Get the last record inserted
$oid = pg_getlastoid($result);
  if (!$oid) {echo "An OID error occurred.\n"; exit;}
// Select the record that was last entered
$result = pg_Exec($conn,"SELECT cid FROM contacts WHERE oid=$oid;");
  if (!$result) {echo "A SELECT query error occurred.\n"; exit;}
// Place the result into the variable $CID
$CID = pg_Result($result, 0, "cid");
  if (!$CID) {echo "There is a problem returning the Contact ID.\n"; exit;}
// Print out the Contact ID
  else { echo "The record was successfully entered and the Contact ID is:
        $CID \n";}
// Free the result
pg_FreeResult($result);
// Close the connection
pg_Close($conn);
```

```
?>
</body>
</html>
```

The code for this example first inserts the information from the form into the database and then uses the pg_getlastoid() function to get the last record entered. It then uses the retrieved object identifier (OID) to query the database, and returns the customer identifier (CID) of the last record. If all goes well, the contact ID is printed to the browser window. The last part of this example is not needed to insert records using PHP, but it is included to illustrate the use of the pg_getlastoid() function.

Select Queries with PHP

We gave you a taste of a select query in the previous section. This section takes the result set from the select query and formats it for presentation in a Web page. The select query often displays information that you would like to either change or delete. Notice in the following example that edit and delete links are included. We will create these pages later in this chapter. For now, let's look at this example:

```
<html>
<head>
<title>Select Query</title>
<?
$conn = pg_Connect("localhost", "5432", "", "", "test");
    if (!$conn) {echo "An database connection error occurred.\n"; exit;}
$result = pg_Exec($conn,"SELECT cid, name, address, city, state, zip, phone,
                 fax, email FROM contacts ORDER BY name");
    if (!$result) {echo "A query error occurred.\n"; exit;}
$ContactNum = pg_NumRows($result);
    $i = 0;
    while ($i < $ContactNum) {
        $CID[$i] = pg_Result($result, $i, "cid");
        $CName[$i] = pg_Result($result, $i, "name");
        $CAddress[$i] = pg_Result($result, $i, "address");
        $CCity[$i] = pg_Result($result, $i, "city");
        $CState[$i] = pg_Result($result, $i, "state");
        $CZip[$i] = pg_Result($result, $i, "zip");
        $CPhone[$i] = pg_Result($result, $i, "phone");
        $CFax[$i] = pg_Result($result, $i, "fax");
        $CEmail[$i] = pg_Result($result, $i, "email");
        $i++;
    }
```

```
pg_FreeResult($result);
pg_Close($conn);
?>
</head>
<body>
<table>
<TR>
    <TD></TD>
    <TD><b>Full Name</b></TD>
    <TD><b>Address</b></TD>
    <TD><b>City</b></TD>
    <TD><b>State</b></TD>
    <TD><b>Zip</b></TD>
    <TD><b>Phone</b></TD>
    <TD><b>Fax</b></TD>
    <TD><b>Email</b></TD>
</TR>
<?
    $i = 0;
    while ($i < $ContactNum) {
        echo "<TR><TD><A href=editform.php?ID=".$CID[$i].">[Edit]</A>";
        echo "<A href=delete.php?ID=".$CID[$i].">[Delete]</A></TD>";
        echo "<TD>".$CName[$i]."</TD>";
        echo "<TD>".$CAddress[$i]."</TD>";
        echo "<TD>".$CCity[$i]."</TD>";
        echo "<TD>".$CState[$i]."</TD>";
        echo "<TD>".$CZip[$i]."</TD>";
        echo "<TD>".$CPhone[$i]."</TD>";
        echo "<TD>".$CFax[$i]."</TD>";
        echo "<TD>".$CEmail[$i]."</TD></TR>";
    $i++;
}
?>
</table>
</body>
</html>
```

The next section examines this example and explains how to work with the data that is
returned from the query.

Working with the Result Set

One of the main features of the preceding example is the use of an array to store the items that are returned from the select query. The while loop uses the pg_Result() function to get the records that are returned from the select query and stores them in variables. These variables are used later in the script to present the information to the Web browser. The pg_NumRows() function is used to return the number of returned records and, therefore, the number of times that the while loop should be executed to store all the returned information. Notice that a while loop is once again used to step through the array and print the variables in the appropriate place in an HTML table. The CID is used as an identifier in all the returned rows. After the edit and delete links are completed, this identifier will be used in subsequent queries to keep track of the record.

Update Queries

This section continues with the example that was started with the select query. After you click on the Edit hyperlink on the Select Query page, the CID is passed to the Edit Record page. The code listing for this page follows:

```
<html>
<head>
<title>Edit Record Form</title>
<?
$conn = pg_Connect("localhost", "5432", "", "", "test");
    if (!$conn) {echo "An database connection error occurred.\n"; exit;}
$result = pg_Exec($conn,"SELECT cid, name, address, city, state, zip,
                phone, fax, email FROM contacts WHERE cid = $ID");
    if (!$result) {echo "A query error occurred.\n"; exit;}
 $CID = pg_Result($result, $i, "cid");
 $CName = pg_Result($result, $i, "name");
 $CAddress = pg_Result($result, $i, "address");
 $CCity = pg_Result($result, $i, "city");
 $CState = pg_Result($result, $i, "state");
 $CZip = pg_Result($result, $i, "zip");
 $CPhone = pg_Result($result, $i, "phone");
 $CFax = pg_Result($result, $i, "fax");
 $CEmail = pg_Result($result, $i, "email");
pg_FreeResult($result);
pg_Close($conn);
?>
</head>
<body>
    <b>Please update the following:</b></font>
```

Select, Insert, Update, and Delete Queries

```
<p><font size="2" face="Arial, Helvetica, sans-serif">
<form action="edit.php?ID=<? echo $CID ?>" method="POST" enablecab="Yes">
Full Name (Last, First MI):<br>
<input type="Text" name="FullName" align="LEFT" required="Yes" size="59"
 value="<? echo $CName ?>"><br>
Address:<br>
<input type="Text" name="Address" align="LEFT" required="Yes" size="59"
 value="<? echo $CAddress ?>"><br>
City:<br>
<input type="Text" name="City" align="LEFT" required="Yes" size="29"
 value="<? echo $CCity ?>"><br>
State:<br>
<input type="Text" name="State" align="LEFT" required="Yes" size="2"
 value="<? echo $CState ?>"><br>
Zip:<br>
<input type="Text" name="Zip" align="LEFT" required="Yes" size="10"
 value="<? echo $CZip ?>"><br>
Phone:<br>
<input type="Text" name="Phone" align="LEFT" required="No" size="25"
 value="<? echo $CPhone ?>"><br>
Fax:<br>
<input type="Text" name="Fax" align="LEFT" required="Yes" size="25"
 value="<? echo $CFax ?>"><br>
Email:<br>
<input type="Text" name="Email" align="LEFT" required="Yes" size="59"
 value="<? echo $CEmail ?>"><br>
<input type="Submit" name="Submit" value="Submit" align="MIDDLE">
</form>
</body>
</html>
```

This script's first task is to determine, through the CID, which record is to be edited. This is done with a simple select query. The result set of this query is placed into variables to be used later in the HTML form. Notice that because only one record is to be returned, we do not need to use a while loop and an array to return multiple records. The returned variables are placed into the HTML input tag as the value of the field. This places the information in the input field and enables the end user to edit the information.

After the Submit button is pressed, the second part of this script performs the update query. The form variables are passed to this script and are used to create the update query that is sent to the database.

```
<html>
<head>
<title>Edit Record</title>
<?
$conn = pg_Connect("localhost", "5432", "", "", "test");
  if (!$conn) {echo "An database connection error occurred.\n"; exit;}
$result = pg_Exec($conn,"UPDATE contacts SET name='$FullName',
          address='$Address', city='$City', state='$State', zip='$Zip',
          phone='$Phone', fax='$Fax', email='$Email' WHERE cid='$ID'");
  if (!$result) {echo "An UPDATE query error occurred.\n"; exit;}
$result = pg_Exec($conn,"SELECT cid, name, address, city, state, zip,
          phone, fax, email FROM contacts WHERE cid=$ID;");
  if (!$result) {echo "A query error occurred.\n"; exit;}
 $CID = pg_Result($result, $i, "cid");
 $CName = pg_Result($result, $i, "name");
 $CAddress = pg_Result($result, $i, "address");
 $CCity = pg_Result($result, $i, "city");
 $CState = pg_Result($result, $i, "state");
 $CZip = pg_Result($result, $i, "zip");
 $CPhone = pg_Result($result, $i, "phone");
 $CFax = pg_Result($result, $i, "fax");
 $CEmail = pg_Result($result, $i, "email");
pg_FreeResult($result);
pg_Close($conn);
?>
</head>
<body>
<b>The information has been changed to:</b><br>
   Full Name (Last, First MI):<br>
   <b><? echo $CName ?></b><br>
   Address:<br>
   <b><? echo $CAddress ?></b><br>
   City:<br>
   <b><? echo $CCity ?></b><br>
   State:<br>
   <b><? echo $CState ?></b><br>
   Zip:<br>
   <b><? echo $CZip ?></b><br>
   Phone:<br>
```

```
    <b><? echo $CPhone ?></b><br>
    Fax:<br>
    <b><? echo $CFax ?></b><br>
    Email:<br>
    <b><? echo $CEmail ?></b><br><br>
<a href=select.php>Back to Select Page</a>
</body>
</html>
```

Notice that this script verifies that information in the database was changed by performing a select query, which displays the changed information in the browser window.

Delete Queries

The delete query is the last of our simple examples. If the delete link is clicked from the initial select query page, the CID ID is passed to the following script:

```
<title>Delete Record</title>
<?
$conn = pg_Connect("localhost", "5432", "", "", "test");
  if (!$conn) {echo "An database connection error occurred.\n"; exit;}
$result = pg_Exec($conn,"DELETE FROM contacts WHERE cid='$ID'");
  if (!$result) {echo "A DELETE query error occurred.\n"; exit;}
pg_FreeResult($result);
pg_Close($conn);
?>
</head>
<body>
<b>The record was deleted</b><br><br>
<a href=select.php>Back to Select Page</a>
</body>
</html>
```

This script simply deletes the record defined by the CID from the database. You can click the Back to Select Page link to verify that the record was deleted.

This concludes the four functions that all database applications perform. We illustrated how PHP accomplishes insert, select, update, and delete queries using PostgreSQL as the database. We also gave some examples of how to use PHP to display and manipulate the information in the Web browser.

Other Database Functions

Many other database functions can be performed other than the basic queries that
were demonstrated earlier. The PHP interface to PostgreSQL enables you to specify
how the information is returned from the database. You can return information as an
array by using `pg_Fetch_Array()` or `pg_Fetch_Row()`. You can return information as an
object by using `pg_Fetch_Object()`. Other functions will return the size and type of
the field or column or the name or number of fields. The description and use of each
of these functions is included in Chapter 10, "Database Extensions." Many useful bits
of information and properties can be returned through the use of these database
functions. A detailed description with examples of each of these functions is beyond
the scope of this book, but each is fairly straightforward and should be easy to
implement.

Error Messages

It is always a good idea to capture and print all error messages. The PHP interface to
PostgreSQL includes a function that allows for this functionality. This function is
`pg_errormessage()` and it accepts the database connection handle and returns the
string of the error. This string is the text of the error message that is generated from
the database back end.

The following example illustrates how to use the `pg_errormessage()` function to
return an error string. The `pg_Connect()` function in the example attempts to connect
to a database that does not exist. If the function returns an error (as it does in this
case), the connection handle is used in the `pg_errormessage()` function to echo the
string to the browser.

```
<html>
<head>
    <title>Generate an Error</title>
</head>
<body>
<?
// Generate an error connecting to a Postgres Database
$conn = pg_Connect("localhost", "5432", "", "", "testerror");
  if (!$conn) {echo pg_errormessage($conn); exit;}
?>
</body>
</html>
```

This example prints out the following error message to the browser window:

```
FATAL 1: Database testerror does not exist in pg_database
```

Transaction Management

As your database-enabled Web applications become bigger and more complex, you will find the need to lock tables and manage the transactions on the database to eliminate data corruption. When two queries access the same tables to perform any operation other than a simple select query, there is the possibility for the data to become corrupted.

The following simple example illustrates how to set up a transaction, perform the query or set of queries, and then commit the transaction. If the transaction fails at any point, the entire sequence is rolled back.

```html
<html>
<head>
    <title>Managing the Transaction</title>
</head>
<body>
<?
// Connect to the Postgres Database
$conn = pg_Connect("localhost", "5432", "", "", "test");
  if (!$conn) {echo "An database connection error occurred.\n"; exit;}
// Begin the Transaction
$result = pg_exec($conn, "begin work;");
  if (!$result) {echo "An error occurred beginning the transaction.\n"; exit;}
// Lock the table
$result = pg_exec($conn, "lock contacts;");
  if (!$result) {echo "An error occurred locking the contacts table.\n"; exit;}
// Insert the static values into the database
$result = pg_Exec($conn,"INSERT INTO contacts VALUES (NEXTVAL('c'),
        'Test Name','Test Address','Test City','TS','11111','111.222.3333',
        '444.555.6666','me@email.com');");
  if (!$result) {echo "An INSERT query error occurred.\n"; exit;}
// Get the last record inserted
$oid = pg_getlastoid($result);
  if (!$oid) {echo "An OID error occurred.\n"; exit;}
// Select the record that was last entered
$result = pg_Exec($conn,"SELECT cid FROM contacts WHERE oid=$oid;");
  if (!$result) {echo "A SELECT query error occurred.\n"; exit;}
```

```php
// Place the result into the variable $CID
$CID = pg_Result($result, 0, "cid");
  if (!$CID) {echo "There is a problem returning the Contact ID.\n"; exit;}
// Print out the Contact ID
  else { echo "The record was successfully entered and the Contact ID is:
        $CID \n";}
// Commit the transaction
pg_exec($conn, "commit work;");
// End the transaction
pg_exec($conn, "end work;");
// Free the result
pg_FreeResult($result);
// Close the connection
pg_Close($conn);
?>
</body>
</html>
```

Notice that the new portions of this insert query include a BEGIN statement that denotes the start of the transaction. The transaction in this example is named work. The next statement is the LOCK statement. This particular statement locks the entire table while the transaction is being performed. There are many types of locks—both table level and row level—that can be placed on a database while transactions are being performed. A discussion of the pros and cons of each of these types of locks is beyond the scope of this book. Please consult your database documentation for a description of the locks that are available.

In the preceding example, the next bit of code performs the database insert and query. This section of code is very elementary, but it is included for illustration purposes. The next two pg_exec() statements end the transaction; the first commits the work transaction, and the second ends the transaction.

Persistent Database Connections

One of the biggest performance increases that you can make to your database application is to use persistent connections. The establishment of a database connection can often take 90% of the total time of the query. In other words, if you can reuse database connections, your application can make all the queries 90% faster. If your application is database intensive, the overall speed of the application can be affected in a positive manner by using persistent connections.

The pg_pConnect() function is the mechanism that you can use to make a persistent database connection. When a connection to the database is requested, PHP checks for an existing connection. If one exists, PHP does not open another connection but reuses the existing connection. If a connection does not exist, PHP opens one.

From the user's perspective, the `pg_pConnect()` function works exactly the same as its nonpersistent counterpart, `pg_connect()`.

Large Objects

Sometimes it might be necessary to store binary objects in a database. PostgreSQL enables you to do this through the use of inversion of large objects. This is the method used to store images, PDF files, and entire Web pages in a database. The use of large objects requires the database table to be set up to accept an object identifier (OID). The `create table` statement looks something like this:

```
create table contacts (
    cid             int4  DEFAULT NEXTVAL('a'),
    name            char (50),
    address         char (50),
    city            char (50),
    state           char (2),
    zip             char (10),
    phone           char (25),
    fax             char (25),
    email           char (50),
    resume          oid,
primary key (cid));
```

This script creates a contacts table with the usual information and another item called resume that is of type oid.

To enter data in this table, including the resume field, the insert query looks like this:

```
INSERT INTO contacts VALUES (NEXTVAL('c'),'Test Name','Test Address',
    'Test City', 'TS','11111','111.222.3333','444.555.6666','me@email.com',
    lo_import('/resumes/rcox.doc'));
```

This query takes a file named rcox.doc from the /resumes directory and imports it into the database as a large object.

Similarly, a select query to pull the resume out of the database looks like this:

```
SELECT cid, name, address, city, state, zip, phone, fax, email,
    lo_export(resume,'/resumes/rcox.doc') FROM contacts WHERE cid=101;
```

This exports the resume from the database, places it in the /resumes directory, and names the file rcox.doc.

The following example illustrates how to use the PHP large object functionality to insert a large object into the database:

```
<html>
<head>
<title>Large Objects</title>
</head>
<body>
<?
// Connect to the Postgres Database
$conn = pg_Connect("localhost", "5432", "", "", "test");
  if (!$conn) {echo "An database connection error occurred.\n"; exit;}
// Begin the Transaction
$result = pg_exec($conn, "begin;");
  if (!$result) {echo "An error occurred beginning the transaction.\n"; exit;}
// Lock the table
$oid = pg_locreate($conn);
 echo ("The Large Object is created with Object ID = $oid<br>");
$handle = pg_loopen ($conn, $oid, "w");
echo ("The Large Object is opened in Write mode with Handle = $handle<br>");
pg_lowrite ($handle, "/resumes/rcox.doc");
pg_loclose ($handle);
pg_exec ($conn, "INSERT INTO contacts VALUES (NEXTVAL('c'),'Test Name',
         'Test Address','Test City','TS','11111','111.222.3333',
         '444.555.6666','me@email.com', $oid);");
pg_exec ($conn, "commit;");
pg_exec ($conn, "end;");
// Free the result
pg_FreeResult($result);
// Close the connection
pg_Close($conn);
?>
</body>
</html>
```

The output of this script should look something like this:

```
The Large Object is created with Object ID = 24097
The Large Object is opened in Write mode with Handle = Resource id #3
```

The ordinary Web programmer would not use large objects on a regular basis. Instead of directly storing binaries in the database, it is usually preferable to store the link to the file and allow the binary to reside on the operating system's filesystem. Storing only the link allows the database to stay lean, and when the information is served to the Web browser, the Web server can include the path to the binary on the filesystem.

PART II

Syntax Reference

CHAPTER 4

The Core PHP 4 Language

Part of understanding a programming language is comprehending its semantics and syntax, and one of the most important parts of any language to digest is its core language elements. Core elements are syntax or concepts that you generally see across multiple languages. These can be anything from how to specify comments to how to control looping.

In this chapter, we take a look at these elements as they pertain to the PHP language. We dive into the following topics:

- Basic syntax
- Constants
- Control structures
- Escape characters
- Objects and functions
- Operators
- Predefined variables

Basic Syntax

Basic syntax is syntax that covers the three most basic elements of the PHP language. These include the tag that signifies PHP code and the two types of comments.

Tags

Tags refer to PHP identifier tags, which, in a sense, are much like HTML tags that direct the interpreter's actions. In this section, we document those tags and how they work with the language.

<?..?>

Syntax

```
<? code ?>
```

Description

The `<?..?>` identifier represents the beginning and ending tags used to identify PHP code, and are shorthand for the `<?php..?>` method. The PHP parser will look for instances of this identifier so that it can execute the *code* within it. Also check out the entries of `<?php..?>`, `<script language="php">..</script>`, and `<%..%>` for additional methods of signifying PHP code.

<?php..?>

Syntax

```
<?php code ?>
```

Description

The `<?php..?>` identifier, which is the default, represents the beginning and ending tags used to identify PHP code. The PHP parser will look for instances of this identifier so that it can execute the *code* within it. Also check out the entries of `<?..?>`, `<script language="php">..</script>`, and `<%..%>` for additional methods of signifying PHP code.

<?php_track_vars?>

Syntax

```
<?php_track_vars?>
```

Description

The `<?php_track_vars?>` execution directive was used in versions of PHP prior to 4.0.1, but was officially removed in that version. Although it was included in PHP 4.0, it did not function, so it is safe to say that it has not been used at all in PHP 4. `<?php_track_vars?>` was simply a directive that told the engine to track certain variables while interpreting. If you want to obtain more information about this directive, please see the PHP Web site at `http://www.php.net`.

<%..%>

Syntax

```
<% code %>
```

Description

The `<%..%>` identifier represents the beginning and ending tags used to identify PHP code when `asp_tags=1` in the PHP configuration file. This is used to help developers who have worked previously with Microsoft's Active Server Pages (ASP) ease into the PHP language. Several applications, such as earlier versions of Macromedia's Dreamweaver, understand ASP tags and know that they should leave them alone, but do not understand the PHP tags.

For these tags, the PHP parser will look for instances of this identifier so that it can execute the *code* within it. Also check out the entries of `<?..?>`, `<?php..?>`, and `<script language="php">..</script>` for additional methods of signifying PHP code.

<script language="php">..</script>

Syntax

```
<script language="php">
  code
</script>
```

Description

The `<script language="php">..</script>` identifier represents the beginning and ending tags used to identify PHP code. The PHP parser will look for instances of this identifier so that it can execute the *code* within it. Also check out the entries of `<?..?>`, `<?php..?>`, and `<%..%>` for additional methods of signifying PHP code.

Comments

If you have been in the programming world at all, you are aware of the need for comments in your code. As in any other language, PHP provides several methods of signifying comments, which are disregarded by the interpreting engine. Comments are covered in this section of the chapter.

//

Syntax

```
// comment
```

Description

The `//` PHP element, which is commonly referred to as a "one-line comment," enables programmers to include comments in their code. This particular style is the same as seen in other languages such as C, C++, Java, and JavaScript; *comment* must appear on only one line and after the `//` indicator. Here is a quick example of using this method of commenting:

```
// C, Java, and JavaScript programmers should understand how this method works
// in the PHP programming language.
```

/*..*/

Syntax

```
/*
   comment
*/
```

Description

The `/*..*/` PHP element is another method of defining a comment in the PHP language. This method enables you to write comments that span multiple lines, so you can format your comments without using multiple // instances. Be careful when using this syntax and avoid nesting any comments. Here is a quick example of using this method of commenting:

```
/*
Title: Understanding comments
Description: In your comments you may wish to have comments that span
more than one line. If so, this is the method you should use.
*/
```

#

Syntax

```
# comment
```

Description

The # PHP element, which is commonly referred to as a "UNIX shell-style comment," enables programmers to include one-line comments in their code. This particular style is the same as the one seen in UNIX shells and, likewise, *comment* must appear on only one line and after the # indicator. Here is a quick example of using this method of commenting:

```
# You Perl programmers should understand how this method works
# in the PHP programming language.
```

Constants

Constants are a way for a programmer to define constant values for variables by using the define() method at runtime. The difference between these variables and other variables that you might have in your code is that these cannot be changed.

In this section of the book, we look at several predefined PHP constants that reflect the environment in which the PHP interpreter is running.

__FILE__

Syntax

```
__FILE__
```

Description

The __FILE__ constant reflects the name of the current file being parsed by the PHP interpreter.

__LINE__

Syntax

__LINE__

Description

The __LINE__ constant reflects the line number of the current file being parsed by the PHP interpreter.

E_ERROR

Syntax

E_ERROR

Description

The E_ERROR constant contains a nonparsing and nonrecoverable error that has occurred. Additionally, you can use the error_reporting() function to specify the level of error reports you want out of this function.

E_NOTICE

Syntax

E_NOTICE

Description

The E_NOTICE constant contains what may or may not be an error in your PHP code, but either way, it does not prevent the code from completing execution. Additionally, you can use the error_reporting() function to specify the level of error reports you want out of this function.

E_PARSE

Syntax

E_PARSE

Description

The E_PARSE constant reflects the fact that the PHP parser failed because of a syntax problem and cannot recover. Additionally, you can use the error_reporting() function to specify the level of error reports you want out of this function.

E_WARNING

Syntax

E_WARNING

Description

The E_WARNING constant contains an error in your PHP code, but does not prevent the code from completing execution. Additionally, you can use the error_reporting() function to specify the level of error reports you want out of this function.

PHP_OS

Syntax

PHP_OS

Description

The PHP_OS constant reflects the name of the operating system that is currently parsing and interpreting the PHP code. If you are running scripts across multiple platforms, this enables you to check the operating system before performing any system-specific tasks.

PHP_VERSION

Syntax

PHP_VERSION

Description

The PHP_VERSION constant contains a string that reflects the exact version of the PHP interpreter.

FALSE

Syntax

FALSE

Description

The FALSE constant reflects a Boolean false value.

TRUE

Syntax

TRUE

Description

The TRUE constant reflects a Boolean true value.

Control Structures and Statements

Control structures and statements are items that all programmers use to control the flow of their programs. This includes most looping commands, such as if or while statements, and other commands, such as break and continue, that can be used to control the program execution in the body of a control structure.

break

Syntax

break [int num]

Description

The break statement enables you to break out of an if, switch, or while control structure. The optional num value can be used to tell the parser how many control structures to break out of. For instance, if you used a break statement inside an if statement that was inside a while statement itself, you could use break 2 to break out of both statements. Using break 1, which is the default implied value when not passed, would simply break you out of the if statement.

```
if($num == 5){
  // do something here
  if($string == "go"){
    // do more here
    break 2; // breaks outside of both if statements
  }
}
// the break 2 will start back here if executed
```

continue

Syntax

```
continue [int num]
```

Description

The continue statement enables you to stop the execution of the current control iteration and break out to the beginning for the next iteration. The optional num value can be used to tell the parser how many control structures to continue out of. For instance, if you used a continue statement inside a while statement that was inside a second while statement itself, you could use continue 2 to break out of both statements. Using continue 1, which is the default implied value when not passed, would simply cause you to continue out of the second, or nested, while statement.

```
if($num == 5){ // continue statement will come back here if executed
  // do something here
  if($string == "go"){
    // do more here
    $string = "stop";
    continue 2; // breaks outside of both if statements back to first if
  }
  $num++;
}
```

do..while

Syntax

```
do{
    code
}while(condition)
```

Description

The do..while loop is just like the while loop except that it evaluates the condition after the execution of the loop rather than before. The effect of this is that you are guaranteed that the loop will execute at least once, whereas the while loop does not allow for this.

else

Syntax

```
if(condition){
    code
[
}elseif(condition){
    code
]
}else{
    code
}
```

Description

The else statement, which extends the if or elseif statements, provides a default set of code to be executed if previous if or elseif statements fail condition. The brackets around the elseif portion of the syntax example show that this is an optional part of a statement, whereas the if portion is required for the else statement.

elseif

Syntax

```
if(condition){
    code
```

```
}elseif(condition){
  code
[
}else{
  code
]
}
```

Description

The elseif statement, which extends the if statement, provides a second evaluation on a second *condition* before a set of *code* is to be executed. This assumes that previous if or other elseif statements fail their respective *condition*. The brackets around the else portion of the syntax example show that this is an optional part of a statement, whereas the if portion is required for the elseif statement.

for

Syntax

```
for([assignment];[condition];[change_assignment]{
  code
}
```

Description

The for loop has been labeled as the most complex looping structure not only in PHP, but in other programming languages as well. This loop takes an initial *assignment* where a variable is assigned a value. The second parameter specifies a *condition* that is evaluated before each iteration of the loop. If the *condition* evaluates to true, the *code* is executed and the *change_assignment*, such as increasing or decreasing the *assignment* by 1, is performed. At that time, the *condition* is reevaluated with the new value of the *assignment* and the process repeats itself. This continues until *condition* is false.

These parameters are all optional, which might come as a surprise. Leaving them, or even just *condition*, blank will cause the for to loop indefinitely, but does allow you to use an internal break statement to end the loop. You can also see the for..:..endfor entry for a different syntactical way to use the for loop.

> **Note**
> If you want to get extra tricky with the for loop, you can also include comma-separated
> code to be executed in the *change_assignement*. For instance, you could use print
> $counter, $counter++ to print the $counter value on each iteration through the loop. For
> more information about what the ++ means in this example, see the "Incrementing and
> Decrementing" section later in this chapter.

for..:..endfor

Syntax

```
for([assignment];[condition];[change_assignment]):
  code
endfor
```

Description

The for..:..endfor loop is an alternative syntax for the for loop. Using this method,
the opening and closing braces are replaced with : and endfor, respectively. See the
for entry for more information on *condition* and *code*.

foreach

Syntax

```
foreach(array as current_value){
  code
}

foreach(array as current_key => current_value){
  code
}
```

Description

The foreach loop, which was added in PHP4, has two syntactical definitions. In both
definitions the loop takes an *array* and iterates through it. In doing so, it stores the
current_value so that it can be referenced and processed in *code*. For associative
arrays, you can use the second syntactical definition to also store the corresponding
current_key for processing in *code*. The following example should help clarify:

```
// create an array
$weekdays = array (
  "Sunday" => 0,
  "Monday" => 1,
  "Tuesday" => 2,
  "Wednesday" => 3,
  "Thursday" => 4,
  "Friday" => 5,
  "Saturday" => 6
  );

// print out each day with the number it is associated with
foreach($weekday as $day => $number) {
  print "\$weekday = $day.\n";
}
```

if

Syntax

```
if(condition){
  code
}
[
elseif(condition){
  code
}else{
  code
}
]
```

Description

The if statement enables you to execute *code* based on successful validation of *condition*. This statement is one of the most widely used statements in any programming language, and PHP is no different. Optionally, as the syntax description shows, it is often used in conjunction with elseif and/or else statements to provide addition levels of control over *code* execution.

if..:..endif

Syntax

```
if(condition):
    code
endif;
```

Description

The if..:..endif statement is an alternative syntax for the if statement. Using this method, the opening and closing braces are replaced with : and endif, respectively. See the entry for if for more information on condition and code.

include()

Syntax

```
include(string filename)
```

Description

The include() function enables you to include other files specified by filename. These secondary files can be valid PHP code or any text, such as HTML. If you do have additional PHP code that needs to be executed, be sure that you use the proper beginning and ending PHP tags or the parser will not execute the code.

The require() language construct has similar capabilities. The major difference is that include() is executed each time it is encountered, whereas require() pulls in the contents of the included file once. You can see the difference if you place these functions in the body of a loop statement.

Tip
You can place a return statement in the included file to terminate the parsing of the file and return to the file that performed the inclusion.

---

require()

Syntax

```
require(string filename)
```

Description

The require() language construct, which is similar to the Server Side Include (SSI) #include directive, enables you to include other files specified by *filename*. These secondary files can be valid PHP code or any text, such as HTML. If you do have additional PHP code that needs to be executed, be sure that you use the proper beginning and ending PHP tags or the parser will not execute the code.

The difference between this and include() is that include() calls are executed each time they are encountered, whereas require() pulls in the contents of the included file always and only once. This means it will pull in the file even if it is not executed (such as in the body of an if statement that did not pass its condition). This is unlike include(), which pulls in the file only when executed.

> **Note**
> PHP3 enabled programmers to execute return statements in the included file, but PHP4 has deprecated that feature, so avoid using it.

switch..case

Syntax

```
switch(variable){
   case value1:
     code
     [break;]
   case value2:
     code
     [break;]
   case valueN:
     code
     [break;]
[  default:
     code]
}
```

Description

The switch..case statement has an effect similar to that of multiple if statements. For *variable*, the statement will look at each case (*value1*, *value2*,..., *valueN*) to determine where *variable* is equal. When a match is found, *code* under that case is executed. If you want to break out of the statement completely after you have found a match, you need to include the optional break command; otherwise, every portion of code will be executed—not just the code under the case it matched.

If you want to include a default value in case of no matches, include the default section. The code under this section will be executed if none of the previous case statements match.

switch..:..endswitch

Syntax

```
switch(variable):
  case value1:
    code
    [break;]
  case value2:
    code
    [break;]
  case valueN:
    code
    [break;]
[ default:
    code]
endswitch;
```

Description

The switch..:..endswitch statement is an alternative syntax for the switch..case loop. Using this method, the opening and closing braces are replaced with : and endswitch, respectively. See the switch..case entry for more information on variable, value(s), and code.

```
switch($num):
  case 0:
    echo "The number is 0";
    break;
  case 1:
    echo "The number is 1";
    break;
  default:
    echo "The number is not 0 or 1";
endswitch;
```

while

Syntax

```
while(condition){
  code
}
```

Description

The while loop evaluates the condition and if it evaluates to true, executes code. This will continue until condition no longer evaluates to true. This loop is similar to the do..while loop except that it is not guaranteed to execute at least once, whereas the do..while loop is.

while:..endwhile

Syntax

```
while(condition):
  code
endwhile;
```

Description

The while..:..endwhile statement is an alternative syntax for the while loop. Using this method, the opening and closing braces are replaced with : and endwhile, respectively. See the while entry for more information on condition and code.

Escape Characters

Escape characters are signified by a \ before one of several reserved characters that signify noncharacter data, such as a tab or space. These characters are often used when parsing through strings or outputting text that requires these characters.

\n

Syntax

```
\n
```

Description

The \n escape character represents a newline character. This is often thought of as the character entered when pressing the Return or Enter key on your keyboard.

\r

Syntax

\r

Description

The \r escape character represents a carriage return. In the Macintosh world, this is the character entered when pressing the Return or Enter key on your keyboard.

\t

Syntax

\t

Description

The \t escape character is used to represent the entry of a tab.

\\

Syntax

\\

Description

The \\ escape character does not escape a non-character–based entry, but rather is used to represent a backslash, "\". This is necessary only because the backslash is a reserved character in the PHP language and must be escaped when you are literally referring to that character.

\$

Syntax

\$

Description

The \$ escape character is used to represent the dollar sign.

\"

Syntax

\"

Description

The \" escape character does not escape a non-character–based entry, but rather is used to represent a double quotation mark (").

\[0-7]{1,3}

Syntax

\[0-7]{1,3}

Description

The \[0-7]{1,3} syntax specifies that the sequence of characters matching ([0-7]) the regular expression is a character in octal notation that contains one or three characters (defined by the {1,3}).

\x[0-9A-Fa-f]{1,2}

Syntax

\x[0-9A-Fa-f]{1,2}

Description

The \x[0-9A-Fa-f]{1,2} syntax specifies that the sequence of characters matching ([0-9A-Fa-f]) the regular expression is a character in hexadecimal notation that contains one or two characters (defined by the {1,2}).

Objects and Functions

Some groups of PHP's syntax, such as functions and classes, revolve around the ability of the programmer to define his own functionality. This could be anything from a piece of code to be reused for repetitive calculations to the creation of actual objects. These language elements are defined in this section of the chapter.

class

Syntax

```
class name {
  [variable]
  [function name(){
  }]
}
```

Description

A class is a set of *variables* and the *named* functions (that operate on the *variables*) which make up an object. After the object is defined, new instances can be created using the new constructor.

A vehicle object, for instance, could contain certain properties (defined by the *variables* in a PHP class), such as a color or the number of doors. Additionally, this vehicle object could move or stop—these actions can be defined by the *named* functions in the PHP class.

class..extends

Syntax

```
class new_class extends base_class{
  [variable]
  [function name(){
  }]
}
```

Description

The class..extends provides the ability to derive new classes, referenced by *new_class*, out of an existing *base_class*. In these instances, all the variables and functions are inherited from the *base_class* in addition to the ones defined by *variable* and *named* functions.

create_function()

Syntax

```
string create_function(string arguments, string code)
```

Description

The create_function() function, which was added in PHP 4.0.1, creates an anonymous function and returns a unique name for it. The created function performs the *code* that is passed and can accept any *arguments*. Because you might need to create a function with more than one argument, you can pass *arguments* as a single quote, comma-delimited string. For instance, you could do the following:

```
create_function('$arg1,$arg2', 'echo "You passed in $arg1 $arg2");
```

function

Syntax

```
function name([params]){
  code
}
```

Description

A function enables a programmer to define a reusable piece of code. This code could potentially take an optional number of *params* and potentially return a result.

For instance, if you wanted to check the Celsius or Fahrenheit temperature of a number passed, you could create a function that took the numeric temperature value and the type (Celsius or Fahrenheit). This function could then return the corresponding value based in the other unit of measurement. Defining this as a function enables you to reuse the code over and over for an unlimited number of computations.

In PHP3, these functions must be defined before they are used, but in PHP4 this has changed. Additionally, PHP4 adds support for variable-length argument lists.

> **Note**
> In addition to `function`, PHP also has an `old_function`, which allows for support of PHP/FI2 syntax. However, this feature has been deprecated and should be avoided. We wanted to mention it only in case you run across the function in some legacy applications.

new

Syntax

variable = new *class*

Description

The new keyword creates a new instance named *variable* of the *class* specified.

Operators

Operators are language elements that enable you to evaluate or impose conditions on items, such as variables, in your program. There are also operators that enable you to perform mathematical functions, incrementing and decrementing, and logical operations.

An important part of using operators, which were covered in Chapter 1, "Basic PHP," is understanding precedence. Precedence determines the order in which the operators are performed in a given equation. We all remember from grade school that multiplication and division occur before addition and subtraction, which outlines the precedence of these operators. Table 4.1 lists the operator precedence in PHP.

Table 4.1 *Operator Precedence in PHP*

Associativity	Operators
Non-associative	new
Right	[
Right	!, ~, ++, --, (int), (double), (string), (array), (object), @
Left	*, /, %
Left	+, -, .
Left	<<, >>
Non-associative	<, <=, >, >=

Table 4.1   *(continued)*

Associativity	Operators
Non-associative	==, !=, ===
Left	&
Left	^
Left	|
Left	&&
Left	||
Left	?, :
Left	=, +=, -=, *=, /=, .=, %=, &=, |=, ^=, ~=, <<=, >>=
Right	print
Left	and
Left	xor
Left	or
Left	,

Arithmetic

The list of arithmetic operators contains the list of mathematical operations that are common in all programming languages. These operators enable you to perform the basic adding, subtracting, division, multiplication, and modulus of numerical (and sometimes string) values.

+ (Addition)

Syntax

num1 + num2

Description

The + operator is used when you want to add *num1* to *num2*. These values are numerical.

- (Subtraction)

Syntax

num1 - num2

Description

The - operator is used when you want to subtract *num2* from *num1*. These values are numerical.

* (Multiplication)

Syntax

*num1 * num2*

Description

The * operator is used when you want to multiply *num1* by *num2*. These values are numerical.

/ (Division)

Syntax

num1 /num2

Description

The / operator is used when you want to divide *num1* by *num2*. These values are numerical.

% (Modulus)

Syntax

num1 %num2

Description

The % operator is used to obtain the integer remainder of dividing *num1* by *num2*. For instance, if *num1*=5 and *num2*=3, the integer returned from this operation will be 2. These values are numerical.

```
$result = 5 % 3; // returns 2 into $result
```

Assignment

Assignment operators are some of the most powerful operators available. They enable you to assign a value, which might be the result of a computation, to a variable. After the value is in a variable, it can be used for later processing. This section of the chapter outlines the assignment operators in PHP and how they can be used.

=

Syntax

```
variable = num

variable = string

variable1 = variable2

variable1 = &variable2
```

Description

The = operator will assign *variable* to the *num* or *string* on the right side of the operand. The second syntactical definition shows how a variable can be assigned the same value as another variable—a "copy" is made. The final definition shows the assignment of *variable2* to *variable1* as a reference, which means that if *variable2* changes, so does *variable1*.

```
$first = 5;
$second = $first; // $second = 5 now
```

+=

Syntax

```
num1 += num2
```

Description

The += operator is used when you want to add *num1* to *num2* and assign the new value to *num1*. These values are numerical.

```
$num = 5;
$num += 3; // $num now equals 8
```

-=

Syntax

num1 -= *num2*

Description

The -= operator is used when you want to subtract *num2* from *num1* and assign the new value to *num1*. These values are numerical.

*=

Syntax

num1 *= *num2*

Description

The *= operator is used when you want to multiply *num1* by *num2* and assign the new value to *num1*. These values are numerical.

```
$num = 5;
$num *= 3; // $num now equals 15
```

/=

Syntax

num1 /=*num2*

Description

The /= operator is used when you want to divide *num1* by *num2* and assign the new value to *num1*. These values are numerical.

%=

Syntax

num1 %=num2

Description

The %= operator is used to obtain the integer remainder of dividing *num1* by *num2* and assign the new value to *num1*. For instance, if *num1*=5 and *num2*=3, the integer returned from this operation will be 2 and it would be stored in *num1*. These values are numerical.

Bitwise

Bitwise operators are one of the most difficult operations to understand for new programmers. In short, they convert the items into their binary equivalents, such as and and or, for operations that they are to perform.

> **Note**
> Going into detail on the overall concept of bitwise operations is beyond this scope of this book, but the descriptions and examples contained in this section should provide enough information to enable you to perform any bitwise tasks you need.

& (and)

Syntax

variable1 & variable2

Description

The & operator, after the conversion of *variable1* and *variable2* to their binary equivalents, will check to see where bit instances are both equal to 1. To help you understand this, let's take a look, in Table 4.2, at the binary representation of 5 and 6 and see how applying the & operator effects the result.

Table 4.2 *Example of Using the & Operator*

Number	Binary Equivalent
5	101
6	110
Result	100 = 4

As you can see in the table, the result is true only when both binary positions are 1.

| (or)

Syntax

variable1 | *variable2*

Description

The | operator, after the conversion of *variable1* and *variable2* to their binary equivalents, will check to see where either bit instances are equal to 1. To help you understand this, let's take a look, in Table 4.3, at the binary representation of 5 and 6 and see how applying the | operator effects the result.

Table 4.3 *Example of Using the | Operator*

Number	Binary Equivalent
5	101
6	110
Result	111 = 7

As you can see in the table, the result is true when either binary position is 1.

^ (xor)

Syntax

variable1 ^ *variable2*

Description

The ^ operator, after the conversion of *variable1* and *variable2* to their binary equivalents, will check to see where either bit instances, but not both, is equal to 1.

To help you understand this, let's take a look, in Table 4.4, at the binary representation of 5 and 6 and see how applying the ^ operator effects the result.

Table 4.4   *Example of Using the ^ Operator*

Number	Binary Equivalent
5	101
6	110
Result	011 = 3

As you can see in the table, the result is true only when either binary position is 1 and not both.

~ (not)

Syntax

~variable

Description

The ~ operator, after the conversion of *variable* to its binary equivalent, will reverse the bit instances. For instance, if you had the number 4 in binary (100) and you applied the ~ operator, the new value would be 2 (011).

<< (Shift Left)

Syntax

variable1 << variable2

Description

The << operator will shift *variable1* by *variable2* bits to the left. This means that the right side of the binary version of *variable1* will become "padded" with *variable2* number of zeros. This is often used to multiply by two for each *variable2* (that is, if *variable2*=2, it will multiply by 4).

>> (Shift Right)

Syntax

`variable1 >> variable2`

Description

The >> operator will shift `variable1` by `variable2` bits to the right. This means that the left side of the binary version of `variable1` will become "padded" with `variable2` number of zeros. This is often used to divide by two for each `variable2` (that is, if `variable2=2`, it will divide by 4).

Comparison

The lists of comparison operators are most often used in conjunction with the control structures. Within the control structure, programmers use comparison operators to compare variables, strings, numeric values, and so on to check whether the body of the control structure should be performed. For example, you might want to know whether a variable was greater than 10 before performing, and it is the comparison operators that enable you to do this.

== (Equal)

Syntax

`variable1 == variable2`

Description

The == operator compares `variable1` to `variable2` to see whether they are equal. If they are, true is returned.

=== (Identical)

Syntax

`variable1 === variable2`

Description

The === operator compares `variable1` to `variable2` to see whether they are identical and are of the same data type. If they are, true is returned.

```
$num1 = 5;
$num2 = 5;
$string = "5";
$result1 = ($num1 === $num2); // returns 1
$result2 = ($num1 === $string); // returns 0
```

!= (Not Equal)

Syntax

variable1 != *variable2*

Description

The != operator compares *variable1* to *variable2* to see whether they are not equal. If they are not equal, true is returned.

< (Less Than)

Syntax

variable1 < *variable2*

Description

The < operator checks whether *variable1* is less than *variable2*. If so, true is returned.

> (Greater Than)

Syntax

variable1 > *variable2*

Description

The > operator checks whether *variable1* is greater than *variable2*. If so, true is returned.

<= (Less Than or Equal)

Syntax

```
variable1 <= variable2
```

Description

The <= operator checks whether *variable1* is less than or equal to *variable2*. If so, true is returned.

```
$num1 = 5;
$num2 = 4;
$result = ($num1 <= $num2); // returns 0
```

>= (Greater Than or Equal)

Syntax

```
variable1 >= variable2
```

Description

The >= operator checks to see if *variable1* is greater than or equal to *variable2*. If so, true is returned.

Incrementing and Decrementing

The incrementing and decrementing operators are used to increase or decrease the values of the items to which they are applied. This process can occur in a pre- or post-timeframe, and is most often used to increase or decrease counters, such as in loops.

++*num* (Pre-Increment)

Syntax

```
++num
```

Description

The ++*num* operator increases the value of *num* by one. If *num*=0 and ++*num* is applied, *num* will now equal 1. Because the ++ operator is applied before *num*, the increase is applied before anything else. For instance, if you tried to print ++*num* when *num*=0, it would print 1. This is the opposite of post-increment, where 0 would be printed and the value would be adjusted after the print statement.

--*num* (Pre-Decrement)

Syntax

--num

Description

The *--num* operator decreases the value of *num* by one. If *num*=1 and *--num* is applied, *num* will now equal 0. Because the *--* operator is applied before *num*, the decrease is applied before anything else. For instance, if you tried to print *--num* when *num*=1, it would print 0. This is the opposite of post-decrement, where 1 would be printed and the value would be adjusted after the print statement.

num++ (Post-Increment)

Syntax

num++

Description

The *num++* operator increases the value of *num* by one. If *num*=0 and *num++* is applied, *num* will now equal 1. Because the *++* operator is applied after *num*, the increase is applied after anything else. For instance, if you tried to print *num++* when *num*=0, it would print 0. This is the opposite of pre-increment, where 1 would be printed and the value would be adjusted before the print statement.

num-- (Post-Decrement)

Syntax

num--

Description

The *num--* operator decreases the value of *num* by one. If *num*=1 and *num--* is applied, *num* will now equal 0. Because the *--* operator is applied after *num*, the decrease is applied after anything else. For instance, if you tried to print *num--* when *num=1*, it would print 1. This is the opposite of pre-decrement where 0 would be printed and the value would be adjusted before the print statement.

Other

Some groups of operators, such as error control, have only one language element in them. For organization reasons, we have included these items in this section of this chapter.

@ (Error Control)

Syntax

@expression

Description

The @ operator, which can be prepended to any PHP expression, tells the interpreter to ignore any error messages that it might encounter.

> **Note**
> Any errors that are encountered will be stored in the `$php_errormsg` variable if the `track_errors` option is set in the configuration file. If there is an error, this enables you to stop the program, access the error, and write it to the page. See the `die()` entry in Chapter 5, "PHP Language Extensions," for more information.

`..` (Execution)

Syntax

`` `command` ``

Description

The `` `..` `` operator will attempt to execute the shell *command*. If you set a variable equal to this operator, the results of running *command* will be stored in the variable.

> **Warning**
> These are backticks, *not* single quotes.

Logical

Logical operators are very similar to comparison operators and are used to evaluate Boolean expressions. When using this type of operator, it is important to understand the corresponding truth tables. In this section of the chapter, we discuss these operators and each entry will contain its corresponding truth table.

and

Syntax

variable1 and *variable2*

Description

The and operator evaluates whether both *variable1* and *variable2* are true, or equal. Table 4.5 contains the truth table for the possible values. In understanding the truth table, you can see the only time the equation returns true is when both *variable1* and *variable2* are true.

> **Note**
> The only difference between this operator and the && operator is order precedence.

Table 4.5   *Truth Table for the* and *Operator*

variable1	variable2	Result
False	False	False
False	True	False
True	False	False
True	True	True

or

Syntax

variable1 or *variable2*

Description

The or operator evaluates whether either *variable1* or *variable2* is true. Table 4.6 contains the truth table for the possible values. In understanding the truth table, you can see the only time the equation returns false is when both *variable1* and *variable2* are false.

> **Note**
> The only difference between this operator and the || operator is order precedence.

Table 4.6   *Truth Table for the* or *Operator*

variable1	variable2	Result
False	False	False
False	True	True
True	False	True
True	True	True

xor

Syntax

variable1 xor *variable2*

Description

The xor, or exclusive or operator, evaluates whether either *variable1* and *variable2*, but not both, is true. Table 4.7 contains the truth table for the possible values. In understanding the truth table, you can see when *variable1* and *variable2* are the same, false is returned.

Table 4.7   *Truth Table for the* xor *Operator*

variable1	variable2	Result
False	False	False
False	True	True
True	False	True
True	True	False

! (not)

Syntax

!*variable*

Description

The !, or not operator, returns the opposite of *variable*. For instance, if *variable* is true, applying the ! operator will return false.

&& (and)

Syntax

variable1 && *variable2*

Description

The && operator evaluates whether *variable1* and *variable2* are true, or equal. Table 4.8 contains the truth table for the possible values. In understanding the truth table, you can see the only time the equation returns true is when both *variable1* and *variable2* are true.

> **Note**
> The only difference between this operator and the and operator is order precedence.

Table 4.8   *Truth Table for && Operator*

variable1	variable2	Result
False	False	False
False	True	False
True	False	False
True	True	True

|| (or)

Syntax

variable1 || variable2

Description

The || operator evaluates whether either *variable1* or *variable2* is true. Table 4.9 contains the truth table for the possible values. In understanding the truth table, you can see the only time the equation returns false is when both *variable1* and *variable2* are false.

Note
The only difference between this operator and the or operator is order precedence.

Table 4.9   *Truth Table for the || Operator*

variable1	variable2	Result
False	False	False
False	True	True
True	False	True
True	True	True

String

The string operators are used to perform manipulation on the string data types. Although some of the previous operators discussed in this section can be performed on strings as well, these are limited to strings only.

. (Concatenation)

Syntax

string1 . *string2*

Description

The ., or concatenation operator, will "add" *string2* to *string1* when applied. For instance, if *string1*="P" and *string2*="HP", string1 . string2 would equal "PHP".

```
$string1 = "hel";
$string2 = "p";
$string3 = "lo";
$result1 = $sting1 . $string2; // $result1 has "help"
$result2 = $sting1 . $string3; // $result2 has "hello"
```

.= (Concatenating Assignment)

Syntax

string1 .= *string2*

Description

The ., or concatenating assignment operator, will "add" *string2* to *string1* when applied and then store the new string in *string1*. For instance, if *string1*="P" and *string2*="HP", then string1 .= string2 would equal "PHP" and that would be the new value of *string1*.

Predefined Variables

Predefined variables in PHP refer to language elements that are consistent across all applications run in that environment. This is very much like the environment variables you see within the UNIX and Windows operating systems. (Type env at a command line to see a list of your operating system variables.)

Apache

The Apache predefined variables reflect the environment settings of your Apache Web server when running PHP. There are also variables that reflect information about a request of a given user-agent, or browser. This enables you to grab the requested URL, query string, or another element of the HTTP request.

DOCUMENT_ROOT

Syntax

```
string DOCUMENT_ROOT
```

Description

The DOCUMENT_ROOT variable contains the document root, as defined in the PHP configuration file, under which the current script is being parsed.

GATEWAY_INTERFACE

Syntax

```
string GATEWAY_INTERFACE
```

Description

The GATEWAY_INTERFACE variable contains the version of the Common Gateway Interface (CGI) specification that the server is using. For instance, CGI/1.1 is a valid GATEWAY_INTERFACE.

HTTP_ACCEPT

Syntax

```
string HTTP_ACCEPT
```

Description

The HTTP_ACCEPT variable contains the contents of the HTTP Accept: header if the user-agent sent it to the server.

HTTP_ACCEPT_CHARSET

Syntax

```
string HTTP_ACCEPT_CHARSET
```

Description

The `HTTP_ACCEPT_CHARSET` variable contains the contents of the HTTP `Accept-Charset:` header if the user-agent sent it to the server.

HTTP_ACCEPT_LANGUAGE

Syntax

```
string HTTP_ACCEPT_LANGUAGE
```

Description

The `HTTP_ACCEPT_LANGUAGE` variable contains the contents of the HTTP `Accept-Language:` header if the user-agent sent it to the server.

HTTP_CONNECTION

Syntax

```
string HTTP_CONNECTION
```

Description

The `HTTP_CONNECTION` variable contains the contents of the HTTP `Connection:` header if the user-agent sent it to the server.

HTTP_ENCODING

Syntax

```
string HTTP_ENCODING
```

Description

The `HTTP_ENCODING` variable contains the contents of the HTTP `Accept-Encoding:` header if the user-agent sent it to the server.

HTTP_HOST

Syntax

```
string HTTP_HOST
```

Description

The HTTP_HOST variable contains the contents of the HTTP Host: header if the user-agent sent it to the server.

HTTP_REFERER

Syntax

```
string HTTP_REFERER
```

Description

The HTTP_REFERER variable contains the URL of the page from which the user-agent came. This might not be sent by the user-agent.

HTTP_USER_AGENT

Syntax

```
string HTTP_USER_AGENT
```

Description

The HTTP_USER_AGENT variable contains the contents of the HTTP User_Agent: header if the user-agent sent it to the server. For instance, if you access this when an Internet Explorer 5.5 browser on Windows NT 4 makes a request, you get the following:

```
echo HTTP_USER_AGENT; // writes "Mozilla/4.0 (compatible; MSIE 5.5; Windows NT
4.0)"
```

PATH_TRANSLATED

Syntax

```
string PATH_TRANSLATED
```

Description

The PATH_TRANSLATED variable contains the actual filesystem path to the file being processed.

QUERY_STRING

Syntax

```
string QUERY_STRING
```

Description

The QUERY_STRING variable contains everything sent to the server after the ? character in a URL. So, if http://www.mcp.com/createuser.php?name=allen&gender=male were sent, the value of this variable would be name=allen&gender=male.

REMOTE_ADDR

Syntax

```
string REMOTE_ADDR
```

Description

The REMOTE_ADDR variable contains the IP address of the user-agent making the request to the server.

REMOTE_PORT

Syntax

```
string REMOTE_PORT
```

Description

The REMOTE_PORT variable contains the port number being used by the user-agent making the request to the server.

REQUEST_METHOD

Syntax

```
string REQUEST_METHOD
```

Description

The REQUEST_METHOD variable contains the value of the type of request made. Within the HTTP world, this could be a value such as GET, POST, HEAD, or PUT.

REQUEST_URI

Syntax

```
script REQUEST_URI
```

Description

The REQUEST_URI variable contains the actual PATH_INFO that was requested by the user-agent. For example, it could hold a value such as /sports/baseball/news.html.

SCRIPT_FILENAME

Syntax

```
string SCRIPT_FILENAME
```

Description

The SCRIPT_FILENAME variable contains the complete pathname of the file being parsed by the PHP interpreter.

SCRIPT_NAME

Syntax

```
string SCRIPT_NAME
```

Description

The SCRIPT_NAME variable contains the current script's path.

SERVER_ADMIN

Syntax

```
string SERVER_ADMIN
```

Description

The SERVER_ADMIN variable is an Apache-only setting. It contains the value of the
server's administrator directive setting in the Apache configuration file.

SERVER_NAME

Syntax

```
string SERVER_NAME
```

Description

The SERVER_NAME variable contains the name of the server host processing the PHP
page. If the server is a virtual server, it will contain the virtual host information.

SERVER_PORT

Syntax

```
string SERVER_PORT
```

Description

The SERVER_PORT variable contains the port number on which the server is running.
The default setting for Web servers on the Internet is port 80.

SERVER_PROTOCOL

Syntax

```
string SERVER_PROTOCOL
```

Description

The SERVER_PROTOCOL variable contains the name and version of the protocol used in
the request. For example, HTTP/1.1 is a valid value for SERVER_PROTOCOL.

SERVER_SIGNATURE

Syntax

```
string SERVER_SIGNATURE
```

Description

The SERVER_SIGNATURE variable contains the server host name and version number.

SERVER_SOFTWARE

Syntax

```
string SERVER_SOFTWARE
```

Description

The SERVER_SOFTWARE variable contains the server string, which is similar to a user-agent (or browser) string.

PHP

The last section of this chapter contains PHP variables that are constant within the PHP installation. Additionally, there are a couple of variables that are present when PHP scripts are run on the command line.

argv

Syntax

```
array argv
```

Description

The argv array contains a list of options passed to the PHP script if it was executed on the command line.

argc

Syntax

```
int argc
```

Description

The argc variable contains the number of options that were passed to the PHP script if it was executed on the command line.

PHP_SELF

Syntax

```
string PHP_SELF
```

Description

The PHP_SELF variable contains the filename of the script currently being processed, relative to the document root. Please note that this variable is not available if you are running the PHP interpreter on the command line.

HTTP_COOKIE_VARS

Syntax

```
array HTTP_COOKIE_VARS
```

Description

HTTP_COOKIE_VARS contains an associative array of keys and values passed to the PHP script via cookies, which are available in the HTTP header. This is available only if the tracking variables have been turned on within the PHP environment. This can be accomplished in either of the following ways:

- <?php_track_vars?> (no longer supported in PHP 4)

- track_vars configuration file directive

HTTP_GET_VARS

Syntax

```
array HTTP_GET_VARS
```

Description

HTTP_GET_VARS contains an associative array of keys and values passed to the PHP script via the HTTP GET method of form submission. This is available only if the tracking variables have been turned on within the PHP environment. This can be accomplished in either of the following ways:

- <?php_track_vars?> (no longer supported in PHP 4)

- track_vars configuration file directive

HTTP_POST_VARS

Syntax

array HTTP_POST_VARS

Description

HTTP_POST_VARS contains an associative array of keys and values passed to the PHP script via the HTTP POST method of form submission. This is available only if the tracking variables have been turned on within the PHP environment. This can be accomplished in either of the following ways:

- <?php_track_vars?> (no longer supported in PHP 4)

- track_vars configuration file directive

CHAPTER 5

PHP Language Extensions

This chapter primarily details which functions are available in PHP to work with numbers, arrays, and strings. In addition, this chapter describes functions that provide information about the environment and variables that are available to the PHP script that is currently running.

Arbitrary-Precision Mathematics

PHP's arbitrary-precision mathematics functions enable you to perform mathematical operations on real numbers, which include integers, longs, floats, and doubles. The term *arbitrary-precision* stems from the ability you have with these functions to specify a scale parameter. *Scale* represents the number of digits to the right of the decimal point in a number that should be considered in both the calculation and the output. In PHP, arbitrary-precision numbers are represented as strings for parameters and return values.

These functions are part of the bcmath library, which must be separately compiled into PHP (using `--enable-bcmath` during configuration) because of licensing restrictions. For more information, consult the readme.bcmath file that is included with the PHP source files.

bcadd()

Syntax

```
string bcadd(string left_operand, string right_operand, [int scale])
```

Description

The bcadd() function calculates the sum of the left and right operands and returns the result as a string. The optional *scale* parameter is used to indicate the number of digits to the right of the decimal point in the result. If *scale* is omitted, it defaults to 0.

```
echo bcadd(2.002,2.002,2);//result is 4.00
echo bcadd(2.009,2.009,2);//result is 4.00
```

bccomp()

Syntax

```
int bccomp(string left_operand, string right_operand, [int scale])
```

Description

The bccomp() function performs a numeric comparison on the left and right operands. The result is +1 when the *left_operand* is greater than the *right_operand* and -1 when the *left_operand* is less than the *right_operand*. If both are equal, the result is 0. The optional *scale* parameter is used to indicate the number of digits to the right of the decimal point that should be considered in the comparison. If *scale* is omitted, it defaults to 0.

```
echo bccomp(2.005,2.009,2);//result is 0
echo bccomp(2.00,3.00,2);//result is -1
echo bccomp(3.00,2.00,2);//result is 1
```

bcdiv()

Syntax

```
string bcdiv(string left_operand, string right_operand, [int scale])
```

Description

The bcdiv() function calculates the quotient of the *left_operand* divided by the
right_operand. The optional *scale* parameter indicates the number of digits to the
right of the decimal point in the result. If *scale* is omitted, it defaults to 0. If the
right_operand is 0, a divide-by-zero warning will occur.

```
echo bcdiv(2.005,1.009,2);//result is 2
echo bcdiv(10.00,3.00,2);//result is 3.33
echo bcdiv(2.00,3.00,2);//result is 0.66
echo bcdiv(2.00,0.005,2);//result is a divide by zero warning
```

bcmod()

Syntax

```
string bcmod(string left_operand, string modulus)
```

Description

The bcmod() function divides the *left_operand* by the *modulus* and returns the
remainder.

```
echo bcmod(15,3);//returns 0
echo bcmod(15,4);//returns 3
```

bcmul()

Syntax

```
string bcmul(string left_operand, string right_operand, [int scale])
```

Description

The bcmul() function calculates the product of the left and right operands. The *scale*
parameter is optional and indicates the number of digits to the right of the decimal
point in the result. If *scale* is omitted, it defaults to 0.

```
echo bcmul(2.005,3.009,2);//result is 6.00
echo bcmul(10.00,0.500,2);//result is 5.00
echo bcmul(0.500,0.500,2);//result is 0.25
```

bcpow()

Syntax

```
string bcpow(string x, string y, [int scale])
```

Description

The bcpow() function returns a string that is *x* raised to the power *y*. Note that *y* must have a *scale* of 0 or a warning will occur. The *scale* parameter is optional and indicates the number of digits to the right of the decimal point in the result. If *scale* is omitted, it defaults to 0.

```
echo bcpow(2.005,3,2);//result is 8.00
echo bcpow(4.25,2,2);//result is 18.06
```

bcscale()

Syntax

```
string bcscale(int scale)
```

Description

The bcscale() function sets the *scale* that all subsequent bcmath functions will use when none is explicitly indicated. The *scale* parameter is used to indicate the desired precision in the result—specifically, the number of digits to the right of the decimal point.

bcsqrt()

Syntax

```
string bcsqrt(string operand, int scale)
```

Description

The bcsqrt() function calculates the square root of the *operand*. The *scale* parameter is an optional parameter that indicates the number of digits to the right of the decimal point in the result. If *scale* is omitted, it defaults to 0.

```
echo bcsqrt(4.00,2);//result is 2.00
echo bcsqrt(4.25,2);//result is 2.06
```

bcsub()

Syntax

```
string bcsub(string left_operand, string right_operand, int [scale])
```

Description

The bcsub() function calculates the difference by subtracting the *right_operand* from the *left_operand*. The *scale* parameter is an optional parameter indicating the number of digits to the right of the decimal point in the result. If *scale* is omitted, it defaults to 0.

```
echo bcsub(4.005,2.009,2);//result is 2.00
echo bcsub(1.00,2.00,2);//result is -1.00
```

Array

Arrays in PHP can serve many useful roles, but the main reason to use an array is to organize groups of related values. In PHP, each element in an array has a corresponding index (also referred to as *key*) and a value. The index can be a number or it can be a string, whereas the value can be of any type. Arrays of multiple dimensions are possible because an array element itself can in turn be an array. When an array is created, an internal pointer is initialized to the first element of an array. This pointer is used in several functions to traverse the elements of the array. Other roles that arrays can play in PHP include representing a stack or a queue data structure. The array functions provide powerful tools for managing and processing related data.

array()

Syntax

```
array array(...)
```

Description

The array() language construct returns an array made up of the given parameters. The parameters can indicate an index or key with the => operator. Each element in an array is comprised of a key and a value. If a key isn't defined when creating an array, the position of the element in the array will be used with the first element of the array at 0.

```
$array1 = array(1,1);//indexed array starting at zero
$array2 = array("heads"=>1,"tails"=>0);//associative array
$array3 = array($array1,$array2);//array of arrays
```

array_count_values()

Syntax

```
array array_count_values(array input)
```

Description

The array_count_values() function, which was added in PHP 4.0b4, returns an array indicating the frequency of values in the *input* array. The resulting array has the values in the *input* array as the keys and the corresponding frequency of each key in the *input* array as its value.

```
$somearray  = array(1, "ABC", 1);
array_count_values($somearray);//returns array( 1=>2, "ABC"=>1 )
```

array_diff()

Syntax

```
array array_diff(array array1, array array2 [, array ...])
```

Description

The array_diff() function, which was added in PHP 4.0.1, returns all the values contained in *array1* that are not in any of the other arrays given.

```
$array1 = array(1,2,3);
$array2 = array(2,3);
$array3 = array_diff($array1,$array2);//$array3 = (1)
```

array_flip()

Syntax

```
array array_flip(array trans)
```

Description

The `array_flip()` function, which was added in PHP 4.0b4, returns an array that is made up of all the flipped values in the *trans* array. To *flip* means to swap the values with their corresponding keys.

```
$array1 = array("a"=>"1");
$array2 = array_flip($array1);
echo $array2["1"];//returns a
```

array_intersect()

Syntax

```
array array_intersect(array array1 array array2 [, array ...])
```

Description

The `array_intersect()` function, which was added in PHP 4.0.1, returns an array containing the values of *array1* that are also present in all the other given parameters.

```
$array1 = array(1,2,3);
$array2 = array(2,3);
$array3 = array(3,4);
$array4 = array_intersect($array1,$array2,$array3);//$array3 = (3)
```

array_keys()

Syntax

```
array array_keys(array input, mixed [search_value])
```

Description

The `array_keys()` function, which was added in PHP 4.0, returns both numeric and string keys from the *input* array. The *search_value* parameter is optional and it indicates that only keys with this corresponding value should be returned.

```
$inarray = array(1,"two"=>1,0,1,1);
$outarray = array_keys($inarray,1);//$outarray = (0,"two",2,3)
```

array_merge()

Syntax

```
array array_merge(array array1, array array2, [ ...])
```

Description

The array_merge() function, which was added in PHP 4.0, appends multiple arrays together to form one single array. In the case that more than one array shares the same string key, the latter array will overwrite the previous array. With similar numeric keys, this doesn't happen—the arrays are simply appended.

```
$array1 = array(1,2,"two"=>3);
$array2 = array("one"=>1,"two"=>2);
$array3 = array_merge ($array1,$array2);
//$array3 =(1,2,"two"=>2,"one"=>1)
```

array_merge_recursive()

Syntax

```
array array_merge_recursive(array array1, array array2, [ ...])
```

Description

The array_merge_recursive() function, which was added in PHP 4.0, appends multiple arrays together to form one single array. If one of the array parameters contains further arrays, it is also merged.

```
$array1 = array ("type" => array ("values" => "long"), 1);
$array2 = array (2, "type" => array ("values" => "int","blob");
$array3 = array_merge_recursive ($array1, $array2);
//$array3 = ("type" => array("values"=>array("int","blob"),"long"),1,2)
```

array_multisort()

Syntax

```
array array_multisort(array ar1 [, mixed arg [, mixed ... [, array ...]]])
```

Description

The `array_multisort()` function, which was added in PHP 4.0b4, is used to sort multiple arrays as well as multidimensional arrays. The first parameter must be an array, but subsequent parameters can be either an array or a sorting flag. Sort order flags are either SORT_ASC or SORT_DESC, indicating a sort in ascending or descending order, respectively. Possible sort order flag types include SORT_REGULAR, SORT_STRING, and SORT_NUMERIC. The defaults are SORT_ASC and SORT_REGULAR, and the flags apply to only the previously specified array—not every array in the parameter list.

array_pad()

Syntax

```
array array_pad(array input, int pad_size, mixed pad_value)
```

Description

The `array_pad()` function, which was added in PHP 4.0b4, expands the *input* array with *pad_value* to reach the *pad_size*. If the *pad_size* is positive, padding occurs on the right, and padding occurs on the left if the *pad_size* is negative. If the *input* array size is greater than the *pad_size*, no padding takes place.

array_pop()

Syntax

```
mixed array_pop(array array)
```

Description

The `array_pop()` function, which was added in PHP 4.0, removes and returns the last element from *array*. This allows an array to act as a stack data structure with the stack top at the end of the array.

```
$array1 = array (1,2,3);
$top = array_pop($array1);//$top = 3, $array1=(1,2)
```

array_push()

Syntax

```
int array_push(array array, mixed var, [...])
```

Description

The `array_push()` function, which was added in PHP 4.0, appends the passed-in variables to the end of the *array*. This allows the array to act as a stack or queue data structure. Items can be either pushed onto the stack or enqueued at the end of the queue.

```
$array1 = array (1,2);
array_push ($array1,3);//$array1 = (1,2,3)
```

array_rand()

Syntax

```
int array_rand(array input [, int num_req])
```

Description

The `array_rand()` function, which was added in PHP 4.0, randomly picks a key or keys from the *input* array. If *num_req* is 1 or not specified, one key will be returned; if *num_req* is greater than 1, an array with the keys will be returned. The `srand()` function should be called to generate a new random seed before using this function.

array_reverse()

Syntax

```
array array_reverse(array array)
```

Description

The `array_reverse()` function, which was added in PHP 4.0b4, returns an array that is the passed-in *array* with its element order reversed.

array_shift()

Syntax

```
mixed array_shift(array array)
```

Description

The `array_shift()` function, which was added in PHP 4.0, removes the first element of the array and returns it. This could be used to implement a queue data structure in order to dequeue items from the queue.

```
$array1 = array (1,2,3);
$front = array_shift($array1);//$front = 1, $array1=(2,3)
```

array_slice()

Syntax

```
array array_slice(array array, int offset, int [length] )
```

Description

The `array_slice()` function, which was added in PHP 4.0, returns a subset of the parameter *array* beginning at the *offset* and extending for the *length*. If *offset* is positive, the subset is based on the start of the array. If *offset* is negative, the subset is based on the end of the array. The *length* parameter is optional, and when positive, results in the subset containing the *length* number of elements. When *length* is negative, it indicates the subset should stop *length* away from the end of the array. If *length* is omitted, the subset will contain everything from the *offset* until an *array* boundary has been reached.

```
$array1 = array (1,2,3,4,5);
$slice = array_slice($array1,1,3);//$slice = (2,3,4)
```

array_splice()

Syntax

```
array array_splice(array inpt, int offset, int [length] , array [replacement])
```

Description

The `array_splice()` function, which was added in PHP 4.0, removes a subset of *input* bounded by the *offset* and *length* parameters. Optionally, the elements can be replaced with *replacement*. If *offset* is positive, the *offset* is measured from the beginning of *input*. If *offset* is negative, it is measured from the end of *input*.

If the optional *length* parameter is omitted, removal occurs from *offset* to a boundary of *input*. If *length* is positive, the corresponding number of elements will be removed. If *length* is negative, the last element of the removed portion of the *input* array will be *length* number of elements from the end of the array. To remove everything from the *offset* to the end of the array, specify count($input) as the *length* parameter.

The optional *replacement* array will be put in place of any deleted elements. If *offset* and *length* don't account for the removal of any elements, *replacement* is inserted at the *offset* location. When *replacement* is just one element and not an array itself, it is not necessary to place an array() around it.

```
$array1 = array (1,2,3,4,5);
$array2 = array (4,3,2);
$array3 = array_splice($array1,1,3,$array2);//$array3 = (2,3,4),$array1 =
(1,4,3,2,5)
```

array_unique()

Syntax

```
int array_unique(array array)
```

Description

The array_unique() function, which was added in PHP 4.0.1, returns an array that is the *array* parameter with any duplicates removed.

array_unshift()

Syntax

```
int array_unshift(array array, mixed var,[, mixed ...])
```

Description

The array_unshift() function, which was added in PHP 4.0, adds to the *array* any of the parameters passed in to the front of the array. The return value is the number of elements prepended to *array*.

array_values()

Syntax

```
array array_values(array input)
```

Description

The array_values() function returns all the values (not keys) of the *input* array.

array_walk()

Syntax

```
int array_walk(array arr, string func, mixed userdata)
```

Description

The array_walk() function, which was added in PHP 3.0.3 and PHP 4.0, executes the function *func* with each element in the array. Each *func* call will have the array value as the first parameter and the array key as the second parameter. When *userdata* is present, it will be passed as the third parameter to *func*. Note that when *func* encounters errors, a warning will be generated each time. To suppress these warnings, call array_walk() with an @ sign in front of it. Also, array_walk() doesn't reset the *array* by default, so you might need to call reset() between subsequent calls of array_walk().

arsort()

Syntax

```
void arsort(array array)
```

Description

The arsort() function sorts the *array* in reverse order, based on the values in the array with the corresponding indices (keys) being maintained.

```
$array1 = array("c"=>"1","b"=>"2","a"=>"3");
arsort($array1);//array1 = ("a"=>"3","b"=>"2","c"=>"1")
```

asort()

Syntax

```
void asort(array array)
```

Description

The `asort()` function sorts the array based on the values in the array with the corresponding indices (keys) being maintained.

```
$array1 = array("a"=>"3","b"=>"2","c"=>"1");
asort($array1);//array1 = ("c"=>"1","b"=>"2","a"=>"3")
```

compact()

Syntax

```
array compact(string varname | array varnames, [...] )
```

Description

The `array_compact()` function, which was added in PHP 4.0, takes both names of variables and arrays that contain the names of variables, and looks up these variable names in the current symbol table. Each variable name becomes a key and the variable's content becomes the value for a new array, which is created and returned.

count()

Syntax

```
int count(mixed var)
```

Description

The `count()` function returns the number of elements in *var* which is typically an array. If *var* is not an array, the function will return 1; if *var* is not set, `count()` will return 0.

current()

Syntax

```
mixed current(array array)
```

Description

The current() function returns the element in *array* that is currently being pointed to by an internal pointer. Every array has this internal pointer, which is initialized to point to the first element of the array. If the internal pointer points beyond the element list, the function returns false.

each()

Syntax

```
array each(array array)
```

Description

The each() function returns the current key and value pair from *array* and advances the internal pointer to the next key and value pair. The return array consists of four elements, where the elements are comprised of the keys: 0, 1, key, and value. Elements 0 and key contain the key name of the current *array* element, and 1 and value contain the data. If the internal pointer for *array* extends past the end of *array*'s contents, each() returns false.

end()

Syntax

```
end(array array)
```

Description

The end() function moves the internal pointer for *array* to the last element in *array*.

extract()

Syntax

```
void extract(array var_array, int [extract_type] , string [prefix] )
```

Description

The extract() function, which was added in PHP 3.0.7 and PHP 4.0, imports variables from an array into the current symbol table. It examines *var_array* and takes its keys as variable names and its values as the corresponding variable values. Each key/value pair will result in one new entry in the symbol table. In the case where a collision occurs (the variable already exists in the symbol table), the *extract_type* is taken into consideration. The possible values for *extract_type* are

EXTR_OVERWRITE—Results in existing variables being overwritten

EXTR_SKIP—Results in the existing variable value being preserved in the symbol table

EXTR_PREFIX_SAME—Results in the new variable being inserted into the symbol table with *prefix* prepended to the variable name

EXTR_PREFIX_ALL—Results in all new variables in the symbol table being prefixed with *prefix*

prefix defaults to EXTR_OVERWRITE. EXTR_OVERWRITE and EXTR_SKIP don't require a specified *prefix* value.

in_array()

Syntax

```
bool in_array(mixed needle, array haystack)
```

Description

The in_array() function, which was added in PHP 4.0, searches for *needle* in *haystack* and returns true if the *needle* is found.

```
$array1 = array(1,2,3,4,5);
echo in_array(3,$array1);//displays 1
```

key()

Syntax

```
mixed key(array array)
```

Description

The key() function returns the index element of the current *array* position that is pointed to by the internal pointer.

krsort()

Syntax

```
int krsort(array array)
```

Description

The `krsort()` function, which was added in PHP 3.0.13 and PHP 4.0, sorts the *array* in reverse order based on the keys. Key and value pairs are maintained.

```
$array1 = array("a"=>"3","b"=>"2","c"=>"1");
krsort($array1);//array1 = ("c"=>"1","b"=>"2","a"=>"3")
```

ksort()

Syntax

```
int ksort(array array)
```

Description

The `ksort()` function sorts the *array* based on the keys. Key and value pairs are maintained.

```
$array1 = array("c"=>"1","b"=>"2","a"=>"3");
ksort($array1);//array1 = ("a"=>"3","b"=>"2","c"=>"1")
```

list()

Syntax

```
void list(...)
```

Description

The `list()` language construct is used to assign a list of variables in one operation. The construct `list()` is commonly used to assign multiple return values of a function to variables.

next()

Syntax

```
mixed next(array array)
```

Description

The next() function advances the internal pointer by one and returns the element located at this new location. If there are no more elements in *array* to advance to, the function returns false. Note that this function also returns false if the value of the element at this location is empty.

pos()

Syntax

```
mixed pos(array array)
```

Description

The pos() function is an alias to the current() function. The current() function returns the element in *array* that is currently being pointed to by the internal pointer. Every array has this internal pointer, which is initialized to point to the first element inserted into the array. If the internal pointer points beyond the element list, the function returns false.

prev()

Syntax

```
mixed prev(array array)
```

Description

The prev() function rewinds the internal array pointer by one and returns the element at that location. If there are no previous elements, the function returns false. Note that this function also returns false if the value of the element at this location is empty.

range()

Syntax

```
array range(int low, int high)
```

Description

The range() function, which was added in PHP 3.0.8 and PHP 4.0b4, returns an array of integers from *low* to *high*.

```
$array1 = range(1,4);//returns (1,2,3,4)
```

reset()

Syntax

```
mixed reset(array array)
```

Description

The reset() function moves the internal array pointer to the first element in *array* and returns the value of the first element.

rsort()

Syntax

```
void rsort(array array)
```

Description

The rsort() function sorts the *array* in reverse order (highest to lowest).

shuffle()

Syntax

```
void shuffle(array array)
```

Description

The shuffle() function, which was added in PHP 3.0.8 and PHP 4.0b4, randomizes the order of the elements in *array*.

sizeof()

Syntax

```
int sizeof(array array)
```

Description

The sizeof() function returns the number of elements in the *array*. Empty elements are included in the count. This function is similar to count(), but is used specifically for arrays.

```
$array1 = array (1,2,3,4,5,"pos"=>"",);
echo sizeof ($array1);//displays 6
```

sort()

Syntax

```
void sort(array array)
```

Description

The sort() function orders the elements of *array*. The resulting array is sorted from lowest to highest.

uasort()

Syntax

```
void uasort(array array, function cmp_function)
```

Description

The uasort() function, which was added in PHP 3.0.4 and PHP 4.0, sorts the *array* based on a user-defined comparison function. The *array* indices maintain their relation to the *array* elements with which they are associated.

uksort()

Syntax

```
void uksort(array array, function cmp_function)
```

Description

The uksort() function, which was added in PHP 3.0.4 and PHP 4.0, sorts the *array* by keys using a user-defined comparison function.

usort()

Syntax

```
void usort(array array, function cmp_function)
```

Description

The usort() function, which was added in PHP 3.0.3 and PHP 4.0, sorts the *array* by values using a user-defined comparison function.

Dynamic Loading

Loading additional libraries at runtime can extend the functionality of PHP. After the external libraries have been loaded, you can call functions from this library as though they were part of PHP.

dl()

Syntax

```
int dl(string library)
```

Description

The dl() function loads the *library*, which is a PHP extension. The *library* should be placed in the directory specified by the extension_dir directive.

Hash()

PHP offers many hashing options through the use of the mhash library. To utilize these functions, you must download the library from http://sasweb.de/mhash/ and then compile PHP with the --with-mhash option to enable it. The hashing routines include SHA1, GOST, HAVAL, MD5, RIPEMD160, TIGER, and CRC32 checksums.

mhash_get_hash_name()

Syntax

```
string mhash_get_hash_name(int hash)
```

Description

The mhash_get_hash_name() function, which was added in PHP 3.0.9 and PHP 4.0, returns the name of the hash associated with *hash*, which represents a hash ID. If no hash name corresponds to the hash ID, the function returns false.

mhash_get_block_size()

Syntax

```
int mhash_get_block_size(int hash)
```

Description

The mhash_get_block_size() function, which was added in PHP 3.0.9 and PHP 4.0, returns the block size for a given *hash*.

mhash_count()

Syntax

```
int mhash_count(void )
```

Description

The mhash_count() function, which was added in PHP 3.0.9 and PHP 4.0, returns the highest available hash ID. Hash IDs are numbered beginning with zero.

mhash()

Syntax

```
string mhash(int hash, string data)
```

Description

The mhash() function, which was added in PHP 3.0.9 and PHP 4.0, applies the *hash* function to the *data* and returns the resulting hash string, which is also referred to as a *digest*.

Mathematical

PHP's mathematical function library provides methods for geometric operations, numerical conversions, and numerical operations. Note that when performing geometric operations in PHP, the geometric functions expect parameters expressed in radians, but functions are supplied to convert from radians to degrees and vice versa. You can even supply deg2rad() with a degree value as the radians parameter. The conversion factor for this is π *(~3.14)* radians = 180 degrees.

abs()

Syntax

```
mixed abs(mixed number)
```

Description

The abs() function returns the absolute value of *number*. Return type is float if *number* is a float, and int otherwise.

acos()

Syntax

```
float acos(float arg)
```

Description

The acos() function returns the arc cosine *arg* expressed in radians.

asin()

Syntax

```
float asin(float arg)
```

Description

The asin() function returns the arc sine of *arg* expressed in radians.

atan()

Syntax

```
float atan(float arg)
```

Description

The atan() function returns the arc tangent of *arg* expressed in radians.

atan2()

Syntax

```
float atan2(float y, float x)
```

Description

The atan2() function, which was added in PHP 3.0.5 and PHP 4.0, returns the arc tangent of *x* and *y*. It differs from atan *y/x* because the signs of both parameters are used to determine the quadrant of the result. The result is expressed in radians.

base_convert()

Syntax

```
string base_convert(string number, int frombase, int tobase)
```

Description

The base_convert() function, which was added in PHP 3.0.6 and PHP 4.0, returns a string containing *number* represented with a base of *tobase*. The *frombase* parameter indicates the base *number* with which it should be associated. For digits higher than 10, use the alphabet such that a represents 11 and z represents 35.

```
echo base_convert(15,10,16);//returns f
```

bindec()

Syntax

```
int bindec(string binary_string)
```

Description

The `bindec()` function returns the decimal equivalent of *binary_string*. The largest number that can be converted contains 31 bits of 1s or 2,147,483,647 in decimal. The parameter *binary_string* is an unsigned number.

ceil()

Syntax

```
int ceil(float number)
```

Description

The `ceil()` function returns the next higher integer value above *number*.

```
echo ceil(5.23);//returns 6
```

cos()

Syntax

```
float cos(float arg)
```

Description

The `cos()` function returns the cosine of *arg* in radians.

decbin()

Syntax

```
string decbin( int number)
```

Description

The `decbin()` function returns the binary equivalent string of the decimal *number*. The largest number that can be converted is 2,147,483,647 or 31 bits set to 1.

dechex()

Syntax

```
string dechex(int number)
```

Description

The dechex() function returns the hexadecimal equivalent of *number*. The largest *number* that can be converted is 2,147,483,647 or 7fffffff in hex.

decoct()

Syntax

```
string decoct(int number)
```

Description

The decoct() function returns a string that is the conversion of *number* from decimal to octal format. The largest *number* that can be converted is 2,147,483,647 in decimal resulting to 17777777777 in octal.

deg2rad()

Syntax

```
double deg2rad(double number)
```

Description

The deg2rad() function, which was added in PHP 3.0.4 and PHP 4.0, converts *number* from degrees to the radian equivalent.

exp()

Syntax

```
float exp(float arg)
```

Description

The exp() function returns e raised to the power of *arg*.

```
echo exp(1);//returns ~ 2.72
```

floor()

Syntax

```
int floor(float number)
```

Description

The floor() function returns the next lower integer from *number*.

```
echo floor(2.99);//returns 2
```

getrandmax()

Syntax

```
int getrandmax(void)
```

Description

The getrandmax() function returns the maximum value that can be returned by a call to rand().

hexdec()

Syntax

```
int hexdec(string hex_string)
```

Description

The hexdec() function returns the decimal equivalent of the hexadecimal number represented by *hex_string*. The largest number that can be converted is 7fffffff in hex, which equates to 2,147,483,647 in decimal.

log()

Syntax

```
float log(float arg)
```

Description

The log() function returns the natural log of *arg*.

```
echo log(2.718);//returns ~ 1
```

log10()

Syntax

```
float log10(float arg)
```

Description

The log10() function returns the base 10 logarithm of *arg*.

```
echo log10(100);//returns 2
```

max()

Syntax

```
mixed max(mixed arg1, mixed arg2, mixed argn)
```

Description

The max() function examines the parameter list and returns the numerically highest parameter. If *arg1* is an array, the highest value in the array will be returned.

If *arg1* is an integer, string, or double, you need at least two parameters, and max() returns the largest of these values. You can compare an unlimited number of values.

If one or more of the parameters are of type double, all the parameters will be treated as doubles, and the return value will be a double. If none of the parameters is a double, they all will be treated as integers, and the return value will be an integer.

min()

Syntax

```
mixed min(mixed arg1, mixed arg2, mixed argn)
```

Description

The min() function examines the parameter list and returns the numerically lowest parameter. If *arg1* is an array, the lowest value in the array will be returned.

If *arg1* is an integer, string, or double, you need at least two parameters and min() returns the smallest of these values. You can compare an unlimited number of values.

If one or more of the parameters are of type double, all the parameters will be treated as doubles, and the value returned will be a double. If none of the parameters is of type double, they all will be treated as integers, and the value returned will be an integer.

mt_rand()

Syntax

```
int mt_rand( [int min] , [int max] )
```

Description

The `mt_rand()` function, which was added in PHP 3.0.6 and PHP 4.0, returns a random number utilizing the Mersenne Twister method for generating random numbers instead of the standard `libc` library. The optional parameters of `min` and `max` specify a range you want the random number to fall between (range is inclusive). Note that you should provide a seed before utilizing any random number functions.

For more information, check out `http://www.math.keio.ac.jp/~matumoto/emt.html`. The source for MT is available at `http://www.scp.syr.edu/~marc/hawk/twister.html`.

mt_srand()

Syntax

```
void mt_srand(int seed)
```

Description

The `mt_srand()` function, which was added in PHP 3.0.6 and PHP 4.0, seeds the random number generator with `seed`. This allows the random number generating functions to produce varying results depending on what seed is given.

mt_getrandmax()

Syntax

```
int mt_getrandmax(void )
```

Description

The `mt_getrandmax()` function, which was added in PHP 3.0.6 and PHP 4.0, returns the maximum value that can be returned by a call to `mt_rand()`.

number_format()

Syntax

```
string number_format(float number, int decimals, string dec_point,
                     string thousands_sep)
```

Description

The `number_format()` function returns a formatted version of *number* based on the formatting information supplied in the other parameters. If only one parameter is given, *number* will be formatted with a comma as the thousands separator character.

Two parameters indicate that the number should be formatted with the parameter *decimals* number of decimal places after the decimal point. Also, a comma will be used as the thousands separator character.

Four parameters indicate that *number* should be formatted with the parameter *decimals* number of decimal places. Also, *dec_point* indicates the character that should be used in the decimal point location, namely the separator between the ones and tenths positions. Finally, the *thousands_sep* indicates which character should be used to indicate a group of thousands. In the United States, the decimal point is typically specified as "." and the thousands separator is specified as ",", but in some countries these are reversed.

octdec()

Syntax

```
int octdec(string octal_string)
```

Description

The `octdec()` function returns the decimal equivalent of *octal_string*, which represents an octal number. The largest number that can be converted is 17777777777 octal or 2,147,483,647 in decimal.

pi()

Syntax

```
double pi(void )
```

Description

The pi() function returns an approximate value of pi.

pow()

Syntax

```
float pow(float base, float exp)
```

Description

The pow() function returns the base raised to the power of exp.

```
echo pow(2,3);//returns 8
```

rad2deg()

Syntax

```
double rad2deg(double number)
```

Description

The rad2deg() function, which was added in PHP 3.0.4 and PHP 4.0, takes a number specified in radians and returns its value in degrees.

```
echo rad2deg(pi());//displays 180
```

rand()

Syntax

```
int rand ([int min [, int max]])
```

Description

The rand() function returns a psuedo-random number. The number returned will range between 0 and RAND_MAX or *min* and *max*, if they are specified. The random number should be seeded before using this function.

round()

Syntax

```
double round(double val)
```

Description

The round() function returns the resulting number after rounding *val*. The *val* parameter is rounded up when it has a last digit of 5 or greater, and down when the last digit is less than 5.

sin()

Syntax

```
float sin(float arg)
```

Description

The sin() function returns the sine of *arg* in radians.

sqrt()

Syntax

```
float sqrt(float arg)
```

Description

The sqrt() function returns the square root of *arg*.

```
echo sqrt(16);//displays 4
```

srand()

Syntax

```
void srand(int seed)
```

Description

The `srand()` function seeds the random number generator with *seed*. This allows `rand()` to produce varying results.

tan()

Syntax

```
float tan(float arg)
```

Description

The `tan()` function returns the tangent of *arg* in radians.

Miscellaneous

The functions in this section provide a variety of useful tools that don't lend themselves to a specific group of operations. Some of these tools include information regarding the current status of a connection with a browser along with information about that browser. Additionally, some debugging and language constructs dealing with script execution are included.

connection_aborted()

Syntax

```
int connection_aborted(void )
```

Description

The `connection_aborted()` function, which was added in PHP 3.0.7 and PHP 4.0b4, returns true if the client has disconnected. This is usually due to the user clicking the Stop button on his browser.

connection_status()

Syntax

```
int connection_status(void )
```

Description

The connection_status() function, which was added in PHP 3.0.7 and PHP 4.0b4, returns the connection status bit field. The result could indicate a NORMAL status, an ABORTED status, a TIMEOUT status, or a combination of both an ABORTED and TIMEOUT status, in the case that PHP is set to ignore user aborts and continue processing the script after the user aborts.

connection_timeout()

Syntax

```
int connection_timeout(void )
```

Description

The connection_timeout() function, which was added in PHP 3.0.7 and PHP 4.0b4, returns true if the script has timed out.

define()

Syntax

```
int define(string name, mixed value, int [case_insensitive] )
```

Description

The define() function declares a named constant. Named constants are similar to variables with the following exceptions:

Constants are not referenced with a $ before the name.

Constants do not have scope and therefore may be accessed equally from any part of your code.

Redefinition of constants is not allowed.

Constants may represent only scalar values.

The third parameter, case_insensitive, is optional. If the value 1 is given, the constant will be defined as case insensitive. The default behavior is case sensitive.

defined()

Syntax

```
int defined(string name)
```

Description

The defined() function returns true if *name* represents an existing named constant and returns false otherwise.

die()

Syntax

```
void die(string message)
```

Description

The die() language construct outputs a message and stops parsing the script. There is no return.

```
//if login unsuccessful
die ("Unauthorized Access - Terminating");
```

eval()

Syntax

```
void eval(string code_str)
```

Description

The eval() function executes *code_str* as PHP code. The *code_str* must adhere to the normal PHP requirements, including the statement terminator. Any variables created in *code_str* will persist in the main code after function has executed.

exit()

Syntax

```
void exit(void)
```

Description

The exit() language construct stops the current script from executing and does not return control to the script.

func_get_arg()

Syntax

```
int func_get_arg(int arg_num)
```

Description

The func_get_arg() function, which was added in PHP 4.0b4, returns the argument located at the *arg_num* offset into a user-defined function's argument list. Arguments are numbered with a zero base. If not called from inside a user function, a warning will be generated.

If *arg_num* is greater than the number of arguments the user-defined function has, a warning will be generated and a return value of false will be given.

func_get_args()

Syntax

```
int func_gets_args(void )
```

Description

The func_get_args() function, which was added in PHP 4.0b4, returns an array containing the arguments of the current user-defined function. The array counter is zero-based. This is similar to the argv[] parameter that is specified in the main routine of a C program. A warning will be generated if called from outside a user-defined function definition.

func_num_args()

Syntax

```
int func_num_args(void )
```

Description

The `func_num_args()` function, which was added in PHP 4.0b4, returns a count of the arguments passed into the current user-defined function. A warning will be generated if called from outside a user-defined function definition.

function_exists

Syntax

`int function_exists(string function_name)`

Description

The `function_exists()` function, which was added in PHP 3.0.7 and PHP 4.0b4, returns true if a function named `function_name` has been defined; otherwise, it returns false.

get_browser()

Syntax

`object get_browser(string [user_agent] )`

Description

The `get_browser()` function is used to determine the capabilities of the client's browser that is making the request. The browser capabilities are defined in the browscap.ini file. If the `user_agent` is not set, the `$HTTP_USER_AGENT` environment variable will be used as the key into the browscap.ini file. An object is returned that provides details on the capabilities of the browser, including JavaScript and cookie support.

ignore_user_abort()

Syntax

`int ignore_user_abort(int [setting])`

Description

The `ignore_user_abort()` function, which was added in PHP 3.0.7 and PHP 4.0b4, sets the PHP behavior on whether a client disconnect should cause the script to be aborted. It returns the previous setting. By not specifying a `setting` parameter, the function will simply return the current *setting* without altering it. The *setting* of 1 indicates that user abort is on.

iptcparse()

Syntax

```
array iptcparse(string iptcblock)
```

Description

The iptcparse() function, which was added in PHP 3.0.6 and PHP 4.0b4, parses a binary *iptcblock* into single tags and returns an array using the tag marker as an index and the tag marker's value as the value. If no IPTC data exists, the function returns false. More information regarding iptc blocks can be found at http://www.iptc.org/iptc/.

leak()

Syntax

```
void leak(int bytes)
```

Description

The leak() function leaks the specified amount of memory. This function is normally used to verify the behavior of the memory manager, which automatically cleans up "leaked" memory when each request is completed.

pack()

Syntax

```
string pack(string format, mixed [args] ...)
```

Description

The pack() function returns a binary string containing *args* packed according to the *format*. The *format* string contains formatting codes along with an optional repeater parameter, which can be a number or an * (which indicates repeat until the end of the *args*). These formatting codes are based on the codes defined in Perl. The repeat count for a, A, h, H indicates how many characters of one data argument are taken, and the @ character indicates the absolute location for the next piece of data. For all others, the repeat count specifies how many pieces of data are included and packed into the resulting binary string. The following codes are available:

a—NUL-padded string

A—Space-padded string

h—Hex string, low nibble first

H—Hex string, high nibble first

c—Signed char

C—Unsigned char

s—Signed short (always 16-bit, machine byte order)

S—Unsigned short (always 16-bit, machine byte order)

n—Unsigned short (always 16-bit, big-endian byte order)

v—Unsigned short (always 16-bit, little-endian byte order)

i—Signed integer (machine-dependent size and byte order)

I—Unsigned integer (machine-dependent size and byte order)

l—Signed long (always 32-bit, machine byte order)

L—Unsigned long (always 32-bit, machine byte order)

N—Unsigned long (always 32-bit, big-endian byte order)

V—Unsigned long (always 32-bit, little-endian byte order)

f—Float (machine-dependent size and representation)

d—Double (machine-dependent size and representation)

x—NUL byte

X—Back up one byte

@—NUL-fill to absolute position

register_shutdown_function()

Syntax

```
int register_shutdown_function(string func)
```

Description

The `register_shutdown_function()` function, which was added in PHP 3.0.4 and PHP 4.0b4, specifies the name of the function to be called when script processing is complete. No output to the browser is allowed in the shutdown function.

serialize()

Syntax

```
string serialize(mixed value)
```

Description

The `serialize()` function, which was added in PHP 3.0.5 and PHP 4.0b4, returns a string containing a byte-stream representation of *value* that can be stored anywhere. The type and structure of the variable are maintained.

`serialize()` handles the types integer, double, string, array (multidimensional), and object. Note that when serializing an object, only its properties are preserved. The object's methods are not serialized.

sleep()

Syntax

```
void sleep(int seconds)
```

Description

The `sleep()` function causes script processing to pause for *seconds* seconds. Note that you can specify an expression as the *seconds* value, such as (30 * 60) to indicate 30 minutes.

uniqid()

Syntax

```
int uniqid(string prefix, boolean [lcg])
```

Description

The `uniqid()` function returns a prefixed unique identifier based on the current time in microseconds. *prefix* can be up to 114 characters long. *prefix* is useful in creating unique identifiers across processes or machines where the function could be called at the same microsecond. If *lcg* is set to true, a "combined LCG" entropy will be added to the end of the return value, which should make the result even more unique. LCG stands for *linear congruential generator*, which is another type of psuedo-random number generator. When generating a cookie value for a user, it is recommended that you use something like md5 (unique(rand())) for maximum security.

unpack()

Syntax

```
array unpack(string format, string data)
```

Description

The unpack() function extracts data from a binary string (*data*) and places it into an array according to the *format* parameter. See pack() for formatting code details.

unserialize()

Syntax

```
mixed unserialize(string str)
```

Description

The unserialize() function, which was added in PHP 3.0.5 and PHP 4.0b4, returns the original PHP value of *str* before it was serialized. The value can be an integer, double, string, array, or object. An object's methods cannot be serialized, only its properties.

usleep()

Syntax

```
void usleep(int micro_seconds)
```

Description

The usleep() function causes script processing to pause for the number of microseconds specified by *micro_seconds*.

PHP Options and Information

PHP provides the functions that enable you to examine information about the current version of PHP that is running, along with information from the operating system about the PHP process. Additionally, it allows scripts to interact with the operating system environment.

assert()

Syntax

```
int assert (string|bool assertion)
```

Description

The assert() function, which was added in PHP 4.0b4, examines the given assertion and takes action if the result is false. If the parameter is a string, it will be executed. Assertions should be used only as a debugging feature, and not used for normal runtime operations.

assert_options()

Syntax

```
int assert_options (int what [,mixed value)
```

Description

The assert_options() function, which was added in PHP 4.0b4, enables you both to examine and set the assertion options. The following options are available:

Option	ini Setting	Default	Description
ASSERT_ACTIVE	assert.active	1	assert() is on
ASSERT_WARNING	assert.warning	1	Issues a warning for each failure
ASSERT_BAIL	assert.bail	0	Terminates execution if assertion fails

Option	ini Setting	Default	Description
ASSERT_QUIET_EVAL	assert.quiet_eval	0	Disables error reporting during assertion evaluation
ASSERT_CALLBACK	assert_callback	(null)	Calls a user function on failed assertions

error_log()

Syntax

```
int error_log(string message, int message_type, string [destination] ,
            string [extra_headers] )
```

Description

The error_log() function can send a message to a Web server's error log, a TCP port, or to a file. The *message* parameter represents the information that should be logged. The *message_type* parameter indicates where the message should be directed and has four possible values:

0—*message* is sent to PHP's system logger, which is determined by the setting of the error_log configuration option.

1—*message* is sent via email to the address denoted by the *destination* parameter. The parameter *extra_headers* is used with this option as well. The option behaves similar to mail().

2—*message* is sent through the PHP debugging connection. This is possible only when remote debugging is enabled. For this option, *destination* indicates the host and port of the connection listening for debugging information.

3—*message* is written to the end of the file specified by *destination*.

error_reporting()

Syntax

```
int error_reporting(int [level] )
```

Description

The `error_reporting()` function sets the PHP error-reporting level and returns the previous setting. The parameter *level* is an additive bitmask made up of the following codes:

Value	Internal Name
1	E_ERROR
2	E_WARNING
4	E_PARSE
8	E_NOTICE
16	E_CORE_ERROR
32	E_CORE_WARNING

There also exists an E_ALL name, which is equal to 15 (1 + 2 + 4 + 8). Multiple levels are indicated by adding the values together. For example, to indicate warnings and error messages, specify level 3.

extension_loaded()

Syntax

```
bool extension_loaded(string name)
```

Description

The `extension_loaded()` function, which was added in PHP 3.0.10 and PHP 4.0b4, returns true if the PHP extension called *name* is loaded.

getenv()

Syntax

```
string getenv(string varname)
```

Description

The getenv() function returns the value of the environment variable specified by *varname*, and false if the environment variable doesn't exist.

get_cfg_var()

Syntax

```
string get_cgf_var(string varname)
```

Description

The get_cfg_var() function returns the current value of *varname*, which is the name of a PHP configuration variable. If this variable doesn't exist, false is returned. The function doesn't read compile time settings or variables set from the Apache configuration file. To verify that PHP is utilizing a configuration file, check the return value of the cfg_file_path configuration setting. If this value exists, a configuration file is being used.

get_current_user()

Syntax

```
string get_current_user(void)
```

Description

The get_current_user() function returns the name of the owner of the current PHP script.

get_magic_quotes_gpc()

Syntax

```
long get_magic_quotes_gpc(void)
```

Description

The get_magic_quotes_gpc() function, which was added in PHP 3.0.6 and PHP 4.0, returns the current active configuration setting of magic_quotes_gpc. (0 for off, 1 for on). GPC stands for Get/Post/Cookie, and is used to escape quotes in strings that are returned from function calls. When `magic_quotes_gpc` is active, all ' (singlequotes), " (double quotes), \ (backslashes), and NULs are automatically escaped with a backslash.

get_magic_quotes_runtime()

Syntax

```
long get_magic_quotes_runtime(void)
```

Description

The `get_magic_quotes_runtime()` function, which was added in PHP 3.0.6 and PHP 4.0, returns the current active configuration setting of `magic_quotes_runtime`. (0 for off, 1 for on). GPC stands for Get/Post/Cookie, and is used to escape quotes in strings that are returned from function calls. When `magic_quotes_runtime` is active, all ' (single quotes), " (double quotes), \ (backslashes), and NULs are escaped with a backslash automatically.

getlastmod()

Syntax

```
int getlastmod(void)
```

Description

The `getlastmod()` function returns the UNIX timestamp indicating the last change of the currently executing script. The timestamp is of a format that is suitable for feeding to the `date()` function. If an error occurs in retrieving the last modification date, false will be returned.

getmyinode()

Syntax

```
int getmyinode(void)
```

Description

The `getmyinode()` function returns the current executing script's inode information, or false on error.

getmypid()

Syntax

```
int getmypid(void)
```

Description

The getmypid() function returns the process ID as to which PHP is running, or false on error. Note that when PHP is running as a server module, multiple scripts may share the same process ID.

getmyuid()

Syntax

```
int getmyuid(void)
```

Description

The getmyuid() function returns the user ID under which the current script is running, or false on error.

getrusage()

Syntax

```
array getrusage(int [who] )
```

Description

The getrusage() function, which was added in PHP 3.0.7 and PHP 4.0b2, returns an associative array returned from the system call getrusage(). When who is set to 1, the system call getrusage() will be called with RSUAGE_CHILDREN. The array structure is system-dependent, so you should consult your man pages for more information.

phpcredits()

Syntax

```
void phpinfo(int flag)
```

Description

The phpcredits() function, which was added in PHP 4.0, outputs details about the developers of PHP and its modules. The output is in HTML format and its contents are based on the *flag* parameter. Possible values include:

CREDITS_ALL	All the credit messages.
CREDITS_DOCS	Lists the documentation team members.
CREDITS_FULLPAGE	Indicates that an entire HTML page should be generated. This is used in conjunction with other flags.
CREDITS_GENERAL	Lists language developers, 4.0 authors, and SAPI module.
CREDITS_GROUP	Lists the core developers.
CREDITS_MODULES	Lists the extension module developers.
CREDITS_SAPI	Not implemented.

phpinfo()

Syntax

```
int phpinfo(void)
```

Description

The phpinfo() function outputs details about the current state of PHP. The details include information about PHP compilation options and extensions, the PHP version, server information and server environment (if compiled as a module), PHP environment, OS version information, paths, master and local values of configuration options, HTTP headers, and the GNU Public License.

phpversion()

Syntax

```
string phpversion void)
```

Description

The phpversion() function returns a string containing the version of the currently running PHP parser.

php_logo_guid()

Syntax

```
string php_logo_guid(void)
```

Description

The php_logo_guid() function, which was added in PHP 4.0b4, returns the logo guid.

php_sapi_name()

Syntax

```
string php_sapi_name(void)
```

Description

The php_sapi_name() function, which was added in PHP 4.0.1, returns the type of interface between the Web server and PHP, such as cgi or apache.

putenv()

Syntax

```
void putenv(string setting)
```

Description

The putenv() function adds the setting to the current environment variables.

set_magic_quotes_runtime()

Syntax

```
long set_magic_quotes_runtime(int new_setting)
```

Description

The set_magic_quotes_runtime() function, which was added in PHP 3.0.6 and PHP 4.0, sets the current active configuration setting of magic_quotes_runtime to *new_setting*, which can be either 0 for off, or 1 for on.

set_time_limit()

Syntax

```
void set_time_limit(int seconds)
```

Description

The set_time_limit() function sets the number of seconds a script is allowed to run. The default limit is 30 seconds or, if it exists, the max_execution_time value defined in the configuration file. If *seconds* is set to zero, no time limit is imposed.

If called during the execution of the script, the timer is reset to 0 and the counter starts counting towards this new limit. If PHP is running in safe mode, set_time_limit() has no effect.

zend_logo_guid()

Syntax

```
string zend_logo_guid(void)
```

Description

The zend_logo_guid() function, which was added in PHP 4.0b4, returns the Zend guid.

String

PHP has many string manipulation functions, most of which follow the syntax and operation of their C namesakes.

addcslashes()

Syntax

```
string addcslashes(string str, string charlist)
```

Description

The addcslashes() function, which was added in PHP 4.0b4, returns a string with backslashes placed before characters listed in the *charlist* parameter. Similar to C, it escapes \n, \t, \r, and so on. Any characters with ASCII codes lower than 32 or higher than 126 are converted to octal representation. The *charlist* parameter can also be used to specify a range by indicating the ASCII codes of the characters. The notation is "\<*start*>..\<*end*>" where *start* and *end* are ASCII codes.

addslashes()

Syntax

```
string addslashes(string str)
```

Description

The addslashes() function returns a new version of *str* in which characters that must be quoted for database queries have a backslash in front of them. These characters include single quotes ('), double quotes ("), backslashes (\), and NUL (the null byte).

bin2hex()

Syntax

```
string bin2hex(string str)
```

Description

The bin2hex() function, which was added in PHP 3.0.9 and PHP 4.0, returns an ASCII string containing the hexadecimal equivalent of the binary data represented by the parameter *str*. The conversion is done byte-wise with the high-nibble first, where a nibble is half of a byte.

```
echo bin2hex("12ab");//displays 31326162
```

chop()

Syntax

```
string chop(string str)
```

Description

The chop() function returns the *str* parameter without any trailing whitespace. Whitespace includes "\n", "\r", "\t", "\v", "\0", and a plain space.

chr()

Syntax

```
string chr(int ascii)
```

Description

The chr() function returns a one-character string that corresponds to the ASCII code specified by the parameter.

```
echo chr(65);//displays A
```

chunk_split()

Syntax

```
string chunk_split(string string, int [chunklen] , string [end])
```

Description

The chunk_split() function, which was added in PHP 3.0.6 and PHP 4.0, returns *string* broken up at every *chunklen* characters by the string *end*. The optional parameter *chunklen* defaults to 76, and *end* defaults to ("\r\n"). In other words, the default behavior is to take a long string and break it into multiple lines of length 76. This can be useful for converting base64-endcoded output to match RFC 2045 semantics. Base64 encoding is used to preserve binary data when transferring it via electronic mail.

convert_cyr_string()

Syntax

```
string convert_cyr_string(string str, string from, string to);
```

Description

The convert_cyr_string() function, which was added in PHP 3.0.6 and PHP 4.0, returns *str* converted from one Cyrillic character set to another. The *from* and *to* parameters are single characters that represent Cyrillic character sets. The *str* is the character set to which it should be converted. The supported types of Cyrillic character sets are

k—koi8-r

w—Windows-1251

i—ISO8859-5

a—x-cp866

d—x-cp866

m—x-mac-cyrillic

count_chars()

Syntax

```
mixed count_chars(string string, [mode]);
```

Description

The count_chars() function, which was added in PHP 4.0, counts the number of occurrences of each byte value (0–255) in *string* and returns the information in a format determined by *mode*. If *mode* is not specified, it defaults to 0. The options for *mode* include:

0—An array with the key representing the byte value and the value representing the frequency of each byte.

1—An array similar to 0 but only non-zero frequency byte values are listed.

2—An array similar to 0 but only zero frequency byte values are listed.

3—A string is returned containing only the byte values that are used.

4—A string is returned containing only the byte values that are not used.

crc32()

Syntax

```
int crc32(string str)
```

Description

The crc32() function, which was added in PHP 4.0.1, calculates the crc32 polynomial of the *string*. This is typically used to validate data that has been transmitted.

crypt()

Syntax

```
string crypt(string str, string [salt] )
```

Description

The crypt() function encrypts *str* using the standard UNIX DES encryption method. The *salt* is an optional two-character parameter on which the encryption is based. If *salt* is not provided, PHP will randomly generate one. For some operating systems, an MD5-based encryption algorithm replaces the standard DES encryption. The encryption type is specified by the *salt* parameter. During installation of PHP, it is determined which encryption functions are in use on the system. If *salt* is not specified, PHP will auto-generate a *salt* based on the default encryption type for the system. Either the standard 2-character DES salt or a random MD5-compatible salt is generated. You can determine which encryption method is in use by examining the constant CRYPT_SALT_LENGTH.

The output will contain the *salt* as the first two numbers when using the standard DES encryption crypt() function.

On systems where multiple encryption types are supported, the crypt() function accepts either 0 or 1, depending on whether the given type is available:

CRYPT_STD_DES—Standard DES encryption with a 2-character *salt*

CRYPT_EXT_DES—Extended DES encryption with a 9-char *salt*

CRYPT_MD5—MD5 encryption with a 12-char *salt* where the first characters of the result are 1

CRYPT_BLOWFISH—Extended DES encryption with a 16-char *salt* where the first characters of the result are 2

Note that crypt() is a one-direction algorithm. The original *str* cannot be determined from the resulting string.

echo()

Syntax

```
echo(string arg1, string [argn]... )
```

Description

The echo() language construct outputs all the given parameters to the page. Parentheses are optional with one argument and should not be used with multiple arguments.

```
echo "Hello World!";// display Hello World message to user
```

explode()

Syntax

```
array explode(string separator, string string)
```

Description

The explode() function returns an array of strings where each element is from the *string* parameter, which is broken out by the *separator* field.

```
$array1 = explode(",","1,2,3");//$array1 = (1,2,3)
```

flush()

Syntax

```
void flush(void)
```

Description

The flush() function tries to force the current output to be returned to the user. The actual results depend on the method PHP is using for delivery.

get_html_translation_table

Syntax

```
string get_html_translation_table(int table)
```

Description

The get_html_translation_table() function, which was added in PHP 4.0b4, returns the translation table that is used internally for htmlspecialchars() and htmlentities(). You should use HTML_ENTITIES OR HTML_SPECIALCHARS to specify which table you want.

get_meta_tags()

Syntax

```
array get_meta_tags(string filename, int [use_include_path] )
```

Description

The get_meta_tags() function, which was added in PHP 3.04 and PHP 4.0, opens a file specified by filename and parses it looking for any <meta> HTML tags. In the array that is returned, the name property of each meta tag becomes the key and the contents of each meta tag becomes the value. If any special characters exist in the value of the name property, they are substituted with '_', and the rest of the value is converted to lowercase. Specifying use_include_path as 1 asks PHP to look for the file along the standard include path.

htmlentities()

Syntax

```
string htmlentities(string string)
```

Description

The htmlentities() function returns a version of string in which any reserved HTML characters have been translated into "safe" strings. The characters most often encountered are

'&' (ampersand) becomes '&'

'"' (double quote) becomes '"'

'<' (less than) becomes '<'

'>' (greater than) becomes '>'

However, htmlentities() also translates other characters which have an HTML equivalent. Currently, the translations are based on the ISO-8859-1 character set. This function is often used to preserve text input by a user that will be displayed in a Web page.

htmlspecialchars()

Syntax

```
string htmlspecialchars(string string)
```

Description

The htmlspecialchars() function returns a version of *string* in which any reserved HTML characters have been translated into "safe" strings. The characters translated by htmlspecialchars() are

'&' (ampersand) becomes '&'

'"' (double quote) becomes '"'

'<' (less than) becomes '<'

'>' (greater than) becomes '>'

implode()

Syntax

```
string implode(string glue, array pieces)
```

Description

The implode() function returns a string containing all the *pieces* elements in the same order, with the *glue* parameter between each element.

```
$array1 = array (1,2,3);
echo  implode (",",$array1);//results in "1,2,3"
```

join()

Syntax

```
string join(string glue, array pieces)
```

Description

The join() function returns a string containing all the *pieces* elements in the same order, with the *glue* parameter between each element. The join() function is an alias to implode() and therefore exhibits identical behavior.

levenshtein()

Syntax

```
int levenshtein (string str1, string str2)
```

Description

The levenshtein() function, which was added in PHP 4.0.1, calculates the Levenshtein distance between the two given strings. Note that the strings must be less than 255 characters in length or a -1 will be returned. The distance is defined as the minimum number of characters you have to replace, insert, or delete to transform one string to the other. The complexity of the algorithm is o(m*n), which is rather expensive.

ltrim()

Syntax

```
string ltrim(string str)
```

Description

The ltrim() function returns a string that is *str* with all the leading whitespace removed. Whitespace includes the following characters: "\n", "\r", "\t", "\v", "\0", and a plain space.

md5()

Syntax

```
string md5(string str)
```

Description

The md5() function calculates the MD5 hash of the *str* string parameter using the RSA Data Security, Inc. MD5 Message-Digest Algorithm. For more information, see http://www.faqs.org/rfcs/rfc1321.html.

```
echo md5("PHP Dictionary");//displays 522ac575de5b5d3ee2227b9b5e621b7d
```

metaphone()

Syntax

```
string metaphone(string str)
```

Description

The metaphone() function, which was added in PHP 4.0b4, creates the same key for words that sound similar. Its accuracy is greater than soundex() because it knows the basic rules of English pronunciation. The resulting keys are of variable length.

Lawrence Philips (lphilips@verity.com) developed metaphone(). For more information, consult *Practical Algorithms for Programmers*, Binstock & Rex, Addison Wesley, 1995.

```
echo metaphone("root");//displays RT
echo metaphone("route");//displays RT
echo metaphone("wrote");//displays RT
```

nl2br()

Syntax

```
string nl2br(string string)
```

Description

The nl2br() function returns a string comprised of *string* with <BR> inserted before all new lines.

ob_start()

Syntax

```
void ob_start(void)
```

Description

The `ob_start()` function, which was added in PHP 4, turns on output buffering. This causes all output to be appended to an internal buffer. Use `ob_get_contents()` to access this buffer.

ob_get_contents()

Syntax

```
string ob_get_contents(void)
```

Description

The `ob_get_contents()` function, which was added in PHP 4, returns the contents of the output buffer or false if buffering is not active.

ob_end_flush()

Syntax

```
void ob_end_flush(void)
```

Description

The `ob_end_flush()` function, which was added in PHP 4, sends the output buffer to the client and deactivates output buffering.

ob_end_clean()

Syntax

```
void ob_end_clean(void)
```

Description

The `ob_end_clean()` function, which was added in PHP 4, erases the output buffer and turns off buffering.

ob_implicit_flush()

Syntax

```
void ob_implicit_flush([int flag])
```

Description

The `ob_implicit_flush()` function, which was added in PHP 4.0b4, turns on and off output buffering, depending on the *flag* value. The default is on, which results in a flush operation after every output call.

ord()

Syntax

```
int ord(string string)
```

Description

The `ord()` function returns the ASCII value of the first character of the string parameter. This function complements `chr()`.

```
echo ord("ABCDEF");//displays 65
```

parse_str

Syntax

```
void parse_str(string str)
```

Description

The `parse_str()` function processes *str* as though it were the query string from the page request. This includes setting the variables read into the current scope from *str*.

print()

Syntax

```
print(string arg)
```

Description

The `print()` function outputs *arg*.

```
$avar = "test";
print ($avar);//displays test
```

printf()

Syntax

```
int printf(string format, mixed [args]... )
```

Description

The printf() function displays *args* output according to *format*. The *format* string is made up of zero or more directives: ordinary characters (excluding %) that are copied directly into the result, along with conversion specifications, each of which results in fetching its own parameter. Each conversion specification consists of these elements, in order:

padding specifier is an optional parameter that specifies which character to use if padding is necessary to adjust the string to a larger size. The default is to pad with spaces, but can also be specified as the 0 (zero character). To specify an alternative padding character, precede the character with a single quote (').

alignment specifier is an optional parameter that indicates whether the resulting string should be right- or left-justified. The default is right-justified, and a " - " character is used to indicate left justification.

width specifier is an optional number that specifies the minimum number of characters the result should contain.

precision specifier is an optional parameter that specifies the number of decimal digits that should be displayed for floating-point numbers. This applies only to numbers of type double.

type specifier specifies the type as which the argument should be treated. Possible types as which the argument can be treated are

%—Treat as a percent character. No argument is required.

b—Treat as an integer and present as a binary number.

c—Treat as an integer and present as the character with the corresponding ASCII value.

d—Treat as an integer and present as a decimal number.

f—Treat as a double and present as a floating-point number.

o—Treat as an integer and present as an octal number.

s—Treat and present as a string.

x—Treat as an integer and present as a hexadecimal number (with lowercase letters).

X—Treat as an integer and present as a hexadecimal number (with uppercase letters).

```
$type = "checking";
$balance = 500;
printf("type = %s, balance = %2.2f",$type,$balance);
//displays type = checking, balance= 500.00
```

quoted_printable_decode()

Syntax

```
string quoted_printable_decode(string str)
```

Description

The quoted_printable_decode() function, which was added in PHP 3.0.6 and PHP 4.0, returns an 8-bit binary string that corresponds to the decoded quoted printable str. This function is similar to imap_qprint() except that the IMAP module is not required for this function to work.

quotemeta()

Syntax

```
string quotemeta(string str)
```

Description

The quotemeta() function returns a version of str with a backslash character (\) before every character that is among these

. \\ + * ? [^] ($).

rawurldecode()

Syntax

```
string rawurldecode(string str)
```

Description

The `rawurldecode()` function returns *str* in which any % followed by two hex digit codes are replaced with the literal characters. This is often used to decode URL information that has special characters in it passed in from a browser.

rawurlencode()

Syntax

```
string rawurlencode(string str)
```

Description

The `rawurlencode()` function returns a string in which all nonalphanumeric characters except '-', '_', and '.' in *str* have been replaced with a percent (%) sign followed by two hex digits. The encoding process is detailed in RFC 1738. The purpose of this function is to preserve characters so that they are not interpreted as special URL delimiters.

setlocale()

Syntax

```
string setlocale(string category, string locale)
```

Description

The `setlocale()` function indicates the *locale* that functions in the *category* should use. The *category* parameter has the following possible options:

LC_ALL for everything listed in the following options.

LC_COLLATE for string comparison. This is not currently implemented in PHP.

LC_CTYPE for character classification and conversion such as `strtolower()`, `ucfirst()`, and `strtoupper()`.

LC_MONETARY for `localeconv()`—not currently implemented in PHP.

LC_NUMERIC for decimal separator.

LC_TIME for date and time formatting with `strftime()`.

similar_text()

Syntax

```
int similar_text(string first, string second, [double percent])
```

Description

The `similar_text()` function, which was added in PHP 3.0.7 and PHP 4.0b24, describes the similarity of the `first` and `second` strings. The similarity is based on an algorithm proposed by Oliver in 1993. Also note that the complexity of this algorithm is O(N**3) where N is the length of the longest string. By passing a reference as a third argument, `similar_text()` will calculate the similarity in percent for you. It returns the number of matching characters in both strings.

```
echo similar_text("abcdefg","bbcdefh");//displays 5
```

soundex()

Syntax

```
string soundex(string str)
```

Description

The `soundex()` function returns a key that represents how the string is pronounced. This is useful in searching for a word when the correct spelling is not known. This `soundex()` function returns a string four characters long, starting with a letter. This `soundex()` function is described by Donald Knuth in *The Art of Computer Programming, Vol. 3: Sorting and Searching,* Addison-Wesley (1973), pp. 391–392.

```
echo soundex("their");//displays T600
echo soundex("there");//displays T600
echo soundex("root");//displays R300
echo soundex("route");//displays R300
echo soundex("wrote");//displays W630
```

sprintf()

Syntax

```
string sprintf(string format, mixed [args]...)
```

Description

The sprintf() function returns a string made up of the *args*, which have had the *format* applied to them. The *format* string is made up of zero or more directives: ordinary characters (excluding %) that are copied directly into the result, along with conversion specifications, each of which results in fetching its own parameter. Each conversion specification consists of these elements, in order:

padding specifier is an optional parameter that specifies which character to use if padding is necessary to adjust the string to a larger size. The default is to pad with spaces, but can also be specified as the 0 (zero character). To specify an alternative padding character, precede the character with a single quote (').

alignment specifier is an optional parameter that indicates whether the resulting string should be right- or left-justified. The default is right-justified, and a "-" character is used to indicate left justification.

width specifier is an optional number that specifies the minimum number of characters the result should contain.

precision specifier is an optional parameter that specifies the number of decimal digits that should be displayed for floating-point numbers. This applies only to numbers of type double.

type specifier specifies the type as which the argument should be treated. Possible types as which the argument can be treated are

%—Treat as a percent character. No argument is required.

b—Treat as an integer and present as a binary number.

c—Treat as an integer and present as the character with the corresponding ASCII value.

d—Treat as an integer and present as a decimal number.

f—Treat as a double and present as a floating-point number.

o—Treat as an integer and present as an octal number.

s—Treat and present as a string.

x—Treat as an integer and present as a hexadecimal number (with lowercase letters).

X—Treat as an integer and present as a hexadecimal number (with uppercase letters).

```
$type = "checking";
$balance = 500;
$text = sprintf("type = %s, balance = %2.2f",$type,$balance);
echo $text;//displays type = checking, balance= 500.00
```

strcasecmp()

Syntax

```
int strcasecmp(string str1, string str2)
```

Description

The strcasecmp() function, which was added in PHP 3.0.2 and PHP 4.0, returns a negative number if *str1* < *str2*, a positive number if *str2* > *str1*, and 0 if both strings are equal. The comparison is case insensitive.

```
echo strcasecmp ("abc","xyz");//displays -23
echo strcasecmp ("xyz","abc");//displays +23
echo strcasecmp ("abc","ABC");//displays 0
```

strchr()

Syntax

```
string strchr(string haystack, string needle)
```

Description

The strchr() function finds the first occurrence of a string. It returns all of *haystack* starting at the first occurrence of *needle*. If *needle* is not found in *haystack*, false is returned. If *needle* is not a string, it is converted to an integer and applied as the ordinal value of a character. The ordinal value is the corresponding value from an ASCII table; for example, 65 = 'A'.

```
echo strchr ("XXXXAXXXX",65);//displays AXXXX
```

strcmp()

Syntax

```
int strcmp(string str1, string str2)
```

Description

The strcmp() function returns a negative number if *str1* < *str2*, a positive number if *str1* > *str2*, and 0 if *str1* = *str2*. The strcmp() function is case sensitive.

```
echo strcmp ("abc","ABC");//displays 1
```

strcspn()

Syntax

```
int strcspn(string str1, string str2)
```

Description

The strcspn function, which was added in PHP 3.0.2 and PHP 4.0, returns the length of the initial segment of *str1*, which does not have any characters found in *str2*.

```
echo strcspn("abcdefg","efg");//displays 4
```

strip_tags()

Syntax

```
string strip_tags(string str, [string allowable_tags])
```

Description

The strip_tags() function, which was added in PHP 3.0.8 and PHP 4.0b2, returns a string that is the *str* string without any HTML or PHP tags in it. The *allowable_tags* parameter is used to indicate which tags should not be stripped from the *str*.

```
echo strip_tags ("<TITLE>A Title</TITLE>");//displays A Title
```

stripcslashes()

Syntax

```
string stripcslashes(string str)
```

Description

The `stripcslashes()` function, which was added in PHP 4.0b2, returns a string with any escaped or "C-slashed" characters removed. C-escaped characters include \n, \r, and so on.

stripslashes()

Syntax

```
string stripslashes(string str)
```

Description

The `stripslashes()` function returns a string with all backslashes removed. For example, `"\n"` becomes `"n"`, `"\\"` becomes `"\"`, and so on.

stristr()

Syntax

```
string stristr(string haystack, string needle)
```

Description

The `stristr()` function, which was added in PHP 3.0.6 and PHP 4.0, returns a portion of *haystack*, starting from the first occurrence of *needle* until the end of *haystack*. The comparison is case insensitive. If *needle* is not present in *haystack*, false is returned. If *needle* is not a string, it is converted to an integer and it is applied as the ordinal value of a character. The ordinal value is the ASCII value for the number; for instance, 65 = A.

```
echo stristr("abcdEfg","e");//displays Efg
```

strlen()

Syntax

```
int strlen(string str)
```

Description

The strlen() function returns the length of *str*.

```
echo strlen("123456789");//displays 9
```

strpos()

Syntax

```
int strpos(string haystack, string needle, [int offset] )
```

Description

The strpos() function returns the position of the last occurrence of *needle* in *haystack* as a number indicating the offset. If *needle* is not found, the return value will be false. If *needle* is a number, it is converted to an integer and applied as the ordinal value of a character.

Optionally, the *offset* parameter enables you to specify from where in the *haystack* to start searching. However, the position returned is in relation to the beginning of *haystack*.

strrchr()

Syntax

```
string strrchr(string haystack, string needle)
```

Description

The strrchr() function returns a subset of *haystack*, which begins at the start of the last occurrence of *needle* and goes to the end of *haystack*. If *needle* isn't found in *haystack*, the function returns false. Only the first character of *needle* will be used, and if *needle* is a number, its corresponding ASCII value is used.

```
echo strrchr ("abcdefg","d123");//displays defg
```

str_repeat()

Syntax

```
string str_repeat(string input, int multiplier)
```

Description

The str_repeat() function, which was added in PHP 4.0b4, returns the *input* string repeated the number of times indicated by *multiplier*. The *multiplier* parameter must be greater than 0.

```
echo str_repeat("*",50);//displays 50 asterisks
```

strrev()

Syntax

```
string strrev(string string)
```

Description

The strrev() function returns the *string* in reverse order.

strrpos()

Syntax

```
int strrpos(string haystack, char needle)
```

Description

The strrpos() function returns the numeric position of the last occurrence of *needle* in the string *haystack*. Note that *needle* is a character and, if passed in as a string, only the first character will be used. If *needle* is not a string, it is converted to an integer and applied as the ordinal value of a character. If *needle* is not found in *haystack*, false is returned.

```
$text = "123456";
echo strpos ($text,"4");//displays 3
```

strspn()

Syntax

```
int strspn(string str1, string str2)
```

Description

The strspn() function, which was added in PHP 3.0.3 and PHP 4.0, returns the length of the initial segment of *str1*, which consists of characters found only in *str2*.

strstr()

Syntax

```
string strstr(string haystack, string needle)
```

Description

The strstr() function returns a portion of *haystack* starting from the first occurrence of *needle* to the end of *haystack*. If needle is not found, false is returned. If *needle* is not a string, it is converted to an integer and applied as the ordinal value of a character.

strtok()

Syntax

```
string strtok(string arg1, string arg2)
```

Description

The strtok() function is used to tokenize a string into smaller pieces. *arg1* indicates the string to be tokenized and *arg2* is the field separator to use for tokenizing the string. If *arg2* consists of more than one character, any of the characters found will create a token. An internal pointer is kept between calls of strtok(). To continue tokenizing the same string, you should specify only the separator string and not the original string each time.

```
$connstr = "UID=USER;PWD=PASSWD";
strtok ($connstr,"=");
$userid = strtok (";");
strtok ("=");
$password = strtok (";");
echo $userid."/".$password;//displays USER/PASSWORD
```

strtolower()

Syntax

```
string strtolower(string str)
```

Description

The `strtolower()` function returns *str* with all alphabetic characters converted to lowercase. Note that the alphabet is determined by the current locale setting.

strtoupper()

Syntax

```
string strtoupper(string string)
```

Description

The `strtoupper()` function returns *string* with all alphabetic characters converted to uppercase. Note that the alphabet is determined by the current locale setting.

str_replace()

Syntax

```
string str_replace(string needle, string str, string haystack)
```

Description

The `str_replace()` function, which was added in PHP 3.0.6 and PHP 4.0, returns a string in which all occurrences of *needle* in *haystack* have been replaced by *str*. This is a simplified version of `ereg_replace()` and is the preferred function when possible.

```
echo str_replace("1","2","1212");//displays 2222
```

strtr()

Syntax

```
string strtr(string str, string from, string to)
```

Description

The strtr() function examines *str*, replaces all occurrences of each character in *from* with the corresponding character in *to*, and returns the resulting string. The *from* and *to* parameters should be the same length and if not, the extra characters are ignored.

strtr() can also be called with only two parameters. In this case, *from* should be an array that contains *string -> string* pairs that indicate what should be replaced in *str*. Note that strtr() always looks for the longest possible match first and doesn't work recursively. This two-argument functionality was added in PHP 4.0.

```
echo strtr ("a1b1c1","1","2");//displays a2b2c2
```

substr()

Syntax

```
string substring(string string, int start, int [length])
```

Description

The substr() function returns the portion of *string* specified by the *start* and optional *length* parameters. A positive value of *start* indicates the offset at which to start searching *string* is from the beginning, and a negative value of *start* indicates that the offset at which to start searching is from the end of *string*.

If the optional parameter *length* is positive, the string returned will end *length* characters from *start*. If this will result in a string with negative length (because the start is past the end of the string), the returned string will contain the single character at *start*.

If the optional parameter *length* is negative, the string returned will end *length* characters from the end of *string*. If this will result in a string with negative length, the returned string will contain the single character at *start*.

```
echo substr("12345",1,3);//displays 234
```

substr_replace()

Syntax

```
string substr_replace(string string, string replacement, int start,
                      int [length])
```

Description

The `substr_replace()` function, which was added in PHP 4.0b4, replaces the part of *string* bounded by the *start* and (optional) *length* parameters with the *replacement* string and returns the result.

If *start* is positive, the replacement starts at the *start* location in the *string*.

If *start* is negative, the replacement begins at the position *start* number of characters from the end of *string*.

When the optional parameter *length* is positive, it represents the length of the amount of *string* that should be replaced. When *length* is negative, it represents the position from the end of *string* at which to stop replacing. If *length* is not given, the whole length of *string* is used.

```
echo substr_replace ("12345","432",2,3);//displays 12432
```

trim()

Syntax

```
string trim(string str)
```

Description

The `trim()` function removes whitespace from *str* and returns the resulting string. Whitespace includes "\n", "\r", "\t", "\v", "\0", and a plain space.

ucfirst

Syntax

```
string ucfirst(string str)
```

Description

The `ucfirst()` function capitalizes the first character of *str* if it is alphabetic. The alphabet is determined by the current locale setting.

```
$text = "hello world!";
echo ucfirst($text);//displays Hello world!
```

ucwords()

Syntax

```
string ucwords(string str)
```

Description

The ucwords() function, which was added in PHP 3.0.3 and PHP 4.0, returns a string that is *str* with each word's first letter uppercased if it is alphabetic.

```
$text = "hello world!";
echo ucwords($text);//displays Hello World!
```

Variable

The following functions deal primarily with getting and setting variable types.

doubleval()

Syntax

```
double doubleval(mixed var)
```

Description

The doubleval() function returns the double (floating-point) value of the *var* parameter. The *var* parameter must be a scalar type and not an object or array.

empty()

Syntax

```
int empty(mixed var)
```

Description

The empty() function determines whether a variable is set.It returns false if *var* is set to a nonempty or nonzero value, and true otherwise.

gettype()

Syntax

```
string gettype(mixed var)
```

Description

The gettype() function returns the PHP-defined type of the parameter *var*. Possible PHP types include integer, double, string, array, object, and unknown type.

```
$avar = array(1,2,3);
echo gettype($avar);//displays array
```

intval()

Syntax

```
int intval(mixed var, int [base])
```

Description

The intval() function returns the integer value of the parameter *var* using the specified base for the conversion. *base* is an optional parameter with 10 as the default. The parameter *var* may be any scalar type. Note that you cannot use intval() on arrays or objects.

```
echo (intval("123"));//displays 123
echo (intval("10",16));//displays 16
```

is_array()

Syntax

```
int is_array(mixed var)
```

Description

The is_array() function returns true if *var* is an array and returns false otherwise.

is_boolean()

Syntax

```
int is_bool(mixed var)
```

Description

The is_bool() function, which was added in PHP 4.0b4, returns true if *var* is a Boolean value and returns false otherwise.

is_double()

Syntax

```
int is_double(mixed var)
```

Description

The is_double() function returns true if *var* is a double and returns false otherwise.

is_float()

Syntax

```
int is_float(mixed var)
```

Description

The is_float() function returns true if *var* is a double and returns false otherwise. This function is an alias for is_double().

is_int()

Syntax

```
int is_int(mixed var)
```

Description

The is_int() function returns true if *var* is an integer (long) and returns false otherwise. This function is an alias for is_long().

is_integer()

Syntax

```
int is_integer(mixed var)
```

Description

The is_integer() function returns true if *var* is an integer (long) and returns false otherwise. This function is an alias for is_long().

is_long()

Syntax

```
int is_long(mixed var)
```

Description

The is_long() function returns true if *var* is an integer (long) and returns false otherwise.

is_numeric()

Syntax

```
int is_numeric(mixed var)
```

Description

The is_numeric() function, which was added in PHP 4.0RC1, returns true if *var* is a number or a numeric string and returns false otherwise.

is_object()

Syntax

```
int is_object(mixed var)
```

Description

The is_object() function returns true if *var* is an object and returns false otherwise.

is_real()

Syntax

```
int is_real(mixed var)
```

Description

The is_real() function returns true if *var* is a double, and returns false otherwise. This function is an alias for is_double().

is_string()

Syntax

```
int is_string(mixed var)
```

Description

The is_string() function returns true if *var* is a string and returns false otherwise.

isset()

Syntax

```
int isset(mixed var)
```

Description

The isset() function returns true if *var* exists and returns false otherwise.

```
$avar = 100;
echo isset($avar);//displays 1
```

print_r()

Syntax

```
void print_r(mixed expression);
```

Description

The print_r() function, which was added in PHP 4.0, displays human-readable information about the values of variables. If *expression* is a string, integer, or double, the value itself will be printed. If *expression* is an array, the keys and values will be displayed. Similar notation is used for objects.

```
$array1 = array (1,2,3);
print_r($array1);
//displays Array ( [0] => 1 [1] => 2 [2] => 3 )
```

settype()

Syntax

```
int settype(string var, string type)
```

Description

The settype() function sets the type of *var* to that of *type*. Possible values of *type* are "integer", "double", "string", "array", and "object". The return value is true if the type could be set, and false otherwise.

strval()

Syntax

```
string strval(mixed var)
```

Description

The strval() function returns the string representation of *var*. *var* must be a scalar type and not an array or object.

unset()

Syntax

```
int unset(mixed var)
```

Description

The unset() function destroys the specified variable and returns true.

var_dump()

Syntax

```
void var_dump(mixed expression)
```

Description

The var_dump() function, which was added in PHP 3.0.5 and PHP 4.0, displays structured information about an expression, including its type and value. Arrays are processed recursively with values indented to show structure.

```
$array1 = array (1,2,3);
var_dump($array1);
//displays array(3) { [0]=> int(1) [1]=> int(2) [2]=> int(3) }
```

CHAPTER 6

Protocol Extensions

On the Internet, there are lots of methods, called *protocols*, of moving files and data around from place to place. These protocols are what enable us to move files, send and receive email, download Web pages, manage networks, and much more.

Within the PHP programming language are several sets of functions that provide the ability to use these protocols. They are the focus of this chapter and are as follows:

- FTP
- HTTP
- IMAP, POP3, and NNTP
- LDAP
- SNMP

FTP

The File Transfer Protocol (FTP) is a standard Internet protocol that is used to exchange files. Generally speaking, FTP commands are issued either on a command-line interface or through an application. You can read the Request For Comments (RFC) on FTP at `http://www.ietf.org/rfc/rfc0959.txt`.

> **Note**
> For those of you using PHP 3, this library of functions was not added until 3.0.13.

ftp_cdup()

Syntax

```
int ftp_cdup(int ftp_stream)
```

Description

The `ftp_cdup()` function instructs the connection to change to the parent directory of the current working directory in *ftp_stream*, which is the name handle of a previously opened stream using `ftp_connect()`. If successful, 1 is returned. If the function fails, 0 is returned.

The following short example moves up one directory on the system, whose connection is defined by $my_conn. The result of the operation is stored in $status. If successful, this will contain 1; otherwise, it will contain an error message.

```
$status = ftp_cdup($my_conn);
```

ftp_chdir()

Syntax

```
int ftp_chdir(int ftp_stream, string directory)
```

Description

The `ftp_chdir()` function changes the current working directory of *ftp_stream*, which is the name handle of a previously opened stream using `ftp_connect()`, to *directory*. If successful, 1 is returned; otherwise 0 is returned on an error.

ftp_connect()

Syntax

```
int ftp_connect(string host, int [port] )
```

Description

The ftp_connect() function opens an FTP connection to *host* when successful. If the optional *port* is specified, the function attempts to open a connection to that specific port rather than to the default port 21. If the function fails, an error is returned.

The following short example shows how you would connect to ftp.mcp.com and store the FTP stream reference in $my_conn. The result of the operation is stored in $status. If successful, this will contain 1; otherwise, it will contain an error message.

```
$status = ftp_connect('ftp.mcp.com');
```

ftp_delete()

Syntax

```
int ftp_delete(int ftp_stream, string file)
```

Description

The ftp_delete() function deletes *file*, which can include the absolute path as well, on the machine connected to through *ftp_stream*. If the deletion is successful, 1 is returned; otherwise, 0 is returned on an error.

ftp_fget()

Syntax

```
int ftp_fget(int ftp_stream, int file_pointer, string remote_file, int mode)
```

Description

The ftp_fget() function retrieves *remote_file* and writes it to *file_pointer* from *ftp_stream*. If FTP_ASCII is passed as *mode*, the file is transferred in ASCII, or "text" mode. If FTP_BINARY is passed, the file is transferred in binary, or "source" mode. This function returns 1 if successful, and 0 if an error occurs.

ftp_fput()

Syntax

```
int ftp_fput(int ftp_stream, string remote_file, int file_pointer, int mode)
```

Description

The `ftp_fput()` function puts the data defined by *file_pointer* and stores it as *remote_file* on the machine connected to by *ftp_stream*. If FTP_ASCII is passed as *mode*, the file is transferred in ASCII, or "text" mode. If FTP_BINARY is passed, the file is transferred in binary, or "source" mode. This function returns 1 if successful, and 0 if an error occurs.

ftp_get()

Syntax

```
int ftp_get(int ftp_stream, string local_file, string remote_file, int mode)
```

Description

The `ftp_get()` function retrieves *remote_file* and stores it as *local_file* from *ftp_stream*. If FTP_ASCII is passed as *mode*, the file is transferred in ASCII, or "text" mode. If FTP_BINARY is passed, the file is transferred in binary, or "source" mode. This function returns 1 if successful, and 0 if an error occurs.

Here is a quick example that puts `local.txt` on the remote system, whose connection is defined by $my_conn. On the remote system, the file—which is transferred in ASCII mode—is named `remote.txt`.

```
$status = ftp_get($my_conn, 'local.txt', 'remote.txt', FTP_ASCII);
```

ftp_login()

Syntax

```
int ftp_login(int ftp_stream, string username, string password)
```

Description

The `ftp_login()` function takes the passed *ftp_stream*, which is the name handle of a previously opened stream using `ftp_connect()`, and passes it *username* and *password* to login. If the function is successful, 1 is returned; otherwise, 0 is returned when an error has occurred.

ftp_mdtm()

Syntax

```
int ftp_mdtm(int ftp_stream, string remote_file)
```

Description

The ftp_mdtm() function returns the last modified timestamp of *remote_file* connected to through *ftp_stream*. A UNIX timestamp is returned if successful; otherwise, a -1 is returned on error.

> **Note**
> Not all FTP servers support this feature.

ftp_mkdir()

Syntax

```
string ftp_mkdir(int ftp_stream, string directory)
```

Description

The ftp_mkdir() function creates *directory* in the current working directory of *ftp_stream*, which is the name handle of a previously opened stream using ftp_connect(). If successful, the name of the new directory created is returned. If the function is unsuccessful, 0 is returned.

ftp_nlist()

Syntax

```
int ftp_nlist(int ftp_stream, string directory)
```

Description

The ftp_nlist() function, like ftp_rawlist(), returns the list of files, in an array, in *directory* through *ftp_stream*, which is the name handle of a previously opened stream using ftp_connect(). If the operation was unsuccessful, 0 is returned.

ftp_pasv()

Syntax

```
int ftp_pasv(int ftp_stream, int boolean)
```

Description

The ftp_pasv() function turns on passive mode (data connection initiated by client rather than server) on the machine connected to by *ftp_stream* if *boolean* is 1, and turns it off if *boolean* is 0. If an error occurs, 0 is returned by the function.

ftp_put()

Syntax

```
int ftp_put(int ftp_stream, string remote_file, string local_file, int mode)
```

Description

The ftp_put() function puts *local_file* and stores it as *remote_file* on the machine connected to by *ftp_stream*. If FTP_ASCII is passed as *mode*, the file is transferred in ASCII, or "text" mode. If FTP_BINARY is passed, the file is transferred in binary, or "source" mode. This function returns 1 if successful, and 0 if an error occurs.

ftp_pwd()

Syntax

```
int ftp_pwd(int ftp_stream)
```

Description

The ftp_pwd() function returns the path of the working directory, on the remote machine, for *ftp_stream*, which is the name handle of a previously opened stream using ftp_connect(). If the function call fails, 0 is returned.

The following example shows how you can print the current directory of an open FTP connection, defined by $my_conn.

```
echo ftp_pwd($my_conn);
```

ftp_quit()

Syntax

```
int ftp_quit(int ftp_stream)
```

Description

The ftp_quit() function closes the *ftp_stream* connection that was opened by ftp_connect().

ftp_rawlist()

Syntax

```
int ftp_rawlist(int ftp_stream, string directory)
```

Description

The ftp_rawlist() function, as with ftp_list(), returns the list of files, in an array, in *directory* through *ftp_stream*, which is the name handle of a previously opened stream using ftp_connect(). The difference is that ftp_rawlist() executes a LIST FTP command for the array and each line returned represents one line of text from the command execution. If the operation was unsuccessful, 0 is returned.

> **Note**
> If you want to know what kind of information is returned in the list, you can use the ftp_systype() function to return the system type identifier.

ftp_rename()

Syntax

```
int ftp_rename(int ftp_stream, string old_name, string new_name)
```

Description

The ftp_rename() function renames the *old_name* file to *new_name* on the machine connected to through *ftp_stream*. If the renaming was successful, 1 is returned; otherwise, 0 is returned on an error.

ftp_rmdir()

Syntax

```
int ftp_rmdir(int ftp_stream, string directory)
```

Description

The ftp_rmdir() function deletes *directory* in the current working directory of *ftp_stream*, which is the name handle of a previously opened stream using ftp_connect(). If successful, 1 is returned. If the function is unsuccessful, 0 is returned.

ftp_site()

Syntax

```
int ftp_site(int ftp_stream, string command)
```

Description

The ftp_site() function, which was added in PHP 3.0.15, sends *command* to the machine connected to through *ftp_stream*. Because the function actually passed a SITE FTP command, the commands that can be executed vary depending on the server.

ftp_size()

Syntax

```
int ftp_size(int ftp_stream, string remote_file)
```

Description

The ftp_size() function returns the size of *remote_file* connected to by *ftp_stream*. If an error occurs, -1 is returned.

> **Note**
> Not all FTP servers support this feature.

ftp_systype()

Syntax

```
int ftp_systype(int ftp_stream)
```

Description

The `ftp_systype()` function, when successful, returns the system type identifier of the remote machine that is connected to through `ftp_stream`. If the function fails, 0 is returned. The following line will write this information based on the connection defined by $my_conn:

```
echo ftp_systype($my_conn);
```

HTTP

The Hypertext Transfer Protocol (HTTP) is another standard Internet protocol. It is generally used to transfer the Hypertext Markup Language (HTML) pages and related elements, such as images, that make up today's Web pages. You can find more information on HTTP at `http://www.w3.org/Protocols` and more information on HTML at `http://www.w3.org/MarkUp`.

> **Note**
> This library of functions was added in PHP 3.

header()

Syntax

```
int header(string header_directive)
```

Description

The `header()` function enables you to specify a single header directive, in `header_directive`, when fulfilling HTTP requests. If you want to specify several directives, you have to use this function multiple times. When specifying header information, you must send it before sending the HTTP body of the request.

For instance, you can pass back a `"Location: /newpage.html"` if you want to redirect users to `newpage.html` rather than the page they requested. For more information on HTTP headers, you can read the Request For Comments (RFC) at `http://www.ietf.org/rfc/rfc2616.txt`.

setcookie()

Syntax

```
int setcookie(string name, [string value], [int expire], [string path],
    [string domain], [int secure])
```

Description

The `setcookie()` function, which must be sent before any headers (see `header()`), enables you to set a cookie (*name*) with a specific *value*. You also can set when the cookie *expires* and what *path* has the right to read it under what *domain*.

To format *expire* correctly, you can use the UNIX time integer as returned by the `time()` or `mktime()` function. The *domain* field can hold an absolute machine and domain name, such as `"machine.domain.com"` or it can hold just the domain portion (if you want all machines to be able to read the cookie in that domain), such as `".domain.com"`. Finally, *secure* takes a 1 or 0 to signify whether the cookie should be transmitted over HTTPS (secure) connections.

> **Note**
> You *must* be within the *domain* to set a cookie. Although PHP might try to set the cookie, the browser will not accept it. In other words, you can't build a PHP application to run on `www.mcp.com` and set a cookie readable by `.php.net`.

IMAP, POP3, and NNTP

The Internet Message Access Protocol (IMAP) and Post Office Protocol version 3 (POP3) are used for email, and the Network News Transfer Protocol (NNTP) performs tasks that revolve around newsgroups. All these are standard Internet protocols that focus on different types and methods of messaging.

You can read the Request For Comments (RFC) on NNTP at `http://www.ietf.org/rfc/rfc0977.txt`; on IMAP at `http://www.ietf.org/rfc/rfc2192.txt`; and on POP3 at `http://www.ietf.org/rfc/rfc2384.txt`. Because of the semantics of creating and checking emails and mailboxes, we **highly** recommend that you read through these specifications. Otherwise, many of the terms and overall functioning defined in this section might not be clear.

Note

Although all the PHP functions in this section start with `imap_`, they are not limited to just IMAP, as the title of the section indicates. Also, it is worth noting that this library of functions was added in PHP 3.

To get these extensions to work, you must compile PHP with the `--with-imap` parameter, which requires a C IMAP library to work. You can obtain the latest and greatest version of this library from `ftp://ftp.cac.washington.edu/imap`.

imap_8bit()

Syntax

```
string imap_8bit(string string)
```

Description

The `imap_8bit()` function takes an 8-bit string and returns a quoted-printable string according to section 6.7 in the Request For Comments (RFC) 2045. You can read more about this at `http://www.ietf.org/rfc/rfc2045.txt`.

```
imap_8bit('    '); //passing a tab returns "=09"
```

imap_alerts()

Syntax

```
array imap_alerts()
```

Description

The `imap_alerts()` function, which was added in PHP 3.0.12, returns an array of all IMAP alert messages that have occurred since the last call to the function.

imap_append()

Syntax

```
int imap_append(int imap_stream, string mailbox, string message,
    [string flags])
```

Description

The `imap_append()` function appends a string `message` to a specified `mailbox`. If the function is successful, 1 is returned; otherwise, 0 is returned on an error. If the optional `flags` are passed, they are written to `mailbox` as well.

> **Note**
> When using a Cyrus IMAP server, you must use "\r\n" to signify your End Of Line (EOL) instead of the normal "\n". Not doing so will cause the operation to fail.

imap_base64()

Syntax

```
string imap_base64(string text)
```

Description

The `imap_base64()` function takes Base64-encoded `text` and decodes it. If you want to read more about Base64 encoding, see section 6.8 in the Request For Comments (RFC) 2045 at http://www.ietf.org/rfc/rfc2045.txt.

imap_binary()

Syntax

```
string imap_binary(string string);
```

Description

The `imap_binary()` function, which was added in PHP 3.0.2, takes the 8-bit *text* and returns a Base64 string. If you want to read more about Base64 encoding, see section 6.8 in the Request For Comments (RFC) 2045 at http://www.ietf.org/rfc/rfc2045.txt.

imap_body()

Syntax

```
string imap_body(int imap_stream, int num, [int flags]);
```

Description

The imap_body() function returns the body of the message specified by *num* from the mailbox connected to by *imap_stream*. This function takes some optional *flags*, which is a bit mask of one or more of the items in Table 6.1.

Table 6.1   *Values for the* flags *Parameter*

Value	Description
FT_INTERNAL	Specifies the return string is in internal format. This forces it not to standardize to CRLF.
FT_PEEK	Tells the request not to set the \Seen flag, assuming that it is not already set.
FT_UID	Specifies that *num* is the UID and not the message ID.

imap_check()

Syntax

```
object imap_check(int imap_stream);
```

Description

The imap_check() function returns an object with various properties that define the mailbox connected to by *imap_stream*. These properties are as follows:

- Date—Contains the last change of the mailbox contents.

- Driver—Returns the protocol used to access this mailbox, which could be POP3, IMAP, or NNTP.

- Mailbox—Gives you the name of the mailbox.

- Nmsgs—Returns the number of messages in the mailbox.

- Recent—Returns the number of new messages in the mailbox.

If the function fails, FALSE will be returned.

imap_clearflag_full()

Syntax

```
string imap_clearflag_full (int imap_stream, string sequence, string flag,
    string options);
```

Description

The `imap_clearflag_full()` function, which was added in PHP 3.0.3, clears the *flags* on a message connected to by *imap_stream*. The *flags* can be any of the entries in the following list. (You can check Request For Comments (RFC) 2060 at `http://www.ietf.org/rfc/rfc2060.txt` for more information on these flags.)

- `\\Seen`
- `\\Answered`
- `\\Flagged`
- `\\Deleted`
- `\\Draft`
- `\\Recent`

The *options* field contains a bit mask with one or more ST_UIDs, which are sequence arguments that contain UIDs instead of sequence numbers.

imap_close()

Syntax

```
int imap_close(int imap_stream [, int flag])
```

Description

The `imap_close()` function closes the previously opened *imap_stream*. This function takes an optional CL_EXPUNGE *flag* that will cause the removal of all messages marked for deletion.

imap_createmailbox()

Syntax

```
int imap_createmailbox(int imap_stream, string mailbox)
```

Description

The `imap_createmailbox()` function creates a new mailbox, named *mailbox*, on the system connected to by *imap_stream*. The function returns 1 if successful, or 0 if unsuccessful.

imap_delete()

Syntax

```
int imap_delete(int imap_stream, int message_num [, int flag])
```

Description

The `imap_delete()` function, which returns 1 if successful, marks the message located at *message_num* for deletion. The optional *flag* is FT_UID and tells the function to treat *message_num* as a UID.

After you have marked messages for deletion, you must either call the `imap_expunge()` function, or pass CL_EXPUNGE to `imap_close()` when closing the connection, to delete the marked messages.

Tip
If you are connecting to a POP3 mailbox, you need to expunge your marked messages before you close your connection. Marked deletions are not carried across connections as in IMAP.

---

imap_deletemailbox()

Syntax

```
int imap_deletemailbox(int imap_stream, string mailbox)
```

Description

The `imap_deletemailbox()` function deletes the specified *mailbox* from the *imap_stream*. If successful, 1 is returned; otherwise, a 0 is returned on error.

Tip
Check out `imap_open()` for more information on the formatting of mailbox names.

---

imap_errors()

Syntax

```
array imap_errors()
```

Description

The imap_errors() function, which was added in PHP 3.0.12, is an array of all the error messages that have been generated since the beginning of the page or the last time you called the function.

imap_expunge()

Syntax

```
int imap_expunge(int imap_stream)
```

Description

The imap_expunge() function removes all messages marked for deletion in the mailbox connected to by imap_stream. Messages can be marked using the imap_delete(), imap_move_mail(), or imap_setflag_full() functions.

imap_fetch_overview()

Syntax

```
array imap_fetch_overview(int imap_stream, string sequence [, int flag])
```

Description

The imap_fetch_overview() function, which was added in PHP 3.0.4, grabs the message headers for a given sequence and returns an overview of their contents. The sequence is a list of message IDs unless flag is set to FT_UID, in which case it represents UIDs.

The array returned is an array of objects with the properties specified in Table 6.5.

Table 6.5 *Object Properties*

Property	Description
subject	The subject of the messages.
from	Who sent the message.
date	When the message was sent.
message_id	The message ID.
references	A reference to this message ID.
size	Size of the message in bytes.
uid	UID of the message in the mailbox.
msgno	Message sequence number in the mailbox.
recent	The message has been flagged as recent.
flagged	The message has been flagged.
answered	The message has been flagged as answered.
deleted	The message has been flagged for deletion.
seen	The message has been flagged as read.
draft	The message has been flagged as a draft.

The following example shows how you can grab messages 1–3 and 7 using this function.

```
$overview = imap_fetch_overview($mailbox,"1:3,7",0);
```

imap_fetchbody()

Syntax

```
string imap_fetchbody(int imap_stream, int num, string part_num
    [, flags flags])
```

Description

The imap_fetchbody() function will fetch the part—defined by *part_num*—of the message at *num*. You can optionally pass one or more of the *flags* in Table 6.2 to complete this procedure.

Table 6.2 *Values for the* flags *Parameter*

Value	Description
FT_INTERNAL	Specifies the return string is in internal format. This forces it not to standardize to CRLF.
FT_PEEK	Tells the request not to set the \Seen flag, assuming that it is not already set.
FT_UID	Specifies that *num* is the UID and not the message ID.

Note

You can find more information on this topic in the IMAP specification in section 2.3 of the Request For Comments (RFC) 2060 at http://www.ietf.org/rfc/rfc2060.txt.

---

imap_fetchheader()

Syntax

```
string imap_fetchheader(int imap_stream, int num, [int flags])
```

Description

The imap_fetchheader() function will grab and return the complete and unfiltered RFC822 (http://www.ietf.org/rfc/rfc0822.txt) format header of the message at *num*. The option *flags* can be any of the items in Table 6.3.

Table 6.3 *Values for the* flags *Parameter*

Value	Description
FT_INTERNAL	Specifies the return string is in internal format. This forces it not to standardize to CRLF.
FT_PREFETCHTEXT	The RFC822.TEXT should be pre-fetched at the same time. This avoids an extra RTT on an IMAP connection if a full message text is desired (for example, in a "save to local file" operation).
FT_UID	Specifies that *num* is the UID and not the message ID.

imap_fetchstructure()

Syntax

```
object imap_fetchstructure(int imap_stream, int num [, int flag])
```

Description

The `imap_fetchstructure()` function will fetch all the structure information of the message located at *num* and return an object containing its envelope, internal date, size, flags, and body structure. It will also return a similar object for each MIME attachment to the message. The optional *flag* must be FT_UID, which specifies that *num* is the UID and not the message ID.

The returned object itself has the properties defined in Table 6.4.

Table 6.4   *Properties Contained in the Object Returned by the* `imap_fetchstructure()` *Function*

Property	Description	Notes
type	Contains the primary body type	This type can be any of the following:
		0—Text
		1—Multipart
		2—Message
		3—Application
		4—Audio
		5—Image
		6—Video
		7—Other
encoding	Contains the body transfer encoding	This encoding can be any of the following:
		0—7BIT
		1—8BIT
		2—BINARY
		3—BASE64
		4—QUOTED-PRINTABLE
		5—OTHER
ifsubtype	Contains true if there is a subtype string	
subtype	Contains the MIME subtype	
ifdescription	Contains true if there is a description string	

Table 6.4   *(continued)*

Property	Description	Notes
description	Contains content description string	
ifid	Contains true if there is an identification string	
id	Contains identification string	
lines	Contains the number of lines in the message	
bytes	Contains the number of bytes in the message	
ifdisposition	Contains true if there is a disposition string	
disposition	Contains the disposition string if it exists	
ifdparameters	Contains true if the dparameters array exists	
dparameters	Contains the disposition parameter array, if it exists	This is an array of objects, where each object has an attribute and value property.
ifparameters	Contains true if the parameters array exists	
parameters	Contains the MIME parameters array if it exists	This is an array of objects, where each object has an attribute and value property.
parts	Contains an array of objects describing each message part	This is the same as the top-level object returned except that it does not contain another, nested parts property.

imap_getmailboxes()

Syntax

```
array imap_getmailboxes(int imap_stream, string ref, string pattern)
```

Description

The imap_getmailboxes() function, which was added in PHP 3.0.12, obtains a list of objects, stored in a returned array, of the mailboxes to which the user has access. This is accomplished by looking at the connection defined by imap_stream and passing the server name as ref. This is the same server name that you used when you opened the stream with the imap_open() function. You define which mailboxes to obtain information about by passing a pattern for the function to look for.

For pattern, you can use * or % to represent two different wildcards. When used, * will return all mailboxes. %, on the other hand, will return only the top-level mailboxes.

The array of objects themselves will contain three items. It will contain the fullname of the mailbox, the hierarchy delimiter, and a bit mask attribute field. These attributes can be tested against the items in Table 6.6.

Table 6.6 *Values of the Attributes*

Value	Description
LATT_NOINFERIORS	The mailbox has no subfolders under it.
LATT_NOSELECT	The mailbox is only a container, not a mailbox you can open.
LATT_MARKED	The mailbox is marked, and is used only by UW-IMAPD.
LATT_UNMARKED	The mailbox is not marked, and is used only by UW-IMAPD.

Here is a quick example of how you would call this function:

```
$mailboxes = imap_getmailboxes($mbox, "{imap.mcp.com}", "*");
```

imap_getsubscribed()

Syntax

```
array imap_getsubscribed(int imap_stream, string ref, string pattern)
```

Description

The `imap_subscribed()` function, which was added in PHP 3.0.12, obtains a list of objects, stored in a returned array, of the mailboxes to which the user is subscribed. This is accomplished by looking at the connection defined by *imap_stream* and passing the server name as *ref*. This is the same server name that you used when you opened the stream with the `imap_open()` function. You define which mailboxes to obtain information about by passing a *pattern* for the function to look for.

For *pattern*, you can use * or % to represent two different wildcards. When used, * will return all mailboxes. %, on the other hand, will return only the top-level mailboxes.

The array of objects themselves will contain three items. It will contain the *fullname* of the mailbox, the hierarchy *delimiter*, and a bit mask *attribute* field. These attributes can be tested against the items in Table 6.7.

Table 6.7   *Values of the Attributes*

Value	Description
LATT_NOINFERIORS	The mailbox has no subfolders under it.
LATT_NOSELECT	The mailbox is only a container, not a mailbox you can open.
LATT_MARKED	The mailbox is marked, and is used only by UW-IMAPD.
LATT_UNMARKED	The mailbox is not marked, and is used only by UW-IMAPD.

Here is a quick example of how you would call this function:

```
$mailboxes = imap_subscribed($mbox, "{imap.mcp.com}", "*");
```

imap_header()

Syntax

```
object imap_header(int imap_stream, int message_num [, int from_length
   [, int subject_length [, string default_host]]])
```

Description

The `imap_header()` function reads the various header information of the message located at *message_num*, and returns an object containing the values of these elements. This object contains the elements and subobjects discussed in Table 6.8.

Table 6.8   *Properties of the Returned Object*

Property	Comments
remail	
date	
Date	
subject	
Subject	
in_reply_to	
message_id	
newsgroups	
followup_to	
references	
message flags	The types of message flags that can be returned are • Recent: R if the message is recent and seen; N if it is recent and not seen; and null, ' ', if it is not recent • Unseen: U if the message is not seen AND not recent, and null, ' ', if it is seen OR not seen and recent • Answered: A if the message is answered, and null, ' ', if it is unanswered • Deleted: D if the message is deleted, and null, ' ', if it has not been deleted • Draft: X if message is a draft, and null, ' ', if it is not a draft • Flagged: F if the message is flagged, and null, ' ', if it is not flagged
to address	Returns the full to: line, up to 1,024 characters
to[]	Returns an array of objects from the To line, containing • personal • adl • mailbox • host
fromaddress	Returns the full from: line, up to 1,024 characters
from[]	Returns an array of objects from the From line, containing • personal • adl • mailbox • host

Table 6.8 *(continued)*

Property	Comments
ccaddress	Returns the full cc: line, up to 1,024 characters.
cc[]	Returns an array of objects from the Cc line, containing • personal • adl • mailbox • host
bccaddress	Returns full bcc: line, up to 1,024 characters.
bcc[]	Returns an array of objects from the Bcc line, containing • personal • adl • mailbox • host
reply_toaddress	Returns full reply_to: line, up to 1,024 characters
reply_to[]	Returns an array of objects from the Reply_to line, containing • personal • adl • mailbox • host
senderaddress	Returns full sender: line, up to 1,024 characters
sender[]	Returns an array of objects from the sender line, containing • personal • adl • mailbox • host
return_path	Returns full return-path: line, up to 1,024 characters.
return_path[]	Returns an array of objects from the return_path line, containing • personal • adl • mailbox • host
udate	Returns mail message date in UNIX time

Table 6.8 *(continued)*

Property	Comments
fetchfrom	Returns from line formatted to fit fromlength characters
fetchsubject	Returns subject line formatted to fit subjectlength characters

imap_headers()

Syntax

```
array imap_headers(int imap_stream)
```

Description

The imap_headers() function returns an array of strings with header information. There will be one array element per mail message.

imap_last_error()

Syntax

```
string imap_last_error()
```

Description

The imap_last_error() function, which was added in PHP 3.0.12, returns the last IMAP error that occurred on the page. Calling this function does not clear the error, so subsequent calls will return the same error.

imap_listmailbox()

Syntax

```
array imap_listmailbox(int imap_stream, string ref, string pattern)
```

Description

The imap_listmailbox() function returns an array that contains the names of the mailboxes connected to by *imap_stream*. The *ref* parameter is the same server name that you used when you opened the stream with the imap_open() function. You define which mailboxes to obtain information about by passing a *pattern* for the function to look for.

For *pattern*, there you can use * or % to represent two different wildcards. When used, * will return all mailboxes. %, on the other hand, will return only the top-level mailboxes.

imap_listsubscribed()

Syntax

```
array imap_listsubscribed(int imap_stream, string ref, string pattern)
```

Description

The `imap_listsubscribed()` function returns an array that contains the names of all subscribed mailboxes connected to by *imap_stream*. The *ref* parameter is the same server name that you used when you opened the stream with the `imap_open()` function. You define which mailboxes to obtain information about by passing a *pattern* for the function to look for.

For *pattern*, you can use * or % to represent two different wildcards. When used, * returns all mailboxes. %, on the other hand, returns only the top-level mailboxes.

imap_mail()

Syntax

```
string imap_mail(string to, string subject, string message
    [, string additional_headers [, string cc [, string bcc
    [, string rpath]]]])
```

Description

The `imap_mail()` function, which was added in PHP 3.0.14, will send an email *message* to the address specified in *to* with *subject*. You can also pass any *additional_headers*, which are any additional addresses you want to *cc* or *bcc*.

imap_mail_compose()

Syntax

```
string imap_mail_compose(array envelope, array body)
```

Description

The imap_mail_compose() function, which was added in PHP 3.0.5, creates a MIME message based on the *envelope* and *body* passed. Within the *envelope*, you assign values to matching keys, such as to, subject, and from.

imap_mail_copy()

Syntax

```
int imap_mail_copy(int imap_stream, string message_list, string mailbox
    [, int flags])
```

Description

The imap_mail_copy() function copies the specified *message_list* to a particular *mailbox*. The optional *flags* are a bit mask field of one or more of the items in Table 6.10.

Table 6.10 *Possible Values of the Bit Mask Field*

Value	Description
CP_MOVE	Deletes the messages from the current mailbox after the copying is complete.
CP_UID	The sequence numbers in *message_list* contains UIDs.

imap_mail_move()

Syntax

```
int imap_mail_move(int imap_stream, string message_list, string mailbox
    [, int flag])
```

Description

The imap_mail_move() function moves the specified *message_list* to a particular *mailbox*. The optional *flag* is a bit mask field that can contain CP_UID, which specifies that the sequence numbers in *message_list* contain UIDs.

imap_mailboxmsginfo()

Syntax

```
object imap_mailboxmsginfo(int imap_stream)
```

Description

The imap_mailboxmsginfo() function, which was added in PHP 3.0.2, will return information about the current mailbox connected to by *imap_stream*. If an error occurs, FALSE will be returned. The function, when successful, returns its information in an object with the properties listed in Table 6.9.

Table 6.9   *Properties of the Returned Object*

Property	Description
Date	Date the mailbox last changed.
Driver	Driver.
Mailbox	Name of the mailbox.
Nmsgs	Number of messages in the mailbox.
Recent	Number of recent messages in the mailbox.
Unread	Number of unread messages in the mailbox.
Deleted	Number of deleted messages in the mailbox.
Size	Total size of mailbox.

imap_msgno()

Syntax

```
int imap_msgno(int imap_stream, int uid)
```

Description

The imap_msgno() function, which was added in PHP 3.0.3, returns a message sequence number for the *uid* passed.

imap_num_msg()

Syntax

```
int imap_num_msg(int imap_stream)
```

Description

The imap_num_msg() function returns the number of messages in the current mailbox.

imap_num_recent()

Syntax

```
int imap_num_recent(int imap_stream)
```

Description

The imap_num_recent() function returns the number of recent messages in the current mailbox.

imap_open()

Syntax

```
int imap_open(string mailbox, string username, string password [, int flags])
```

Description

The imap_open() function opens an IMAP stream to the specified *mailbox*. To accomplish this connection, you must pass the appropriate *username* and *password*. If the attempt fails, an error will be returned.

When using this function, the syntax for *mailbox* is important. The first portion of the *mailbox* value is the server name, path, and port number, which are contained in brackets, "{}". Following the brackets, you can specify a folder or group name depending on the type of server to which you are connecting.

The optional *flags* parameter is a bit mask that can contain one or more of the items in Table 6.11.

Table 6.11   *Values for the Bit Mask*

Value	Description
CL_EXPUNGE	Expunge mailbox automatically when closing connection.
OP_ANONYMOUS	Don't use or update an .newsrc for news (NNTP only).
OP_HALFOPEN	Open a connection but not a mailbox (for IMAP and NNTP names).
OP_READONLY	Open mailbox in read-only mode.

This function can be used to connect to an IMAP, POP3, or NNTP server. Sample syntax for these connections are as follows:

```
$mbox = imap_open("{imap.mcp.com:143}INBOX", "raw", "mypass"); //IMAP
$mbox = imap_open("{pop3.mcp.com/pop3:110", "raw", "mypass"); //POP3
$mbox = imap_open("{news.mcp.com/nntp:119}comp.lang", "raw", "mypass"); //NNTP
```

imap_ping()

Syntax

```
int imap_ping(int imap_stream)
```

Description

The imap_ping() function will check whether *imap_stream* is still active and will return 1. If not, 0 will be returned.

imap_qprint()

Syntax

```
string imap_qprint(string string)
```

Description

The imap_qprint() function will convert a quoted-printable string to an 8-bit string, which it returns. For more information on this conversion, you can check out Section 6.7 in the Request For Comments (RFC) 2045, which can be found at http://www.ietf.org/rfc/rfc2045.txt.

imap_renamemailbox()

Syntax

```
int imap_renamemailbox(int imap_stream, string old_name, string new_name)
```

Description

The imap_renamemailbox() function will rename the specified mailbox from *old_name* to *new_name*. Check the entry for imap_open() for how to format these names, which include the server name, port, and mailbox name.

imap_reopen()

Syntax

```
int imap_reopen(int imap_stream, string mailbox [, string flags])
```

Description

The imap_reopen() function will reopen the imap_stream, but to a new mailbox. The optional flags parameter is a bit mask that can contain one or more of the items in Table 6.12.

Table 6.12 *Values for the Bit Mask*

Value	Description
CL_EXPUNGE	Expunge mailbox automatically when closing connection.
OP_ANONYMOUS	Don't use or update an .newsrc for news (NNTP only).
OP_HALFOPEN	Open a connection but not a mailbox (for IMAP and NNTP names).
OP_READONLY	Open mailbox in read-only mode.

imap_rfc822_parse_adrlist()

Syntax

```
array imap_rfc822_parse_adrlist(string address, string default_host)
```

Description

The imap_rfc822_parse_adrlist() function, which was added in PHP 3.0.2, parses the address on the default_host and returns an array of objects with the properties in Table 6.13.

Table 6.13 *Properties of the Returned Object*

Property	Description
mailbox	The username of the mailbox.
host	The host name.
personal	The personal name.
adl	At domain source route.

The following is a quick example of how this works:

```
$address = "John Doe, mcp.com, jdoe";
$adrlist = imap_rfc822_parse_adrlist($address,"mcp.com");
reset($adrlist);
while(list($key,$value)=each($adrlist)){
  print "mailbox: ".$value->mailbox."<br>\n";
  print "host: ".$value->host."<br>\n";
  print "personal: ".$value->personal."<br>\n";
  print "adl: ".$value->adl."<p>\n";
}
```

imap_rfc822_parse_headers()

Syntax

```
object imap_rfc822_parse_headers(string headers [, string default_host])
```

Description

The `imap_rfc822_parse_headers()` function, which was added in PHP 4.0, returns an object with information on the *headers*. You can use the optional *default_host* parameter to specify the default host for the function to use.

imap_rfc822_write_address()

Syntax

```
string imap_rfc822_write_address(string mailbox, string host, string personal)
```

Description

The `imap_rfc822_write_address()` function, which was added in PHP 3.0.2, returns a properly formatted email address according to the Request For Comments (RFC) 822.

```
// writes "John Doe <jdoe@mcp.com>"
echo imap_rfc822_write_address('jdoe', 'mcp.com', 'John Doe')
```

imap_scanmailbox()

Syntax

```
array imap_scanmailbox (int imap_stream, string text)
```

Description

The `imap_scanmailbox()` function searches the mailbox connected to by *imap_stream* for the occurrence of *text* in the mailbox. All matching occurrences are stored in the returned array. If you do not want to limit the returned data by specifying *text*, use the `imap_listmailbox()` function.

imap_search()

Syntax

```
array imap_search(int imap_stream, string criteria, int flags)
```

Description

The `imap_search()` function, which was added in PHP 3.0.12, searches the mailbox connected to by *imap_stream* for the occurrence of *criteria* in the mailbox. *criteria* is a list of space-separated keywords and values. If one of the values must contain a value, such as `"John Doe"`, you must include that value in quotes. The possible keywords that can be used are in Table 6.14.

Table 6.14   *Keywords That Can Be Used with* `imap_search()`

Keyword	Description
ALL	All messages matching the rest of the criteria.
ANSWERED	Match messages with the \\ANSWERED flag.
BCC "*string*"	Match messages with "*string*" in the Bcc field.
BEFORE "*date*"	Match messages with Date: before "*date*".
BODY "*string*"	Match messages with "*string*" in the body of the message.
CC "*string*"	Match messages with "*string*" in the Cc field.
DELETED	Match deleted messages.
FLAGGED	Match messages with \\FLAGGED set.
FROM "*string*"	Match messages with "*string*" in the From field.
KEYWORD "*string*"	Match messages with "*string*" as a keyword.
NEW	Match new messages.
OLD	Match old messages.
ON "*date*"	Match messages with Date matching "*date*".
RECENT	Match messages with \\RECENT set.
SEEN	Match messages with \\SEEN set.

Table 6.14   *(continued)*

Keyword	Description
SINCE "*date*"	Match messages with Date after "*date*".
SUBJECT "*string*"	Match messages with "*string*" in the Subject field.
TEXT "*string*"	Match messages with text "*string*".
TO "*string*"	Match messages with "*string*" in the To field.
UNANSWERED	Match messages that have not been answered.
UNDELETED	Match messages that are not deleted.
UNFLAGGED	Match messages that are not flagged.
UNKEYWORD "*string*"	Match messages that do not have the keyword "*string*".
UNSEEN	Match messages that have not been read yet.

All matching occurrences from the *criteria* used are stored in the returned array.

imap_setflag_full()

Syntax

```
string imap_setflag_full(int imap_stream, string sequence,
    string message_flag [, string flag])
```

Description

The imap_setflag_full() function, which was added in PHP 3.0.3, sets the *message_flag* on the messages specified by *sequence*. The optional *flag* is a bit mask that can be ST_UID, which specifies that *sequence* contains UIDs instead of sequence numbers. The *sequence* itself can be any of the following:

- \\Seen

- \\Answered

- \\Flagged

- \\Deleted

- \\Draft

- \\Recent

imap_sort()

Syntax

```
array imap_sort(int imap_stream, int sort, int reverse, int flags)
```

Description

The imap_sort() function, which was added in PHP 3.0.3, returns an array of message headers sorted based on *sort*. If *reverse* is 1, the sorting is based on *sort*, but in reverse order. The *sort* itself can be based on any one of the items in Table 6.15.

Table 6.15 *Possible Sort Criteria*

Value	Description
SORTDATE	Message date.
SORTARRIVAL	Arrival date.
SORTFROM	Mailbox in first From address.
SORTSUBJECT	Message subject.
SORTTO	Mailbox in first To address.
SORTCC	Mailbox in first cc address.
SORTSIZE	Size of message in octets.

The *flags* are a bit mask of one or more of the items in Table 6.16.

Table 6.16 *Possible Bit Mask Values*

Value	Description
SE_UID	Return UIDs instead of sequence numbers.
SE_NOPREFETCH	Don't prefetch searched messages.

imap_status()

Syntax

```
object imap_status(int imap_stream, string mailbox, int flags)
```

Description

The `imap_status()` function, which was added in PHP 3.0.4, returns the status information on a given *mailbox*. This information is in the form of an object. Possible *flags* are shown and defined in Table 6.17.

Table 6.17   *Flags That Can Be Passed to the* `imap_status()` *Function*

Property	Description
SA_ALL	Set all the properties defined in this table.
SA_MESSAGES	Set status->messages to the number of messages in *mailbox*.
SA_RECENT	Set status->recent to the number of recent messages in *mailbox*.
SA_UIDNEXT	Set status->uidnext to the next UID to be used in *mailbox*.
SA_UIDVALIDITY	Set status->uidvalidity to a constant that changes when UIDs for *mailbox* may no longer be valid.
SA_UNSEEN	Set status->unseen to the number of new messages in *mailbox*.

imap_subscribe()

Syntax

```
int imap_subscribe(int imap_stream, string mailbox)
```

Description

The `imap_subscribe()` function enables you to subscribe to a new *mailbox* on the *imap_stream*. If successful, the function returns 1; otherwise it returns 0 on error.

imap_uid()

Syntax

```
int imap_uid(int imap_stream, int message_num)
```

Description

The `imap_uid()` function, which was added in PHP 3.0.3, returns the UID for the message specified by *message_num*. Because the *message_num* can change, this function is often used to obtain a truly unique identifier specified by the UID.

imap_undelete()

Syntax

```
int imap_undelete(int imap_stream, int message_num)
```

Description

The `imap_undelete()` function removes the deletion flag from the specified *message_num*. If the function is successful, it will return 1; otherwise, 0 will be returned in the instance of an error.

> **Note**
> In some releases of PHP 3, you might find that this function does not appear to work. If so, try passing a third, empty parameter to the function.

imap_unsubscribe()

Syntax

```
int imap_unsubscribe(int imap_stream, string mailbox)
```

Description

The `imap_unsubscribe()` function will unsubscribe to *mailbox*. If the function is successful, it will return 1; otherwise, 0 will be returned in the instance of an error.

imap_utf7_decode()

Syntax

```
string imap_utf7_decode(string text)
```

Description

The `imap_utf7_decode()` function, which was added in PHP 3.0.15, decodes the modified UTF-7 *text* and returns 8-bit data. If the *text* passed was not valid, then false will be returned. You can find more information on the modified UTF-7 encoding in Section 5.1.3 of the Request For Comments (RFC) 2060, which can be found at `http://www.ietf.org/rfc/rfc2060.txt`.

imap_utf7_encode()

Syntax

```
string imap_utf7_encode(string text)
```

Description

The `imap_utf7_encode()` function, which was added in PHP 3.0.15, coverts 8-bit data, specified by *text*, into modified UTF-7 text. If the *text* passed was not valid, false will be returned. You can find more information on the modified UTF-7 encoding in Section 5.1.3 of the Request For Comments (RFC) 2060, which can be found at `http://www.ietf.org/rfc/rfc2060.txt`.

imap_utf8()

Syntax

```
string imap_utf8(string text)
```

Description

The `imap_utf8()` function, which was added in PHP 3.0.13, converts *text* to UTF-8, as defined in the Request For Comments (RFC) 2044. You can read more about UTF-8 at `http://www.ietf.org/rfc/rfc2044.txt`.

LDAP

The Lightweight Directory Access Protocol (LDAP) is used to locate people, organizations, and resources, such as files, on a network. These directory servers are a special kind of database that holds its information in a tree-like structure.

Unlike files that are stored on a filesystem and referenced by a path, LDAP entries are referenced by their distinguished name, or DN. For instance, the following might be an entry:

```
cn=John Doe,o=PHP Programmers Corp,st=NC,countryname=USA
```

Because the sequence is read from right to left, you see the tree appear as follows:

- countryname—Name of the country in which John works

- st—Name of the state John works in (assuming that he works in the United States, of course)

- o—Name of the company for which John works

- cn—Full name of John

This, of course, enables you to sort by the values easily, without entries losing their place in the overall structure, or tree. You can read the Request For Comments (RFC) at http://www.ietf.org/rfc/rfc1959.txt.

ldap_add()

Syntax

```
int ldap_add(int ldap_pointer, string distinguished_name, array fields)
```

Description

The ldap_add() function adds additional *fields* to the entry defined by *distinguished_name*. If the function was successful, it will return 1; otherwise, it will return 0 on error.

ldap_bind()

Syntax

```
int ldap_bind(int ldap_pointer [, string rdn [, string password]])
```

Description

The ldap_bind() function binds the directory to a specified relative distinguished name (RDN) and password. If *rdn* and *password* are not passed, an anonymous bind is attempted. If the function is successful, 1 is returned; otherwise, an error is returned.

ldap_close()

Syntax

```
int ldap_close(int ldap_pointer)
```

Description

The ldap_close() function closes a link to a specified LDAP server. If successful, 1 is returned; otherwise, an error is returned.

ldap_connect()

Syntax

```
int ldap_compare(int ldap_pointer, string distinguished_name,
    string attribute, string value)
```

Description

The `ldap_compare()` function, which was added in PHP 4.0.2, compares the `value`—which cannot be binary—of `attribute` to the same attribute value in the entry specified with the `distinguished_name`. If the function is successful, 1 is returned; otherwise, -1 is returned on error.

ldap_count_entries()

Syntax

```
int ldap_count_entries(int ldap_pointer, int result)
```

Description

The `ldap_count_entries()` function returns the count on an internal LDAP search `result`. A `false` is returned on error.

ldap_delete()

Syntax

```
int ldap_delete(int ldap_pointer, string distinguished_name)
```

Description

The `ldap_delete()` function deletes the entry specified by `distinguished_name` in an LDAP directory. If the function fails, `false` is returned.

ldap_dn2ufn()

Syntax

```
string ldap_dn2ufn(string distinguished_name)
```

Description

The `ldap_dn2ufn()` function converts *distinguished_name* into user-friendly naming (UFN) format, which might be a little easier for you to read. This conversion is accomplished by removing the type names from the *distinguished_name*.

ldap_err2str()

Syntax

```
string ldap_err2str(int error_num)
```

Description

The `ldap_err2str()` function, which was added in PHP 3.0.13, takes a LDAP *error_num* and returns the string equivalent or description of the error. The actual *error_num* values are standardized in LDAP, but the messages could return slightly different descriptions when converted to strings.

ldap_errno()

Syntax

```
int ldap_errno(int ldap_pointer)
```

Description

The `ldap_errno()` function, which was added in PHP 3.0.12, returns the error number of the last LDAP command. When called, these errors will be written to your HTML output unless you prefix your LDAP function calls with @ to suppress error messages.

ldap_error()

Syntax

```
string ldap_error(int ldap_pointer)
```

Description

The `ldap_error()` function, which was added in PHP 3.0.12, returns the error message of the last LDAP command. When called, these errors will be written to your

HTML output unless you prefix your LDAP function calls with @ to suppress error messages.

ldap_explode_dn()

Syntax

```
array ldap_explode_dn(string distinguished_name, int with_attribute)
```

Description

The ldap_explode_dn() function splits up the components of the distinguished_name into its component parts (that is, it splits on commas), and returns an array. If with_attribute is equal to 1, each array element will contain both the type name and value in typename=value format. If set to 0, each array element will contain only the values.

ldap_first_attribute()

Syntax

```
string ldap_first_attribute(int ldap_pointer, int result, int ber)
```

Description

The ldap_first_attribute() function will return the first attribute of the internal LDAP search result. The ber parameter is a pass-by-reference value for the internal memory state of the pointer, which increments on subsequent ldap_next_attribute() function calls.

ldap_first_entry()

Syntax

```
int ldap_first_entry(int ldap_pointer, int result)
```

Description

The ldap_first_entry() function will return the first entry of the internal LDAP search result. If the call fails, false will be returned.

ldap_free_result()

Syntax

```
int ldap_free_result(int result)
```

Description

The `ldap_free_result()` function will free the internal LDAP search *result* from memory. By default, this freeing of memory happens at the end of a page, but this function enables you to free the memory yourself during long scripts that could absorb excessive amounts of memory.

ldap_get_attributes()

Syntax

```
array ldap_get_attributes(int ldap_pointer, int result)
```

Description

The `ldap_get_attributes()` function will return a multi-dimensional array of attributes and values for the internal LDAP search *result*. The first column in the array contains the attribute identifier and the second column contains the value of that attribute. Use the following methods to find out how many array items are contained in each column:

```
$result_array["count"]; //total number of attributes (first column)
$result_array["attribute"]["count"]; //number of values for attribute
```

ldap_get_dn()

Syntax

```
string ldap_get_dn(int ldap_pointer, int result)
```

Description

The `ldap_get_dn()` function returns the distinguished name (DN) of the internal LDAP search *result*.

ldap_get_entries()

Syntax

```
array ldap_get_entries(int ldap_pointer, int result)
```

Description

The ldap_get_entries() function returns all entries of the internal LDAP search
result. If the function call is unsuccessful, false is returned. You can access the items
in the array as follows:

```
$result_array["count"]; //number of entries in result
$result_array[0]; //details of first entry
$result_array[i]["dn"]; //DN of the ith entry
$result_array[i]["count"]; //number of attributes in ith entry
$result_array[i][j]; //jth attribute in the ith entry
$result_array[i]["attribute"]["count"]; //# values for attribute in ith entry
$result_array[i]["attribute"][j]; //jth value of attribute in ith entry
```

> **Note**
> When using this function, all attribute names, or type names, will be converted to lowercase
> for proper ordering in the array. This is not a problem with any LDAP operations because
> LDAP is not case-sensitive.

ldap_get_values()

Syntax

```
array ldap_get_values(int ldap_pointer, int result, string attribute)
```

Description

The ldap_get_values() function returns all values, in an array, of a specified
attribute from an internal LDAP search result.

```
$result_array["count"]; //number of values in result
$result_array[0]; //value of first entry
```

If you want to return binary values, see the entry for the ldap_get_values_len()
function.

ldap_get_values_len()

Syntax

```
array ldap_get_values_len(int ldap_pointer, int result, string attribute)
```

Description

The ldap_get_values_len() function, which was added in PHP 3.0.13, returns all binary values, in an array, of a specified *attribute* from an internal LDAP search *result*.

```
$result_array["count"]; //number of values in result
$result_array[0]; //value of first entry
```

If you want to return string values, see the entry for the ldap_get_values() function.

ldap_list()

Syntax

```
int ldap_list(int ldap_pointer, string base_distinguished_name, string filter
    [, array attributes [, int attributes_only [, int size_limit [, int
    time_limit [, int dereference]]]]])
```

Description

The ldap_list() function performs a single-level search (that is, its scope is LDAP_SCOPE_ONELEVEL, which is one level below the *base_distinguished_name*) for the specified *filter*. The filter is in the format of *attribute=value*. If you want to return entries for all values, you can simply pass * as the value.

If you want to restrict the results of this function, you can do so by limiting it to just the *attributes*, which are optional, specified in an array. If you want only the attribute types returned and not the values, you can set *attributes_only* equal to 1. It is also possible to further limit it by the optional *size_limit*, which is the number of entries to be returned. The optional *time_limit* enables you to specify the number of seconds the function has to complete.

The final attribute, *dereference*, defines how you want aliases in the LDAP server to be handled. Table 6.18 shows the complete list from which you have to choose.

Table 6.18   *Possible Values for the* dereference *Attribute*

Value	Description
LDAP_DEREF_ALWAYS	Aliases should be always dereferenced.
LDAP_DEREF_FINDING	Aliases should not be dereferenced during the search, but rather when locating the base object.
LDAP_DEREF_NEVER	Aliases are never dereferenced. This is the default setting.
LDAP_DEREF_SEARCHING	Aliases should be dereferenced during the search, but not when locating the base object.

> **Note**
> The optional parameters (`attributes_only`, `size_limit`, `time_limit`, `dereference`) were added in PHP 4.0.2.

ldap_mod_add()

Syntax

```
int ldap_mod_add(int ldap_pointer, string distinguished_name, array attributes)
```

Description

The ldap_mod_add() function, which was added in PHP 3.0.8, adds new *attributes* to the specified *distinguished_name*. If the function is successful, it will return 1; otherwise, it will return an error.

ldap_mod_del()

Syntax

```
int ldap_mod_del(int ldap_pointer, string distinguished_name, array attributes)
```

Description

The ldap_mod_del() function, which was added in PHP 3.0.8, deletes *attributes* from the specified *distinguished_name*. If the function is successful, it will return 1; otherwise, it will return an error.

ldap_mod_replace()

Syntax

```
int ldap_mod_replace(int ldap_pointer, string distinguished_name,
    array attributes)
```

Description

The `ldap_mod_replace()` function, which was added in PHP 3.0.8, replaces *attributes* in the specified *distinguished_name*. If the function is successful, it will return 1; otherwise, it will return an error.

ldap_modify()

Syntax

```
int ldap_modify(int ldap_pointer, string distinguished_name, array fields)
```

Description

The `ldap_modify()` function modifies the *fields* in the entry defined by *distinguished_name*. If the function is successful, it will return 1; otherwise, it will return an error.

ldap_next_attribute()

Syntax

```
string ldap_next_attribute(int ldap_pointer, int result, int ber)
```

Description

The `ldap_next_attribute()` function returns the next entry of the internal LDAP search *result*. The *ber* parameter is a pass-by-reference value for the internal memory state of the pointer, which increments on function calls.

ldap_next_entry()

Syntax

```
int ldap_next_entry(int ldap_pointer, int result)
```

Description

The ldap_next_entry() function returns an identifier for the next entry of an internal LDAP search *result*. This function is first called after a call to ldap_first_entry(), until no more entries exist. At that time, false will be returned.

ldap_read()

Syntax

```
int ldap_read(int ldap_pointer, string base_distinguished_name, string filter
   [, array attributes [, int attributes_only [, int size_limit [, int
   time_limit   [, int dereference]]]]])
```

Description

The ldap_read() function performs a search, with the scope of LDAP_SCOPE_BASE (one entry from a directory), for the specified *filter*. The filter is in the format of *attribute=value*. If you want to return entries for all values, you can simply pass * as the value.

If you want to restrict the results of this function, you can do so by limiting it to just the *attributes*, which are optional, specified in an array. If you want only the attribute types returned and not the values, you can set *attributes_only* equal to 1. It is also possible to further limit the results by the optional *size_limit*, which is the number of entries to be returned. The optional *time_limit* enables you to specify the number of seconds the function has to complete.

The final attribute, *dereference*, defines how you want aliases in the LDAP server to be handled. Table 6.19 shows the complete list from which you have to choose.

Table 6.19   *Possible Values for the* dereference *Attribute*

Value	Description
LDAP_DEREF_ALWAYS	Aliases should be always dereferenced.
LDAP_DEREF_FINDING	Aliases should not be dereferenced during the search, but rather when locating the base object.
LDAP_DEREF_NEVER	Aliases are never dereferenced. This is the default setting.
LDAP_DEREF_SEARCHING	Aliases should be dereferenced during the search, but not when locating the base object.

> **Note**
> The optional parameters (`attributes_only`, `size_limit`, `time_limit`, `dereference`) were added in PHP 4.0.2.

ldap_search()

Syntax

```
int ldap_search(int ldap_pointer, string base_distinguished_name, string filter
    [, array attributes [, int attributes_only [, int size_limit [, int
    time_limit   [, int dereference]]]]])
```

Description

The `ldap_search()` function performs a search, with the scope of `LDAP_SCOPE_SUBTREE` (the entire directory), for the specified `filter`. The filter is in the format of *attribute=value*. If you want to return entries for all values, you can simply pass * as the value.

If you want to restrict the results of this function, you can do so by limiting it to just the `attributes`, which are optional, specified in an array. If you want only the attribute types returned and not the values, you can set `attributes_only` equal to 1. It is also possible to further limit the results by the optional `size_limit`, which is the number of entries to be returned. The optional *time_limit* enables you to specify the number of seconds the function has to complete.

The final attribute, `dereference`, defines how you want aliases in the LDAP server to be handled. Table 6.20 shows the complete list from which you have to choose.

Table 6.20 *Possible Values for the* dereference *Attribute*

Value	Description
LDAP_DEREF_ALWAYS	Aliases should be always dereferenced.
LDAP_DEREF_FINDING	Aliases should not be dereferenced during the search, but rather when locating the base object.
LDAP_DEREF_NEVER	Aliases are never dereferenced. This is the default setting.
LDAP_DEREF_SEARCHING	Aliases should be dereferenced during the search, but not when locating the base object.

> **Note**
>
> The optional parameters (`attributes_only`, `size_limit`, `time_limit`, `dereference`) were added in PHP 4.0.2.

ldap_unbind()

Syntax

```
int ldap_unbind(int ldap_pointer)
```

Description

The `ldap_unbind()` function unbinds the LDAP directory pointed to by `ldap_pointer`. If successful, 1 will be returned; otherwise, `false` on error.

SNMP

The Simple Network Management Protocol (SNMP) is a protocol for building network management framework. On UNIX, you must also install the UCD SNMP package for this work. You can obtain this from `http://ucd-snmp.ucdavis.edu`. On Windows NT/2000, these functions do not require any additional components to be installed, but do note that they do not work on the Windows 95/98/Me platforms.

You can read more about SNMP in the Request For Comments (RFC) 2571, which you can find at `http://www.ietf.org/rfc/rfc2571.txt`.

snmp_get_quick_print()

Syntax

```
boolean snmp_get_quick_print()
```

Description

The `snmp_get_quick_print()` function, which was added in PHP 3.0.8, grabs the value of the UCD library's `quick_print` setting and returns `true` if on, or `false` if off.

> **Note**
>
> This function is present only when using the UCD library, which is a UNIX-only function.

snmp_set_quick_print()

Syntax

```
snmp_set_quick_print(int quick_print)
```

Description

The snmp_set_quick_print() function, which was added in PHP 3.0.8, sets the value of the UCD library's *quick_print* setting. If 1, which stands for true, is passed as *quick_print*, this setting will be turned on. 0 is used to turn it off.

Note
This function is present only when using the UCD library, which is a UNIX-only function.

---

snmpget()

Syntax

```
string snmpget(string hostname, string community, string object_id
    [, int timeout [, int retries]])
```

Description

The snmpget() function reads the object at *object_id* on *hostname* in the read *community*. It will return the object value if successful, or false on an error. The optional *timeout* parameter enables you to provide a timeout in seconds, and if used, you can also provide the number of *retries* that you want to try.

snmpset()

Syntax

```
bool snmpset(string hostname, string community, string object_id, string type,
    mixed value [, int timeout [, int retries]])
```

Description

The snmpset() function sets the *value* of the *object_id* on *hostname* within the read *community*. The *type* parameter must be one of the following, depending on the type of variable set on the SNMP host:

- i—INTEGER
- u—Unsigned INTEGER
- t—TIMETICKS
- a—IPADDRESS
- o—OBJID
- s—STRING
- x—HEX STRING
- d—DECIMAL STRING

If you defined OPAQUE_SPECIAL_TYPES when compiling the SNMP library, you will also have access to the following types:

- U—Unsigned int64
- I—Signed int64
- F—Float
- D—Double

The optional *timeout* parameter enables you to provide a timeout in seconds, and if used, you can also provide the number of *retries* that you want to attempt.

snmpwalk()

Syntax

```
array snmpwalk(string hostname, string community, string object_id
    [, int timeout [, int retries]])
```

Description

The snmpwalk() function returns an array of objects' values, starting with *object_id*, from *hostname* and the read *community*. If a null value is passed for *object_id*, the root object is assumed, and if the value does not exist, an error is returned.

The optional *timeout* parameter enables you to provide a timeout in seconds, and if used, you can also provide the number of *retries* that you want to attempt.

snmpwalkoid()

Syntax

```
array snmpwalkoid(string hostname, string community, string object_id
   [, int timeout [, int retries]])
```

Description

The snmpwalkoid() function, which was added in PHP 3.0.8, returns an associative array of objects' values, starting with *object_id*, from *hostname* and the read *community*. If a null value is passed for *object_id*, the root object is assumed, and if the value does not exist, an error is returned.

The optional *timeout* parameter enables you to provide a timeout in seconds, and if used, you can also provide the number of *retries* that you want to attempt.

CHAPTER 7

Internet-Related Extensions

This chapter describes a group of functions that are specific to the Internet. This group includes functions dealing with Internet applications such as the Apache Web server, WDDX, and VMailMgr. The chapter also discusses functions that provide network, mail, and session access.

Apache Specific

The Apache Web server is a highly configurable, powerful, HTTP server. Apache is the most popular Web server on the Internet for reasons that include Apache's extensibility with add-on modules, which provide extra functionality. Another reason for Apache's popularity is its multiplatform support. Apache runs on most flavors of UNIX, Windows NT/9x/2000, NetWare 5.x, and OS/2. The set of Internet-related functions described in this section provide information about the Apache resource, headers, and other functionality.

> **Note**
> This section assumes that the PHP module is installed as an Apache module. Most of these functions are not supported if Apache is used as a CGI.

apache_lookup_uri()

Syntax

```
apache_lookup_uri(filename);
```

Description

This function performs a request for the URI defined by `filename`. `apache_lookup_uri()` requests enough information about the resource to return a class with the properties shown in Table 7.1.

Table 7.1 *Properties Returned by the* `apache_lookup_uri()` *Function*

Status	Handler	Boundary
the_request	Uri	No_cache
status_line	Filename	No_local_copy
Method	Path_info	Allowed
Content_type	Args	send_bodyct
Bytes_sent	Clength	Mtime
Byterange	Unparsed_uri	Request_time

apache_note()

Syntax

```
apache_note(note_name, [note_value]);
```

Description

The `apache_note()` function sends and receives information to the request's notes table. When the function is passed one argument, it returns the value of *note_name*. If `apache_note()` is called with two arguments, it sets the value of *note_name* to *note_value* and returns the previous value of *note_name*.

getallheaders()

Syntax

```
getallheaders();
```

Description

The getallheaders() function returns an associative array of all the HTTP headers in the current HTTP request. All the header variables are available to you as individual PHP variables, but this function presents those variables to you in a single array.

virtual()

Syntax

```
virtual(filename);
```

Description

The virtual() function is used to include a file defined by *filename* into the PHP request. This is equivalent to the Server Side Include (SSI) syntax <!--#include virtual *filename* -->. This function cannot be used to include a PHP file, and if it encounters an error, false (0) is returned.

Mail

Sending an email from a PHP script can be a very powerful tool. It is often used to alert users or administrators to specific conditions specified within the application. The single mail() function described in the following section is the interface to SMTP- and sendmail-compatible applications on a UNIX system and SMTP-compatible mail servers on Windows.

mail()

Syntax

```
mail(recipient, subject, message, [additional_headers]);
```

Description

The mail() function is used to send an email with the body of the email specified by the *message* parameter to the email address defined in *recipient*. The subject for the email is defined by the *subject* parameter. Multiple recipients can be specified by a comma-delimited list in *recipient*. The optional parameter *additional_headers* is used to define additional header information that can be inserted at the end of the original email header. Multiple *additional_headers* are delimited with the carriage return linefeed characters, "\r\n". Additional header information can be used to specify the senders address or the format of the email.

Calling the mail() function in a UNIX environment invokes the sendmail shell command. The Windows environment will establish a connection with the SMTP server to send the mail. Specific mail parameters are set in the [mail function] section of the php.ini configuration file.

If the mail() function encounters an error, false (0) is returned.

Network

This section describes a set of functions that use standard Internet protocols to communicate and return information about network resources. Debugging functions are also described in this section because of their method of implementation.

checkdnsrr()

Syntax

```
checkdnsrr(host, [type]);
```

Description

The checkdnsrr() function searches DNS records for a hostname defined by *host* having a specific *type*. It returns true, 1, if any records are found and returns false, 0, if no records were found or if an error occurred. Table 7.2 shows the valid DNS record types.

Table 7.2   *Valid DNS Record Types*

Type	Description
A	IP Address
MX	Mail Exchanger (Default)
NS	Name Server
SOA	Start of Authority
PTR	Pointer to other information
CNAME	Canonical Name
ANY	Any records

A valid value for *host* is the IP address in dotted-quad notation or the hostname.

closelog()

Syntax

```
closelog();
```

Description

The closelog() function closes the file descriptor that is used to write to the system logger. The use of this function is optional, but recommended.

debugger_off()

Syntax

```
debugger_off();
```

Description

The debugger_off() function tells PHP to stop sending information to the internal debugger.

debugger_on()

Syntax

```
debugger_on(address);
```

Description

The debugger_on() function tells PHP to start sending diagnostic information to the internal debugger. The *address* attribute is the IP address of the host used for debugging. The port is set in the [Debugger] section of the php.ini file.

fsockopen()

Syntax

```
fsockopen(hostname, port, [errno], [errstr], [timeout]);
```

Description

The fsockopen() function establishes a TCP socket connection to *port* running on *hostname*. The optional *timeout* parameter defines the timeout for the connect() system call.

If fsockopen() is not successful, it will return false, 0. The optional variables used for *errno* and *errstr* will be set to indicate the system-level error number and string of system errors that occurred. If fsockopen() is successful, it will return a file pointer that can then be used by other file-related functions, such as fputs(), fgets(), fclose(), and so on.

gethostbyaddr()

Syntax

```
gethostbyaddr(ip_address);
```

Description

The gethostbyaddr() function returns the hostname specified by *ip_address*. If the function is not successful, it will return false, 0.

gethostbyname()

Syntax

```
gethostbyname(hostname);
```

Description

The gethostbyname() function returns the IP address in dotted-quad notation of the Internet host specified by *hostname*.

gethostbynamel()

Syntax

```
gethostbynamel(hostname);
```

Description

The gethostbynamel() function returns an array containing a list of the IP addresses to which the Internet host specified by *hostname* resolves.

getmxrr()

Syntax

```
getmxrr(hostname, mxhosts, [weight]);
```

Description

The getmxrr() function searches DNS for all MX (Mail Exchanger) records for the host defined by *hostname*. This function will return true, 1, if any records are found, and false, 0, is returned if no records were found or an error occurred.

The list of the records found is placed into the *mxhosts* array. Optionally, if the weight for the MX records is returned, the array *weight* will contain this information.

getprotobyname()

Syntax

```
getprotobyname(name);
```

Description

The getprotobyname() function returns the number associated with the protocol name defined by *name*. This number is retrieved from /etc/protocols.

getprotobynumber()

Syntax

```
getprotobynumber(number);
```

Description

The getprotobynumber() function returns the name associated with the protocol number defined by *number*. The name is retrieved from /etc/protocols.

getservbyname()

Syntax

```
getservbyname(service, protocol);
```

Description

The getservbyname() function returns the port that corresponds to *service* and *protocol*. The services are retrieved from /etc/services file. Valid protocols are specified as TCP or UDP.

getservbyport()

Syntax

```
getservbyport(port, protocol);
```

Description

The getservbyport() function returns the service which corresponds to *port* and *protocol*. The services are retrieved from /etc/services. Valid protocols are specified as TCP or UDP.

openlog()

Syntax

```
openlog(ident, option, facility);
```

Description

The openlog() function opens a connection to the system logger. The string, *ident*, is added to each entry sent to the system log. Valid values for *option* are given in Table 7.3 and valid values for *facility* are given in Table 7.4. These values are also found in the manpage for syslog(3).

> **Note**
> The *option* LOG_PID is the only valid option in the Windows environment.

Table 7.3 *Valid Values for* option

Options	Description
LOG_PID	Add the PID to each message.
LOG_CONS	If a message cannot be sent to the system log, send the message to the system console.
LOG_ODELAY	Delay opening the log until the first call to syslog. This is true by default.
LOG_NDELAY	Open the log immediately. Do not wait for the first call to syslog.
LOG_NOWAIT	Do not wait for child processes. The use of this flag is discouraged.
LOG_PERROR	Log all messages to stderr.

> **Note**
> LOG_USER is the only value for *facility* that is valid in the Windows environment.

Table 7.4 *Valid Values for* facility

Facility	Description
LOG_KERN	Kernel messages
LOG_USER	Generic user-level messages (default)
LOG_MAIL	Mail subsystem
LOG_DAEMON	Other system daemons
LOG_AUTH	Security/authorization messages (deprecated; use LOG_AUTHPRIV instead)
LOG_SYSLOG	Messages generated internally by syslogd
LOG_LPR	Line printer subsystem
LOG_NEWS	Usenet news subsystem

Table 7.4 *(continued)*

Facility	Description
LOG_UUCP	UUCP subsystem
LOG_CRON	Clock daemon (cron and at)
LOG_AUTHPRIV	Security/authorization messages

pfsockopen()

Syntax

```
pfsockopen(hostname, port, [errno], [errstr], [timeout]);
```

Description

The pfsockopen() function is the persistent version of fsockopen(). Both functions establish a socket connection as a file stream. A TCP socket connection is established to *hostname* and *port*. The optional *timeout* parameter defines the timeout for the connect() system call.

The pfsockopen() function does not close the socket connection upon completion of a read or write to the socket.

If pfsockopen() is not successful, it will return false, 0. The optional variables *errno* and *errstr* will be set to indicate the system-level error that occurred. If pfsockopen() is successful, it will return a file pointer that can then be used by other file-related functions such as fputs(), fgets(), fclose(), and so on.

set_socket_blocking()

Syntax

```
set_socket_blocking(socket descriptor, mode);
```

Description

The set_socket_blocking() function sets the blocking mode for the socket. If *mode* is false, 0, the socket descriptor will be switched to nonblocking mode. Setting *mode* to true, 1, will set the socket to blocking mode. In nonblocking mode, calls that get information from the socket will return immediately with data that is in the input buffer. In blocking mode, socket reads will halt execution until all the data available on the socket is received.

syslog()

Syntax

```
syslog(priority, message);
```

Description

The syslog() function adds *message* with *priority* to the system log. Valid priorities are given in Table 7.5.

> **Note**
> On Windows NT, the syslog service is provided through an emulator. The messages are logged in the NT Event Log and can be viewed by using the Event Viewer.

Table 7.5 *Priorities*

Priority	Description
LOG_EMERG	This is a panic situation; the system is unstable. The message may be broadcast by the operating system to all users of the system. This message is translated to a warning on Windows.
LOG_ALERT	This is a situation that requires action to be taken immediately. It is translated into an error on Windows.
LOG_CRIT	This is a critical condition that can by be caused by external or hardware problems. This is translated to a warning on Windows.
LOG_ERR	These are general error conditions. These are translated to warnings on Windows.
LOG_WARNING	These are warnings, less severe than errors.
LOG_NOTICE	A notice is not an error, but is a significant condition requiring attention. This is translated to a warning on Windows.
LOG_INFO	Informational messages do not require any special action to be taken.
LOG_DEBUG	These messages are only debug-level messages. They are translated to warnings on Windows.

Session Handling

This section describes the session-handling functions that are included in the base PHP4 distribution. These functions allow session variables to be established and tracked per visitor. This functionality allows the user experience to vary depending on permissions, user-defined options, or environment. Sessions do not require variables to be stored in cookies, although it is possible, but rather session IDs are passed via the URL. In either case, these variables are stored and retrieved on the server through these PHP functions.

session_start()

Syntax

```
session_start();
```

Description

The session_start() function, which always returns true, allocates memory and establishes a session for the user.

session_destroy()

Syntax

```
session_destroy();
```

Description

The session_destroy() function, which always returns true, terminates the session and destroys all the data associated with the user's session.

session_name()

Syntax

```
session_name([name]);
```

Description

The session_name() function returns the name of the current session as a string. If *name* is specified, the name of the current session is changed to *name*.

session_module_name

Syntax

```
session_module_name([module]);
```

Description

The session_module_name() function returns the name of the current session module as a string. If *module* is specified, that module will be used.

session_save_path()

Syntax

```
session_save_path([path]);
```

Description

The session_save_path() function returns the path of the directory that session data is currently being saved. If the *path* is specified, the session data storage will be changed to *path*.

session_id()

Syntax

```
session_id([id]);
```

Description

The session_id() function returns the session ID for the current session as a string. If *id* is specified, it will replace the current session ID with that value.

session_register()

Syntax

```
session_register(name,[...]);
```

Description

The session_register() function registers variables with the current session. This function accepts a variable number of parameters and returns true, 1, if the session variable is successfully registered. The parameters can be a string holding the variable name, an array containing variable names, or arrays themselves. For each variable name sent to `session_register()` as a parameter, a global variable is created in the current session.

session_unregister()

Syntax

```
session_unregister(name);
```

Description

The `session_unregister()` function unregisters the variable defined by *name* from the current session. This function returns true, 1, if the variable is successfully unregistered from the session.

session_is_registered()

Syntax

```
session_is_registered(name);
```

Description

The `session_is_registered()` function returns true, 1, if the variable *name* is registered with the current session.

session_decode()

Syntax

```
session_decode(data);
```

Description

The `session_decode()` function decodes the string defined by *data* into variables and inserts these variables into the current session.

session_encode()

Syntax

```
session_encode();
```

Description

The session_encode() function returns an encoded string containing all current session data and associated variables.

URL

This section deals with functions that encode, decode, or parse URL data. This is often used when submitting forms to CGI programs or passing variables from a URL to a program.

base64_decode()

Syntax

```
base64_decode(encoded_data);
```

Description

The base64_decode() function decodes a string defined by *encoded_data* and returns the original data as a string.

base64_encode()

Syntax

```
base64_encode(data);
```

Description

The base64_encode() function encodes the string defined by *data* and returns the data as a string in base64 encoding. This encoded string is designed to minimize the corruption of raw binary data. Because of error checking, the encoded string is approximately 33% larger than the original data. Base64 encoding is described in RFC-2045 section 6.8. Table 7.6 illustrates the encoding that occurs.

Table 7.6 *Base64 Conversions*

Val	Encod	Val	Encod	Val	Encod	Val	Encod
0	A	17	R	34	I	51	z
1	B	18	S	35	j	52	0
2	C	19	T	36	k	53	1
3	D	20	U	37	l	54	2
4	E	21	V	38	m	55	3
5	F	22	W	39	n	56	4
6	G	23	X	40	o	57	5
7	H	24	Y	41	p	58	6
8	I	25	Z	42	q	59	7
9	J	26	a	43	r	60	8
10	K	27	b	44	s	61	9
11	L	28	c	45	t	62	+
12	M	29	d	46	u	63	/
13	N	30	e	47	v		
14	O	31	f	48	w	(pad)	=
15	P	32	g	49	x		
16	Q	33	h	50	y		

parse_url()

Syntax

```
parse_url(url);
```

Description

The parse_url() function returns an associative array containing the components of the *url*. The array will contain one or all of the following elements:

- scheme
- host
- port
- user

- pass

- path

- query

- fragment

urldecode()

Syntax

```
urldecode(str);
```

Description

The urldecode() function converts str from URL-encoded format into plain text. This places any nonalphanumeric characters, encoded with a percent sign (%) followed by the two-digit hexadecimal ASCII value of the character, back to their character representations. Plus signs are converted to spaces.

urlencode()

Syntax

```
urlencode(str);
```

Description

The urlencode() function returns a string that has been converted from plain text to URL format. This conversion replaces any nonalphanumeric characters with a percent sign (%) followed by the two-digit hexadecimal ASCII value of the character. Spaces are converted to plus (+) signs.

VMailMgr

VMailMgr (Virtual Mail Manager) is an assortment of programs designed to manage multiple email domains and mailboxes on a single host. VMailMgr operates in conjunction with the qmail application. qmail is a sendmail alternative that offers more options and program control than sendmail.

The following functions build on the established VMailMgr and qmail functionality. For this reason, VMailMgr and qmail must be installed for these functions to work.

Resource

The qmail application and information are available at `http://www.qmail.org`.

The VMailMgr application and information are available at `http://www.vmailmgr.org`.

---

vm_adduser()

Syntax

```
vm_adduser(vdomain, basepwd, newusername, newuserpassword);
```

Description

The vm_adduser() function adds a new virtual user with *newusername* and *newuserpassword* to *vdomain*. The *vdomain* parameter is defined as the domain name of the user's virtual domain. The string *basepwd* is the password of the master user that administers the virtual users.

This function returns the following:

- O—Okay
- 1—Bad
- 2—Error
- 3—Error connecting

vm_addalias()

Syntax

```
vm_addalias(vdomain, basepwd, username, alias);
```

Description

The vm_addalias() function adds *alias* to the virtual user defined by *username*. The *vdomain* parameter is defined as the domain name of the user's virtual domain. The string *basepwd* is the password of the master user that administers the virtual users.

This function returns the following:

- O—Okay
- 1—Bad
- 2—Error
- 3—Error connecting

vm_passwd()

Syntax

```
vm_passwd(vdomain, username, password, newpassword);
```

Description

The vm_passwd() function changes the password of the virtual user defined by *username* to *newpassword*. The old password for this virtual user must be specified in *password* for this operation to be successful. The *vdomain* parameter is defined as the domain name of the user's virtual domain.

This function returns the following:

- O—Okay
- 1—Bad
- 2—Error
- 3—Error connecting

vm_delalias()

Syntax

```
vm_delalias(vdomain, basepwd, alias);
```

Description

The vm_delalias() function removes *alias* from the virtual domain. The *vdomain* parameter is defined as the domain name of the user's virtual domain. The string *basepwd* is the password of the master user that administers the virtual users.

This function returns the following:

- O—Ok
- 1—Bad
- 2—Error
- 3—Error connecting

vm_deluser()

Syntax

```
vm_deluser(vdomain, username);
```

Description

The vm_deluser() function removes the virtual user, *username*, from the virtual domain defined by *vdomain*.

This function returns the following:

- O—Okay
- 1—Bad
- 2—Error
- 3—Error connecting

WDDX

WDDX is freely available, XML-based technology developed by the Allaire Corporation. WDDX is used to exchange complex data between varieties of Web programming languages.

All standard programming environments on the Web (ColdFusion, Perl, ASP, Java, JavaScript, PHP, and so on) have native data structures such as arrays and record sets. WDDX provides a module for each language that will automatically serialize or translate the native data structures into a WDDX packet, or deserialize the WDDX packet into a native data structure. WDDX can be used with HTTP, SMTP, POP, FTP, and other Internet protocols that support transferring textual data.

> **Resource**
>
> You can receive more information on Allaire at http://www.allaire.com.
>
> Additional information about WDDX is available at http://www.wddx.org.

wddx_serialize_value()

Syntax

```
wddx_serialize_value(var, [comment]);
```

Description

The wddx_serialize_value() function creates a WDDX packet from the value defined by *var*. Optionally, a comment string, defined by *comment*, can be added to the packet. This comment will appear in the packet header. wddx_serialize_value() returns the WDDX packet.

wddx_serialize_vars()

Syntax

```
wddx_serialize_vars(var_name, [...] );
```

Description

The wddx_serialize_vars() function creates a WDDX packet from a variable number of parameters. Each of the parameters can be a variable name, an array containing variable names, or an array.

wddx_packet_start()

Syntax

```
wddx_packet_start([comment]);
```

Description

The wddx_packet_start() function, which accepts an optional *comment* string, is used to define the start of the WDDX packet. This function returns an integer that is defined as the WDDX packet ID.

wddx_packet_end()

Syntax

```
wddx_packet_end(packet_id);
```

Description

The wddx_packet_end() function, which returns the string with the WDDX packet, ends the WDDX packet defined by packet_id.

wddx_add_vars()

Syntax

```
wddx_add_vars(packet_id, name_var, [...]);
```

Description

The wddx_add_vars() function, which accepts a variable number of arguments that can be of any type, adds serialized variables to the WDDX packet defined by packet_id. The variables are serialized exactly like the wddx_serialize_vars() function. The packet is initialized by first calling wddx_packet_start() and ended by calling wddx_packet_end().

wddx_deserialize()

Syntax

```
wddx_deserialize(packet);
```

Description

The wddx_deserialize() function takes the WDDX packet defined by packet and deserializes it. The returned result can be a string, integer, or array.

CHAPTER 8

Document-Related
Extensions

PHP enables you to take advantage of the many external libraries that have been developed to accomplish very specific document-related tasks. This chapter provides a quick reference to the functions available in each of the document-related extensions libraries. But, for an in-depth understanding of the libraries, you need to consult the library-specific documentation. To understand how the PHP function calls are translated into the specific library function calls, you should examine the appropriate .c file in the extension directory for that library, such as `/php-4.0.2/ext/cpdf/cpdf.c` for the ClibPDF library. You will often find that not every available library function has been implemented in PHP, and those that have been implemented might not have the same features and functionality as those in the library.

Aspell

The Aspell library provides you access to dictionary functions from PHP. You can verify the spelling of a word as well as get possible matching words based on a particular spelling. The library is not part of the standard source, but can be obtained from `http://aspell.sourceforge.net`. However, this is an outdated library, and you will likely want to use the Pspell library functions instead.

aspell_new()

Syntax

```
int aspell_new (string master, string personal)
```

Description

The aspell_new() function, which was added in PHP 3.0.7, returns a handle to the dictionary for use with other aspell functions.

aspell_check()

Syntax

```
Boolean aspell_check (int dictionary_link, string word)
```

Description

The aspell_check() function, which was added in PHP 3.0.7, checks the spelling of the word against the dictionary indicated by the dictionary_link parameter. If the word is spelled correctly, TRUE is returned; otherwise, FALSE is returned.

aspell_check_raw()

Syntax

```
Boolean aspell_check_raw (int dictionary_link, string word)
```

Description

The aspell_check_raw() function, which was added in PHP 3.0.7, checks the spelling of the word parameter against the dictionary specified by the dictionary_link parameter. The word parameter is not trimmed or case adjusted before the lookup is made. If the spelling is correct, TRUE is returned; otherwise, FALSE is returned.

aspell_suggest()

Syntax

```
array aspell_suggest (int dictionary_link, string word)
```

Description

The `aspell_suggest()` function, which was added in PHP 3.0.7, returns an array of words with similar spellings to the *word* parameter as found in the *dictionary_link*.

Pspell

The Pspell library, which is preferred over Aspell, also provides you access to dictionary functions from PHP. You can verify the spelling of a word as well as get possible matching words based on a particular spelling. You can obtain both the Aspell and Pspell libraries from `http://aspell.sourceforge.net` and `http://pspell.sourceforge.net`. To include this library, compile with `--with-pspell=<dir above Aspell and Pspell libraries>`.

pspell_new()

Syntax

```
int pspell_new (string language [, string spelling [, string jargon
[, string encoding [, int mode ]]]])
```

Description

The `pspell_new()` function, which was added in PHP 4, returns a handle to the dictionary for use with other Pspell functions. The *language* code represents the two-letter ISO 639 language code along with an optional two-letter ISO 3166 country code. The *spelling* parameter is used when more than one version of the language exists, such as American, British, and Canadian for English. The *jargon* parameter is used when a language has words with similar spelling. The *encoding* parameter represents what type of encoding the word is stored in. The *mode* parameter dictates how the library will operate:

PSPELL_FAST—Fast operation; least number of hints

PSPELL_NORMAL—Normal mode with more hints

PSPELL_BAD_SPELLERS—Slow mode with lots of hints

PSPELL_RUN_TOGETHER—Treats run-together words as acceptable

pspell_check()

Syntax

```
boolean pspell_check (int dictionary_link, string word)
```

Description

The `pspell_check()` function, which was added in PHP 4.0, checks the spelling of the *word* against the dictionary indicated by the *dictionary_link* parameter. If the word is spelled correctly, TRUE is returned; otherwise, FALSE is returned.

pspell_suggest()

Syntax

```
array pspell_suggest (int dictionary_link, string word)
```

Description

The `pspell_suggest()` function, which was added in PHP 4, returns an array of words with similar spellings to the *word* parameter as found in the *dictionary_link*.

ClibPDF

The ClibPDF functions allow you to generate PDF documents dynamically from your PHP code. The ClibPDF library is available from `http://www.fastio.com`, but it is not freeware, so you should consult the licensing agreement before implementing it in your code. The documentation that accompanies ClibPDF contains further details about each of the functions mentioned in this section.

To understand the mapping from PHP to ClibPDF, you should examine the cpdf.c file typically found in the `/php-4.x/ext/cpdf/` directory. Note that the ClibPDF library is not currently available as part of the Windows distribution. To include ClibPDF add `--with-cpdflib=<directory above /lib/libcpdf.a>` in your configure arguments. All PDF documents created with ClibPDF must include the following functions: `cpdf_open()`, `cpdf_pageinit()`, `cpdf_finalize()`, and `cpdf_close()`. Another alternative to the ClibPDF library is the PDF library documented later in this section. There are licensing differences between the two libraries as well as some feature differences—most notably, the ability to create the entire document in memory by using ClibPDF.

cpdf_global_set_document_limits()

Syntax

```
void cpdf_global_set_document_limits (int maxpages, int maxfonts,
 int maximages, int maxannotations, int maxobjects)
```

Description

The `cpdf_global_set_document_limits()` function, which was added in PHP 4.0.b4, sets the limits for all PDF documents that follow this call. This function must be called before the `cpdf_open()` function is called. The parameter names indicate which options can be set globally. This is an optional function, and the default values can be found in cpdflib.h.

cpdf_set_creator()

Syntax

```
void cpdf_set_creator (string creator)
```

Description

The `cpdf_set_creator()` function, which was added in PHP 3.0.8 and PHP 4.0.b4, sets the *creator* field of the PDF document that is stored in its info object. Note that the *creator* string will be truncated at 62 characters.

cpdf_set_title()

Syntax

```
void cpdf_set_title(string title)
```

Description

The `cpdf_set_title()` function, which was added in PHP 3.0.8 and PHP 4.0.b4, sets the *title* field of the PDF document that is stored in its info object. Note that the *title* string will be truncated at 62 characters.

cpdf_set_subject()

Syntax

```
void cpdf_set_subject (string subject)
```

Description

The cpdf_set_subject() function, which was added in PHP 3.0.8 and PHP 4.0.b4, sets the *subject* field of the PDF document that is stored in its info object. Note that the *subject* string will be truncated at 62 characters.

cpdf_set_keywords()

Syntax

```
void cpdf_set_keywords(string keywords)
```

Description

The cpdf_set_keywords() function, which was added in PHP 3.0.8 and PHP 4.0.b4, sets the *keywords* field of the PDF document that is stored in its info object. Note that the *keywords* string will be truncated at 120 characters.

cpdf_open()

Syntax

```
int cpdf_open (int compression, string filename)
```

Description

The cpdf_open() function, which was added in PHP 3.0.8 and PHP 4.0.b4, creates a new PDF document. A *compression* parameter value other than 0 indicates that compression should be used. The optional *filename* parameter names the file to which the contents should be written. By not specifying a filename, you can have the document created in memory, and then later decide to write it to a file or stream back to the client through standard out. Use cpdf_save_to_file() to save a copy of the file, and use cpdf_output_buffer() to send the contents to standard out. The ClibPDF library does accept "-" as a *filename* parameter to indicate standard out, but when PHP is used as an Apache module, you must use the cpdf_output_buffer() function instead of this shortcut. The return value is used as a handle to most other ClibPDF functions.

cpdf_close()

Syntax

```
void cpdf_close (int pdf document)
```

Description

The cpdf_close() function, which was added in PHP 3.0.8 and PHP 4.0.b4, closes an active *pdf document*. Make sure to call this function when you have finished processing the PDF document because doing so releases all memory and file resources allocated by the library during processing. You also need to free any additional resources you created—such as plots—because this is not done automatically.

cpdf_page_init()

Syntax

```
void cpdf_page_init (int pdf document, int page number,
 int orientation, double height, double width, double unit)
```

Description

The cpdf_page_init() function, which was added in PHP 3.0.8 and PHP 4.0.b4, initializes an individual page for writing. The *pdf_document* parameter is the handle returned from cpdf_open(). The *page_number* parameter indicates the page to which you want to write. For a single-page document, this should be 1; for a multi-page document, you can start with 1 or any larger number. The *orientation* parameter enables you to indicate whether the page should be written in landscape (1) or portrait (0) format. The *height* and *width* parameters specify the size of the page based on the *unit* parameter, which is the number of points per unit. This defaults to 72, which is the number of points in one inch. The following code will initialize page 1, set the page orientation to portrait, and set the dimensions to 8.5×11 inches.

```
cpdf_page_init($cpdf, 1, 0, 792,612);
```

cpdf_finalize_page()

Syntax

```
void cpdf_finalize_page (int pdf document, int page number)
```

Description

The cpdf_finalize_page() function, which was added in PHP 3.0.10 and PHP 4.0.b4, ends the page specified by *page_number*. A page cannot be modified after it has been finalized. This should be used with longer documents for efficient memory use, but isn't necessary for shorter documents (3 pages or fewer).

cpdf_finalize()

Syntax

```
void cpdf_finalize (int pdf document)
```

Description

The cpdf_finalize() function, which was added in PHP 3.0.8 and PHP 4.0.b4, finishes the document so that it can be streamed to the client or stored in a file.

cpdf_output_buffer()

Syntax

```
void cpdf_outpuf_buffer (int pdf document)
```

Description

The cpdf_output_buffer() function, which was added in PHP 3.0.9 and PHP 4.0.b4, dumps the contents of the current buffer to stdout. This is used when the cpdf_open() is called without a filename parameter, which causes the contents to be held in memory.

cpdf_save_to_file()

Syntax

```
void cpdf_save_to_file (int pdf document, string filename)
```

Description

The cpdf_save_to_file() function, which was added in PHP 3.0.8 and PHP 4.0.b4, dumps the contents of the current buffer to a file designated by the filename parameter. This is useful when no filename is specified with the cpdf_open() function, which causes the document to be created and stored in memory.

cpdf_set_current_page()

Syntax

```
void cpdf_set_current_page (int pdf document, int page number)
```

Description

The `cpdf_set_current_page()` function, which was added in PHP 3.0.9 and PHP 4.0.b4, specifies the page in the document to which subsequent commands pertain. You can switch between multiple pages in a document, but after the `cpdf_finalize_page()` function is called, you can no longer modify that page. Note that if you switch pages, the domain will revert back to the default domain for that page. Domains are commonly used to enable you to switch easily between coordinate systems.

cpdf_begin_text()

Syntax

```
void cpdf_begin_text(int pdf document)
```

Description

The `cpdf_begin_text()` function, which was added in PHP 3.0.8 and PHP 4.0.b4, marks the beginning of a text section in a PDF page. The `cpdf_end_text()` function is called when the text section is complete. Multiple lines of text can be drawn within a text section as long as they share the same font.

```
<?pdf cpdf_begin_text($pdf);

cpdf_set_font($pdf, 12,"Times-Roman","WinAnsiEncoding");
cpdf_text($pdf,50,50,"First line of text");
cpdf_text($pdf,50,100,"Second line of text");
cpdf_end_text($pdf) ?>
```

cpdf_end_text()

Syntax

```
void cpdf_end_text (int pdf document)
```

Description

The `cpdf_end_text()` function, which was added in PHP 3.0.8 and PHP 4.0.b4, marks the end of the text section. All text sections must start with `cpdf_begin_text()` and end with `cpdf_end_text()`.

cpdf_show()

Syntax

```
void cpdf_show (int pdf document, string text)
```

Description

The cpdf_show() function, which was added in PHP 3.0.8 and PHP 4.0.b4, outputs the text parameter at the current text point. The lower-left corner of text is aligned with the current point. The current text point is updated to be the end of the text string.

cpdf_show_xy()

Syntax

```
void cpdf_show_xy (int pdf document, string text,
 double x-coor, double y-coor, int mode)
```

Description

The cpdf_show_xy() function, which was added in PHP 3.0.8 and PHP 4.0.b4, outputs the text parameter at the position indicated by the x-coor and y-coor parameters. The optional mode parameter is used to indicate the unit length in points (72 points per inch). Omitting a value or specifying 0 causes the default page unit to be used.

cpdf_text()

Syntax

```
void cpdf_text (int pdf document, string text,
 double x-coor, double y-coor, int mode, double orientation, int alignmode)
```

Description

The cpdf_text() function, which was added in PHP 3.0.8 and PHP 4.0.b4, outputs the text parameter at the position indicated by the x-coor and y-coor parameters. The optional mode parameter is used to indicate the unit length in points (72 points per inch). Omitting a value or specifying 0 causes the default page unit to be used. The optional parameter orientation is used to indicate that text should be rotated orientation degrees from the horizontal axis. The optional *alignmode* parameter indicates how the text should be placed relative to the current text point. Align modes are defined in the cpdflib.h file. The possible values are formed with "TEXT_POS_" and a location indicator concatenated together. Possible values are UL, ML, LL, UM, MM, LM, UR, MR, LR, where L is left or lower, M is middle, U is upper, and R is right. For example, TEXT_POS_LL indicates that the lower-left corner of *text* should be located at the x and y coordinates.

cpdf_set_font()

Syntax

```
void cpdf_set_font (int pdf document,
string font name, double size, string encoding)
```

Description

The cpdf_set_font() function, which was added in PHP 3.0.8 and PHP 4.0.b4, is used to specify a font's *name*, *size*, and *encoding*. Forty-one Roman fonts are supported along with many international varieties—consult the ClibPDF manual for details. Commonly used Roman fonts that are available include Helvetica, Times Roman, and Courier. The *size* parameter indicates the font size in points. The possible values for *encoding* are MacRomanEncoding, MacExpertEncoding, WinAnsiEncoding, and NULL, where NULL is the specified font's built-in encoding. If you don't have a preference, WinAnsiEncoding should be used because it is the most efficient.

cpdf_set_leading()

Syntax

```
void cpdf_set_leading (int pdf document, double distance)
```

Description

The cpdf_set_leading() function, which was added in PHP 3.0.8 and PHP 4.0.b4, is used to set the spacing between lines of text, where *distance* is specified in points (72 points = 1 inch). This is useful when using the cpdf_continue_text() function to display text.

cpdf_set_text_rendering()

Syntax

```
void cpdf_set_text_rendering (int pdf document, int mode)
```

Description

The cpdf_set_text_rendering() function, which was added in PHP 3.0.8 and PHP 4.0.b4, sets the *mode* for character outline. The default is 0, which indicates to fill the character outline with the current fill color. Other values include 1=stroke text, 2=fill and stroke text, 3=invisible, 4=fill text and add it to clipping path, 5=stroke text and add it to clipping path, 6=fill and stroke text and add it to clipping path, and 7=add it to clipping path.

cpdf_set_horiz_scaling()

Syntax

```
void cpdf_set_horiz_scaling (int pdf document, double scale)
```

Description

The cpdf_set_horiz_scaling() function, which was added in PHP 3.0.8 and PHP 4.0.b4, sets the horizontal scaling factor to *scale*, which is a percentage. This can be used to stretch or skew the horizontal length of a string. The default value is 100 percent.

cpdf_set_text_rise()

Syntax

```
void cpdf_set_text_rise (int pdf document, double value)
```

Description

The cpdf_set_text_rise() function, which was added in PHP 3.0.8 and PHP 4.0.b4, sets the offset *value* of text from the base line measured in points (72 points = 1 inch). Use a positive *value* for superscript and a negative value for subscript.

cpdf_set_text_matrix()

Syntax

```
void cpdf_set_text_matrix (int pdf document, array matrix)
```

Description

The cpdf_set_text_matrix() function, which was added in PHP 3.0.8 and PHP 4.0.b4, enables you to associate a transformation matrix with the current text font. A matrix can be used to set the current point, rotation, and skewing.

cpdf_set_text_pos()

Syntax

```
void cpdf_set_text_pos (int pdf document,
 double x-koor,  double y-koor, int mode)
```

Description

The cpdf_set_text_pos() function, which was added in PHP 3.0.8 and PHP 4.0.b4, sets the location where the next call to cpdf_show() will output text. The optional *mode* parameter can be used to set the unit length in points. If *mode* is 0 or not specified, the page's default unit length will be used.

cpdf_set_char_spacing()

Syntax

```
void cpdf_set_char_spacing (int pdf document, double space)
```

Description

The cpdf_set_char_spacing() function, which was added in PHP 3.0.8 and PHP 4.0.b4, is used to add further spacing between characters. The *space* parameter should be specified in points (72 points = 1 inch).

cpdf_set_word_spacing()

Syntax

```
void cpdf_set_word_spacing (int pdf document, double space)
```

Description

The `cpdf_set_word_spacing()` function, which was added in PHP 3.0.8 and PHP 4.0.b4, is used to add further spacing between words. The *space* parameter should be specified in points (72 points = 1 inch).

cpdf_continue_text()

Syntax

```
void cpdf_continue_text (int pdf document, string text)
```

Description

The `cpdf_continue_text()` function, which was added in PHP 3.0.8 and PHP 4.0.b4, outputs text at the beginning of the next line. The effect is like performing a carriage return and line feed before outputting the text.

cpdf_stringwidth()

Syntax

```
double cpdf_stringwidth (int pdf document, string text)
```

Description

The `cpdf_stringwidth()` function, which was added in PHP 3.0.8 and PHP 4.0.b4, returns the width of the current font for *text* in points. A font value must already be set for this function to work properly.

cpdf_save()

Syntax

```
void cpdf_save (int pdf document)
```

Description

The `cpdf_save()` function, which was added in PHP 3.0.8 and PHP 4.0.b4, is used to save the current graphics state. It enables you to work easily with one object without impacting other objects.

cpdf_restore()

Syntax

```
void cpdf_restore (int pdf document)
```

Description

The cpdf_restore() function, which was added in PHP 3.0.8 and PHP 4.0.b4, is used to restore the graphics state you saved with cpdf_save(). It enables you to work easily with one object without impacting other objects.

cpdf_translate()

Syntax

```
void cpdf_translate (int pdf document, double x-koor, double y-koor, int mode)
```

Description

The cpdf_translate() function, which was added in PHP 3.0.8 and PHP 4.0.b4, is used to shift the origin of the coordinate system to the x-koor and y-koor values. The optional parameter mode can be used to specify the unit length. If mode is 0 or not specified, the page's default unit length will be used.

cpdf_scale()

Syntax

```
void cpdf_scale (int pdf document, double x-scale, double y-scale)
```

Description

The cpdf_scale() function, which was added in PHP 3.0.8 and PHP 4.0.b4, is used to scale the coordinate system for both the x- and y-axes, by the x-scale and y-scale factors.

cpdf_rotate()

Syntax

```
void cpdf_rotate (int pdf document, double angle)
```

Description

The cpdf_rotate() function, which was added in PHP 3.0.8 and PHP 4.0.b4, is used to rotate the current coordinate system by the *angle* parameter specified in degrees. The rotation is centered at the current origin and a positive value for *angle* indicates clockwise rotation.

cpdf_setflat()

Syntax

```
void cpdf_setflat (int pdf document, double value)
```

Description

The cpdf_setflat() function, which was added in PHP 3.0.8 and PHP 4.0.b4, sets the flatness with a minimum value of 0 and a maximum of 100.

cpdf_setlinejoin()

Syntax

```
void cpdf_setlinejoin (int pdf document, long value)
```

Description

The cpdf_setlinejoin() function, which was added in PHP 3.0.8 and PHP 4.0.b4, sets the linejoin *value*, which must be between 0 and 2. Possible values are 0 for miter, 1 for round, and 2 for bevel.

cpdf_setlinecap()

Syntax

```
void cpdf_setlinecap (int pdf document, int value)
```

Description

The cpdf_setlinecap() function, which was added in PHP 3.0.8 and PHP 4.0.b4, sets the linecap value, which must be between 0 and 2. Possible values are 0 for butt end, 1 for round, and 2 for projecting square.

cpdf_setmiterlimit()

Syntax

```
void cpdf_setmiterlimit (int pdf document, double value)
```

Description

The `cpdf_setmiterlimit()` function, which was added in PHP 3.0.8 and PHP 4.0.b4, is used to specify the behavior when two line segments meet at a corner, including how pointed the corner should be when the lines meet at a sharp angle. The minimum for `value` is 1.

cpdf_setlinewidth()

Syntax

```
void cpdf_setlinewidth (int pdf document, double width)
```

Description

The `cpdf_setlinewidth()` function, which was added in PHP 3.0.8 and PHP 4.0.b4, sets the current line width. The `width` parameter is a value specified in points (72 points = 1 inch).

cpdf_setdash()

Syntax

```
void cpdf_setdash (int pdf document, double white, double black)
```

Description

The `cpdf_setdash()` function, which was added in PHP 3.0.8 and PHP 4.0.b4, sets a pattern for dashed lines where `white` and `black` are the lengths of the segments in points. Zero values indicate a solid line.

cpdf_moveto()

Syntax

```
void cpdf_moveto (int pdf document, double x-koor, double y-koor, int mode)
```

Description

The cpdf_moveto() function, which was added in PHP 3.0.8 and PHP 4.0.b4, moves the current point to the location specified by *x-koor* and *y-koor* coordinates. The optional parameter *mode* is used to specify a unit length other than the page default.

cpdf_rmoveto()

Syntax

```
void cpdf_rmoveto (int pdf document, double x-koor, double y-koor, int mode)
```

Description

The cpdf_rmovteto() function, which was added in PHP 3.0.9 and PHP 4.0.b4, moves the current point to the offset specified by the *x-koor* and *y-koor* values. The optional parameter *mode* is used to specify a unit length other than the page default.

cpdf_curveto()

Syntax

```
void cpdf_curveto (int pdf document, double x1,
  double y1, double x2, double y2, double x3, double y3, int mode)
```

Description

The cpdf_curveto() function, which was added in PHP 3.0.8 and PHP 4.0.b4, draws a Bézier cubic curve using the current point as the starting point, *x3* and *y3* as the end point, and *(x1,y1),(x2,y2)* as the control points. The optional parameter *mode* is used to specify a unit length other than the page default.

cpdf_lineto()

Syntax

```
void cpdf_lineto (int pdf document,  double x-koor, double y-koor, int mode)
```

Description

The cpdf_lineto() function, which was added in PHP 3.0.8 and PHP 4.0.b4, draws a line from the current point to the location indicated by the x and y coordinates. The optional parameter *mode* is used to specify a unit length other than the page default.

cpdf_rlineto()

Syntax

```
void cpdf_rlineto (int pdf document, double x-koor, double y-koor, int mode)
```

Description

The cdpf_rlineto() function, which was added in PHP 3.0.8 and PHP 4.0.b4, draws a line from the current point to the relative location indicated by the x and y coordinates. The optional parameter *mode* is used to specify a unit length other than the page default.

cpdf_circle()

Syntax

```
void cpdf_circle (int pdf document,
  double x-koor, double y-koor, double radius, int mode)
```

Description

The cpdf_circle() function, which was added in PHP 3.0.8 and PHP 4.0.b4, draws a circle centered at the x and y coordinates with a radius of *radius*. The optional parameter *mode* is used to specify a unit length other than the page default.

cpdf_arc()

Syntax

```
void cpdf_arc (int pdf document, double x-koor,
  double y-koor, double radius, double start, double end, int mode)
```

Description

The cpdf_arc()function, which was added in PHP 3.0.8 and PHP 4.0.b4, draws an arc centered at the x and y coordinates beginning at the *start* angle and finishing at the *end* angle measure in degrees. The optional parameter *mode* is used to specify a unit length other than the page default.

cpdf_rect()

Syntax

```
void cpdf_rect (int pdf document, double x-koor,
 double y-koor, double width, double height, int mode)
```

Description

The cpdf_rect() function, which was added in PHP 3.0.8 and PHP 4.0.b4, draws a rectangle with dimensions *width* and *height* with its lower-left corner at the x and y coordinates. The optional parameter *mode* is used to specify a unit length other than the page default.

cpdf_closepath()

Syntax

```
void cpdf_closepath(int pdf document)
```

Description

The cpdf_closepath() function, which was added in PHP 3.0.8 and PHP 4.0.b4, connects the first and last points in the path currently being drawn.

cpdf_stroke()

Syntax

```
void cpdf_stroke (int pdf document)
```

Description

The cpdf_stroke() function, which was added in PHP 3.0.8 and PHP 4.0.b4, strokes the current paths with current stroke color and line width.

cpdf_closepath_stroke()

Syntax

```
void cpdf_closepath_stroke (int pdf document)
```

Description

The cpdf_closepath_stroke() function, which was added in PHP 3.0.8 and PHP 4.0.b4, combines the functionality of cpdf_close_path() and cpdf_stroke(). It also clears the path.

cpdf_fill()

Syntax

```
void cpdf_fill (int pdf document)
```

Description

The cpdf_fill() function, which was added in PHP 3.0.8 and PHP 4.0.b4, fills inside the current path with the current fill color.

cpdf_fill_stroke()

Syntax

```
void cpdf_fill_stroke(int pdf document)
```

Description

The cpdf_fill_stroke() function, which was added in PHP 3.0.8 and PHP 4.0.b4, fills the inside of the current path with the current fill color, and then strokes the current path with the current stroke color.

cpdf_closepath_fill_stroke()

Syntax

```
void cpdf_closepath_fill_stroke(int pdf document)
```

Description

The cpdf_closepath_fill_stroke() function, which was added in PHP 3.0.8 and PHP 4.0.b4, combines the functions of cpdf_closepath(), cpdf_fill(), and cpdf_stroke() into one operation. This closes the current path, fills the interior with the current fill color, and draws the current path.

cpdf_clip()

Syntax

```
void cpdf_clip (int pdf document)
```

Description

The cpdf_clip() function, which was added in PHP 3.0.8 and PHP 4.0.b4, clips all further drawing to the current path.

cpdf_setgray_fill()

Syntax

```
void cpdf_setgray_fill(int pdf document, double value)
```

Description

The cpdf_setgray_fill() function, which was added in PHP 3.0.8 and PHP 4.0.b4, sets the gray value with which to fill a path, where *value* is a number between 0 and 1, inclusive.

cpdf_setgray_stroke()

Syntax

```
void cpdf_setgray_stroke (int pdf document, double gray value)
```

Description

The cpdf_setgray_stroke() function, which was added in PHP 3.0.8 and PHP 4.0.b4, sets the gray stroke value, where *value* is a number between 0 and 1, inclusive.

cpdf_setgray()

Syntax

```
void cpdf_setgray (int pdf document, double gray value)
```

Description

The cpdf_setgray() function, which was added in PHP 3.0.8 and PHP 4.0.b4, sets both the stroke and fill gray colors, where *value* is a number between 0 and 1, inclusive.

cpdf_setrgbcolor_fill()

Syntax

```
void cpdf_setrgbcolor_fill (int pdf document,
double red value, double green value, double blue value)
```

Description

The cpdf_setrgbcolor_fill() function, which was added in PHP 3.0.8 and PHP 4.0.b4, sets the RGB color to use to fill a path. Each *value* is a number between 0 and 1, inclusive.

cpdf_setrgbcolor_stroke()

Syntax

```
void cpdf_setrgbcolor_stroke (int pdf document,
 double red value, double green value, double blue value)
```

Description

The cpdf_setrgbcolor_stroke() function, which was added in PHP 3.0.8 and PHP 4.0.b4, sets the RGB color to use to draw a path. Each *value* is a number between 0 and 1, inclusive.

cpdf_setrgbcolor()

Syntax

```
void cpdf_setrgbcolor (int pdf document,
 double red value, double green value, double blue value)
```

Description

The cpdf_setrgbcolor() function, which was added in PHP 3.0.8 and PHP 4.0.b4, sets the RGB color used to draw and fill a path. Each *value* is a number between 0 and 1, inclusive.

cpdf_add_outline()

Syntax

```
void cpdf_add_outline(int pdfdoc, int lastoutline,
 int sublevel, int open, int pagenr, string title)
```

Description

The `cpdf_add_outline()` function, which was added in PHP 3.0.9 and PHP 4.0.b4, adds an outline entry to the document, which is also called a bookmark. The *pdfdoc* parameter identifies the document with which you are working. The *lastoutline* parameter is a reference to the previous outline assigned to the document. You must always add to the bottom of the list—you can't do any insertions or deletions. If *sublevel* is nonzero, the new entry will be below the *lastoutline*; if zero, the new entry will be at the same level. If *open* is nonzero, the entry will be visible when the page is first opened. The *pagenr* parameter represents the destination page for this entry. The *title* parameter represents a string for the outline.

cpdf_set_page_animation()

Syntax

```
void cpdf_set_page_animation (int pdf document,
 int transition, double duration)
```

Description

The `cpdf_set_page_animation()` function, which was added in PHP 3.0.9 and PHP 4.0.b4, specifies the type and parameters for the transition effects of the current page. The transition happens when going from another page to the current page. The *duration* parameter represents the number of seconds between pages. The *transition* parameter can have the following values:

0—No transition

1—Two lines sweeping across the display to reveal the page

2—Multiple lines sweeping across the display to reveal the page

3—A box reveals the page

4—A single line that reveals the page sweeping across the display

5—The previous page dissolves and shows the next page

6—The dissolve effect moves from one screen edge to another

7—The old page is replaced by the new page, which is the default

cpdf_import_jpeg()

Syntax

```
int cpdf_open_jpeg (int pdf document, string
file name, double x-koor, double y-koor, double angle,
 double width, double height, double x-scale, double y-scale, int mode)
```

Description

The cpdf_open_jpeg() function, which was added in PHP 3.0.9 and PHP 4.0.b4, imports a JPEG image from a file with scaling and optional rotation. The image is placed at the location specified by the x-koor and y-koor coordinates. The angle parameter is the angle of rotation in degrees. The height, width, x-scale, and y-scale parameters are used to size the image and may be set to stretch or skew the image, or set to 0 not to alter the image. The optional parameter mode is used to specify a unit length other than the page default.

cpdf_place_inline_image()

Syntax

```
void cpdf_place_inline_image (int pdf document,
 int image, double x-koor, double y-koor, double angle,
 double width, double height, int mode)
```

Description

The cpdf_place_inline_image() function, which was added in PHP 3.0.9 and PHP 4.0.b4, inserts an image generated from PHP image functions into the page at the location specified by the x and y coordinates. The height and width parameters enable you to scale the image to meet a necessary size. The angle parameter enables you to rotate the images by a value specified in degrees. The optional parameter mode is used to specify a unit length other than the page default.

cpdf_add_annotation()

Syntax

```
void cpdf_add_annotation (int pdf document,
 double llx, double lly, double urx, double ury,
 string title, string content, int mode)
```

Description

The cpdf_add_annotation() function, which was added in PHP 3.0.12 and PHP 4.0.b4, adds an annotation in the rectangle bounded by the *llx,lly* and *urx,ury* points. The parameters *title* and *content* set the values of the annotation, respectively. The optional parameter *mode* is used to specify a unit length other than the page default.

Forms Data Format

The Forms Data Format library enables you to interact with forms that are part of PDF documents. Details on the purpose and use of this library can be found at http://partners.adobe.com/asn/developer/acrosdk/forms.html. To include this library with PHP, you should have --with-fdftk=<*directory above /lib/libFdfTk.so*> as a configure argument. Working with PDF forms is similar to HTML forms except that the form variables and values are not available directly, and must be written to file first, and then read out of the file. In addition to reading form field data, the library also enables you to populate PDF form values.

fdf_open()

Syntax

```
int fdf_open (string filename)
```

Description

The fdf_open() function, which was added in PHP 3.0.6 and PHP 4.0, opens a forms data file for processing. The file must consist only of data returned from a PDF form. Because data from the form is not available from the environment in a manner similar to HTML forms, the form results must first be written to a file and then read in using this function before processing. An example of this follows:

```php
<?php
$fp = fopen (formdata.fdf","w");//create a file to hold the form data
fwrite($fp, $HTTP_FDF_DATA, strlen($HTTP_FDF_DATA));
//write the form data to the file
fclose ($fp);//close file
$fpfdf = fdf_open("formdata.fdf");//open the form data file
//…do some processing
fdf_close($fdpfd);//close the file
?>
```

fdf_close()

Syntax

```
void fdf_close (int fdf document)
```

Description

The fdf_close() function, which was added in PHP 3.0.6 and PHP 4.0, closes an FDF document that was opened by using the fdf_open() function.

fdf_create()

Syntax

```
int fdf_create(void)
```

Description

The fdf_create() function, which was added in PHP 3.0.6 and PHP 4.0, creates a new FDF document. Use this function to populate input fields in a PDF document with data.

fdf_save()

Syntax

```
int fdf_save(string filename)
```

Description

The fdf_save() function, which was added in PHP 3.0.6 and PHP 4.0, saves an FDF document. The filename parameter is used to name the output file. Although the toolkit supports using "-" to write to stdout, this is not supported when using PHP as an Apache module. In that case, you should use the fpassthru() function to output the FDF.

fdf_get_value()

Syntax

```
string fdf_get_value (int fdf document, string fieldname)
```

Description

The `fdf_get_value()` function, which was added in PHP 3.0.6 and PHP 4.0, returns the value of a field from an FDF document.

fdf_set_value()

Syntax

```
void fdf_set_value (int fdf document,
 string fieldname, string value, int isName)
```

Description

The `fdf_set_value()` function, which was added in PHP 3.0.6 and PHP 4.0, sets the value of a field in an FDF document. The `isName` parameter is used to indicate whether the field value should be converted to a PDF name (1) or PDF string (0).

fdf_next_field_name()

Syntax

```
string fdf_next_field_name (int fdf document, string fieldname)
```

Description

The `fdf_next_field_name()` function, which was added in PHP 3.0.6 and PHP 4.0, returns the next field name after `fieldname`. If `fieldname` is NULL, the name of the first field will be returned.

fdf_set_ap()

Syntax

```
void fdf_set_ap (int fdf document, string field name,
 int face, string filename, int page number )(e)Description
```

The `fdf_set_ap()` function, which was added in PHP 3.0.6 and PHP 4.0, specifies the appearance value of a field. This is referred to as the /AP key. The `face` parameter can have these values: 1 for `FDFNormalAP`, 2 for `FDFRolloverAP`, and 3 for `FDFDownAP`.

fdf_set_status()

Syntax

```
void fdf_set_status (int fdf document, string status)
```

Description

The fdf_set_status() function, which was added in PHP 3.0.6 and PHP 4.0, is used to set the value of the /STATUS key.

fdf_get_status()

Syntax

```
string fdf_get_status (int fdf document)
```

Description

The fdf_get_status() function, which was added in PHP 3.0.6 and PHP 4.0, is used to determine the value of the /STATUS key.

fdf_set_file()

Syntax

```
void fdf_set_file (int fdf document, string filename)
```

Description

The fdf_set_file() function, which was added in PHP 3.0.6 and PHP 4.0, is used to set the value of the /F key. The /F key is a handle (URL) to the PDF form that should be populated with data.

fdf_get_file()

Syntax

```
string fdf_get_file (int fdf document)
```

Description

The fdf_get_file() function, which was added in PHP 3.0.6 and PHP 4.0, is used to determine the value of the /F key.

Hyperwave

Hyperwave Information Server (HIS) is similar to a database server, except that it is used to store and retrieve entire documents instead of individual data fields. Detailed information about HIS can be found at http://www.hyperwave.com, along with the PHP manual. The necessary library for including Hyperwave support is included with PHP and can be activated by passing --with-hyperwave as an argument to configure, but the server component must be purchased from Hyperwave. If you are implementing a Hyperwave solution, keep in mind that when dealing with external document retrieval from a data source external to Hyperwave, PHP might have a simpler interface than Hyperwave offers.

hw_array2objrec()

Syntax

string hw_array2objrec (array *object_array*)

Description

The hw_array2objrec() function, which was added in PHP 3.0.4 and PHP 4.0, converts the given *object_array* into an object record.

hw_children()

Syntax

array_hw_children (int *connection*, int *objectID*)

Description

The hw_children() function, which was added in PHP 3.0.3 and PHP 4.0, examines the collection identified by the *objectID* and returns an array of object IDs for all the child documents and collections for that *objectID*.

hw_childrenobj()

Syntax

array hw_childrenobj (int *connection*, int *objectID*)

Description

The hw_childrenobj() function, which was added in PHP 3.0.3 and PHP 4.0, examines the collection identified by the *objectID* and returns an array of object records for all the child documents and collections for that *objectID*.

hw_close()

Syntax

```
int hw_close (int connection)
```

Description

The hw_close() function, which was added in PHP 3.0.3 and PHP 4.0, closes the connection to a Hyperwave server specified by the *connection* index. Returns TRUE if successful, and FALSE otherwise.

hw_connect()

Syntax

```
int hw_connect (string host, int port, string username, string password)
```

Description

The hw_connect() function, which was added in PHP 3.0.3 and PHP 4.0, tries to establish a connection with a Hyperwave server. If successful, the function returns the index of the connection that is used for subsequent calls to the server; if a connection cannot be established, the function returns FALSE. All string parameters should be quoted. If the optional *username* and *password* are omitted, an anonymous connection attempt will be made.

hw_cp()

Syntax

```
int hw_cp (int connection, array object id array, int destination id)
```

Description

The hw_cp() function, which was added in PHP 3.0.3 and PHP 4.0, copies the objects specified in the *object_id_array* to the collection specified by the *destination_id*. The return value represents the number of objects that were copied.

hw_deleteobject()

Syntax

```
int hw_deleteobject (int connection, int object_to_delete)
```

Description

The hw_deleteobject() function, which was added in PHP 3.0.3 and PHP 4.0, deletes the object referenced by the *object_to_delete* parameter and returns TRUE if successful, FALSE otherwise.

hw_docbyanchor()

Syntax

```
int hw_docbyanchor (int connection, int anchorID)
```

Description

The hw_docbyanchor() function, which was added in PHP 3.0.3 and PHP 4.0, returns the object ID of the document to which the *anchorID* belongs.

hw_docbyanchorobj()

Syntax

```
string hw_docbyanchorobj (int connection, int anchored)
```

Description

The hw_docbyanchorobj() function, which was added in PHP 3.0.3 and PHP 4.0, returns the object record of the document to which the *anchorID* belongs.

hw_documentattributes()

Syntax

```
string hw_documentattributes (int hw document)
```

Description

The hw_documentattributes() function, which was added in PHP 3.0.3 and PHP 4.0, returns the object record for the document specified by the *hw_document* parameter.

hw_documentbodytag()

Syntax

```
string hw_documentbodytag (int hw_document)
```

Description

The hw_documentbodytag() function, which was added in PHP 3.0.3 and PHP 4.0, returns the corresponding BODY tag for the document specified by the *hw_document* parameter. If the document is comprised of HTML, the BODY tag should be printed before the document.

hw_documentcontent()

Syntax

```
string hw_documentcontent(int hw_document)
```

Description

The hw_documentcontent() function, which was added in PHP 3.0.3 and PHP 4.0, returns the contents for the *hw_docoment*. If the document is HTML based, everything after the BODY tag is returned because the contents of the HEAD and BODY tags are stored in the document's object record.

hw_documentsetcontent()

Syntax

```
string hw_documentsetcontent (int hw_document, string content)
```

Description

The hw_documentsetcontent() function, which was added in PHP 3.0.8, is used to set the contents of the *hw_document* to *content* if it doesn't exist, or replace the contents of the document if it already does exist. If the document is HTML, the content refers to everything after the BODY tag because the HEAD and BODY tags are stored in the object record.

hw_documentsize()

Syntax

```
int hw_documentsize (int hw document)
```

Description

The hw_documentsize() function, which was added in PHP 3.0.3 and PHP 4.0b1, returns the size of the *hw_document* in bytes.

hw_errormsg()

Syntax

```
string hw_errormsg (int connection)
```

Description

The hw_errormsg() function, which was added in PHP 3.0.3 and PHP 4.0, returns a string containing the error message that was generated for the specified *connection*'s last command or "No Error" if the last command was successful.

hw_edittext()

Syntax

```
int hw_edittext (int connection, int hw_document)
```

Description

The hw_edittext() function, which was added in PHP 3.0.3 and PHP 4.0, uploads the text-only *hw_document* to the server. The object record of this document cannot be changed while the document is being edited. Note that the control connection is blocked during the upload to the server.

hw_error()

Syntax

```
int hw_error (int connection)
```

Description

The hw_error() function, which was added in PHP 3.0.3 and PHP 4.0, returns the error number that was generated for the specified *connection*'s last command or 0 if the last command was successful.

hw_free_document()

Syntax

```
int hw_free_document (int hw_document)
```

Description

The hw_free_document() function, which was added in PHP 3.0.3 and PHP 4.0, releases the memory allocated for the *hw_document*.

hw_getparents()

Syntax

```
array hw_getparents (int connection, int objectID)
```

Description

The hw_getparents() function, which was added in PHP 3.0.3 and PHP 4.0, returns an array of object IDs that represent the parents of the given *objectID*.

hw_getparentsobj()

Syntax

```
array hw_getparentsobj (int connection, int objectID)
```

Description

The hw_getparentsobj() function, which was added in PHP 3.0.3 and PHP 4.0, returns an indexed array of object records that represent the parents of the specified *objectID*. The last element of the array returned is an associative array containing statistical details about the object records.

hw_getchildcoll()

Syntax

```
array hw_getchildcoll (int connection, int objectID)
```

Description

The hw_getchildcoll() function, which was added in PHP 3.0.3 and PHP 4.0, returns an array of object IDs representing a child collection of the collection indicated by the *objectID* parameter.

hw_getchildcollobj()

Syntax

```
array hw_getchildcollobj( int connection, int objectID)
```

Description

The hw_getchildcollobj() function, which was added in PHP 3.0.3 and PHP 4.0, returns an array of object records representing a child collection of the collection indicated by the *objectID* parameter.

hw_getremote()

Syntax

```
int hw_getremote (int connection, int objectID)
```

Description

The hw_getremote() function, which was added in PHP 3.0.3 and PHP 4.0, retrieves a document that is stored in an external source. Remote documents are accessed using the Hyperwave Gateway Interface (HGI), which enables you to obtain documents from other HTTP, FTP, and some database servers. If this functionality is needed, consider accessing the documents directly using PHP instead of utilizing the HGI.

hw_getremotechildren()

Syntax

```
int hw_getremotechildren (int connection, string object record)
```

Description

The hw_getremotechildren() function, which was added in PHP 3.0.3 and PHP 4.0, returns the children of a remote document. If only one child exists, the document itself is returned; if multiple child documents exist, an array of virtual objects' records is returned and their handling depends on the HGI implementation. If you need this functionality, considering accessing the documents by using PHP instead of the HGI.

hw_getsrcbydestobj()

Syntax

```
array hw_getsrcbydestobj (int connection, int objectID)
```

Description

The array_hw_getsrcbydestobj() function, which was added in PHP 3.0.3 and PHP 4.0, returns an array of object records that represent all anchors pointing to the object specified by the *objectID* parameter. The *objectID* can be either a document or a destination anchor.

hw_getobject()

Syntax

```
array hw_getobject (int connection, [int|array] objectID, string query)
```

Description

The hw_getobject() function, which was added in PHP 3.0.3 and PHP 4.0, returns the corresponding object record for the *objectID* referenced if the *objectID* is an integer; otherwise, it returns an array of object records. The array of object records is based on the *query* parameter, which indicates further criteria for record searching. The *query* parameter allows the following syntax:

```
<expr> ::= "(" <expr> ")" |
"!" <expr> | /* NOT */
<expr> "||" <expr> | /* OR */
<expr> "&&" <expr> | /* AND */
<attribute> <operator> <value>
<attribute> ::= /* any attribute name (Title, Author, DocumentType ...) */
<operator> ::= "=" | /* equal */
"<" | /* less than (string compare) */
```

```
">" | /* greater than (string compare) */
"~" /* regular expression matching */
```

hw_getandlock()

Syntax

```
string hw_getandlock (int connection, int objectID)
```

Description

The hw_getandlock() function, which was added in PHP 3.0.3 and PHP 4.0, returns the object record for the specified *objectID* parameter and locks access to the object.

hw_gettext()

Syntax

```
int hw_gettext (int connection, int objectID [,mixed rootID/prefix])
```

Description

The hw_gettext() function, which was added in PHP 3.0.3 and PHP 4.0, retrieves the document with corresponding *objectID*. Any anchors in the document will already be inserted before retrieval. If *rootID/prefix* is an integer value of 0, the links will be constructed from the name of the link's destination object. If *rootID/prefix* is a nonzero integer, the link is built from all the names starting at the object with the ID *rootID/prefix* separated by a slash relative to the current object. If *rootID/prefix* is a string, that string will be prepended to the location. This function works only for pure text documents and blocks the control connection during the transfer.

hw_getobjectbyquery()

Syntax

```
array hw_getobjectbyquery (int  connection, string query, int max hits)
```

Description

The hw_getobjectbyquery() function, which was added in PHP 3.0.3 and PHP 4.0, returns an array of object IDs that match the search specified by the *query* parameter. The *max_hits* parameter enables you to cap the number of search results returned (-1 is unlimited). Note that the search works only with indexed attributes.

hw_getobjectbyqueryobj()

Syntax

```
array hw_getobjectbyqueryobj (int connection, string query, int max hits)
```

Description

The hw_getobjectbyqueryobj() function, which was added in PHP 3.0.3 and PHP 4.0, returns an array of object records that match the search specified by the *query* parameter. The *max_hits* parameter enables you to cap the number of search results returned (-1 is unlimited). Note that the search works only with indexed attributes.

hw_getobjectbyquerycoll()

Syntax

```
array hw_getobjectbyquerycoll (int connection,
  int objectID, string query, int max hits)
```

Description

The hw_getobjectbyquerycoll() function, which was added in PHP 3.0.3 and PHP 4.0, returns an array of object IDs that match the search specified by the *query* parameter. The scope is limited to the collection specified by the *objectID* parameter. The *max_hits* parameter enables you to cap the number of search results returned (-1 is unlimited). Note that the search works only with indexed attributes.

hw_getobjectbyquerycollobj()

Syntax

```
array hw_getobjectbyquerycollobj( int connection,
  int objectID, string query, int max hits)
```

Description

The hw_getobjectbyquerycollobj() function, which was added in PHP 3.0.3 and PHP 4.0, returns an array of object records that match the search specified by the *query* parameter. The scope is limited to the collection specified by the *objectID* parameter. The *max_hits* parameter enables you to cap the number of search results returned (-1 is unlimited). Note that the search works only with indexed attributes.

hw_getchilddoccoll()

Syntax

```
array hw_getchilddoccoll (int connection, int objectID)
```

Description

The hw_getchilddoccoll() function, which was added in PHP 3.0.3 and PHP 4.0, returns an array of object IDs that are children of the collection denoted by *objectID*.

hw_getchilddoccollobj()

Syntax

```
array hw_getchilddoccollobj (int connection, int objectID)
```

Description

The hw_getchilddoccollobj() function, which was added in PHP 3.0.3 and PHP 4.0, returns an array of object records that are children of the collection denoted by *objectID*.

hw_getanchors()

Syntax

```
array hw_getanchors (int connection, int objectID)
```

Description

The hw_getanchors() function, which was added in PHP 3.0.3 and PHP 4.0, returns an array of object IDs that are anchors of the document specified by *objectID*.

hw_getanchorsobj()

Syntax

```
array hw_getanchorsobj (int connection, int objectID)
```

Description

The hw_getanchorsobj() function, which was added in PHP 3.0.3 and PHP 4.0, returns an array of object records that are anchors of the document specified by *objectID*.

hw_mv()

Syntax

```
int hw_mv (int connection, array object id array,
 int source id, int destination id)
```

Description

The hw_mv() function, which was added in PHP 3.0.3 and PHP 4.0, moves the objects in the *object_id_array* parameter from the *source_id* to the *destination_id*. If the *destination_id* parameter is set to 0, the objects in the *object_id_array* will be unlinked from the *source_id* collection. If this is the last instance of the object, it will also be deleted.

hw_identify()

Syntax

```
int hw_identify (string username, string password)
```

Description

The hw_identify() function, which was added in PHP 3.0.3 and PHP 4.0, enables you to identify which user is making the request. This is most often handled at the time that the connection to the server is established.

hw_incollections()

Syntax

```
array hw_incollections (int connection, array object_id_array,
 array collection_id_array, int return-collections)
```

Description

The hw_incollections() function, which was added in PHP 3.0.3 and PHP 4.0, verifies whether the objects listed in the *object_id_array* are part of the *collection_id_array.* If the *return-collections* parameter is 0, the intersection of object IDs is returned in an array; if set to 1, the object IDs of the collections that have corresponding children in the *object_id_array* are returned.

hw_info()

Syntax

```
string hw_info (int connection)
```

Description

The hw_info() function, which was added in PHP 3.0.3 and PHP 4.0, supplies information on the current status of the specified *connection*. The return string is formatted as follows: "*<Serverstring>, <Host>, <Port>, <Username>, <Port of Client>, <Byte swapping>*".

hw_inscoll()

Syntax

```
int hw_inscoll (int connection, int objectID, array object array)
```

Description

The hw_inscoll() function, which was added in PHP 3.0.3 and PHP 4.0, inserts a new collection specified by the *object_array* parameter into the *objectID* collection.

hw_insdoc()

Syntax

```
int hw_insdoc (int connection, int parentID,
string object record, string text)
```

Description

The hw_insdoc() function, which was added in PHP 3.0.3 and PHP 4.0, places a new document with attributes specified in the *object_record* parameter into the collection specified by the *parentID* parameter. An object record will be inserted as well as the *text* parameter, if it is present. The hw_insertdocument() is more flexible and often used instead.

hw_insertdocument()

Syntax

```
int hw_insertdocument (int connection, int parent id, int hw document)
```

Description

The hw_insertdocument() function, which was added in PHP 3.0.3 and PHP 4.0, places a new document into the collection specified by the *parentID* parameter. The document has to be created using hw_newdocument() prior to calling this function. The object record of the *hw_document* should contain Type, DocumentType, Title, and Name at a minimum, with MimeType also recommended. The return value is the new object ID or FALSE is unsuccessful.

hw_insertobject()

Syntax

```
int hw_insertobject (int connection, string object rec, string parameter)
```

Description

The hw_insertobject() function, which was added in PHP 3.0.3 and PHP 4.0, inserts an object into the server. The *object_rec* represents the object record of the Hyperwave object to be inserted. Consult the Hyperwave documentation for *parameter* specifications.

hw_mapid()

Syntax

```
int hw_mapid (int connection, nt server id, int object id)
```

Description

The hw_mapid() function, which was added in PHP 3.0.13 and PHP 4.0b4, enables you to map a global object ID on any Hyperwave server to a virtual object ID, even if you did not connect to the server. The global ID is comprised of the server ID as well as its object ID, where the server ID is the integer representation of the server's IP address. Note that to utilize this functionality, Hyperwave must be compiled using the F_DISTRIBUTED flag in the hc_comm.c file.

hw_modifyobject()

Syntax

```
in hw_modifyobject (int connection, int object to change,
 array remove, array add, int mode)
```

Description

The hw_modifyobject() function, which was added in PHP 3.0.7 and PHP 4.0b2, enables you to modify attributes of an object's record. The *array* parameters specify attributes to remove and add, respectively. To modify an existing attribute, you must remove the old one and add it back. The *mode* parameter specifies whether to process the changes recursively, with 1 indicating yes. The following example modifies an attribute:

```
// $objid is the ID of the object to modify

    // $connect is an existing HIS connection
        $removearray = array("Name" => "oldname");
        $addarray = array("Name" => "newname");
        $hw_modifyobject($connect, $objid, $removearray, $addarray);
```

hw_new_document()

Syntax

```
int hw_new_document (string object record,
string document data, int document size, int document size)
```

Description

The hw_new_document() function, which was added in PHP 3.0.3 and PHP 4.0, creates a new Hyperwave document whose data and object record are set to *document_data* and *object_record*, respectively. The length of the *document_data* has to be specified in the *document_size* parameter. This functions only creates the document, and does not insert it into the server.

hw_objrec2array()

Syntax

```
array hw_objrec2array (string object record)
```

Description

The `hw_objrec2array()` function, which was added in PHP 3.0.3 and PHP 4.0, generates an object array based on the *object_record* parameter. The attribute names of the *object_record* are stored as the keys in the array. Multiple similar attributes are placed into a subarray. Currently, only the `Title`, `Description`, `Group`, and `Keyword` attributes are handled properly.

hw_outputdocument()

Syntax

```
int hw_outputdocument (int hw document)
```

Description

The `hw_outputdocument()` function, which was added in PHP 3.0.3 and PHP 4.0b1, outputs the document specified by the *hw_document* parameter excluding the `BODY` tag.

hw_pconnect()

Syntax

```
int hw_pconnect (string host, int port, string username, string password)
```

Description

The `hw_pconnect()` function, which was added in PHP 3.0.3 and PHP 4.0, attempts to make a persistent connection to the specified server using the *username* and *password* parameters for authentication. The return value is the connection index if successful, and FALSE otherwise. You can attempt anonymous access by not specifying a *username* or *password*. Also note that multiple connections can exist at one time.

hw_pipedocument()

Syntax

```
int hw_pipedocument (int connection, int objectID)
```

Description

The `hw_pipedocument()` function, which was added in PHP 3.0.3 and PHP 4.0, returns the Hyperwave document (including anchors) indicated by the *objectID* parameter. The contents will be returned on a special data connection that does not block the control connection.

hw_root()

Syntax

```
int hw_root()
```

Description

The hw_root() function, which was added in PHP 3.0.3 and PHP 4.0, currently always returns 0, which represents the object ID of the hyperroot collection. The root collection of the connected server is the child collection of the hyperroot.

hw_unlock()

Syntax

```
int hw_unlock (int connection, int objectID)
```

Description

The hw_unlock() function, which was added in PHP 3.0.3 and PHP 4.0, releases a lock on the object specified by the *objectID* parameter so that others may gain access.

hw_who()

Syntax

```
int hw_who (int connection)
```

Description

The hw_who() function, which was added in PHP 3.0.3 and PHP 4.0, returns an array listing users currently logged on to the server. Each array entry represents a user and contains the elements id, name, system, onSinceDate, onSinceTime, TotalTime, and self, where self=1 if the entry corresponds to the user who made the hw_who() request.

hw_username()

Syntax

```
string hw_getusername (int connection)
```

Description

The hw_getusername() function, which was added in PHP 3.0.3 and PHP 4.0, returns the username corresponding to the current *connection*.

PDF

The PDF library functions enable you to generate PDF documents dynamically from your PHP code. The PDF library is available from http://www.pdflib.com. It is not freeware, so you should consult the licensing agreement before implementing it in your code. To understand the mapping from PHP to the PDF library, you should examine the pdf.c file typically found in the /php-4.x/ext/pdf/ directory. Note that the PDF library is not currently available as part of the Windows distribution. To include the PDF library, use the following in your configure arguments:

```
--with-pdflib=<directory above /lib/pdflib.so>
--with-zlib-dir=<directory above /lib/libz.so
--with-jpeg-dir=<directory above /lib/libjpeg.so>
--with-png-dir=<directory above /lib/libpng.so
--with-tiff-dir=<directory above /lib/libtiff.so>
```

The PDF library requires the JPEG, PNG, Tiff, and Zlib libraries as indicated by running configure --help. An alternative to the PDF library is the ClibPDF library documented earlier in this chapter. There are licensing differences between the two libraries as well as some feature differences. You should consult the documentation that comes with the PDF and ClibPDF libraries for more details.

pdf_get_info()

Syntax

```
info pdf_get_info (string filename)
```

Description

The pdf_get_info() function, which was added in PHP 3.0.6 and PHP 4.0b1, returns an empty info structure for a PDF document. The info structure can be filled with document details such as subject, author, and so on.

pdf_set_info()

Syntax

```
info pdf_set_info (int pdf_document, string fieldname, string value)
```

Description

The pdf_set_info() function, which was added in PHP 4.0.1, is used to set the information fields of a PDF document. Possible fieldname parameter values include Subject, Title, Creator, Author, Keywords, and one user-defined name. This function must be called before pdf_begin_page().

pdf_open()

Syntax

```
int pdf_open (int file)
```

Description

The pdf_open() function, which was added in PHP 3.0.6 and PHP 4.0, opens a new PDF document. The corresponding file has to be opened with fopen() and the resulting file descriptor passed as the file parameter. The return value is used as an argument to subsequent PDF functions that access the document.

pdf_close()

Syntax

```
void pdf_close (int pdf document)
```

Description

The pdf_close() function, which was added in PHP 3.0.6 and PHP 4.0, closes the specified pdf_document.

pdf_begin_page()

Syntax

```
void pdf_begin_page (int pdf document, double width, double height)
```

Description

The pdf_begin_page() function, which was added in PHP 3.0.6 and PHP 4.0, creates a new page with the dimensions *width* and *height*. This function must be called at the beginning of every PDF page.

pdf_end_page()

Syntax

```
void pdf_end_page (int pdf document)
```

Description

The pdf_end_page() function, which was added in PHP 3.0.6 and PHP 4.0, ends a PDF page, which frees resources and prevents any further modification of the page.

pdf_show()

Syntax

```
void pdf_show (int pdf document, string text)
```

Description

The pdf_show() function, which was added in PHP 3.0.6 and PHP 4.0, prints out the string *text* at the current position using the current font and then advances the current pointer to the end of the text.

pdf_show_boxed()

Syntax

```
int pdf_show_boxed (int pdf document, string text,
  double x-coor, double y-coor, double width, double height,  string mode)
```

Description

The pdf_show_boxed() function, which was added in PHP 4.0RC1, prints out the *text* parameter inside a box whose lower-left corner is located at the x and y coordinates. The dimensions of the box are specified by the *height* and *width* parameters. If both coordinates are zero, *mode* can be 'left', 'right', or 'center'; and if both are unequal, *mode* can be 'justify' or 'filljustify'. The return value indicates the number of characters in *text* that did not fit inside the box.

pdf_show_xy()

Syntax

```
void pdf_show_xy (ind pdf document, string text, double x-coor, double y-coor)
```

Description

The pdf_show_xy() function, which was added in PHP 3.0.6 and PHP 4.0, outputs the *text* parameter at the location specified by the x and y coordinates.

pdf_set_font()

Syntax

```
void pdf_set_font (int pdf document, string font name,
  double size, string encoding [,int embed ])
```

Description

The pdf_set_font() function sets the current font type, face, and encoding. If you are using a version of pdflib prior to 2.20, *encoding* should be set to a number between 0 and 4, inclusive, where 0 is builtin, 1 is pdfdoc, 2 is macroman, 3 is macexpert, and u is winansi. For versions of pdflib higher than 2.20, *encoding* should be one of the following string values: builtin, host, pdfdoc, macroman, macexpert, or winansi. The *embed* parameter specifies whether the font should be included with the document's contents. This is a good idea if you are using a nonstandard font to ensure that the reader can properly view the document. This function should be called after the pdf_begin_page() function is called.

pdf_set_leading()

Syntax

```
void pdf_set_leading (int pdf document, double distance)
```

Description

The pdf_set_leading() function, which was added in PHP 3.0.6 and PHP 4.0, specifies the distance that should be between text lines when using the pdf_continue_text() function.

pdf_set_parameter()

Syntax

void pdf_set_parameter (int *pdf document*, string *name*, string *value*)

Description

The pdf_set_parameter() function, which was added in PHP 4.0RC1, is used to set parameters for the pdflib library where *name* is the key and *value* is the value of the parameter.

pdf_set_text_rendering()

Syntax

void pdf_set_text_rendering (int *pdf document*, int *mode*)

Description

The pdf_set_text_rendering() function, which was added in PHP 3.0.6 and PHP 4, sets how text should be rendered according to the *mode* parameter. The *mode* parameter can take these values: 0 for fill text, 1 for stroke text, 2 for fill and stroke text, 3 for invisible, 4 for fill text and add it to clipping path, 5 for stroke text and add it to clipping path, 6 for fill and stroke text and add it to clipping path, 7 for add it to clipping path.

pdf_set_horiz_scaling()

Syntax

void pdf_set_horiz_scaling (int *pdf document*, double *scale*)

Description

The pdf_set_horiz_scaling() function, which was added in PHP 3.0.6 and PHP 4.0, sets the horizontal scaling factor to *scale*, which is a percentage. This can be used to stretch or skew the horizontal length of a string. The default value is 100 percent.

pdf_set_text_rise()

Syntax

```
void pdf_set_text_rise (int pdf document, double rises)
```

Description

The pdf_set_text_rise() function, which was added in PHP 3.0.6 and PHP 4.0 sets the offset *value* of text from the base line measured in points (72 = 1 inch). Use a positive *value* for a superscript and a negative value for a subscript.

pdf_set_text_matrix()

Syntax

```
void pdf_set_text_matrix (int pdf document, array matrix)
```

Description

The pdf_set_text_matrix() function, which was added in PHP 3.0.8 and PHP 4.0.b4, enables you to associate a transformation *matrix* with the current text font. A matrix can be used to set the current point, rotation, and skewing. Consult the PostScript documentation for further matrix details.

pdf_set_text_pos()

Syntax

```
void pdf_set_text_pos (int pdf document, double x-coor, double y-coor)
```

Description

The pdf_set_text_pos() function, which was added in PHP 3.0.6 and PHP 4.0, sets the location where the next call to cpdf_show() will output text.

pdf_set_char_spacing()

Syntax

```
void pdf_set_char_spacing (int pdf document, double space )
```

Description

The `pdf_set_char_spacing()` function, which was added in PHP 3.0.6 and PHP 4.0, is used to add further spacing between characters. The *space* parameter should be specified in points (72 points = 1 inch).

pdf_set_word_spacing()

Syntax

```
void pdf_set_word_spacing (int pdf_document, double space)
```

Description

The `pdf_set_word_spacing()` function, which was added in PHP 3.0.6 and PHP 4.0, is used to add further spacing between words. The *space* parameter should be specified in points (72 points = 1 inch).

pdf_skew()

Syntax

```
void pdf_skew (int pdf document, double alpha, double beta)
```

Description

The `pdf_skew()` function, which was added in PHP 4.0RC1, skews the coordinate system by *alpha* and *beta* degrees. Angles are measured counterclockwise from the positive x-axis of the current coordinate system. Note that neither *alpha* nor *beta* can be 90 or 270 degrees.

pdf_continue_text()

Syntax

```
void pdf_continue_text (int pdf document, string text)
```

Description

The `pdf_continue_text()` function, which was added in PHP 3.0.6 and PHP 4.0, outputs text at the beginning of the next line. The effect is similar to performing a carriage return and line feed before outputting the text.

pdf_stringwidth()

Syntax

```
double pdf_stringwidth (int pdf document, string text)
```

Description

The pdf_stringwidth() function, which was added in PHP 3.0.6 and PHP 4, returns the width of the current font for *text* in points. A font value must have been set previously for this function to work properly.

pdf_save()

Syntax

```
void pdf_save (int pdf document)
```

Description

The pdf_save() function, which was added in PHP 3.0.6 and PHP 4, is used to save the current graphics state. It enables you to work easily with one object without impacting other objects.

pdf_restore()

Syntax

```
void pdf_restore (int pdf document )
```

Description

The pdf_restore() function, which was added in PHP 3.0.6 and PHP 4, is used to restore the graphics state you saved with pdf_save(). It enables you to work easily with one object without impacting other objects.

pdf_translate()

Syntax

```
void pdf_translate (int pdf document, double x-coor, double y-coor)
```

Description

The `pdf_translate()` function, which was added in PHP 3.0.6 and PHP 4, is used to shift the origin of the coordinate system to the *x-coor* and *y-coor* values. You need to call `pdf_moveto()` to set the current point after using this function.

pdf_scale()

Syntax

```
void pdf_scale (int pdf document, double x-scale, double y-scale)
```

Description

The `pdf_scale()` function, which was added in PHP 3.0.6 and PHP 4, is used to scale the coordinate system for both the x and y axes, by the *x-scale* and *y-scale* factors.

pdf_rotate()

Syntax

```
void pdf_rotate (int pdf document, double angle)
```

Description

The `pdf_rotate()` function, which was added PHP 3.0.6 and PHP 4, is used to rotate the current coordinate system by the *angle* parameter, which is specified in degrees. The rotation is centered at the current origin and a positive value for *angle* indicates clockwise rotation.

pdf_setflat()

Syntax

```
void pdf_setflat (int pdf document, double value )
```

Description

The `pdf_setflat()` function, which was added in PHP 3.0.6 and PHP 4.0, sets the flatness with a minimum value of 0 and a maximum of 100.

pdf_setlinejoin()

Syntax

```
void pdf_setlinejoin (int pdf document, long value)
```

Description

The pdf_setlinejoin() function, which was added in PHP 3.0.6 and PHP 4.0, sets the linejoin *value*, which must be between 0 and 2. Possible values are 0 for miter, 1 for round, and 2 for bevel.

pdf_setlinecap()

Syntax

```
void pdf_setlinecap (int pdf document, int value)
```

Description

The pdf_setlinecap() function, which was added in PHP 3.0.6 and PHP 4.0, sets the linecap value, which must be between 0 and 2. Possible values are 0 for butt end, 1 for round, and 2 for projecting square.

pdf_setmiterlimit()

Syntax

```
void pdf_setmiterlimit (int pdf document, double value)
```

Description

The pdf_setmiterlimit() function, which was added in PHP 3.0.6 and PHP 4.0, is used to specify the behavior when two line segments meet at a corner, including how pointed the corner should be when they meet at a sharp angle. The minimum for *value* is 1.

pdf_setlinewidth()

Syntax

```
void pdf_setlinewidth (int pdf document, double width)
```

Description

The `pdf_setlinewidth()` function, which was added in PHP 3.0.6 and PHP 4.0, sets the current line width. The *width* parameter is a value specified in points (72 points = 1 inch).

pdf_setdash()

Syntax

```
void pdf_setdash (int pdf document, double white, double black)
```

Description

The `pdf_setdash()` function, which was added in PHP 3.0.6 and PHP 4.0, sets a pattern for dashed lines where *white* and *black* are the lengths of the segments in points. A zero value indicates a solid line.

pdf_moveto()

Syntax

```
void pdf_moveto (int pdf document, double x-coor, double y-coor)
```

Description

The `pdf_moveto()` function, which was added in PHP 3.0.6 and PHP 4.0, moves the current point to the location specified by *x-coor* and *y-coor* coordinates.

pdf_curveto()

Syntax

```
void pdf_curveto (int pdf document, double x1,
  double y1, double x2, double y2, double x3, double y3)
```

Description

The `pdf_curveto()` function, which was added in PHP 3.0.6 and PHP 4.0 draws a Bézier cubic curve using the current point as the starting point, *x3* and *y3* as the end point and (*x1,y1*),(*x2,y2*) as the control points.

pdf_lineto()

Syntax

```
void pdf_lineto (int pdf document, double x-coor, double y-coor)
```

Description

The pdf_lineto() function, which was added in PHP 3.0.6 and PHP 4.0, draws a line from the current point to the location indicated by the x and y coordinates.

pdf_circle()

Syntax

```
void pdf_circle (int pdf document, double x-coor, double y-coor, double radius)
```

Description

The pdf_circle() function, which was added in PHP 3.0.6 and PHP 4.0, draws a circle centered at the x and y coordinates with a radius of radius.

pdf_arc()

Syntax

```
void pdf_arc (int pdf document, double x-coor,
double y-coor, double radius, double start, double end)
```

Description

The pdf_arc() function, which was added in PHP 3.0.6 and PHP 4.0, draws an arc centered at the x and y coordinates starting at the start angle and ending at the end angle measured in degrees.

pdf_rect()

Syntax

```
void pdf_rect (int pdf document, double x-coor,
double y-coor, double width, double height)
```

Description

The pdf_rect() function, which was added in PHP 3.0.6 and PHP 4.0, draws a rectangle with dimensions *width* and *height* with its lower-left corner at the x and y coordinates.

pdf_closepath()

Syntax

```
void pdf_closepath (int pdf document)
```

Description

The pdf_closepath() function, which was added in PHP 3.0.6 and PHP 4.0, connects the first and last points in the path currently being drawn.

pdf_stroke()

Syntax

```
void pdf_stroke(int pdf document)
```

Description

The pdf_stroke() function, which was added in PHP 3.0.6 and PHP 4.0, strokes the current paths with current stroke color and line width.

pdf_closepath_stroke()

Syntax

```
void pdf_closepath_stroke (int pdf document)
```

Description

The pdf_closepath_stroke() function, which was added in PHP 3.0.6 and PHP 4.0, combines the functionality of pdf_close_path() and pdf_stroke(). It also clears the path.

pdf_fill()

Syntax

```
void pdf_fill (int pdf document)
```

Description

The pdf_fill() function, which was added in PHP 3.0.6 and PHP 4.0, fills the inside of the current path with the current fill color.

pdf_fill_stroke()

Syntax

```
void pdf_fill_stroke (int pdf document)
```

Description

The pdf_fill_stroke() function, which was added in PHP 3.0.6 and PHP 4.0, fills the inside of the current path with the current fill color and then strokes the current path with the current stroke color.

pdf_closepath_fill_stroke()

Syntax

```
void pdf_closepath_fill_stroke (int pdf document )
```

Description

The pdf_closepath_fill_stroke() function, which was added in PHP 3.0.6 and PHP 4.0, combines the functions of pdf_closepath(), pdf_fill(), and pdf_stroke() into one operation. This closes the current path, fills the interior with the current fill color, and draws the current path.

pdf_endpath()

Syntax

```
void pdf_endpath (int pdf document)
```

Description

The pdf_endpath() function, which was added in PHP 3.0.6 and PHP 4.0, ends the current path, but it does not close the path.

pdf_clip()

Syntax

```
void pdf_clip (int pdf document)
```

Description

The `pdf_clip()` function, which was added in PHP 3.0.6 and PHP 4.0, clips all further drawing to the current path.

pdf_setgray_fill

Syntax

```
void pdf_setgray_fill (int pdf document, double gray value)
```

Description

The `pdf_setgray_fill()` function, which was added in PHP 3.0.6 and PHP 4.0, sets the gray value with which to fill a path, where *value* is a number between 0 and 1, inclusive.

pdf_setgray_stroke()

Syntax

```
void pdf_setgray_stroke (int pdf document, double gray value)
```

Description

The `pdf_setgray_stroke()` function, which was added in PHP 3.0.6 and PHP 4.0, sets the gray stroke value, where *value* is a number between 0 and 1, inclusive.

pdf_setgray()

Syntax

```
void pdf_setgray (int pdf document, double gray value)
```

Description

The `pdf_setgray()` function, which was added in PHP 3.0.6 and PHP 4.0, sets both the stroke and fill gray colors, where *value* is a number between 0 and 1, inclusive.

pdf_setrgbcolor_fill()

Syntax

```
void pdf_setrgbcolor_fill (int pdf document,
double red value, double green value, double blue value)
```

Description

The pdf_setrgbcolor_fill() function, which was added in PHP 3.0.6 and PHP 4.0, sets the RGB color to use to fill a path. Each value is a number between 0 and 1, inclusive.

pdf_setrgbcolor_stroke()

Syntax

```
void pdf_setrgbcolor_stroke (int pdf document,
 double red value, double green value, double blue value)
```

Description

The pdf_setrgbcolor_stroke() function, which was added in PHP 3.0.6 and PHP 4.0, sets the RGB color to use to draw a path. Each value is a number between 0 and 1, inclusive.

pdf_setrgbcolor()

Syntax

```
void pdf_setrgbcolor (int pdf document, double red value,
 double green value, double blue value)
```

Description

The pdf_setrgbcolor() function, which was added in PHP 3.0.6 and PHP 4.0, sets the RGB color used to draw and fill a path. Each value is a number between 0 and 1, inclusive.

pdf_add_outline()

Syntax

```
int pdf_add_outline (int pdf document,
string text [, int parent [, int open ]])
```

Description

The pdf_add_outline() function, which was added in PHP 3.0.6 and PHP 4.0, adds an outline entry to the document which is also referred to as a bookmark. The *pdf_document* parameter identifies the document with which you are working. The *parent* parameter is a reference to the previous outline assigned to the document. You must always add to the bottom of the list—you can't do any insertions or deletions. If *open* is nonzero, the entry will be visible when the page is first opened. The *text* parameter represents a string for the outline.

pdf_set_transition()

Syntax

```
void pdf_set_transition (int pdf document, int transition)
```

Description

The pdf_set_transition() function, which was added in PHP 3.0.6 and PHP 4.0, specifies the type and parameters for transition effects of the current page. The transition happens when going from another page to the current page. The transition parameter can have the following values:

0—No transition

1—Two lines sweeping across the display to reveal the page

2—Multiple lines sweeping across the display to reveal the page

3—A box that reveals the page

4—A single line sweeping across the display that reveals the page

5—The previous page dissolves and shows the next page

6—The dissolve effect moves from one screen edge to another

7—The old page is replaced by the new page, which is the default

pdf_set_duration()

Syntax

```
void pdf_set_duration (int pdf document, double duration)
```

Description

The `pdf_set_duration()` function, which was added in PHP 3.0.6 and PHP 4.0, sets the amount of time elapsed between page changes. This can be used in combination with the `pdf_transition()` function.

pdf_open_gif

Syntax

```
int pdf_open_gif (int pdf document, string filename)
```

Description

The `pdf_open_gif()` function, which was added in PHP 3.0.6 and PHP 4.0, opens a GIF file specified by the `filename` parameter. The return value is a PDF image identifier that can be used for subsequent calls.

pdf_open_memory_image()

Syntax

```
int pdf_open_memory_image (int pdf document, int image)
```

Description

The `pdf_open_memory_image()` function, which was added in PHP 3.0.10 and PHP 4.0b2, makes an image that was created using PHP's image functions available for the PDF document. The return value is a PDF image identifier.

pdf_open_jpeg()

Syntax

```
int pdf_open_jpeg (int pdf docment, string filename)
```

Description

The `pdf_open_jpeg()` function, which was added in PHP 3.0.7 and PHP 4.0b2, imports a JPEG image from a file specified by the `filename` parameter and returns a PDF image identifier.

pdf_close_image()

Syntax

```
void pdf_close_image (int image)
```

Description

The pdf_close_image() function, which was added in PHP 3.0.7 and PHP 4.0b2, closes any image opened with a PDF image open function.

pdf_place_image()

Syntax

```
void pdf_place_image (int pdf document, int image,
 double x-coor, double y-coor, double scale)
```

Description

The pdf_place_image() function, which was added in PHP 3.0.7 and PHP 4.0b2, places an image on the page at the location specified by the x and y coordinates. The scale parameter enables you to adjust the image size. Scaling adjusts the size of pixels but doesn't do any down sampling.

pdf_put_image()

Syntax

```
void pdf_put_image (int pdf document, int image)
```

Description

The pdf_put_image() function, which was added in PHP 3.0.7 and was removed after PHP 4.0b4, enables the image to be placed into a PDF file without showing it until the pdf_execute_function() is called. This function is not used for pdflib versions higher than 2.01.

pdf_execute_image()

Syntax

```
void pdf_execute_image (int pdf document, int image,
 double x-coor, double y-coor, double scale)
```

Description

The `pdf_execute_image()` function, which was added in PHP 3.0.7 and was removed after PHP 4.0b4, causes an image placed in a PDF document with `pdf_put_image()` to display at the x and y coordinates. The image can be scaled at the time of display by using the *scale* parameter, where a value of 1 indicates original size.

pdf_add_annotation()

Syntax

```
void pdf_add_annotation (int pdf document, double llx,
  double lly, double urx, double ury, string title, string content)
```

Description

The `pdf_add_annotation()` function, which was added in PHP 3.0.12 and PHP 4.0.b2, adds an annotation in the rectangle bounded by the *llx,lly* and *urx,ury* points. The parameters *title* and *content* set the title and content values of the annotation, respectively.

XML Parser

The XML parser functions available in PHP enable you to parse, but not validate, XML documents. The extension lets you create parsers that have corresponding handlers for each XML event. Note that case-folding, in XML parlance, simply means uppercasing, and all element names that are passed to the handlers are uppercased. To include XML support using Apache 1.3.7 or later, just pass `--with-xml` as an argument to PHP's configure. Prior versions of Apache require that you include the expat library, which can be found at `http://www.jclark.com/xml/`.

xml_parser_create()

Syntax

```
int xml_parser_create ([string encoding ])
```

Description

The `xml_parser_create()` function, which was added in PHP 3.0.6 and PHP 4, establishes an XML parser using the specified *encoding* method, which can be

ISO-8859-1 (default), US-ASCII, or UTF-8, and returns a handle to the parser for subsequent XML function calls.

xml_set_object()

Syntax

```
void xml_set_object (int parser, object &object)
```

Description

The xml_set_object() function, which was added in PHP 4.0b4, enables you to use the *parser* inside the *object*. This allows you to reference the parser created with xml_parser_create() inside your class.

```php
<?php

class xmlobject   {
var $parser;
function xmlobject() {
    $this->parser = xml_parser_create();
    xml_set_object($this->parser,&$this);
    xml_set_element_handler($this->parser,"tag_open","tag_close");
    xml_set_character_data_handler($this->parser,"cdata");
}
//xmlobject methods…
} // end of class xml
?>
```

xml_set_element_handler()

Syntax

```
int xml_set_element_handler (int parser,
string startElementHandler, string endElementHandler)
```

Description

The xml_set_element_handler() function, which was added in PHP 3.0.6 and PHP 4.0, identifies the *startElementHandler* and *endElementHandler* functions for the XML parser *parser*. If either handler string is FALSE or empty, the *parser* will be disabled. The return value is TRUE if the handlers were set up successfully and FALSE if the parser is invalid. The *startElementHandler* function must have three parameters:

- parser—An integer value that is a reference to the XML parser that called the handler function.

- name—A string that contains the name of the element for which this handler is called. Case-folding will cause the name to be in uppercase characters.

- attribs—An associative array with the element's attributes, where the name is the key and values are the attribute's values. The attribute name values may be case-folded along with the element names, but the attribute values are not case-folded.

The *endElementHandler* function must have two parameters:

- parser—An integer value that is a reference to the XML parser that called the handle.

- name—A string that contains the name of the element for which this handler is called. Case-folding will cause the name to be in uppercase characters.

xml_set_character_data_handler()

Syntax

```
int xml_set_character_data_handler (int parser, string handler)
```

Description

The xml_set_character_data_handler() function, which was added in PHP 3.0.6 and PHP 4, defines the character data-handler function for the XML parser *parser*. The *handler* parameter contains the name of a function that must exist when xml_parse() is called for *parser*. If the handler function is empty or FALSE, the *parser* will be disabled. A return value of TRUE indicates that the *handler* function was set properly, and FALSE indicates that *parser* is invalid. The *handler* function must take two parameters:

- parser—A reference to the XML parser which called the handler

- data—The character string

xml_set_processing_instruction_handler()

Syntax

```
int xml_set_processing_instruction_handler (int parser, string handler)
```

Description

The xml_set_processing_instruction_handler() function, which was added in PHP 3.0.6 and PHP 4.0, sets the processing instruction handler for the given *parser*. The processing function must follow this format:

```
<?

    target
    data?>
```

You can also put PHP code into the tag, but the limitation is that in an XML processing instruction (PI), the PI end tag '?>' cannot be quoted. If the handler function is empty or FALSE, the *parser* will be disabled. A return value of TRUE indicates that the *handler* function was set properly, and FALSE indicates that *parser* is invalid. The *handler* function must take three parameters:

- parser—An integer value that is a reference to the XML parser that called the handler function

- target—A string that contains the PI target

- data—A string that contains the PI data

xml_set_default_handler()

Syntax

```
int xml_set_default_handler (int parser, string handler)
```

Description

The xml_set_default_handler() function, which was added in PHP 3.0.6 and PHP 4.0, sets the default *handler* function for the given *parser*. If the handler function is empty or FALSE, the *parser* will be disabled. A return value of TRUE indicates that the *handler* function was set properly, and FALSE indicates that *parser* is invalid. The *handler* function must take two parameters:

- parser—An integer value that is a reference to the XML parser that called the handler function

- data—A string that contains the character data. This handles any data for which no previous handler has been specified.

xml_set_unparsed_entity_decl_handler()

Syntax

```
int xml_set_unparsed_entity_decl_handler (int parser, string handler)
```

Description

The xml_set_unparsed_entity_decl_handler() function, which was added in PHP 3.0.6 and PHP 4.0, sets the unparsed entity declaration *handler* function for a given *parser*. The handler is utilized when the parser sees an external entity declaration containing an NDATA declaration, such as

```
<!ENTITY name {publicId | systemId}

     NDATA notationName>
```

If the handler function is empty or FALSE, the *parser* will be disabled. A return value of TRUE indicates that the *handler* function was set properly, and FALSE indicates that *parser* is invalid. The *handler* function must take six parameters:

- parser—An integer that references the XML parser that called the handler.

- entityName—A string that names the entity you are defining.

- base—A string that resolves the system identifier (systemID) of an external entity. Current implantations support only an empty string for this value.

- systemId—A string that is the system identifier for the external entity.

- publicId—A string that is the public identifier for the external entity.

- notationName—A string that is the notation of this entry.

xml_set_notation_decl_handler()

Syntax

```
int xml_set_notation_decl_handler (int parser, string handler)
```

Description

The `xml_set_notation_decl_handler()` function, which was added in PHP 3.0.6 and PHP 4.0, sets the notation declaration *handler* for a given *parser*. The notation declaration handler is found in a document's DTD and is formatted as follows:

```
<!NOTATION

name {systemId |
publicID}>
```

If the handler function is empty or FALSE, the *parser* will be disabled. A return value of TRUE indicates that the *handler* function was set properly, and FALSE indicates that *parser* is invalid. The *handler* function must take five parameters:

- parser—An integer that references the XML parser that called the handler.

- notationname—A string that is the notation's name. This format is described earlier.

- base—A string that resolves the system identifier (systemID) of the notation declaration. Current implementations support only an empty string for this value.

- systemId—A string that is the system identifier for the external notation declaration.

- publicId—A string that is the public identifier for the external notation declaration.

xml_set_external_entity_ref_handler()

Syntax

```
int xml_set_external_entity_ref_handler (int parser, string handler)
```

Description

The xml_set_external_entity_ref_handler() function, which was added in PHP 3.0.6 and PHP 4, sets the external entity reference handler for the specified *parser*. If the handler function is empty or FALSE, the handler will be disabled. A return value of TRUE indicates that the *handler* function was set properly, and FALSE indicates that *parser* is invalid. The *handler* function must take five parameters:

- parser—An integer that references the XML parser that called the handler.

- openEntityName—A string that is a space-separated list of the names of the entities that are open for the parse of this entity.

- base—A string that resolves the system identifier (systemID) of the notation declaration. Current implementations support only an empty string for this value.

- systemId—A string that is the system identifier for the external notation declaration.

- publicId—A string that is the public identifier for the external notation declaration.

xml_parse()

Syntax

```
int xml_parse (int parser, string data [,int isFinal])
```

Description

The xml_parse() function, which was added in PHP 3.0.6 and PHP 4.0, begins the parsing of an XML document. The *parser* parameter identifies which parser to use and the *data* parameter is the piece of data to be parsed. The *isFinal* parameter is used to indicate the last piece of the data to parse (TRUE). The function returns TRUE on success and FALSE otherwise.

xml_get_error_code()

Syntax

```
int xml_get_error_code (int parser)
```

Description

The `xml_get_error_code()` function, which was added in PHP 3.0.6 and PHP 4, returns the XML error code. It returns FALSE if *parser* is invalid.

xml_error_string()

Syntax

```
string xml_error_string (int code)
```

Description

The `string_xml_error_string()` function, which was added in PHP 3.0.6 and PHP 4.0, returns the textual description of the error code parameter *code*, or FALSE if no description for the code exists.

xml_get_current_line_number()

Syntax

```
int xml_get_current_line_number (int parser)
```

Description

The `xml_get_current_line_number()` function, which was added in PHP 3.0.6 and PHP 4.0, returns the line number that the *parser* is currently processing.

xml_get_current_column_number()

Syntax

```
int xml_get_current_column_number (int parser)
```

Description

The `xml_get_current_column_number()` function, which was added in PHP 3.0.6 and PHP 4.0, returns the column number on the current line that the *parser* is currently processing.

xml_get_current_byte_index()

Syntax

```
int xml_get_current_byte_index (int parser)
```

Description

The `xml_get_current_byte_index()` function, which was added in PHP 3.0.6 and PHP 4.0, returns the byte index that the *parser* is currently processing.

xml_parser_free()

Syntax

```
string xml_parser_free (int parser)
```

Description

The `xml_parser_free()` function, which was added in PHP 3.0.6 and PHP 4.0, frees the *parser* and returns TRUE if successful; otherwise, it returns FALSE.

xml_parser_set_option()

Syntax

```
int xml_parser_set_option (int parser, int option, mixed value)
```

Description

The `xml_parser_set_option()` function, which was added in PHP 3.0.6 and PHP 4.0, sets an option for the specified *parser*. The possible option values are `XML_OPTION_CASE_FOLDING`, which is an integer used to turn case-folding on and off (on by default), and `XML_OPTION_TARGET_ENCODING`, a string used set the target encoding type. Encoding types include `ISO-8859-1`, `US-ASCII`, and `UTF-8`.

xml_parser_get_option()

Syntax

```
mixed xml_parser_get_option (int parser, int option)
```

Description

The xml_parser_get_option() function, which was added in PHP 3.0.6 and PHP 4.0, returns the value of the specified *option*. See xml_parser_set_option() for the possible values.

utf8_decode()

Syntax

```
string utf8_decode (string data)
```

Description

The utf8_decode() function, which was added in PHP 3.0.6 and PHP 4.0, decodes a character string with UTF-8 encoding to single-byte ISO-8859-1 encoding.

utf8_encode()

Syntax

```
string utf8_encode (string data)
```

Description

The utf8_encode() function, which was added in PHP 3.0.6 and PHP 4.0, encodes a character string with ISO-8859-1 encoding to UTF-8 encoding.

CHAPTER 9

System Extensions

This chapter describes the PHP functions that interact with the operating system. These functions return information about users, directories, files, and processes. They provide information about the system and allow access to files and directories.

This chapter also contains specific information about how to interact with NIS and retrieve information from POSIX system calls. There are also functions that enable you to manage shared memory, semaphores, and execute external scripts or programs and return the information to PHP.

Directory

This section describes the functions that are used to open, read, change, rewind, and close directories. Remember that permissions are important when using these functions. If the user that is running the PHP script does not have permissions to perform the operation, the function will return an error.

chdir()

Syntax

```
int chdir(string directory);
```

Description

The chdir() function changes the current working directory to *directory*. This function returns true, 1, if the function is successful; false, 0, is returned if there is a problem changing directories.

dir()

Syntax

```
new dir(string directory);
```

Description

The dir() function uses object-oriented methodology for creating a directory object defined by *directory*. This function returns two properties: *handle* and *path*. The *handle* property can be used with other directory functions, such as readdir() and closedir(). It behaves exactly as if the directory were opened using the opendir() function. The *path* property is set to the directory that was opened. This should always be the same as the string *directory* that was used to call the function. There are three methods—read, rewind, and close—available with this function. They operate the same as readdir(), rewinddir(), and closedir().

closedir()

Syntax

```
void closedir(int dir_handle);
```

Description

The closedir() function closes the directory defined by *dir_handle*. The stream must have previously been opened by opendir() or dir().

opendir()

Syntax

```
int opendir(string path);
```

Description

The opendir() function opens the directory defined by *path* and returns a directory handle. This directory handle is used when calling closedir(), readdir(), and rewinddir().

readdir()

Syntax

```
string readdir(int dir_handle);
```

Description

The readdir() function returns the name of the next file from the directory defined by *dir_handle*. The filenames returned are not ordered or sorted in any particular way.

rewinddir()

Syntax

```
void rewinddir(int dir_handle);
```

Description

The rewinddir() function resets the pointer for the directory defined by *dir_handle* to the beginning of the directory stream.

Filesystem

This section describes functions that provide information about a system's files, directories, permissions, and users. These functions enable you to read files, change and set permissions, create links, and return statistics about files and directories. Permissions are important when using these functions; if the user who is running PHP does not have permissions to perform the operation, an error will be returned.

> **Note**
> Remember that PHP typically runs as the user nobody, or some other user with limited system access.

basename()

Syntax

```
string basename(string path);
```

Description

The `basename()` function returns the filename portion of the path defined by `path`. Given a string containing a path to a file, this function will return only the name of the file.

chgrp()

Syntax

```
int chgrp(string filename, mixed group);
```

Description

The `chgrp()` function changes the group to which the file defined by `filename` belongs to the group defined by `group`. All UNIX permissions apply to the execution of this function. Users can only change the group to another group of which the user is a member. This function returns false, 0, if it encounters a problem.

Because Windows systems do not have an equivalent, this function always returns true, 1, and the function does nothing.

chmod()

Syntax

```
int chmod(string filename, int mode);
```

Description

The chmod() function changes the permissions of the file specified by *filename* to the mode defined by *mode* (see Tables 9.1 and 9.2). The parameter passed as *mode* is not assumed to be octal unless it is preceded with a zero.

Table 9.1 *Permissions on a UNIX System*

Mode	Permission
0(000)	No permissions
1(001)	Execute
2(010)	Write
3(011)	Write and execute
4(100)	Read
5(101)	Read and execute
6(110)	Read and write
7(111)	Read, write, and execute

Table 9.2 *Permissions on a Windows system*

Mode	Permission
1(0000100)	Execute
2(0000200)	Write
4(0000400)	Read

> **Note**
> The only permission used on a Windows system is the read-only permission. This is because all files on a Windows system are readable and writeable (if the directory is accessible). Execution is determined by the extension of the file (that is, .com, .exe, .bat, and so on) and not by an execute permission.

chown()

Syntax

```
int chown(string filename, mixed user);
```

Description

The chown() function changes the owner of the file defined by *filename* to the user specified by *user*. If the function is successful, true, 1, is returned. UNIX permissions apply to the execution of this function such that only root (or a user with superuser privileges) can change the owner of a file.

Because Windows systems do not have an equivalent, this function always returns true, 1, and the function does nothing.

clearstatcache()

Syntax

```
void clearstatcache(void);
```

Description

The clearstartcache() function clears the stat cache. Because of the resources required when executing stat or lstat system calls, PHP caches the results of the last call and those results are used in each subsequent call. This function takes no parameters and returns no status, but is used to force a new status check when calling the following functions:

stat()	lstat()	file_exists()
is_writeable()	is_readable()	is_executable()
is_file()	is_dir()	is_link()
filectime()	fileatime()	filemtime()
fileinode()	filegroup()	fileowner()
filesize()	filetype()	fileperms()

copy()

Syntax

```
int copy(string source, string dest);
```

Description

The copy() function makes a copy of the file specified in *source* and places it in the destination defined by *dest*. The function returns true, 1, if it is successful and false, 0, if it fails.

dirname()

Syntax

```
string dirname(string path);
```

Description

The dirname() function returns the directory portion of the string passed as *path*.

On Windows, both the forward slash (/) and the backslash (\) are used as path separator characters. In UNIX environments, only the forward slash (/) is used.

diskfreespace()

Syntax

```
float diskfreespace(string directory);
```

Description

The diskfreespace() function takes a string, *directory*, and returns the number of bytes available on the corresponding disk.

fclose()

Syntax

```
int fclose(int fp);
```

Description

The fclose() function closes the file corresponding to the file pointer *fp*. The function returns true, 1, on success and false, 0, if the file pointer is invalid or was not successfully opened with fopen() or fsockopen().

feof()

Syntax

```
int feof(int fp);
```

Description

The foef() function returns true, 1, if the file pointer specified by *fp* reached an End of File (EOF) or if an error occurs.

> **Note**
> The file referenced by *fp* must point to a file successfully opened by fopen(), popen(), or fsockopen().

fgetc()

Syntax

```
string fgetc(int fp);
```

Description

The fgetc() function returns a string containing a single character read from the file pointed to by *fp* and increments the file pointer, *fp*, one character. This function returns false, 0, if the end of file (EOF) is reached.

fgetcsv()

Syntax

```
array fgetcsv(int fp, int length, string [delimiter]);
```

Description

The fgetcsv() function gets a line of data from a comma-separated value (CSV) file referenced by the file pointer, *fp*. It returns an array with the values separated by the optional *delimiter*. If *delimiter* is not specified, a comma (,) is assumed. The parameter *length* is the longest line of the CSV file allowing for trailing carriage returns and line feeds.

> **Note**
> A blank line in the input CSV file will be translated into an array with one null field. The blank line will not be interpreted as an error.

fgets()

Syntax

```
string fgets(int fp, int length);
```

Description

The fgets() function reads the file referenced by *fp*, and returns a string of *length*–1. If an end of file (EOF) is reached, the *length* parameter is ignored and the string is returned. The function will return false, 0, if there is an error reading the file.

fgetss()

Syntax

```
string fgetss(int fp, int length, string [allowable_tags]);
```

Description

The fgetss() function reads the file referenced by *fp*, and returns a string of *length*–1. If an end of file (EOF) is reached, the *length* parameter is ignored and the string is returned. This function strips out any HTML or PHP tags from the input file. The optional parameter *allowable_tags* defines any tags that are not to be stripped out of the input file. The function will return false, 0, if there is an error reading the file.

file()

Syntax

```
array file(string filename, int [use_include_path]);
```

Description

The `file()` function reads the file specified by *filename* and returns an array containing each line of the file. If the optional parameter *include_path* is set to 1, the file will be searched for in the include path.

file_exists()

Syntax

```
int file_exists(string filename);
```

Description

The `file_exists()` function checks for the file defined by *filename* and if it exists, the function returns true, 1. If the file doesn't exist, false, (0) is returned.

> **Note**
> The results of this function are cached by PHP. Any subsequent calls to `file_exists()` will return the same results even if the environment has changed. The cache is cleared through the `clearstatcache()` function.

fileatime()

Syntax

```
int fileatime(string filename);
```

Description

The `fileatime()` function returns the last access time of the file defined by *filename*. The format of this time is the standard UNIX time format, which is the number of seconds since the start of the UNIX epoch, or January 1, 1970. The function returns false, 0, if an error is returned.

> **Note**
> The results of this function are cached by PHP. Any subsequent calls to `fileatime()` will return the same results even if the environment has changed. The cache is cleared through the `clearstatcache()` function.

filectime()

Syntax

```
int filectime(string filename);
```

Description

The filectime() function returns the last changed time of the file specified by filename. The format of this time is the standard UNIX time format, which is the number of seconds since the start of the UNIX epoch, or January 1, 1970. This function returns false, 0, if an error was encountered.

> **Note**
> The results of this function are cached by PHP. Any subsequent calls to filectime() will return the same results even if the environment has changed. The cache is cleared through the clearstatcache() function.

filegroup()

Syntax

```
int filegroup(string filename);
```

Description

The filegroup() function returns the group identifier (GID) of the owner of the file specified by filename. This function returns false, 0, if an error is encountered. Windows always returns false, 0.

> **Note**
> The results of this function are cached by PHP. Any subsequent calls to filegroup() will return the same results even if the environment has changed. The cache is cleared through the clearstatcache() function.

fileinode()

Syntax

```
int fileinode(string filename);
```

Description

The `fileinode()` function returns the inode number of the file specified by filename. This function returns false, 0, if an error is encountered. Because Windows does not have an equivalent, it always returns false, 0.

Note
The results of this function are cached by PHP. Any subsequent calls to `fileinode()` will return the same results even if the environment has changed. The cache is cleared through the `clearstatcache()` function.

---

filemtime()

Syntax

```
int filemtime(string filename);
```

Description

The `filemtime()` function returns the last modified time of the file specified by *filename*. The format of this time is the standard UNIX time format, which is the number of seconds since the start of the UNIX epoch, or January 1, 1970. This function returns false, 0, if an error is encountered.

Note
The results of this function are cached by PHP. Any subsequent calls to `filemtime()` will return the same results even if the environment has changed. The cache is cleared through the `clearstatcache()` function.

---

fileowner()

Syntax

```
int fileowner(string filename);
```

Description

The `fileowner()` function returns the user identifier (UID) of the owner of the file specified in *filename*. This function returns false, 0, if an error is encountered. Because Windows does not have an equivalent, it always returns false, 0.

> **Note**
> The results of this function are cached by PHP. Any subsequent calls to `fileowner()` will
> return the same results even if the environment has changed. The cache is cleared through
> the `clearstatcache()` function.

fileperms()

Syntax

```
int fileperms(string filename);
```

Description

The `fileperms()` function returns the permissions on the file specified by `filename` (see Tables 9.3 and 9.4). The permissions are returned in the standard octal or binary format. This function returns false, `0`, if an error is encountered.

Table 9.3 *Permissions Returned by* `fileperms()` *on a UNIX System*

Mode	Permission
0(000)	No permissions
1(001)	Execute
2(010)	Write
3(011)	Write and execute
4(100)	Read
5(101)	Read and execute
6(110)	Read and write
7(111)	Read, write, and execute

Table 9.4 *Permissions Returned by* `fileperms()` *on a Windows System*

Mode	Permission
7(111)	Execute—files with a .exe or .bat extension
6(110)	Write—normal files
4(100)	Read—files with the read-only attribute

> **Note**
> The results of this function are cached by PHP. Any subsequent calls to `fileperms()` will return the same results even if the environment has changed. The cache is cleared through the `clearstatcache()`function.

filesize()

Syntax

```
int filesize(string filename);
```

Description

The `filesize()` function returns the size, in bytes, of the file specified in *filename*. This function returns false, 0, if an error is encountered.

> **Note**
> The results of this function are cached by PHP. Any subsequent calls to `filesize()` will return the same results even if the environment has changed. The cache is cleared through the `clearstatcache()` function.

filetype()

Syntax

```
string filetype(string filename);
```

Description

The `filetype()` function returns the type of the file specified in *filename*. The file types returned are `fifo`, `char`, `dir`, `block`, `link`, `file`, and `unknown`. In Windows, this function returns either file or directory. This function returns false, 0, if an error is encountered.

> **Note**
> The results of this function are cached by PHP. Any subsequent calls to `filetype()` will return the same results even if the environment has changed. The cache is cleared through the `clearstatcache()` function.

flock()

Syntax

```
bool flock(int fp, int operation);
```

Description

The flock() function locks the file referenced by *fp*. This function uses a method of locking that requires all other programs to lock the file in the same way. The methods of locking the file are listed in Table 9.5.

Table 9.5   *Operation Parameters Used by the* flock() *Function*

Function	Operation	Binary
Shared lock	1	001
Exclusive lock	2	010
Release a lock	3	011
Shared lock without blocking	5	101
Exclusive lock without blocking	6	110

> **Note**
> The flock() function works on Windows platforms and UNIX platforms.

The flock() function returns true, 1, if the operation is successful.

fopen()

Syntax

```
int fopen(string filename, string mode, int [use_include_path]);
```

Description

The fopen() function opens the file specified by *filename* and a pointer to the file is returned. The *mode* defines the mode in which the file will be opened. The *mode* options are listed in Table 9.6.

Table 9.6   *Modes for the* fopen() *Function*

mode	Description
r	Opens the file in read-only mode and places the file pointer, *fp*, at the beginning of the file.
r+	Opens the file in read/write mode and places the file pointer, *fp*, at the beginning of the file.
w	Creates a new file in write mode and places the file pointer, *fp*, at the beginning of the file. If a file exists, it is overwritten with the new file.
w+	Creates a new file in read/write mode and places the file pointer, *fp*, at the beginning of the file. If the file exists, it is overwritten with the new file.
a	Opens the file in write mode and places the file pointer, *fp*, at the end of the file. If the file does not exist, it will be created.
a+	Opens the file in read/write mode and places the file pointer, *fp*, at the end of the file. If the file does not exist, it will be created.

If *filename* begins with "http://", an HTTP 1.0 connection will be opened to the URL and the file pointer will be placed at the beginning of the response text.

If *filename* begins with "ftp://", an FTP connection will be opened to the specified server and the file pointer will be placed at the beginning of the requested file.

> **Note**
> An error will be returned if the FTP server does not support passive mode.

The optional parameter *use_include_path* can be set to "1" if you want to use the *include_path* to search for the file.

fpassthru()

Syntax

```
int fpassthru(int fp);
```

Description

The fpassthru() function reads the file pointed to by *fp* and writes the file to standard out, which is usually the browser. The file is read until End of File, EOF. This function returns true, 1, if the function is successful.

fputs()

Syntax

```
int fputs(int fp, string str, int [length]);
```

Description

The fputs() function is identical to the fwrite() function. It writes the contents of *string* to the file defined by *fp*. The *length* parameter is optional and if it is not specified, the entire string will be written; otherwise, writing will stop after *length* bytes are written. This function returns false, 0, if an error occurred.

fread()

Syntax

```
string fread(int fp, int length);
```

Description

The fread() function reads *length* bytes from the file referenced by *fp*. Reading stops when *length* bytes have been read or EOF is reached, whichever comes first.

fseek()

Syntax

```
int fseek(int fp, int offset);
```

Description

The fseek() function sets the file pointer, *fp*, to *offset* bytes from the start of the file.

Note
The fseek() function will not return an error if you seek past the end of the file, EOF.

---

ftell()

Syntax

```
int ftell(int fp);
```

Description

The ftell() function returns the position of the file pointer referenced by *fp*. The function returns false, 0, if it is not successful.

fwrite()

Syntax

```
int fwrite(int fp, string string, int [length]);
```

Description

The fwrite() function writes the contents of *string* to the file defined by *fp*. The *length* parameter is optional and if it is not specified, the entire string will be written; otherwise, writing will stop after *length* bytes are written.

set_file_buffer()

Syntax

```
int fwrite(int fp, int buffer);
```

Description

The set_file_buffer() function sets the buffering for write operations to the file referenced by *fp* to *buffer* bytes. If the *buffer* parameter is 0, write operations are unbuffered.

is_dir()

Syntax

```
bool is_dir(string filename);
```

Description

The is_dir() function returns true, 1, if *filename* exists and is a directory.

> **Note**
> The results of this function are cached by PHP. Any subsequent calls to is_dir() will
> return the same results even if the environment has changed. The cache is cleared through
> the clearstatcache() function.

is_executable()

Syntax

```
bool is_executable(string filename);
```

Description

The is_executable() function returns true, 1, if the *filename* exists and is executable.
On UNIX systems, this will also return true, 1, if a directory has the execute
permission set.

> **Note**
> The results of this function are cached by PHP. Any subsequent calls to is_executable()
> will return the same results even if the environment has changed. The cache is cleared
> through the clearstatcache()function.

is_file()

Syntax

```
bool is_file(string filename);
```

Description

The is_file() function returns true, 1, if the *filename* exists and is a file.

> **Note**
> The results of this function are cached by PHP. Any subsequent calls to is_file() will
> return the same results even if the environment has changed. The cache is cleared through
> the clearstatcache() function.

is_link()

Syntax

```
bool is_link(string filename);
```

Description

The is_link() function returns true, 1, if the *filename* exists and is a symbolic link.

> **Note**
> The results of this function are cached by PHP. Any subsequent calls to is_link() will return the same results even if the environment has changed. The cache is cleared through the clearstatcache() function.

is_readable()

Syntax

```
bool is_readable(string filename);
```

Description

The is_readable() function returns true, 1, if the *filename* exists and is readable. On UNIX systems, this will also return true, 1, if a directory has the read permission set. On Windows, this function always returns true, 1.

> **Note**
> The results of this function are cached by PHP. Any subsequent calls to is_executable() will return the same results even if the environment has changed. The cache is cleared through the clearstatcache() function.

is_writeable()

Syntax

```
bool is_writeable(string filename);
```

Description

The is_writeable() function returns true, 1, if the *filename* exists and is writeable. On UNIX systems, this will also return true, 1, if a directory has the write permission set.

> **Note**
> The results of this function are cached by PHP. Any subsequent calls to is_writeable() will return the same results even if the environment has changed. The cache is cleared through the clearstatcache() function.

link()

Syntax

```
int link(string target, string link);
```

Description

The link() function creates a hard link from *target* to *link*. This function does nothing on Windows.

linkinfo()

Syntax

```
int linkinfo(string path);
```

Description

The linkinfo() function verifies the existence of the link referenced by *path*. This function returns true, 1, if the link exists.

mkdir()

Syntax

```
int mkdir(string pathname, int mode);
```

Description

The mkdir() function creates the directory specified by *pathname*.

The *mode* parameter specifies the permission on the directory and should be in octal format (see Table 9.7). For example, all permissions for the user, read and execute for the group, and read and execute for the world would be represented by 0755.

Table 9.7   *Valid Modes on a UNIX System*

Mode	Permission
0	No permissions
1	Execute
2	Write
3	Write and execute
4	Read
5	Read and execute
6	Read and write
7	Read, write, and execute

> **Note**
> The *mode* argument is ignored on a Windows system.

pclose()

Syntax

```
int pclose(int fp);
```

Description

The pclose() function closes the file pointer, *fp*, to a pipe opened by popen().

This function returns the termination status of the process that was run through the popen() function.

popen()

Syntax

```
int popen(string command, string mode);
```

Description

The popen() function forks the process defined by *command* and opens a pipe to the output. The *mode* parameter can be either r or w and the function returns a file pointer that is placed at the beginning of the piped output. This function returns false, 0, if an error is returned.

readfile()

Syntax

```
int readfile(string filename, int [use_include_path]);
```

Description

The readfile() function reads an entire file defined by *filename* and writes it to standard out, which is usually the browser. This function returns the number of bytes read. False is returned if an error occurs.

If *filename* begins with "http://" or "ftp://", a connection is opened to the appropriate server and the text of the response is written to standard output.

The optional parameter *use_include_path* can be set to "1", if you want to search for the file in the include path.

readlink()

Syntax

```
string readlink(string path);
```

Description

The readlink() function returns the destination of the symbolic link defined by *path*. This function returns false, 0, if there is an error.

rename()

Syntax

```
int rename(string oldname, string newname);
```

Description

The rename() function renames the file or directory defined by *oldname* to the name specified in *newname*. This function returns true, 1, if the process is successful.

rewind()

Syntax

```
int rewind(int fp);
```

Description

The rewind() function sets the file pointer, *fp*, to the beginning of the file. This function returns false, 0, if there is an error.

rmdir()

Syntax

```
int rmdir(string dirname);
```

Description

The rmdir() function removes the directory defined by *dirname*. Permissions must be adequate for the operation to be completed and the directory must not contain any files. This function returns true, 1, if the function is successful.

stat()

Syntax

```
array stat(string filename);
```

Description

The stat() function returns the information shown in Table 9.8 on the file defined by *filename*.

Table 9.8 *Contents of the* stat() *Array*

Name	Description
Device/drive Letter	This is the device on which the file resides or the drive number (0, 1, 2, ...) on a Windows system.
Inode	The inode of the file. Zero in Windows.
Inode mode	The read, write, execute permissions on the file.
Number of links	The number of links to the file. Windows always returns 1.
User	The user ID (UID) of the owner of the file. Windows always returns 0.
Group	The group ID (GID) of the owner of the file. Windows always returns 0.
Device type/drive letter	This is the device type on a UNIX system. Windows returns the drive letter.
Size	The size of the file in bytes.
Last access time	The last time the file was accessed.
Last modified time	The last time the file was modified.
Last changed time	The last time the file was changed. On Windows, this is the creation time.
Block size	The block size for file I/O. This is −1 in the Windows environment.
Number of blocks	Number of blocks used by the file. Windows returns a −1.

> **Note**
> The results of this function are cached by PHP. Any subsequent calls to stat() will return the same results even if the environment has changed. The cache is cleared through the clearstatcache() function.

lstat()

Syntax

```
array lstat(string filename);
```

Description

The lstat() function is identical to the stat() function except that this function also returns information about a symbolic link defined by *filename*. If the link is a symbolic link, the information about the link, shown in Table 9.9, is returned.

Table 9.9   *Contents of the* lstats() *Array*

Name	Description
Device/drive letter	This is the device on which the file resides or the drive number (0, 1, 2, ...) on a Windows system.
Inode	The inode of the file. Zero in Windows.
Number of links	The number of links to the file. Windows always returns 1.
User	The user ID (UID) of the owner of the file. Windows always returns 0.
Group	The Group ID (GID) of the owner of the file. Windows always returns 0.
Device type/drive letter	This is the device type on a UNIX system. Windows returns the drive letter.
Size	The size of the file in bytes.
Last access time	The last time the file was accessed.
Last modified time	The last time the file was modified.
Last changed time	The last time the file was changed. On Windows, this is the creation time.
Block size	The block size for file I/O. This is –1 in the Windows environment.
Number of blocks	Number of blocks used by the file. Windows returns a –1.

> **Note**
> The results of this function are cached by PHP. Any subsequent calls to lstat() will return the same results even if the environment has changed. The cache is cleared through the clearstatcache() function.

symlink()

Syntax

```
int symlink(string target, string link);
```

Description

The symlink() function creates a symbolic link from *target* to the destination specified by *link*.

tempnam()

Syntax

```
string tempnam(string dir, string prefix);
```

Description

The `tempnam()` function creates a unique filename in the directory specified by *dir*. If the directory doesn't exist, the file will be created in the system's temporary directory. The optional string defined by *prefix* will be prepended to the filename.

This function will read the environment of the operating system if *dir* is not supplied and will place the file in the temporary directory. This is defined by the `TMPDIR` environment variable in UNIX and the `TMP` environment variable in Windows.

touch()

Syntax

```
int touch(string filename, int time);
```

Description

The `touch()` function changes the last modified time of the file defined by *filename* to *time*. If no time is given, the last modified time of the file is set to the current time. The format of this time is the standard UNIX time format, which is the number of seconds since the start of the UNIX epoch, or January 1, 1970. If the file does not exist, one is created. This function returns true, 1, if successful.

umask()

Syntax

```
int umask(int mask);
```

Description

The `umask()` function sets PHP's umask to *mask*. This function is used to define the default permissions on a file when it is created. This function returns the old umask if successful and false, 0, if an error is encountered. If the function is called without any options, the current umask is returned.

unlink()

Syntax

```
int unlink(string filename);
```

Description

The unlink() function deletes the file defined by *filename*. The function returns true, 1, if the operation is successful.

NIS

Network Information System, NIS, was developed by Sun Microsystems in the 1980s as a tool to help network administrators centralize the administration critical system files. NIS evolved into an architecture that provides a distributed database service for managing any file or groups of files on a network. NIS provides centralized administration of these files and makes it easy to propagate a single change to every machine in the NIS domain.

This section assumes that you have a working knowledge of NIS and understand what NIS domains, NIS maps, masters, slaves, and netgroups are.

yp_get_default_domain()

Syntax

```
int yp_get_default_domain(void);
```

Description

The yp_get_default_domain() function returns the default domain of the node. This is often used for retrieving the domain parameter for subsequent NIS calls. This function returns false, 0, if the function encounters an error.

yp_order()

Syntax

```
int yp_order(string domain, string map);
```

Description

The yp_order() function returns the order number for a *map* in the specified *domain*. This function returns false, **0**, if an error occurs.

yp_master()

Syntax

```
string yp_master(string domain, string map);
```

Description

The yp_master() function returns the machine name of the master NIS server for a *map* in the specified *domain*. This function returns false, **0**, if it is not successful.

yp_match()

Syntax

```
string yp_match(string domain, string map, string key);
```

Description

The yp_match() function returns the value associated with the parameter *key* from the specified *map* for the specified *domain*. This function returns false, **0**, if it is unsuccessful.

yp_first()

Syntax

```
string[] yp_first(string domain, string map);
```

Description

The yp_first() function returns the first key/value pair from the named *map* in the specified *domain*. If the function encounters an error, false (**0**) is returned.

yp_next()

Syntax

```
string[] yp_next(string domain, string map, string key);
```

Description

The yp_next() function returns the next key/value pair in the named *map* after the specified *key* for the specified *domain*. This function returns false, 0, if an error occurred.

yp_errno()

Syntax

```
int yp_errno(void);
```

Description

The yp_errno() function returns the error code if the previous NIS operation failed (see Table 9.10).

Table 9.10 *Possible Errors Returned by* yp_errno()

Number	Description
1	The arguments to the function are not valid.
2	The Remote Procedure Call, RPC, failed. The domain has been unbound.
3	The server in this domain cannot be bound.
4	The specified map in this server's domain is invalid.
5	The specified key is not valid in the specified map.
6	Internal NIS error.
7	Resource allocation error.
8	No more records in the map database.
9	Communication error with the portmapper.
10	Communication error with ypbind.
11	Communication error with ypserv.
12	The local domain name is not set.
13	The yp database is corrupt.
14	There is a yp version conflict.
15	Access violation.
16	The database is busy.

yp_err_string()

Syntax

```
string yp_err_string(void);
```

Description

The yp_err_string() function returns the error message if the previous NIS operation failed (see Table 9.11).

Table 9.11   *Possible Errors Returned by* yp_err_string()

Number	Description
1	The arguments to the function are not valid.
2	The Remote Procedure Call, RPC, failed. The domain has been unbound.
3	The server in this domain cannot be bound.
4	The specified map in this server's domain is invalid.
5	The specified key is not valid in the specified map.
6	Internal NIS error.
7	Resource allocation error.
8	No more records in the map database.
9	Communication error with the portmapper.
10	Communication error with ypbind.
11	Communication error with ypserv.
12	The local domain name is not set.
13	The yp database is corrupt.
14	There is a yp version conflict.
15	Access violation.
16	The database is busy.

POSIX

This section describes the POSIX commands included in PHP4. POSIX (Portable Operating System Interface) is an IEEE standard that was designed to make code easier to port between UNIX operating systems. Ultimately, POSIX is an attempt by a group of vendors to create a single standard program interface for every version of UNIX. The POSIX standard defines how a system function will be called, what information will be returned, and how the information will be formatted.

posix_kill()

Syntax

```
bool posix_kill(int pid, int sig);
```

Description

The posix_kill() function sends the signal specified by *sig* to the process identified by *pid*. This function returns false, 0, if the function is not successful.

posix_getpid()

Syntax

```
int posix_getpid(void);
```

Description

The posix_getpid() function returns the process identifier (PID) of the current process. This function returns false, 0, if the function is not successful.

posix_getppid()

Syntax

```
int posix_getppid(void);
```

Description

The posix_getppid() function returns the process identifier (PID) of the parent process of the current process. This function returns false, 0, if the function is not successful.

posix_getuid()

Syntax

```
int posix_getuid(void);
```

Description

The `posix_getuid()` function returns the numeric real user ID (UID) of the current process. This function returns false, **0**, if the function is not successful.

posix_geteuid()

Syntax

```
int posix_geteuid(void);
```

Description

The `posix_geteuid()` function returns the numeric effective user ID (UID) of the current process. This function returns false, **0**, if the function is not successful.

posix_getgid()

Syntax

```
int posix_getgid(void);
```

Description

The `posix_getgid()` function returns the numeric real group ID (GID) of the current process. This function returns false, **0**, if the function is not successful.

posix_getegid()

Syntax

```
int posix_getegid(void);
```

Description

The `posix_getegid()` function returns the numeric effective group ID (GID) of the current process. This function returns false, **0**, if the function is not successful.

posix_setuid()

Syntax

```
bool posix_setuid(int uid);
```

Description

The `posix_setuid()` function sets the real user ID (UID) of the current process. This function returns false, 0, if the function is not successful.

> **Note**
> This function requires sufficient rights to complete successfully. These privileges usually require root access to the system.

posix_setgid()

Syntax

```
bool posix_setgid(int gid);
```

Description

The `posix_setgid()` function sets the real group ID (GID) of the current process. This function returns false, 0, if the function is not successful.

> **Note**
> This function requires sufficient rights to complete successfully. These privileges usually require root access to the system.

posix_getgroups()

Syntax

```
array posix_getgroups(void);
```

Description

The `posix_getgroups()` function returns an array of integers containing the numeric group IDs of the current process. This function returns false, 0, if the function is not successful.

posix_getlogin()

Syntax

```
string posix_getlogin(void);
```

Description

The posix_getlogin() function returns the login name of the user owning the current process. This function returns false, 0, if the function is not successful.

posix_getpgrp()

Syntax

```
int posix_getpgrp(void);
```

Description

The posix_getpgrp() function returns the process group identifier of the current process. This function returns false, 0, if the function is not successful.

posix_setsid()

Syntax

```
int posix_setsid(void);
```

Description

The posix_setsid() function makes the current process a session leader. This function returns the session ID or false, 0, if the function is not successful.

posix_setpgid()

Syntax

```
int posix_setpgid(int pid, int pgid);
```

Description

The posix_setpgid() function allows the process pid to join the process group pgid. This function returns false, 0, if the function is not successful.

posix_getpgid()

Syntax

```
int posix_getpgid(int pid);
```

Description

The posix_getpgid() function returns the process group identifier of the process *pid*. This is not an official POSIX function. If your system does not support this function, it will always return false, 0.

posix_setsid()

Syntax

```
int posix_getsid(int pid);
```

Description

The posix_setsid() function returns the SID of the process *pid*. If the *pid* is 0, the SID of the current process is returned. This is not an official POSIX function. If your system does not support this function, it will always return false, 0.

posix_uname()

Syntax

```
array posix_uname(void);
```

Description

The posix_uname() function returns an associative array containing a hash of strings with information about the system. The items in the array are listed in Table 9.12.

Table 9.12 *List of Indices Returned by* posix_uname()

Name	Description
sysname	The operating system name
nodename	The system name
release	The operating system release
version	The operating system version
machine	The machine architecture

posix_times()

Syntax

```
array posix_times(void);
```

Description

The `posix_times()` function returns an associative array containing information about the current process CPU usage. The items in the array are listed in Table 9.13.

Table 9.13   *List of Items Returned by* `posix_uname()`

Name	Description
ticks	The number of clock ticks since the system was rebooted
utime	The user time of the current process
stime	The system time of the current process
cutime	The user time of the current process and child processes
cstime	The system time of the current process and child processes

posix_ctermid()

Syntax

```
string posix_ctermid(void);
```

Description

The `posix_ctermid()` function retrieves the pathname of controlling terminal.

posix_ttyname()

Syntax

```
string posix_ttyname(int fd);
```

Description

The `posix_ttyname()` function retrieves the terminal device name associated with the file descriptor, fd.

posix_isatty()

Syntax

```
bool posix_isatty(int fd);
```

Description

The `posix_isatty()` function determines whether the file descriptor, *fd*, is an interactive terminal.

posix_getcwd()

Syntax

```
string posix_getcwd(void);
```

Description

The `posix_getcwd()` function returns the pathname of current working directory.

posix_mkfifo()

Syntax

```
bool posix_getcwd(string pathname, int mode);
```

Description

The `posix_mkfifo()` function creates a named pipe file specified by *pathname* with the mode specified by *mode*.

posix_getgrnam()

Syntax

```
array posix_getgrnam(string name);
```

Description

The `posix_getgrnam()` function returns an associative array with information about the group defined in *name*. The associative array contains the entries listed in Table 9.14.

Table 9.14   *Associative Array Returned by* posix_getgrnam()

Entry	Description
name	The name of the group
gid	The numeric group ID for the group
number[n]	The member list for the group
members	The number of members in the group

posix_getgrgid()

Syntax

```
array posix_getgrgid(int gid);
```

Description

The posix_getgrgid() function returns an associative array with information about the group defined by the numeric *gid* (group ID). The associative array contains the entries listed in Table 9.15.

Table 9.15   *Associative Array Returned by* posix_getgrnam()

Entry	Description
name	The name of the GID's group
gid	The numeric group ID for the group
number[n]	The member list for the GID
members	The number of members in the GID

posix_getpwnam()

Syntax

```
array posix_getpwnam(string name);
```

Description

The posix_getpwnam() function returns an associative array with information about the username defined by *name* (see Table 9.16). This is the same information that is contained in the /etc/passwd file.

Table 9.16   *Associative Array Returned by* posix_getpwnam()

Entry	Description
name	The username for the user
passwd	The encrypted password for the user
uid	The user ID for the user
gid	The group ID for the user
gecos	The real name for the user
dir	The user's home directory
shell	The user's preferred shell

posix_getpwuid()

Syntax

```
array posix_getpwuid(int uid);
```

Description

The posix_getpwuid() function returns an associative array with information about the username defined by *uid* (see Table 9.17). This is the same information that is contained in the /etc/passwd file.

Table 9.17   *Associative Array Returned by* posix_getpwnam()

Entry	Description
name	The username for the *uid*
passwd	The encrypted password for the *uid*
uid	The user ID for the *uid*
gid	The group ID for the *uid*
gecos	The real name for the *uid*
dir	The *uid*'s home directory
shell	The *uid*'s preferred shell

posix_getrlimit()

Syntax

```
array posix_getrlimit(void);
```

Description

The posix_getrlimit() function returns an associative array about the resource limits of the operating system. The associative array returns the items listed in Table 9.18.

Table 9.18   *Associative Array Returned by* posix_getrlimit()

Number	Description
core	Maximum core file size
data	Maximum data size
stack	Maximum stack size
virtualmem	Maximum virtual memory size
totalmem	Total system memory
rss	Maximum resident set size
maxproc	Maximum number of processes
memlock	Maximum locked-in-memory address space
cpu	CPU time in seconds
filesize	Maximum file size
openfiles	Maximum number of open files

Program Execution

This section describes functions that allow external programs to return information to PHP. These functions differ in the way they return information to PHP, to the browser, or how they format the output. These are very powerful functions and allow PHP to employ any external executable that is available to the operating system.

escapeshellcmd()

Syntax

```
string escapeshellcmd(string command);
```

Description

The escapeshellcmd() function escapes any characters in the string *command*. Escaping characters places backslashes in front of special characters before they are passed to the exec() or system() function.

exec()

Syntax

```
string exec(string command, string [array], int [return_var]);
```

Description

The exec() function executes the given *command* and returns the last line from the result of the execution. The optional argument *array* will contain the entire output of the command. The optional argument *return_val* will return the actual return the status of the command.

passthru()

Syntax

```
string passthru(string command, int [return_var]);
```

Description

The passthru() function executes the *command* and passes binary data, such as an image stream, directly back to the browser. The optional parameter *return_var* will return the status of the UNIX command.

system()

Syntax

```
string system(string command, int [return_var]);
```

Description

The system() function executes the given *command* and returns the last line of the command's result. The optional parameter *return_var* will contain the result status of the command.

Semaphore and Shared Memory

This section describes the functions that are used to manage shared memory. Shared memory provides an efficient method of sharing memory between multiple processes.

Because the data resides in the same physical RAM space and is accessible to multiple processes, a method must be devised to allow synchronous access to this memory. This method is achieved through the use of semaphores that provide synchronous access to shared memory segments by multiple processes and applications.

This section assumes that you have a thorough understanding of semaphores and shared memory and the methods, processes, and techniques used to acquire semaphores and shared memory.

sem_get()

Syntax

```
int sem_get(int key, int [max_acquire], int [perm]);
```

Description

The sem_get() function returns a semaphore ID that can be used to access semaphore defined by *key*. The optional parameter *max_acquire* is used to define the maximum number of processes that can acquire the semaphore at the same time. The optional parameter *perm* sets the permission bits for the semaphore. The default is 0666, read/write. The function returns false, 0, if an error occurred.

> **Note**
> Calling sem_get() a second time will return a different semaphore ID. However, both identifiers access the same semaphore.

sem_acquire()

Syntax

```
int sem_acquire(int sem_identifier);
```

Description

The sem_acquire() function blocks processing until the semaphore defined by *sem_identifier* can be acquired. The function returns false, 0, if there is an error.

> **Note**
> Remember to release all semaphores after use. Failure to do so will result in a warning.

sem_release()

Syntax

```
int sem_release(int sem_identifier);
```

Description

The sem_release() function releases the semaphore defined by *sem_identifier*. The function returns false, 0, if there is an error.

shm_attach()

Syntax

```
int shm_attach(int key, int [memsize], int [perm]);
```

Description

The shm_attach() function returns an ID that that can be used to access shared memory defined by *key*. The optional parameters *memsize* and *perm* create the shared memory segment of *memsize* with permissions defined by *perm*. The function returns false, 0, if an error occurred.

> **Note**
> Calling shm_attach() a second time will return a different shared memory ID; however, both identifiers access the same shared memory. The *memsize* and *perm* arguments will be ignored.

shm_detach()

Syntax

```
int shm_detach(int shm_identifier);
```

Description

The shm_detach() function disconnects from the shared memory identified by *shm_identifier*. The shared memory must have been previously created by shm_attach(). The function returns false, 0, on error.

shm_remove()

Syntax

```
int shm_remove(int shm_identifier);
```

Description

The shm_remove() function removes shared memory identified by *shm_identifier* and destroys all data. This function returns false, 0, on error.

shm_put_var()

Syntax

```
int shm_put_var(int shm_identifier, int variable_key, mixed variable);
```

Description

The shm_put_var() function inserts or updates a variable in the shared memory identified by *shm_identifier*. The defined *variable_key* is updated with the value of *variable*.

shm_get_var()

Syntax

```
mixed shm_get_var(int shm_identifier, int variable_key);
```

Description

The shm_get_var() function returns the variable in the shared memory space defined by *shm_identifier* with a given *variable_key*.

shm_remove_var()

Syntax

```
int shm_remove_var(int shm_identifier, int variable_key);
```

Description

The shm_remove_var() function removes a variable in the shared memory space defined by *shm_identifier* with a given *variable_key* and frees the memory taken up by the variable.

CHAPTER 10

Database Extensions

This chapter provides a reference for all the database-related functions available with PHP. All the major—and many of the minor—relational databases are supported, both natively and in some cases, through ODBC drivers. Database support is one of the most important features of PHP and is constantly being updated, so be sure to consult the latest documentation for new functions and features.

Several commonalities exist between many of the different databases supported. One commonality is connection handling. Most major databases offer both persistent and non-persistent connections. A non-persistent connection is destroyed automatically at the end of script processing, whereas a persistent connection remains even after a script has finished. Because the amount of overhead involved in establishing a connection can be significant, you will generally have better performance by using persistent connections, but you can do this only when PHP is running as a server module and not as a CGI program. Another commonality is that when a connection attempt is made, PHP looks for a similar connection and returns the reference to it instead of creating a new connection, if possible. This is true for both persistent and non-persistent connections.

Some terms you should be familiar with when consulting this chapter include transaction, commit, rollback, cursor, and fetch. A *transaction* is a set of SQL queries that are related, typically because they build upon each other. A transaction is used to ensure that a particular process completes successfully. The typical transaction example is this: Imagine transferring money from your savings account to your checking account. The first part of the transaction would debit your savings account and the second part would credit your checking account. Of course, if either of these actions fails, you want the entire process to fail; otherwise, your money could disappear into thin air. This is the purpose of a transaction: to ensure that the entire process finishes. When you complete the transaction or process, you can call *commit*, which tells the database that you have finished and are confirming your changes. *Rollback* means to reverse your previous transaction or query. Finally, a *cursor* refers to the result of a query and *fetch* means to examine a row of the result set. For a more complete understanding of these concepts, consult any of the database vendors' reference material.

Database Abstraction Layer

The Database Abstraction Layer functions provide a means to work with many of the file-based databases that are available. These include Dbm, Gdbm, SleepyCat Software DB2 and DB3, and others. The underlying structure of these databases is based on key/value pairs, which provide for simple and efficient lookups. For many applications, this is all the database functionality you will need, and enables you to avoid the task of maintaining a relational database, which can often be daunting. The following example opens a database, reads the value of user123's password, and returns it to the screen:

```php
<?php

$dba_handle = dba_open ("/usr/local/users.db","n","db2");
if (!$dba_handle ) {echo "user database open failed\n");
exit; }
echo "Password for user123 is:\n";
echo dba_fetch ("user123",$dba_handle);
dba_close ($dba_handle);
?>
```

dba_close()

Syntax

```
void dba_close(int handle)
```

Description

The dba_close() function, which was added in PHP 3.0.8 and PHP 4.0b2, closes the connection to a database indicated by the *handle* parameter. All resources utilized by this *handle*, which is created by the dba_open() function, are freed. No return value is available for this function.

dba_delete()

Syntax

```
string dba_delete(string key, int handle)
```

Description

The dba_delete() function, which was added in PHP 3.0.8 and PHP 4.0b2, deletes the entry with the corresponding *key* from the database specified by the *handle* parameter. The return value is TRUE if the *key* is deleted and FALSE otherwise.

dba_exists()

Syntax

```
bool dba_exists(string key, int handle)
```

Description

The dba_exists() function, which was added in PHP 3.0.8 and PHP 4.0b2, checks for the existence of an entry with *key* in the database specified by the *handle* parameter. The return value is TRUE if the *key* is found and FALSE otherwise.

dba_fetch()

Syntax

```
string dba_fetch (string key, int handle)
```

Description

The dba_fetch() function, which was added in PHP 3.0.8 and PHP 4.0b2, returns the data associated with the *key* in the database referenced by the *handle*. If the *key* is found, its data value is returned, and FALSE is returned otherwise.

dba_firstkey()

Syntax

```
string dba_firstkey (int handle)
```

Description

The `dba_firstkey()` function, which was added in PHP 3.0.8 and PHP 4.0b2, returns the first key in the database referenced by the *handle* parameter. It also resets an internal key pointer to the first item in the database, which is useful when performing a linear search. The return value is the first key, or FALSE if no key is found.

dba_insert()

Syntax

```
bool dba_insert (string key, string value, int handle)
```

Description

The `dba_insert()` function, which was added in PHP 3.0.8 and PHP 4.0b2, inserts an entry into the database referenced by the *handle* parameter. The entry is comprised of the *key* and *value* parameters. If the *key* already exists in the database, FALSE is returned; otherwise, TRUE is returned.

dba_nextkey()

Syntax

```
string dba_nextkey (int handle)
```

Description

The `dba_nextkey()` function, which was added in PHP 3.0.8 and PHP 4.0b2, returns the value of the next key in the database referenced by the *handle* parameter. The internal key pointer is also incremented. The key value is returned if successful, and FALSE is returned otherwise.

dba_open()

Syntax

```
int dba_open (string path, string mode, string handler [,...])
```

Description

The dba_open() function, which was added in PHP 3.0.8 and PHP 4.0b2, is used to open a connection to a database. The *path* parameter represents a regular path in the filesystem. The *mode* parameter can be one of four options: 'r' for read access, 'w' for read/write access to an existing database, 'c' for read/write and creation, or 'n' for create, read/write, and truncate. The parameter *handler* represents the name of the handler that will be used to access the *path*. The handler is passed any optional parameters that are supplied. An example of a handler is 'gdbm'. The return value is a handle to the database, or FALSE if the connection fails.

dba_optimize()

Syntax

```
bool dba_optimize (int handle)
```

Description

The dba_optimize() function, which was added in PHP 3.0.8 and PHP 4.0b2, optimizes the database referenced by the *handle* parameter. The return value is TRUE for a successful optimization and FALSE otherwise.

dba_popen()

Syntax

```
int dba_popen (string path, string mode, string handler [,...])
```

Description

The dba_popen() function, which was added in PHP 3.0.8 and PHP 4.0b2, is used to open a persistent connection to a database. The *path* parameter represents a regular path in the filesystem. The *mode* parameter can be one of four options: 'r' for read access, 'w' for read/write access to an existing database, 'c' for read/write and creation, or 'n' for create, read/write, and truncate. The parameter *handler* represents the name of the handler that will be used to access the *path*. The *handler* is passed any optional parameters that are supplied. An example of a handler is 'gdbm'. The return value is a handle to the database, or FALSE if the connection fails.

dba_replace()

Syntax

```
bool dba_replace (string key, string value, int handle)
```

Description

The dba_replace() function, which was added in PHP 3.0.8 and PHP 4.0b2, replaces or inserts an entry into the database referenced by the *handle* parameter. The entry is comprised of the *key* and *value* parameters. The return value is TRUE on success and FALSE otherwise.

dba_sync()

Syntax

```
bool dba_sync (int handle)
```

Description

The dba_sync() function, which was added in PHP 3.0.8 and PHP 4.0b2, synchronizes the database referenced by the *handle* parameter. This function typically causes the changes to be written to disk. The return value is TRUE on success and FALSE otherwise.

dBASE

The dBASE functions enable you to interact with records stored in a .dbf file. There is no support for indexes, locking, or memo fields at this time. Because locking doesn't exist, it is very possible that two concurrent processes could damage the database. dBASE files are fixed-length sequential records. Deleting a record in dBASE only causes the record to be marked for deletion; the record is not removed until dbase_pack() is called. Because dBASE doesn't support concurrent users well and has many other limitations, using dBASE is recommended only for testing purposes. The following example opens a dBASE file and dumps the contents of the first record:

```
<?

$dbase_db = dbase_open("users.dbf",0);
$dbase_numfields  = dbase_numfields($db);
```

```
$dbase_record = dbase_get_record($dbase_db,0);
    for ($i=0; $i < $dbase_numfields; $i++) {
            print $dbase_record[$i]."<br>\n";}
$dbase_close($dbase_db);
?>
```

dbase_create()

Syntax

```
int dbase_create (string filename, array fields)
```

Description

The dbase_create() function, which is available in PHP 3.0.16 and prior along with PHP 4.0, creates a dBASE database file. The *filename* parameter is used to name the new file and the *fields* parameter is used to specify the database columns of the file. The *fields* parameter should be an array of arrays, with each array describing one field in the database. Each array consists of four fields: the column name, a character indicating the column type, field length, and precision. Precision represents the number of digits after the decimal point. If creation is successful, a *dbase_identifier* is returned; FALSE is returned otherwise.

Field Types Available

Character	Type	Notes
L	Boolean	These do not have a length or precision.
M	Memo	These are not supported by PHP. They don't have a length or precision.
D	Date	These are stored in the format *YYYYMMDD*. They do not have a length or precision.
N	Number	These have both a length and a precision.
C	String	These are for character data up to the length specified.

```
$tabledef = array(array("userid,"N",8,0)
"username","C",50), array("password","C",50));
dbase_create("users.dbf",$tabledef);
```

dbase_open()

Syntax

```
int dbase_open (string filename, int flags)
```

Description

The dbase_open() function, which is available in PHP 3.0.16 and prior along with PHP 4.0, attempts to open a dBASE file and returns a *dbase_identifier* if successful and FALSE otherwise. The *filename* parameter represents the name of the dBASE file to be opened and the *flags* parameter is used to determine the mode in which the file should be opened. Typical flag values are 0 for read-only, 1 for write-only, and 2 for read and write.

dbase_close()

Syntax

```
bool dbase_close (int dbase_identifier)
```

Description

The dbase_close() function, which is available in PHP 3.0.16 and prior along with PHP 4.0, closes the dBASE file specified by the *dbase_identifier* parameter.

dbase_pack()

Syntax

```
bool dbase_pack (int dbase_identifier)
```

Description

The dbase_pack() function, which is available in PHP 3.0.16 and prior along with PHP 4.0, packs the dBASE file represented by the *dbase_identifier* parameter. When a record is deleted in dBASE using SQL, the record is only marked for deletion and not actually removed. This function causes the record to be removed from the database.

dbase_add_record()

Syntax

```
bool dbase_add_record (int dbase_identifier, array record)
```

Description

The dbase_add_record() function, which is available in PHP 3.0.16 and prior along with PHP 4.0, adds a record to the dBASE database specified by the *dbase_identifier* parameter. The *record* parameter must match the record type of the dBASE database or the call will be unsuccessful and FALSE will be returned.

dbase_replace_record()

Syntax

```
bool dbase_replace_record (int dbase_identifier, array record,
 int dbase_record, int dbase_record_number)
```

Description

The dbase_replace_record() function, which is available in PHP 3.0.16 and prior along with PHP 4.0, replaces the record at the location specified by the *dbase_record_number* parameter in the database referenced by the *dbase_identifier* parameter. The *dbase_record* type must match the record it is replacing; otherwise, the replacement is unsuccessful and FALSE is returned.

dbase_delete_record()

Syntax

```
bool dbase_delete_record (int dbase_identifier, int record)
```

Description

The dbase_delete_record() function, which is available in PHP 3.0.16 and prior versions along with PHP 4.0, marks a record to be deleted from the database referenced by the *dbase_identifier* parameter. The record is not actually removed from the database until dbase_pack() is called.

dbase_get_record()

Syntax

```
array dbase_get_record (int dbase_identifier, int record)
```

Description

The dbase_get_record() function, which is available in PHP 3.0.16 and prior along with PHP 4.0, returns the record indicated by the *record* parameter in the database referenced by the *dbase_identifier* parameter. The record is returned as an array with a starting index of 0 as well as an associative member named 'deleted', which represents whether the record has been marked for deletion with '1' meaning TRUE. Each field is converted into the appropriate PHP data type with dates left as strings.

dbase_get_record_with_names()

Syntax

```
array dbase_get_record_with_names (int dbase_identifier, int record)
```

Description

The dbase_get_record_with_names() function, which is available in PHP 3.0.16 and prior versions along with PHP 4.0, returns the record indicated by the *record* parameter in the database referenced by the *dbase_identifier* parameter. The record is returned as an associative array with a member named 'deleted' which represents whether the record has been marked for deletion with '1' meaning TRUE. Each field is converted into the appropriate PHP data type with dates left as strings.

dbase_numfields()

Syntax

```
int dbase_numfields (int dbase_identifier)
```

Description

The dbase_numfields() function, which is available in PHP 3.0.16 and prior versions along with PHP 4.0, returns the number of fields in a dBASE database referenced by the *dbase_identifier* parameter. Note that field numbers are zero-based and record numbers are one-based.

dbase_numrecords()

Syntax

```
int dbase_numrecords (int dbase_identifier)
```

Description

The dbase_numrecords() function, which is available in PHP 3.0.16 and prior versions along with PHP 4.0, returns the number of rows in a dBASE database referenced by the dbase_identifier parameter. Note that record numbers are one-based and field numbers are zero-based.

DBM

The DBM functions enable you to access data stored in one of the many DBM-style databases such as Berkeley DB, Gdbm, system libraries, and some of the flat-file databases that exist. DBM databases store key and value pairs as opposed to relational databases, which store variable-length records of related data. The following example opens a DBM database and retrieves the password of user123:

```
<?

$dbm_db = dbmopen("users","r");
echo dbm_fetch($dbm_db,"user123");
$dbmclose (dbm_db);
?>
```

dbmopen()

Syntax

```
int dbmopen (string filename, string flags)
```

Description

The dbmopen() function, which is available in PHP 3.0.16 and prior along with PHP 4.0, is used to open a connection to a DBM file. The *path* parameter represents the full path to the DBM file. The *mode* parameter can be one of four options: 'r' for read access, 'w' for read/write access to an existing database, 'c' for read/write and create, or 'n' for create, read/write, and truncate. The returned value can be used as a handle to subsequent DBM function calls. Note that PHP does its own file locking (by creating .lck files) in addition to any file locking done by the database.

dbmclose()

Syntax

```
bool dbmclose (int dbm_identifier)
```

Description

The dbmclose() function, which is available in PHP 3.0.16 and prior versions along with PHP 4.0, closes the DBM file referenced by the *dbm_identifier* parameter and closes any associated locks. The function returns TRUE on success, and FALSE otherwise.

dbmexists()

Syntax

```
bool dbmexists (int dbm_identifier, string key)
```

Description

The dbmexists() function, which is available in PHP 3.0.16 and prior versions along with PHP 4.0, returns TRUE if a value associated with the *key* parameter exists in the DBM file referenced by the *dbm_identifier* parameter.

dbmfetch()

Syntax

```
string dbmfetch (int dbm_identifier, string key)
```

Description

The dbmfetch() function, which is available in PHP 3.0.16 and prior versions along with PHP 4.0, returns the value associated with the *key* parameter from the DBM file referenced by the *dbm_identifier* parameter.

dbminsert()

Syntax

```
int dbminsert (int dbm_identifier, string key, string value)
```

Description

The dbminsert() function, which is available in PHP 3.0.16 and prior versions along with PHP 4.0, inserts the record into the DBM file indicated by the *dbm_identifier* parameter. The record is comprised of the *key* and *value* parameters. The possible return values are 0 for success, 1 for key already exists, and -1 for file opened in read-only mode. You should use dbmreplace() if you want to change an existing value.

dbmreplace()

Syntax

```
bool dbmreplace (int dbm_identifier, string key, string value)
```

Description

The dbmreplace() function, which is available in PHP 3.0.16 and prior versions along with PHP 4.0, replaces the value previously associated with the *key* parameter with the *value* parameter in the database referenced by the *dbm_identifier* parameter. A return value of TRUE indicates success and FALSE indicates otherwise.

dbmdelete()

Syntax

```
bool dbmdelete (int dbm_identifier, string key)
```

Description

The dbmdelete() function, which is available in PHP 3.0.16 and prior versions along with PHP 4.0, deletes the value corresponding to the *key* parameter in the DBM file referenced by the *dbm_identifier* parameter. The return value is TRUE if successful and FALSE otherwise.

dbmfirstkey()

Syntax

```
string dbmfirstkey (int dbm_identifier)
```

Description

The dbmfirstkey() function, which is available in PHP 3.0.16 and prior versions along with PHP 4.0, returns the first key in the database referenced by the dbm_identifier parameter. Note that the DBM file is not required to have a specific order.

dbmnextkey()

Syntax

```
string dbmnextkey (int dbm_identifier, string key)
```

Description

The dbmnextkey() function, which is available in PHP 3.0.16 and prior versions along with PHP 4.0, returns the subsequent key after the key parameter in the DBM file referenced by the dbm_identifier parameter. To traverse the entire DBM file, start with dbmfirstkey() and then call dbmnextkey() repeatedly until FALSE is returned.

dblist()

Syntax

```
string dblist (void)
```

Description

The dblist() function, which is available in PHP 3.0.16 and prior versions along with PHP 4.0, details the DBM-compatible library being utilized.

FilePro

The FilePro functions enable you to access the read-only data stored in a FilePro database. More information on FilePro is available at http://www.fileproplus.com.

filepro()

Syntax

```
bool filepro (string directory)
```

Description

The `filepro()` function, which is available in PHP 3.0.16 and prior along with PHP 4.0, reads and verifies the map file located in `directory`.

filepro_fieldname()

Syntax

```
string filepro_fieldname (int field_number)
```

Description

The `filepro_fieldname()` function, which is available in PHP 3.0.16 and prior versions along with PHP 4.0, returns the name of the field referenced by the `field_number` parameter.

filepro_fieldtype()

Syntax

```
string filepro_fieldtype (int field_number)
```

Description

The `filepro_fieldtype()` function, which is available in PHP 3.0.16 and prior versions along with PHP 4.0, examines the field referenced by the `field_number` parameter and returns its edit type.

filepro_fieldwidth()

Syntax

```
int filepro_fieldwidth (int field_number)
```

Description

The `filepro_fieldwidth()` function, which is available in PHP 3.0.16 and prior versions along with PHP 4.0, examines the field referenced by the *field_number* parameter and returns its width.

filepro_retrieve()

Syntax

```
string filepro_retrieve (int row_number, int field_number)
```

Description

The `filepro_retrieve()` function, which is available in PHP 3.0.16 and prior versions along with PHP 4.0, returns the data at the location indicated by the *row_number* and *field_number* parameters.

filepro_fieldcount()

Syntax

```
int filepro_fieldcount (void)
```

Description

The `filepro_fieldcount()` function, which is available in PHP 3.0.16 and prior versions along with PHP 4.0, returns the number of fields (columns) in the currently open FilePro database.

filepro_rowcount()

Syntax

```
int filepro_rowcount (void)
```

Description

The `filepro_rowcount()` function, which is available in PHP 3.0.16 and prior versions along with PHP 4.0, returns the number of rows in the currently open FilePro database.

Informix

The Informix functions enable you to access data stored in any of the following Informix databases: Informix 7.x, SE 7.x, Universal Server (IUS) 9.x, and IDS 2000. For handling of BLOBs (binary large objects), use BLOB identifiers and the functions ifx_blobinfile(), ifx_get_blob(), ifx_create_blob(), and ifx_update_blob(), which enable you to transfer the BLOB's contents between files and variables along with creating and updating BLOBs. The following example connects to the users database and retrieves user123's password:

```
<?

$ifx_db = ifx_connect("usersdb","username","password");
$result_id  =
ifx_query ("select password from users where username = user123",$ifx_db);
$row = ifx_fetch_row ($result_id);
echo $row[password];
ifx_close ($ifx_db);
?>
```

ifx_connect()

Syntax

```
int ifx_connect ([string database [, string userid [, string password]]])
```

Description

The ifx_connect() function, which is available in PHP 3.0.3 through PHP 3.0.16 along with PHP 4.0 and higher, returns a connection to an Informix server. Each of the parameters is optional and, if not specified, will be taken from the configuration file. If a subsequent call is made with the same parameters, the already-opened link will be returned instead of creating a new handle. The link is automatically closed at the end of a script's processing or when ifx_close() is called. A connection handle is returned on success and FALSE is returned otherwise.

ifx_pconnect()

Syntax

```
int ifx_pconnect ([string database [, string userid [, string password]]])
```

Description

The ifx_pconnect() function, which is available in PHP 3.0.3 through PHP 3.0.16 along with PHP 4.0 and higher, is identical to ifx_connect() when not used with a PHP Web server module. If used as with a PHP server module, the connection will not be terminated with ifx_close() or at the end of script processing. Instead, the existing connection can be used over and over.

ifx_close()

Syntax

```
int ifx_close ([int link_identifier])
```

Description

The ifx_close() function, which is available in PHP 3.0.3 through PHP 3.0.16 along with PHP 4.0 and higher, is used to close a connection identified by the link_identifier parameter. This function always returns TRUE. Note that this function is not usually necessary because non-persistent connections are automatically closed at the end of script processing and persistent connections cannot be closed with this function.

ifx_query()

Syntax

```
int ifx_query (string query, [, int link_identifier
 [, int cursor_type [, mixed blobidarray]]])
```

Description

The ifx_query() function, which is available in PHP 3.0.3 through PHP 3.0.16 along with PHP 4.0 and higher, sends a query to the currently active database on the server indicated by the link_identifier parameter. If no link_identifier is used, an attempt is made to use the last opened link. If no open links are available, the function tries to establish a connection to the database. The optional cursor_type parameter is used to set the cursor processing to scroll, hold, sequential, or a combination of scroll and hold. To set scroll cursor processing, specify IFX_SCROLL and to set hold, use IFX_HOLD—these are constant values that don't need quotes around them. If you want to use both scroll and hold, 'or' these two values together. The default for this parameter is sequential cursor processing. If you have BLOB columns in the query, you should specify their IDs in the blobidarray parameter and substitute question marks in the query statement. If the contents of the TEXT (or BYTE) column allow it, you can also use `ifx_textasvarchar(1)` and `ifx_byteasvarchar(1)`. This enables you to treat TEXT (or BYTE) columns as though they were (long) VARCHAR columns for select queries, thus avoiding the use of BLOB IDs. If the previous shortcut is not used, the query will return BLOB columns as BLOB IDs.

ifx_prepare()

Syntax

```
int ifx_prepare (string query, int conn_id
 [, int cursor_def, mixed blobidarray])
```

Description

The `ifx_prepare()` function, which is available in PHP 3.0.4 through PHP 3.0.16 along with PHP 4.0 and higher, prepares a query on the database indicated by the `conn_id` parameter. The optional `cursor_type` parameter is used to set the cursor processing to scroll, hold, sequential, or a combination of scroll and hold. To set scroll cursor processing, specify `IFX_SCROLL` and to set hold, use IFX_HOLD—these are constant values that don't need quotes around them. If you want to use both scroll and hold, `'or'` these two values together. The default for this parameter is sequential cursor processing. If you have BLOB columns in the query, you should specify their IDs in the `blobidarray` parameter and substitute question marks in the query statement. If the contents of the TEXT (or BYTE) column allow it, you can also use `ifx_textasvarchar(1)` and `ifx_byteasvarchar(1)`. This enables you to treat TEXT (or BYTE) columns as though they were (long) VARCHAR columns for select queries, thus avoiding the use of BLOB IDs. If the previous shortcut is not used, the query will return BLOB columns as BLOB IDs.

ifx_do()

Syntax

```
int ifx_do (int result_id)
```

Description

The `ifx_do()` function, which is available in PHP 3.0.4 through PHP 3.0.16 along with PHP 4.0 and higher, executes a previously prepared statement that was made with the `ifx_prepare()` function. The return value is TRUE on success, and FALSE otherwise.

ifx_error()

Syntax

```
string ifx_error (void)
```

Description

The `ifx_error()` function, which is available in PHP 3.0.3 through PHP 3.0.16 along with PHP 4.0 and higher, returns the error code of the last call made. Informix error codes (SQLSTATE and SQLCODE) are formatted as follows:

```
x [SQLSTATE = aa bbb SQLCODE=cccc]
where x =
space : no error
E : error
N : no more data
W : warning
? : undefined
```

If the x character is anything other than a space, SQLSTATE and SQLCODE describe the error in more detail. See the Informix manual for the description of SQLSTATE and SQLCODE. The return string has one character describing the general results of a statement and both SQLSTATE and SQLCODE associated with the most recent SQL statement executed. The format of the string is `(char) [SQLSTATE=(two digits) (three digits) SQLCODE=(one digit)]`. The first character can be `' '` (space) (indicating success), `'W'` (the statement caused some warning), `'E'` (an error happened when executing the statement), or `'N'` (the statement didn't return any data).

ifx_errormsg()

Syntax

```
string ifx_errormsg ([int errorcode])
```

Description

The `ifx_errormsg()` function, which is available in PHP 3.0.4 through PHP 3.0.16 along with PHP 4.0 and higher, returns the Informix error message that corresponds to the last error that occurred or to the *errorcode* parameter, if it is present.

ifx_affected_rows()

Syntax

```
int ifx_affected_rows (int result_id)
```

Description

The `ifx_affected_rows()` function, which is available in PHP 3.0.3 through PHP 3.0.16 along with PHP 4.0 and higher, returns the number of rows affected when the query referenced by the `result_id` parameter was executed. For insert, update, and delete statements, the returned number is the actual value, but for select statements, the returned number is just an estimation and should not be relied on.

ifx_getsqlca()

Syntax

```
array ifx_getsqlca (int result_id)
```

Description

The `ifx_getsqlca()` function, which is available in PHP 3.0.8 through PHP 3.0.16 along with PHP 4.0 and higher, returns an associative array which is comprised of `sqlca.sqlerr[0]` through `sqlca.sqlerr[5]`, after the query denoted by `result_id` is executed. In the case of inserts, updates, and deletes, the server sets the values after the query is executed, and includes the number of affected rows along with the serial insert value. For select statements, the values are set after the prepare function has been called. Therefore, you get only an estimate of the number of rows affected.

ifx_fetch_row()

Syntax

```
array ifx_fetch_row (int result_id [, mixed position])
```

Description

The `ifx_fetch_row()` function, which is available in PHP 3.0.3 through PHP 3.0.16 along with PHP 4.0 and higher, returns an associative array for the fetched row identified by the `result_id` parameter. If no rows are available, FALSE is returned. BLOB columns are returned as integer blob id values for use with the `ifx_get_blob()`

function, unless you have used `ifx_textasvarchar(1)` or `ifx_byteasvarchar(1)`, which causes the BLOBs to be returned as string values. The optional *position* parameter, which can be used only with scroll cursors, is used to denote which row to fetch. The possible values include `'NEXT'`, `'PREVIOUS'`, `'FIRST'`, `'CURRENT'`, `'LAST'`, or a number indicating a particular row in the cursor. Each row is returned in an array with a base index of zero, and the column name as the key.

ifx_htmltbl_result()

Syntax

```
int ifx_htmltbl_result (int result_id [, string html_table_options])
```

Description

The `ifx_htmltbl_result()` function, which is available in PHP 3.0.3 through PHP 3.0.16 along with PHP 4.0 and higher, is used to return the results of the query referenced by the *result_id* parameter as an HTML table. The optional *html_table_options* parameter is used to indicate any <table> tag options to be used.

ifx_fieldtypes()

Syntax

```
array ifx_fieldtypes (int result_id)
```

Description

The `ifx_fieldtypes()` function, which is available in PHP 3.0.3 through PHP 3.0.16 along with PHP 4.0 and higher, examines the results of the query denoted by the *result_id* parameter. It returns an associative array with the field names as the keys and the field types as the data elements. The return value will be FALSE if an error occurs.

ifx_fieldproperties()

Syntax

```
array ifx_fieldproperties (int result_id)
```

Description

The ifx_fieldproperties() function, which is available in PHP 3.0.3 through PHP 3.0.16 along with PHP 4.0 and higher, examines the results of the query denoted by the *result_id* parameter. It returns an associative array with the field names as the keys and the field properties as the data elements. The return value will be FALSE if an error occurs. The field properties are formatted as follows: SQLTYPE;*length*; *precision*;*scale*;ISNULLABLE, where SQLTYPE is the Informix data type, such as 'SQLVCHAR'; *length* is the field length; *precision* is the number of places after the decimal point; and ISNULLABLE is set to either 'Y' or 'N', which represents whether a field can have a NULL value.

ifx_num_fields()

Syntax

```
int ifx_num_fields (int result_id)
```

Description

The ifx_num_fields() function, which is available in PHP 3.0.3 through PHP 3.0.16 along with PHP 4.0 and higher, returns the number of columns in the prepared or executed query referenced by the *result_id* parameter. The return value will be FALSE on error.

ifx_num_rows()

Syntax

```
int ifx_num_rows (int result_id)
```

Description

The ifx_num_rows() function, which is available in PHP 3.0.3 through PHP 3.0.16 along with PHP 4.0 and higher, returns the number of rows already fetched by the query referenced with *result_id*.

ifx_free_result()

Syntax

```
int ifx_free_result (int result_id)
```

Description

The `ifx_free_result()` function, which is available in PHP 3.0.3 through PHP 3.0.16 along with PHP 4.0 and higher, attempts to release all resources associated with the *result_id* query and returns FALSE on error.

ifx_create_char()

Syntax

```
int ifx_create_char (string param)
```

Description

The `ifx_create_char()` function, which is available in PHP 3.0.3 through PHP 3.0.16 along with PHP 4.0 and higher, creates a character object comprised of the *param* parameter.

ifx_free_char()

Syntax

```
int ifx_free_char (int bid)
```

Description

The `ifx_free_char()` function, which is available in PHP 3.0.6 through PHP 3.0.16 along with PHP 4.0 and higher, deletes the character object referenced by the *bid* parameter. The function returns TRUE on success and FALSE otherwise.

ifx_update_char()

Syntax

```
int ifx_update_char (int bid, string content)
```

Description

The `ifx_update_char()` function, which is available in PHP 3.0.6 through PHP 3.0.16 along with PHP 4.0 and higher, updates the contents of the character object referenced by the *bid* parameter with the contents of the *content* parameter. It returns TRUE on success, and FALSE otherwise.

ifx_get_char()

Syntax

```
int ifx_get_char (int bid)
```

Description

The ifx_get_char() function, which is available in PHP 3.0.6 through PHP 3.0.16 along with PHP 4.0 and higher, returns the contents of the character object indicated by the *bid* parameter.

ifx_create_blob

Syntax

```
int ifx_create_blob (int type, int mode, string param)
```

Description

The ifx_get_char() function, which is available in PHP 3.0.4 through PHP 3.0.16 along with PHP 4.0 and higher, creates a BLOB object and returns FALSE if an error occurred and the new BLOB object ID otherwise. The *type* parameter accepts the value 0 for BYTE or u for TEXT. The *mode* parameter accepts the value 0 for BLOB object content held in memory or 1 for BLOB object content held in a file. The *param* parameter accepts 0 for a pointer to content, and 1 for a pointer to a file string.

ifx_copy_blob()

Syntax

```
int ifx_copy_blob (int bid)
```

Description

The ifx_copy_blob() function, which is available in PHP 3.0.4 through PHP 3.0.16 along with PHP 4.0 and higher, duplicates the BLOB object identified with the *bid* parameter. The return value is the new BLOB object ID, or FALSE on failure.

ifx_free_blob()

Syntax

```
int ifx_free_blob (int bid)
```

Description

The ifx_free_blob() function, which is available in PHP 3.0.4 through PHP 3.0.16 along with PHP 4.0 and higher, deletes the BLOB object referenced by the *bid* parameter, and returns TRUE on success and returns FALSE otherwise.

ifx_get_blob()

Syntax

```
int ifx_get_blob (int bid)
```

Description

The ifx_get_blob() function, which is available in PHP 3.0.4 through PHP 3.0.16 along with PHP 4.0 and higher, returns the contents of a BLOB object referenced by the *bid* parameter.

ifx_update_blob()

Syntax

```
ifx_update_blob (int bid, string content)
```

Description

The ifx_update_blob() function, which is available in PHP 3.0.4 through PHP 3.0.16 along with PHP 4.0 and higher, updates the contents of the BLOB object referenced by the *bid* parameter with the contents of the *content* parameter, and returns TRUE on success and returns FALSE otherwise.

ifx_blobinfile_mode()

Syntax

```
void ifx_blobinfile_mode (int mode)
```

Description

The ifx_blobinfile_mode() function, which is available in PHP 3.0.4 through PHP 3.0.16 along with PHP 4.0 and higher, specifies the default BLOB mode for select statements. A *mode* parameter value of 1 indicates save byte BLOBs in a file, and 0 indicates save byte BLOBs in memory.

ifx_textasvarchar()

Syntax

```
void ifx_textasvarchar (int mode)
```

Description

The ifx_textasvarchar() function, which is available in PHP 3.0.4 through PHP 3.0.16 along with PHP 4.0 and higher, specifies the default text mode for select statements. A *mode* parameter value of 1 indicates to return a varchar with text content, and 0 indicates to return a BLOB ID.

ifx_byteasvarchar()

Syntax

```
void ifx_bytesasvarchar (int mode)
```

Description

The ifx_byteasvarchar() function, which is available in PHP 3.0.4 through PHP 3.0.16 along with PHP 4.0 and higher, specifies the default byte mode for select statements. A *mode* parameter value of 1 indicates to return a varchar with text content, and 0 indicates to return a BLOB ID.

ifx_nullformat()

Syntax

```
void ifx_nullformat (int mode)
```

Description

The ifx_nullformat() function, which is available in PHP 3.0.4 through PHP 3.0.16 along with PHP 4.0 and higher, sets the default return value for NULL data. A *mode* parameter value of 1 indicates to return 'NULL' and 0 indicates to return "".

ifxus_create_slob()

Syntax

```
int ifxus_create_slob (int mode)
```

Description

The ifxus_create_slob() function, which is available in PHP 3.0.4 through PHP 3.0.16 along with PHP 4.0 and higher, creates and opens a SLOB object. Possible *mode* values are 1 = LO_RDONLY, 2 = LO_WRONLY, 4 = LO_APPEND, 8 = LO_RDWR, 16 = LO_BUFFER, 32 = LO_NOBUFFER -> or-mask. You can use the number of the named constant. The return value is the new SLOB object ID on success and FALSE otherwise.

ifx_free_slob()

Syntax

```
int ifxus_free_slob (int bid)
```

Description

The ifx_free_slob() function, which is available in PHP 3.0.3 through PHP 3.0.16 along with PHP 4.0 and higher, deletes the SLOB object referenced by the *bid* parameter. The return value is TRUE on success and FALSE otherwise.

ifxus_close_slob()

Syntax

```
int ifxus_close_slob (int bid)
```

Description

The ifxus_close_slob() function, which is available in PHP 3.0.4 through PHP 3.0.16 along with PHP 4.0 and higher, deletes the SLOB object referenced by the *bid* parameter and returns TRUE on success and FALSE otherwise.

ifxus_open_slob()

Syntax

```
int ifxus_open_slob (long bid, int mode)
```

Description

The ifxus_open_slob() function, which is available in PHP 3.0.4 through PHP 3.0.16 along with PHP 4.0 and higher, opens an existing SLOB object referenced by the *bid* parameter. The *mode* parameter accepts the following values: 1 = LO_RDONLY,

2 = LO_WRONLY, 4 = LO_APPEND, 8 = LO_RDWR, 16 = LO_BUFFER, 32 = LO_NOBUFFER -> or-mask. The return is value is the SLOB object ID or FALSE on error.

ifxus_tell_slob()

Syntax

```
int ifxus_tell_slob (long bid)
```

Description

The ifxus_tell_slob() function, which is available in PHP 3.0.4 through PHP 3.0.16 along with PHP 4.0 and higher, returns the current file or seek position of the open SLOB object referenced by the *bid* parameter. The return value will be FALSE if an error occurs.

ifxus_seek_slob()

Syntax

```
int ifxus_seek_blob (long bid, int mode, long offset)
```

Description

The ifxus_seek_slob() function, which is available in PHP 3.0.4 through PHP 3.0.16 along with PHP 4.0 and higher, sets the current file or seek position of the open SLOB object referenced by the *bid* parameter. The possible *mode* values are 0 for LO_SEEK_SET, 1 for LO_SEEK_CUR, and 2 for LO_SEEK_END. The *offset* parameter is represented in bytes. The return value will be FALSE if an error occurs; otherwise, the return value will be the new seek position.

ifxus_read_slob()

Syntax

```
int ifxus_read_slob (long bid, long nbytes)
```

Description

The ifxus_read_slob() function, which is available in PHP 3.0.4 through PHP 3.0.16 along with PHP 4.0 and higher, reads from the SLOB object referenced by the *bid* parameter the number of bytes indicated by the *nbytes* parameter. The return value is the string on success; otherwise, the return value is FALSE.

ifxus_write_slob()

Syntax

```
int ifxus_write_slob (long bid, string content)
```

Description

The `ifxus_write_slob ()` function, which is available in PHP 3.0.4 through PHP 3.0.16 along with PHP 4.0 and higher, writes the `content` parameter into the SLOB object referenced by the `bid` parameter. The return value is the number of bytes written or FALSE on failure.

InterBase

The InterBase functions enable you to access data in an InterBase database, which is a product of Borland/Inprise. More information can be found at `http://www.interbase.com`.

ibase_connect()

Syntax

```
int ibase_connect (string database [,string username [,string password
[, string charset [, int buffers [, int dialect [, string role ]]]]]])
```

Description

The `ibase_connect()` function, which is available in PHP 3.0.6 through PHP 3.0.16 along with PHP 4.0 and higher, establishes a connection to an InterBase server. The `database` parameter should be a valid path to a database file on the server on which the file resides. If the file is on another machine, it must be prefixed in one of the following manners: `'hostname:'` for TCP/IP, `'//hostname/'` for NetBEUI, or `'hostname@'` for IPX/SPX. The optional `username` and `password` parameters can also be set using the PHP configuration directives `ibase.default_user` and `ibase.default_password`, respectively. The `charset` parameter indicates the default character set for the database and `buffers` indicates the number of database buffers to allocate for the server-side cache. If `buffers` is set to 0 or omitted, the server uses its own default. The `dialect` parameter sets the default SQL dialect for any statement executed within a connection, and defaults to the highest one supported by the client libraries. If another call is made with the same arguments, a previously opened connection will be used if one is available. A connection is destroyed when a script's execution is complete or `ibase_close()` is called. Note that the *buffers*, *dialect*, and *role* parameters were not added until PHP 4.0rc2.

ibase_pconnect()

Syntax

```
int ibase_pconnect (string database [,string username [,string password
[, string charset [, int buffers [, int dialect [, string role ]]]]]])
```

Description

The `ibase_pconnect()` function, which is available in PHP 3.0.6 through PHP 3.0.16 along with PHP 4.0 and higher, is similar to `ibase_connect()` that was described earlier, with one major difference. The difference is that the connection does not close with the end of a script's processing or a call to the `ibase_close()` function.

ibase_close()

Syntax

```
int ibase_close ([int connection_id])
```

Description

The `ibase_close()` function, which is available in PHP 3.0.6 through PHP 3.0.16 along with PHP 4.0 and higher, closes the connection referenced by the *connection_id* parameter. If *connection_id* is not specified, the most recently opened link is closed. The default transaction is committed on close and other transactions are rolled back.

ibase_query()

Syntax

```
int ibase_query ([int link_identifier, string query [, int bind_args[])
```

Description

The `ibase_query()` function, which is available in PHP 3.0.6 through PHP 3.0.16 along with PHP 4.0 and higher, executes the *query* parameter against the database referenced by the *link_identifier* parameter. Although the *bind_args* parameter is available for passing variable values, it is not recommended to do so; instead, you should use the ibase_prepare() and ibase_execute() functions.

ibase_fetch_row()

Syntax

```
array ibase_fetch_row (int result_identifier)
```

Description

The ibase_fetch_row() function, which is available in PHP 3.0.6 through PHP 3.0.16 along with PHP 4.0 and higher, returns the next row from the result set referenced by the *result_identifier* parameter, which is the return value from ibase_query().

ibase_fetch_object()

Syntax

```
object ibase_fetch_object (int result_id)
```

Description

The ibase_fetch_object() function, which is available in PHP 3.0.6 through PHP 3.0.16 along with PHP 4.0 and higher, retrieves a row as a pseudo-object from the result set identified by the *result_id* parameter that is returned from the ibase_query() and ibase_execute() functions.

ibase_free_result()

Syntax

```
int ibase_free_result (int result_identifier)
```

Description

The ibase_free_result() function, which is available in PHP 3.0.6 through PHP 3.0.16 along with PHP 4.0 and higher, frees the result set referenced by the *result_identifier* parameter.

ibase_prepare()

Syntax

```
int ibase_prepare ([int link_identifier, string query])
```

Description

The ibase_prepare() function, which is available in PHP 3.0.6 through PHP 3.0.16 along with PHP 4.0 and higher, prepares the *query* for later binding and execution with the ibase_execute() function. The *link_identifier* is an open database connection.

ibase_execute()

Syntax

```
int ibase_execute (int query [, int bind_args])
```

Description

The ibase_execute() function, which is available in PHP 3.0.6 through PHP 3.0.16 along with PHP 4.0 and higher, executes a previously prepared query. The *bind_args* parameters represent the variables that should be substituted into the query before executing. To prepare a query for execution, use the ibase_query() function.

ibase_free_query()

Syntax

```
int ibase_free_query (int query)
```

Description

The ibase_free_query() function, which is available in PHP 3.0.6 through PHP 3.0.16 along with PHP 4.0 and higher, frees a query created with the ibase_prepare() function.

ibase_timefmt()

Syntax

```
int ibase_timefmt (string format [, int columntype])
```

Description

The ibase_timefmt() function, which is available in PHP 3.0.6 through PHP 3.0.16 along with PHP 4.0 and higher, sets the format for any timestamp, date, or time type columns returned from a query. Internally, the C function strftime() is used to do the formatting, so it might be helpful to consult its documentation as well. The *columntype* parameter, which was added in PHP 4.0, can take the values IBASE_ TIMESTAMP, IBASE_DATE, and IBASE_TIME, and defaults to IBASE_TIMESTAMP. It is also possible to set the defaults using the configuration directives: ibase.timestampformat, ibase.dateformat, and ibase.timeformat.

ibase_num_fields()

Syntax

```
int ibase_num_fields (int result_id)
```

Description

The ibase_num_fields() function, which is available in PHP 3.0.7 through PHP 3.0.16 along with PHP 4.0rc1 and higher, returns the number of fields in the result set denoted by *result_id* parameter.

Microsoft SQL Server

The Microsoft SQL Server functions enable you to access data from a Microsoft SQL Server database. The most commonly used version of MS SQL Server at the time of this writing is 7, but MS SQL 2000 is rapidly gaining in popularity. Note that several vendors offer drivers that enable you to access this database from a UNIX/Linux machine. The following example connects to the user database and retrieves user123's password from the users table:

```
<?

$ms_link_id = mssql_connect('users');
$ms_result_id =
mssql_query ('select password from users where username=user123',$ms_link_id);
echo $ms_result_id[0];
mssql_close($ms_link_id);
?>
```

mssql_close()

Syntax

```
int mssql_close ([int link_identifier])
```

Description

The mssql_close() function, which is available from PHP 3.0 to PHP 3.0.16 along with PHP 4.0 and higher, closes the link to an MS SQL Server indicated by the link_identifier and closes the last opened link if none is specified. A connection will automatically be closed at the end of a script's execution, so it isn't necessary to use this call.

mssql_connect()

Syntax

```
int mssql_connect ([string servername [, string username [,string password]]])
```

Description

The mssql_connect() function, which is available from PHP 3.0 to PHP 3.0.16 along with PHP 4.0 and higher, creates a connection to an MS SQL Server. The servername parameter should be a valid server name as defined in the 'interfaces' file. If a connection is already open with the same arguments, that connection's identifier will be returned instead of opening a new connection. The connection will be closed at the end of the script's processing or when a call to mssql_close() is called.

mssql_data_seek()

Syntax

```
int mssql_data_seek (int result_identifier, int row_number)
```

Description

The mssql_data_seek() function, which is available from PHP 3.0 to PHP 3.0.16 along with PHP 4.0 and higher, moves the internal row pointer for the result set referenced by the result_identifier to the row_number. This is used to set the row that the next call to mssql_fetch_row() will return.

mssql_fetch_array()

Syntax

```
int mssql_fetch_array (int result)
```

Description

The mssql_fetch_array() function, which is available from PHP 3.0 to PHP 3.0.16 along with PHP 4.0 and higher, is similar to mssql_fetch_row() in that it returns a row with data stored with the numerical indices. But mssql_fetch_array() also adds the ability to access the data with associative indices where the field names are the keys. The performance difference between the two functions is negligible.

mssql_fetch_field()

Syntax

```
object mssql_fetch_field (int result [,int field_offset])
```

Description

The mssql_fetch_field() function, which is available from PHP 3.0 to PHP 3.0.16 along with PHP 4.0 and higher, returns an object that has field information for the result set indicated by the result parameter. If no field_offset parameter is specified, the next field is examined. The returned object has the following properties:

- *name*—Column name. If the column is a result of a function, this property is set to computed#N, where #N is a serial number.

- *column_source*—The table from which the column was taken.

- *max_length*—Maximum length of the column.

- *numeric*—1 if the column is numeric.

mssql_fetch_object()

Syntax

```
int msssql_fetch_object (int result)
```

Description

The `mssql_fetch_object()` function, which is available from PHP 3.0 to PHP 3.0.16 along with PHP 4.0 and higher, fetches a row as an object and returns the properties or FALSE if there are no more rows. Use field names to access the data in the returned object.

mssql_fetch_row()

Syntax

```
array mssql_fetch_row (int result)
```

Description

The `mssql_fetch_row()` function, which is available from PHP 3.0 to PHP 3.0.16 along with PHP 4.0 and higher, returns a row as an enumerated array or FALSE if no more rows exist in the result set referenced by the *result* parameter. Each result column is stored in a zero-based array offset.

mssql_field_length()

Syntax

```
int mssql_field_length (int result [, int offset])
```

Description

The `mssql_field_length()` function, which is available from PHP 3.0.3 to PHP 3.0.16 along with PHP 4.0b4 and higher, returns the length of a field in the result set referenced by the *result* parameter at the location indicated by the *offset* parameter.

mssql_field_name()

Syntax

```
int mssql_field_name (int result [,int offset])
```

Description

The `mssql_field_name()` function, which is available from PHP 3.0.3 to PHP 3.0.16 along with PHP 4.0 and higher, returns the name of a field in the *result* set at the *offset* location.

mssql_field_seek()

Syntax

```
int mssql_field_seek (int result, int field_offset)
```

Description

The mssql_field_seek() function, which is available from PHP 3.0 to PHP 3.0.16 along with PHP 4.0 and higher, sets the field position in the result set to the specified offset. If the next call to mssql_fetch_field() doesn't include an offset, this field will be returned.

mssql_field_type()

Syntax

```
string mssql_field_type (int result [, int offset])
```

Description

The mssql_field_type() function, which is available from PHP 3.0.3 to PHP 3.0.16 along with PHP 4.0 and higher, returns the type of a field in the result set at the offset location.

mssql_free_result()

Syntax

```
int mssql_free_result (int result)
```

Description

The mssql_free_result() function, which is available from PHP 3.0 to PHP 3.0.16 along with PHP 4.0 and higher, frees all memory associated with the result set. This will happen automatically at the end of a script's processing, so it is not usually necessary to call this function.

mssql_get_last_message

Syntax

```
string msssql_get_last_message (void)
```

Description

The `mssql_get_last_message()` function, which is available from PHP 3.0 to PHP 3.0.16 along with PHP 4.0 and higher, returns the last message generated from the server.

mssql_min_error_severity()

Syntax

```
void mssql_min_error_severity (int severity)
```

Description

The `mssql_min_error_severity()` function, which is available from PHP 3.0 to PHP 3.0.16 along with PHP 4.0 and higher, sets the minimum threshold for the errors generated by the server.

mssql_min_message_severity()

Syntax

```
void mssql_min_message_severity (int severity)
```

Description

The `mssql_min_message_severity()` function, which is available from PHP 3.0 to PHP 3.0.16 along with PHP 4.0 and higher, sets the maximum threshold for the messages generated by the server.

mssql_num_fields()

Syntax

```
int mssql_num_fields (int result)
```

Description

The `mssql_num_fields()` function, which is available from PHP 3.0 to PHP 3.0.16 along with PHP 4.0 and higher, returns the number of fields in the `result` set.

mssql_num_rows()

Syntax

```
int mssql_num_rows (int result)
```

Description

The mssql_num_rows() function, which is available from PHP 3.0 to PHP 3.0.16 along with PHP 4.0 and higher, returns the number of rows in the *result* set.

mssql_pconnect()

Syntax

```
int mssql_pconnect (string servername [, string username [, string password]]])
```

Description

The mssql_pconnect() function, which is available from PHP 3.0 to PHP 3.0.16 along with PHP 4.0 and higher, acts similar to mssql_connect() except that it first looks for a persistent connection that is already established. If a persistent connection is available, the function uses it instead of opening a new one. Secondly, the connection does not close with the end of a script's processing.

mssql_query()

Syntax

```
int mssql_query (string query [, int link_identifier])
```

Description

The mssql_query() function, which is available from PHP 3.0 to PHP 3.0.16 along with PHP 4.0 and higher, sends a *query* to the database indicated by the *link_identifier* parameter. If no *link_identifier* is specified, a connection attempt is made as if mssql_connect() were called. A *result_identifier* is returned on success; otherwise, FALSE is returned.

mssql_result()

Syntax

```
int mssql_result (int result, int i, mixed field)
```

Description

The mssql_result() function, which is available from PHP 3.0 to PHP 3.0.16 along with PHP 4.0 and higher, returns the contents of one column of a *result* set. The *field* parameter can be one of three values: the offset, the fieldname, or the field's table name dot field name. The column name will be the alias value if specified. If processing several columns or the entire row of the result set, you should use mssql_fetch_row(), mssql_fetch_array(), or mssql_fetch_object() because they are more efficient. Also note that specifying an offset is more efficient than using column names.

mssql_select_db()

Syntax

```
int mssql_select_db (string database_name [, int link_identifier])
```

Description

The mssql_select_db() function, which is available from PHP 3.0 to PHP 3.0.16 along with PHP 4.0 and higher, sets the active database for the server that is referenced by the *link_identifier* parameter. If no *link_identifier* is specified, an attempt will be made to open a connection as though mssql_connect() were called.

mSQL

The mSQL functions enable you access to data in an mSQL database. More information can be found at http://www.Hughes.com.ua. To include support for this database, compile with the --with-msql=[dir] option where *dir* is typically /usr/local/Hughes. The following example connects to the user database and retrieves user123's password from the users table:

```
<?
$msql_link_id = msql_connect("users");
$msql_result_id =
```

```
msql_query ("select password from users where username=user123",$msql_link_id);
$results = msql_fetch(msql_result_id);
echo $results[0];
mssql_close($msql_link_id);
?>
```

msql()

Syntax

```
int msql (string database, string query, int link_identifier)
```

Description

The msql() function, which is available from PHP 3.0 to PHP 3.0.16 along with PHP 4.0 and higher, executes the *query* against the *database* specified using the optional *link_identifier* parameter. If no *link_identifier* is specified, it attempts to create a connection as though msql_connect() were called with no arguments. The return value is an mSQL query identifier to the query result, or FALSE on error.

msql_affected_rows()

Syntax

```
int msql_affected_rows (int query_identifier)
```

Description

The msql_affected_rows() function, which is available from PHP 3.0.6 to PHP 3.0.16 along with PHP 4.0 and higher, returns the number of rows impacted by the execution of the query referenced by the *query_identifier* parameter.

msql_close()

Syntax

```
int msql_close (int link identifier)
```

Description

The msql_close() function, which is available from PHP 3.0 to PHP 3.0.16 along with PHP 4.0 and higher, closes the connection referenced by the *link_identifier* parameter. If no link is specified, an attempt to close the last opened link is made. This function is not normally necessary because non-persistent connections are automatically closed at the end of script processing.

msql_connect()

Syntax

```
int msql_connect ([string hostname [, string hostname[:port]
[, string username, [, string password]]])
```

Description

The `msql_connect()` function, which is available from PHP 3.0 to PHP 3.0.16 along with PHP 4.0 and higher, establishes an mSQL connection. The return value is an mSQL link identifier on success and FALSE otherwise. The *hostname* parameter is optional and defaults to the local host. If a subsequent identical call is made with the same arguments and a link still exists, its link identifier is returned instead of opening a new link. The link created by this function will be destroyed when a script completes processing or when `msql_close()` is called.

msql_create_db()

Syntax

```
int msql_create_db (string database_name [, int link_identifier])
```

Description

The `msql_create_db()` function, which is available from PHP 3.0 to PHP 3.0.16 along with PHP 4.0 and higher, attempts to create a new database on the server referenced by the *link_identifier* parameter, or the last opened connection if *link_identifier* is not present.

msql_createdb()

Syntax

```
int msql_createdb (string database_name [, int link_identifier ])
```

Description

The `msql_createdb()` function, which is available from PHP 3.0 to PHP 3.0.16 along with PHP 4.0 and higher, is identical to the `msqsl_create_db()` function.

msql_data_seek()

Syntax

```
int msql_data_seek (int query_identifier, int row_number )
```

Description

The `msql_data_seek()` function, which is available from PHP 3.0 to PHP 3.0.16 along with PHP 4.0 and higher, moves the internal row pointer for the result set associated with the *query_identifier* to the row *row_number*. The next call to `msql_fetch_row()` will return the specified row.

msql_dbname()

Syntax

```
string msql_dbname (int query_identifier, int i)
```

Description

The `msql_dbname()` function, which is available from PHP 3.0 to PHP 3.0.16 along with PHP 4.0 and higher, returns the database name stored in position *i* of the result set pointed to by *query_identifier* for the `msql_dbname()` function. The `msql_numrows()` function can also be used to determine how many database names are available.

msql_drop_db()

Syntax

```
int msql_drop_db (string database_name, int link_identifier )
```

Description

The `msql_drop_db()` function, which is available from PHP 3.0 to PHP 3.0.16 along with PHP 4.0 and higher, attempts to remove the database *database_name* on the server indicated with the *link_identifier*. The return value is TRUE for success and FALSE otherwise.

msql_dropdb()

Syntax

```
int msql_drop_db (string database_name, int link_identifier )
```

Description

The msql_dropdb() function, which is available from PHP 3.0 to PHP 3.0.16 along with PHP 4.0 and higher, is identical to msql_drop_db().

msql_error()

Syntax

```
string msql_error()
```

Description

The msql_error() function, which is available from PHP 3.0 to PHP 3.0.16 along with PHP 4.0 and higher, returns the error message associated with the last mSQL call.

msql_fetch_array()

Syntax

```
int msql_fetch_array (int query_identifier [, int result_type ])
```

Description

The msql_fetch_array() function, which is available from PHP 3.0 to PHP 3.0.16 along with PHP 4.0 and higher, returns an array that represents the fetched row from the query_identifier, or FALSE if no more rows exist in the result set. This function extends the features of msql_fetch_row() in that it stores the data in not only the numeric indices of the array, but also as associate indices with the field names acting as the keys. The result_type parameter is optional and can take the values MSQL_ASSOC, MSQL_NUM, and MYSQL_BOTH, and is used to indicate what the format of the array returned should take. Note that the performance difference between msql_fetch_row() and msql_fetch_array() is negligible.

msql_fetch_field()

Syntax

```
object msql_fetch_field (int query_identifier, int field_offset)
```

Description

The `msql_fetch_field()` function, which was added in PHP 3.0.7 and PHP 4.0, returns an object containing field information for the result set associated with the `query_identifier` parameter. If no `field_offset` is specified, the next field that would be retrieved by `msql_fetch_field()` is examined. The returned properties of the object are

- *name*—Column name
- *table*—Name of the table to which the column belongs
- *not_null*—1 if the column cannot be null
- *primary_key*—1 if the column is a primary key
- *unique*—1 if the column is a unique key
- *type*—The type of the column

msql_fetch_object()

Syntax

```
int msql_fetch_object (int query_identifier [, int result_type])
```

Description

The `msql_fetch_object()` function, which is available from PHP 3.0 to PHP 3.0.16 along with PHP 4.0 and higher, returns an object that corresponds to the fetched row in the result set referenced by the `query_identifier`. Because an object is returned instead of an array (as with `msql_fetch_array()`), you may access the data only by field names. The optional parameter `result_type` is a constant and can take the values `MSQL_ASSOC`, `MSQL_NUM`, and `MSQL_BOTH`. The performance of this function compared `msql_fetch_array()` is equal or only slightly behind `msql_fetch_row()`, and the difference is effectively negligible.

msql_fetch_row()

Syntax

```
array msql_fetch_row (int query_identifier)
```

Description

The msql_fetch_row() function, which is available from PHP 3.0 to PHP 3.0.16 along with PHP 4.0 and higher, returns an enumerated array that corresponds to the row fetched from the result set referenced by the *query_identifier* parameter. Each result column is stored at the zero-based offset of the array. The return value is FALSE if no more rows exist in the result set.

msql_fieldname()

Syntax

```
string msql_fieldname (int query_identifier, int field)
```

Description

The msql_fieldname() function, which is available from PHP 3.0 to PHP 3.0.16 along with PHP 4.0 and higher, returns the name of the field in the result set referenced by the *query_identifier* and located at the *field* index.

msql_field_seek()

Syntax

```
int msql_field_seek (int query_identifier, int field_offset )
```

Description

The msql_field_seek() function, which is available from PHP 3.0 to PHP 3.0.16 along with PHP 4.0 and higher, seeks to the specified *field_offset* in the result set referenced by the *query_identifier*. The next call to msql_fetch_field() will use this field if no offset is specified.

msql_fieldtable()

Syntax

```
int msql_fieldtable (int query_identifier, int field)
```

Description

The `msql_fieldtable()` function, which is available from PHP 3.0 to PHP 3.0.16 along with PHP 4.0 and higher, returns the name of the table from which the *field* parameter came.

msql_fieldtype()

Syntax

```
string msql_fieldtype (int query_identifier, int i)
```

Description

The `msql_fieldtype()` function, which is available from PHP 3.0 to PHP 3.0.16 along with PHP 4.0 and higher, returns the field type for the field at position *i* in the result set referenced by the *query_identifier*. The return values include `'int'`, `'string'`, and `'real'`.

msql_fieldflags()

Syntax

```
string msql_fieldflags (int query_identifier, int i)
```

Description

The `msql_fieldflags()` function, which is available from PHP 3.0 to PHP 3.0.16 along with PHP 4.0 and higher, returns the field flags for the field located at *i* in the result set referenced by the *query_identifier*. The return value will be `'not null'`, `'primary key'`, a combination of the two, or an empty string (`""`).

msql_fieldlen()

Syntax

```
int msql_fieldlen (int query_identifier, int i)
```

Description

The `msql_fieldlen()` function, which is available from PHP 3.0 to PHP 3.0.16 along with PHP 4.0 and higher, returns the length of the field located at *i* in the result referenced by the *query_identifier* parameter.

msql_free_result()

Syntax

```
int msql_free_result (int query_identifier)
```

Description

The `msql_free_result()` function, which is available from PHP 3.0 to PHP 3.0.16 along with PHP 4.0 and higher, releases the memory associated with the result set referenced by the `query_identifier` parameter. This is not normally necessary because all resources are freed automatically when a script completes its processing.

msql_freeresult()

Syntax

```
int msql_freeresult (int query_identifier)
```

Description

The `msql_freeresult()` function, which is available from PHP 3.0 to PHP 3.0.16 along with PHP 4.0 and higher, is the same as the `msql_free_result()` function. It releases the memory associated with the result set referenced by the `query_identifier` parameter. This is not normally necessary because all resources are freed automatically when a script completes its processing.

msql_list_fields()

Syntax

```
int msql_list_fields (string database, string tablename)
```

Description

The `msql_list_fields()` function, which is available from PHP 3.0 to PHP 3.0.16 along with PHP 4.0 and higher, returns information about the `tablename` in the given `database`. The return value can be used with `msql_fieldflags()`, `msql_fieldlen()`, `msql_fieldname()`, and `msql_fieldtype()`. The return value is FALSE if an error occurred. More information can be found in `$phperrmsg`, along with a printed message, unless the function was called with `@msql_list_fields()`.

msql_listfields()

Syntax

```
int msql_listfields (string database, string tablename )
```

Description

The msql_listfields() function, which is available from PHP 3.0 to PHP 3.0.16 along with PHP 4.0 and higher, is identical to the msql_list_fields() function.

msql_list_dbs()

Syntax

```
int msql_list_dbs(void)
```

Description

The msql_list_dbs() function, which is available from PHP 3.0 to PHP 3.0.16 along with PHP 4.0 and higher, returns a pointer to a list of databases currently available from the msql daemon. Use msql_dbname() to traverse the list.

msql_listdbs()

Syntax

```
int msql_listdbs(void)
```

Description

The msql_listdbs() function, which is available from PHP 3.0 to PHP 3.0.16 along with PHP 4.0 and higher, is identical to the msql_list_dbs() function.

msql_list_tables()

Syntax

```
int msql_list_tables (string database)
```

Description

The `msql_list_tables()` function, which is available from PHP 3.0 to PHP 3.0.16 along with PHP 4.0 and higher, returns a pointer to a list of tables in the msql *database*. The `msql_tablename()` function should be used to traverse the list.

msql_listtables()

Syntax

```
int msql_list_tables (string database)
```

Description

The `msql_listtables()` function, which is available from PHP 3.0 to PHP 3.0.16 along with PHP 4.0 and higher, is identical to `msql_list_tables()`.

msql_num_fields()

Syntax

```
int msql_num_fields (int query_identifier)
```

Description

The `msql_num_fields()` function, which is available from PHP 3.0 to PHP 3.0.16 along with PHP 4.0 and higher, returns the number of fields in the result set referenced by the *query_identifier* parameter.

msql_num_rows()

Syntax

```
int msql_num_rows(int query_identifier)
```

Description

The `msql_num_rows()` function, which is available from PHP 3.0 to PHP 3.0.16 along with PHP 4.0 and higher, returns the number of rows in the result set referenced by the *query_identifier*.

msql_numfields()

Syntax

```
int msql_numfields (int query_identifier)
```

Description

The msql_numfields() function, which is available from PHP 3.0 to PHP 3.0.16 along with PHP 4.0 and higher, is identical to the msql_num_fields() function.

msql_numrows()

Syntax

```
int msql_numrows(int query_identifier)
```

Description

The msql_numrows() function, which is available from PHP 3.0 to PHP 3.0.16 along with PHP 4.0 and higher, is identical to the msql_num_rows() function.

msql_pconnect()

Syntax

```
int msql_pconnect (string hostname [, string hostname[:port]
 [, string username [, string password ]]]])
```

Description

The msql_pconnect() function, which is available from PHP 3.0 to PHP 3.0.16 along with PHP 4.0 and higher, opens a persistent connection to an mSQL database and returns the link identifier on success and returns FALSE otherwise. The function tries to find an existing persistent connection and return its handle instead of opening a new connection, if possible. Also, the connection will not be closed with the end of a script's processing or by calling the msql_close() command.

msql_query()

Syntax

```
int msql_query (string query, int link_identifier)
```

Description

The msql_query() function, which is available from PHP 3.0 to PHP 3.0.16 along with PHP 4.0 and higher, sends the *query* to the server associated with the specified *link_identifier*. If no *link_identifier* is specified, the last opened link is used. If no links are open, a connection attempt is made as if msql_connect() were called. The return value is a link identifier on success and FALSE otherwise.

msql_regcase()

Syntax

```
string msql_regcase (string string)
```

Description

The msql_regcase() function, which is available from PHP 3.0 to PHP 3.0.16 along with PHP 4.0 and higher, makes a regular expression for a case-insensitive match. The return value will be a valid regular expression that matches *string*. The resulting expression is *string* with each character converted to a bracket expression.

msql_result()

Syntax

```
int msql_result (int query_identifier, int i, mixed field)
```

Description

The msql_result() function, which is available from PHP 3.0 to PHP 3.0.16 along with PHP 4.0 and higher, returns the contents of the cell at the row specified by the *i* parameter in the corresponding *field*. The *field* parameter can be the field name, field's offset, or the table name dot field name (*tablename.fieldname*). In the case where a column alias is used, use it instead of the column name. When dealing with large result sets, it is more efficient to fetch a row at a time, than to fetch individual cells. Also, using offsets has better performance than using names.

msql_select_db()

Syntax

```
int msql_select_db (string database_name, int link_identifier)
```

Description

The `msql_select_db()` function, which is available from PHP 3.0 to PHP 3.0.16 along with PHP 4.0 and higher, sets the current active *database_name* for the connection referenced by the *link_identifier* parameter. If no link is specified, the last open link is used; if no link is available, the function attempts to establish a new one. The return value is TRUE on success and FALSE otherwise.

msql_selectdb()

Syntax

```
int msql_selectdb (string database_name, int link_identifier)
```

Description

The `msql_selectdb()` function, which is available from PHP 3.0 to PHP 3.0.16 along with PHP 4.0 and higher, is identical to `msql_selectdb()`.

msql_tablename()

Syntax

```
string msql_tablename (int query_identifier, int field)
```

Description

The `msql_tablename()` function, which is available from PHP 3.0 to PHP 3.0.16 along with PHP 4.0 and higher, uses the *query_identifier* returned by the `msql_list_tables()` function along with the *field* index and returns the corresponding table name for that field. The `msql_numrows()` function can be used to determine the number of tables in the result pointer.

MySQL

The MySQL functions enable you to access data in a MySQL database. More information can be found at http://www.mysql.com. To include MySQL support, use configure with the `--with-mysql=<path to mysql>`. Specifying a *path to mysql* value is optional, but recommended if you are using different versions of PHP at the same time. The following example connects to the user database and retrieves user123's password from the users table:

```
<?
$mysql_link_id = mysql_connect("users");
$mysql_result_id =
mysql_query ("select password from users where
username=user123",$mysql_link_id);
$results = mysql_fetch_row(mysql_result_id);
echo $results[0];
mysql_close($mysql_link_id);
?>
```

mysql_affected_rows()

Syntax

```
int mysql_affected_rows ([int link_identifier])
```

Description

The `mysql_affected_rows()` function, which is available from PHP 3.0 to PHP 3.0.16 along with PHP 4.0 and higher, returns the number of rows affected by the previous MySQL operation (insert, update, or delete) performed on the `link_identifier`. The last open link is assumed if no `link_identifier` is specified. If the previous statement was a delete with no `where` clause (all rows deleted), the return value will be 0. For select statements, you should use the `mysql_num_rows()` function to see how many rows were returned. Also note that when performing an update statement, if the result is that no rows change even though they meet the `where` clause criteria, the return value will be 0. The following example opens the user table in the users database and retrieves user123's password:

```
<?

$mysql_db = mysql_connect ("users");
$mysql_result_id =
mysql_query ("users","select password where username='user123'",mysql_db);
$mysql_row = mysql_fetch_row($mysql_result_id);
echo mysql_row[0];
mysql_close ($mysql_db);
?>
```

mysql_change_user()

Syntax

```
int mysql_change_user (string user, string password,
[, string database [, int link_identifier ]])
```

Description

The mysql_change_user() function, which is available from PHP 3.0.13 to PHP 3.0.16, changes the logged-in user of the active connection to the parameter values specified using the link_identifier connection, or the current connection if none is specified. If the function fails, the currently connected user maintains his connection.

mysql_close()

Syntax

```
int mysql_close ([int link_identifier])
```

Description

The mysql_close() function, which is available from PHP 3.0 to PHP 3.0.16 along with PHP 4.0 and higher, closes the connection referenced by the link_identifier parameter, or the last opened link if none is specified. Closing a link occurs automatically at the end of a script's processing, so this function isn't normally used.

mysql_connect()

Syntax

```
int mysql_connect ([string hostname [:port] [:/path/to/socket]
[, string username [, string password]]])
```

Description

The mysql_connect() function, which is available from PHP 3.0 to PHP 3.0.16 along with PHP 4.0 and higher, returns a link identifier on establishment of a connection and FALSE on failure. The host:port parameter defaults to 'localhost:3306', and username defaults to the owner of the server process, and password defaults to an empty string. The hostname parameter can also include a port or a path/to/socket for the local host. A subsequent identical call to this function will cause an existing link to be returned if available. Also, the link will be closed automatically when a script completes its processing unless it is explicitly closed using the `msql_close()` function.

mysql_create_db()

Syntax

```
int mysql_create_db (string database_name [, int link_identifier])
```

Description

The `mysql_create_db()` function, which is available from PHP 3.0 to PHP 3.0.16 along with PHP 4.0 and higher, attempts to create a new database named *database_name* on the server referenced by the *link_identifier*. Note that for backward compatibility, `mysql_createdb()` can also be used.

mysql_data_seek()

Syntax

```
int mysql_data_seek_ (int result_identifier, int row_number)
```

Description

The `mysql_data_seek()` function, which is available from PHP 3.0 to PHP 3.0.16 along with PHP 4.0 and higher, moves the internal row pointer for the result set referenced by the *result_identifier* to the *row_number*. The next call to `mysql_fetch_row()` would then return that row. Note that row numbers start with 0.

mysql_db_name()

Syntax

```
int mysql_db_name (int result, int row [, mixed field])
```

Description

The `mysql_db_name()` function, which is available from PHP 3.0 to PHP 3.0.16 along with PHP 4.0 and higher, is used to traverse the list of names created by the `mysql_list_dbs()` function. The *result* parameter indicates which result set to use, and the *row* and optional *field* parameters indicate which cell in the result set. A FALSE value is returned on error.

mysql_db_query()

Syntax

```
int mysql_db_query (string database, string query [, int link_identifier])
```

Description

The mysql_db_query() function, which is available from PHP 3.0 to PHP 3.0.16 along with PHP 4.0 and higher, sends the *query* to the *database* for execution utilizing the *link_identifier* or the last opened link. If no link exists, an attempt will be made to create one as though msql_connect() were called with no arguments. This function is equivalent to msql().

mysql_drop_db()

Syntax

```
int mysql_drop_db (string database_name [, int link_identifier])
```

Description

The mysql_drop_db() function, which is available from PHP 3.0 to PHP 3.0.16 along with PHP 4.0 and higher, attempts to remove the *database_name* from the server associated with the *link_identifier*. The return value is TRUE on success and failure otherwise. This function is identical to mysql_dropdb().

mysql_errno()

Syntax

```
int mysql_errno ([int link_identifier])
```

Description

The mysql_errno() function, which is available from PHP 3.0 to PHP 3.0.16 along with PHP 4.0 and higher, returns the numerical value of the error message last generated on the *link_identifier* connection. The return value is 0 if no error occurred.

mysql_error()

Syntax

```
string mysql_error ([int link_identifier])
```

Description

The `mysql_error()` function, which is available from PHP 3.0 to PHP 3.0.16 along with PHP 4.0 and higher, returns the text error of the last message associated with the *link_identifier* connection or an empty string if no error occurred.

mysql_fetch_array()

Syntax

```
array mysql_fetch_array (int result [, int result_type])
```

Description

The `mysql_fetch_array()` function, which is available from PHP 3.0 to PHP 3.0.16 along with PHP 4.0 and higher, fetches a row from the *result* set into an associative array. This extends the `mysql_fetch_row()` function because in addition to storing data in the numeric indices of the array, it also stores the data in associative indices where the field names are the keys. Note that if two columns share the same name, use the numeric index or an alias; otherwise, the last column listed takes precedence. The *result_type* parameter can be MYSQL_ASSOC, MYSQL_NUM, or MYSQL_BOTH.

mysql_fetch_field()

Syntax

```
object mysql_fetch_field (int result [, int field_offset])
```

Description

The `mysql_fetch_field()` function, which is available from PHP 3.0 to PHP 3.0.16 along with PHP 4.0 and higher, retrieves column information from the *result* set and returns it as an object. If a *field_offset* isn't specified, the next field that would be retrieved by `mysql_fetch_field()` is returned. The object has the following properties.

Name	Column Name
table	Name of the table the column belongs to
max_length	Maximum length of the column
not_null	1 if the column cannot be null
primary_key	1 if the column is a primary key

Name	Column Name
unique_key	1 if the column is a unique key
multiple_key	1 if the column is a non-unique key
numeric	1 if the column is numeric
blob	1 if the column is a BLOB
type	The type of the column
unsigned	1 if the column is unsigned
zerofill	1 if the column is zero-filled

mysql_fetch_lengths()

Syntax

```
array mysql_fetch_lengths (int result)
```

Description

The `mysql_fetch_lengths()` function, which is available from PHP 3.0 to PHP 3.0.16 along with PHP 4.0 and higher, returns a zero-based array with the lengths of each field in the last row fetched of the `result` set.

mysql_fetch_object()

Syntax

```
object mysql_fetch_object (int result [, int result_type])
```

Description

The `mysql_fetch_object()` function, which is available from PHP 3.0 to PHP 3.0.16 along with PHP 4.0 and higher, returns an object with properties that belong to the row fetched in the `result` set. To access data in the object, you must use the field names and not their offsets. The optional parameter `result_type` can take the values `MYSQL_ASSOC`, `MYSQL_NUM`, and `MYSQL_BOTH`. The performance of this function matches the `mysql_fetch_array()` function, and is only slightly behind the `mysql_fetch_row()` function; the performance difference is negligible.

mysql_fetch_row()

Syntax

```
array mysql_fetch_row(int result)
```

Description

The mysql_fetch_row() function, which is available from PHP 3.0 to PHP 3.0.16 along with PHP 4.0 and higher, returns an enumerated array for a row in the result set or FALSE if no rows are left. The columns of the row are in the array at a zero-based offset.

mysql_field_name()

Syntax

```
string mysql_field_name (int result, int field_index)
```

Description

The mysql_field_name() function, which is available from PHP 3.0 to PHP 3.0.16 along with PHP 4.0 and higher, returns the name of the field referenced by the field_index in the result set. Note that the index is zero based.

mysql_field_seek()

Syntax

```
int mysql_field_seek (int result, int field_offset)
```

Description

The mysql_field_seek() function, which is available from PHP 3.0 to PHP 3.0.16 along with PHP 4.0 and higher, seeks to the field_offset in the result set. If the next call to mysql_fetch_field() doesn't include an offset, this field will be returned.

mysql_field_table()

Syntax

```
string mysql_field_table (int result, int field_offset)
```

Description

The `mysql_field_table()` function, which is available from PHP 3.0 to PHP 3.0.16 along with PHP 4.0 and higher, returns the name of the table that the field specified by the *field_offset* in the *result* set is in. For backward capability, `mysql_fieldtable()` can also be used.

mysql_field_type()

Syntax

```
string mysql_field_type (int result, int field_offset)
```

Description

The `mysql_field_type()` function, which is available from PHP 3.0 to PHP 3.0.16 along with PHP 4.0 and higher, returns the type of the field specified by the *field_offset* in the *result* set. Possible return values include `int`, `real`, `blob`, and `string`, as well as the others defined in the MySQL documentation.

mysql_field_flags()

Syntax

```
string mysql_field_flags (int result, int field_offset)
```

Description

The `mysql_field_flags()` function, which is available from PHP 3.0 to PHP 3.0.16 along with PHP 4.0 and higher, returns the field flags for field specified by the *field_offset* in the *result* set. The flags are returned as a single-spaced string that can be further manipulated using the `explode()` function. The following flags can be reported `not_null`, `primary_key`, `unique_key`, `multiple_key`, `blob`, `unsigned`, `zerofill`, `binary`, `enum`, `auto_increment`, and `timestamp`. For backward compatibility, `mysql_fieldflags()` can be used.

mysql_field_len()

Syntax

```
int mysql_field_len (int result, int field_offset)
```

Description

The `mysql_field_len()` function, which is available from PHP 3.0 to PHP 3.0.16 along with PHP 4.0 and higher, returns the length the field specified by the *field_offset* parameter in the *result* set.

mysql_free_result()

Syntax

```
int mysql_free_result (int result)
```

Description

The `mysql_free_result()` function, which is available from PHP 3.0 to PHP 3.0.16 along with PHP 4.0 and higher, frees all memory associated with the *result* set. This function is not typically used because a result set is freed automatically when the script completes its processing.

mysql_insert_id()

Syntax

```
int mysql_insert_id ([int link_identifier])
```

Description

The `mysql_insert_id()` function, which is available from PHP 3.0 to PHP 3.0.16 along with PHP 4.0 and higher, returns the ID that was automatically generated for an AUTO_INCREMENT column on the previous insert statement performed on the *link_identifier* connection. If the connection is not specified, the previous link is assumed. The return value will be 0 if no value was generated for the last statement. Note that the last ID generated can be retrieved using the internal MySQL function LAST_INSERT_ID(). If the column type is bigint, you must use the internal MySQL function instead of this function.

mysql_list_fields()

Syntax

```
int mysql_list_fields (string database_name,
string table_name [, int link_identifier ])
```

Description

The mysql_list_fields() function, which is available from PHP 3.0 to PHP 3.0.16
along with PHP 4.0 and higher, returns a pointer to information about the given
table_name in the *database_name* using the *link_identifier*. The resulting list can be
examined using mysql_field_flags(), mysql_field_len(), mysql_field_name(), and
mysql_field_type(). The return value is a positive number representing the result
identifier or FALSE if an error occurs. For backward compatibility,
mysql_listfields() is also supported.

mysql_list_dbs()

Syntax

```
int_mysql_list_dbs ([int link_identifier])
```

Description

The mysql_list_dbs() function, which is available from PHP 3.0 to PHP 3.0.16 along
with PHP 4.0 and higher, returns a pointer to a list of the currently available databases
on the MySQL daemon. Use the mysql_tablename() function to traverse the list.

mysql_list_tables()

Syntax

```
int mysql_list_tables (string database, [, int link_identifier])
```

Description

The mysql_list_tables() function, which is available from PHP 3.0 to PHP 3.0.16
along with PHP 4.0 and higher, returns a pointer to a list of tables for the *database*.
The mysql_tablename() function should be used to traverse the list.

mysql_num_fields()

Syntax

```
int myssql_num_fields (int result)
```

Description

The mysql_num_fields() function, which is available from PHP 3.0 to PHP 3.0.16 along with PHP 4.0 and higher, returns the number of fields in the *result* set. For backward compatibility, mysql_numfields() is also supported.

mysql_num_rows()

Syntax

```
int mysql_num_rows (int result)
```

Description

The mysql_num_rows() function, which is available from PHP 3.0 to PHP 3.0.16 along with PHP 4.0 and higher, returns the number of rows in a result set. This is valid only for select statements. If you need to determine the number of rows affected by an insert, update, or delete statement, you should use the mysql_affected_rows() function. For backward compatibility, the mysql_numrows() function is also supported.

mysql_pconnect()

Syntax

```
int mysql_pconnect ([string hostname [:port] [:/path/to/socket]
[, string username [, string password]]])
```

Description

The mysql_pconnect() function, which is available from PHP 3.0 to PHP 3.0.16 along with PHP 4.0 and higher, is used to establish a persistent connection to a MySQL server. The default *host:port* is localhost:3306, the default *username* is the name of the user that owns the server process, and the default *password* is the empty string. The *hostname* parameter can also include a port or path to socket. If a persistent connection already exists, it will be returned instead and the connection is not closed on completion of a script's processing.

mysql_query()

Syntax

```
int mysql_query (string query [, int link_identifier])
```

Description

The `mysql_query()` function, which is available from PHP 3.0 to PHP 3.0.16 along with PHP 4.0 and higher, sends the *query* to the server referenced by the *link_identifier*. If a link isn't specified, the last opened link is used. If no link is available, an attempt to establish one is made as though `mysql_connect()` were called with no arguments. Note that the *query* string should not end with a semicolon. The return value is TRUE for success and FALSE otherwise, although a TRUE return value doesn't guarantee that the query affected any rows of data or returned a result set.

mysql_result()

Syntax

```
mixed mysql_result (int result, int row [, mixed field])
```

Description

The `mysql_result()` function, which is available from PHP 3.0 to PHP 3.0.16 along with PHP 4.0 and higher, returns the contents of a cell in the *result* set located at the *row* and optional *field* position. The *field* parameter can be the name, offset, or table name dot fieldname (*tablename.fieldname*). If the select statement used aliases, use those names instead of the column names. If obtaining multiple cells for one row, it is often quicker to fetch the entire row. Also, better performance can be achieved by using the offsets instead of the names.

mysql_select_db()

Syntax

```
int mysql_select_db (string database_name [, int link_identifier])
```

Description

The `mysql_select_db()` function, which is available from PHP 3.0 to PHP 3.0.16 along with PHP 4.0 and higher, selects the current active database for the server referenced by the *link_identifier* parameter, and if no link is specified, the last opened link is used. If no link exists, the function tries to establish one. For backward compatibility, the `mysql_selectdb()` function is supported.

mysql_tablename()

Syntax

```
string mysql_tablename int result, int i)
```

Description

The `mysql_tablename()` function, which is available from PHP 3.0 to PHP 3.0.16 along with PHP 4.0 and higher, traverses the list returned from the `mysql_list_tables()` function and returns the name of the table. The parameter *i* is used as an index into the list.

ODBC

The ODBC functions enable you to access data not only from databases for which ODBC drivers exist, but also from databases that have borrowed the semantics of ODBC. Such databases include Adabas D, IBM DB2, iODBC, Solid, and Sybase SQL Anywhere. Although ODBC was originally developed by Microsoft, it is now widely available on several platforms including most UNIX/Linux variations.

odbc_autocommit()

Syntax

```
int odbc_autocommit (int connection_id [, int OnOff])
```

Description

The `odbc_autocommit()` function, which is available from PHP 3.0.6 to PHP 3.0.16 along with PHP 4.0 and higher, returns the autocommit status for the *connection_id* if no *OnOff* value is supplied. A TRUE value means that autocommit is on, and FALSE indicates that it is off or an error occurred. Supply a value for the *OnOff* parameter to set it accordingly. Turning off autocommit is equivalent to starting a transaction.

odbc_binmode()

Syntax

```
int odbc_binmode (int result_id, int mode)
```

Description

The `odbc_binmode()` function, which is available from PHP 3.0.6 to PHP 3.0.16 along with PHP 4.0 and higher, determines how binary data should be handled. The possible *mode* values are as follows:

`ODBC_BINMODE_PASSTHRU`—Passthru BINARY data

`ODBC_BINMODE_RETURN`—Return as is

`ODBC_BINMODE_CONVERT`—Convert to char and return

When binary SQL data is converted to character C data, each byte (8 bits) is expressed as two ASCII characters. The ASCII characters are the hexadecimal equivalent for the binary data. If the *result_id* parameter is set to 0, these settings will be the default for future calls.

odbc_close()

Syntax

```
void obdc_close (int connection_id)
```

Description

The `odbc_close()` function, which is available from PHP 3.0.6 to PHP 3.0.16 along with PHP 4.0 and higher, closes the connection referenced by the *connection_id* unless transactions are still open. In such a case, the connection will remain open.

odbc_close_all()

Syntax

```
void odbc_close_all(void)
```

Description

The `odbc_close_all()` function, which is available from PHP 3.0.6 to PHP 3.0.16 along with PHP 4.0 and higher, closes all server connections unless transactions are still open. In such a case, the connections will remain open.

odbc_commit()

Syntax

```
int odbc_commit (int connection_id)
```

Description

The odbc_commit() function, which is available from PHP 3.0.6 to PHP 3.0.16 along with PHP 4.0 and higher, causes all pending transactions on the connection_id to be committed. The return value is TRUE on success and FALSE otherwise.

odbc_connect()

Syntax

```
int odbc_connect (string dsn, string user, string password [, int cursor_type])
```

Description

The odbc_connect() function, which is available from PHP 3.0.6 to PHP 3.0.16 along with PHP 4.0 and higher, establishes a connection to an ODBC data source. The return value is a connection ID on success and FALSE otherwise. The optional parameter cursor_type can take the values SQL_CUR_USE_IF_NEEDED, SQL_CUR_USE_ODBC, SQL_CUR_USE_DRIVER, and SQL_CUR_DEFAULT. The cursor_type parameter is not normally needed, but can be useful for resolving ODBC driver-related problems. Using SQL_CUR_USE_ODBC will often correct the issue.

odbc_cursor()

Syntax

```
string odbc_cursor (int result_id)
```

Description

The odbc_cursor() function, which is available from PHP 3.0.6 to PHP 3.0.16 along with PHP 4.0 and higher, returns the cursor name for the corresponding result_id.

odbc_do()

Syntax

```
int odbc_do (int conn_id, string query)
```

Description

The `odbc_do()` function, which is available from PHP 3.0.6 to PHP 3.0.16 along with PHP 4.0 and higher, executes the *query* on the *conn_id* connection.

odbc_exec()

Syntax

```
in odbc_exec (int connection_id, string query_string)
```

Description

The `odbc_exec()` function, which is available from PHP 3.0.6 to PHP 3.0.16 along with PHP 4.0 and higher, prepares and executes the statement specified in the *query_string* using the *connection_id* connection. An ODBC result identifier is returned on success and FALSE otherwise.

odbc_execute()

Syntax

```
int odbc_execute (int result_id [, array parameters_array])
```

Description

The `odbc_execute()` function, which is available from PHP 3.0.6 to PHP 3.0.16 along with PHP 4.0 and higher, executes a statement prepared with the `odbc_prepare()` function. The *parameters_array* should be used if there are parameters to pass to the statement. The return value is TRUE on success and FALSE otherwise.

odbc_fetch_into()

Syntax

```
int odbc_fetch_into (int result_id [, int rownumber, array result_array])
```

Description

The odbc_fetch_into() function, which is available from PHP 3.0.6 to PHP 3.0.16 along with PHP 4.0 and higher, fetches a row into the *result_array*, which should be passed by reference. The array will contain the column values starting at index 0. The *rownumber* parameter is used to indicate which row in the result set should be fetched, and the *result_id* references the appropriate result set.

odbc_fetch_row()

Syntax

```
int odbc_fetch_row (int result_id [, int row_number])
```

Description

The odbc_fetch_row() function, which is available from PHP 3.0.6 to PHP 3.0.16 along with PHP 4.0 and higher, fetches a row from the result set referenced by the *result_id* so that it may be accessed with the odbc_result() function. The return value is TRUE if a row was fetched and FALSE otherwise. To iterate through the result set, call this function with 1 as the *row_number* for the first call and omit the *row_number* for subsequent calls.

odbc_field_name()

Syntax

```
string odbc_field_name (int result_id, int field_number)
```

Description

The odbc_field_name() function, which is available from PHP 3.0.6 to PHP 3.0.16 along with PHP 4.0 and higher, returns the name of the column at the position *field_number* in the result set referenced by the *result_id*. The columns are 1-based and FALSE is returned if no columns exist or an error occurs.

odbc_field_type()

Syntax

```
int odbc_field_type (int result_id, string field_number)
```

Description

The odbc_field_type() function, which is available from PHP 3.0.6 to PHP 3.0.16 along with PHP 4.0 and higher, returns the SQL type of the column at the *field_number* in the result set referenced by the *result_id*. Note that the column numbering starts at 1.

odbc_field_len()

Syntax

```
int odbc_field_len (int result_id, int field_number)
```

Description

The odbc_field_len() function, which is available from PHP 3.0.6 to PHP 3.0.16 along with PHP 4.0 and higher, returns the length of the field referenced by the *field_number* in the result set referenced by the *result_id*. Note that the column numbering starts at 1.

odbc_free_result()

Syntax

```
int odbc_free_result (int result_id)
```

Description

The odbc_free_result() function, which is available from PHP 3.0.6 to PHP 3.0.16 along with PHP 4.0 and higher, frees the resources associated with the result set referenced by the *result_id*. Because the result set is automatically freed at the end of a script's processing, it is normally not necessary to call this function. Note that if autocommit is not set, any pending transactions are rolled back when this function is called.

odbc_longreadlen()

Syntax

```
int odbc_longreadlen (int result_id, int length)
```

Description

The odbc_longreadlen() function, which is available from PHP 3.0.6 to PHP 3.0.16 along with PHP 4.0 and higher, sets the number of bytes returned to PHP, where 0 indicates that long column data is passed through to the client.

odbc_num_fields()

Syntax

```
int odbc_num_fields (int result_id)
```

Description

The odbc_num_fields() function, which is available from PHP 3.0.6 to PHP 3.0.16 along with PHP 4.0 and higher, returns the number of columns in the result set referenced by the result_id parameter. The return value will be FALSE if an error occurred.

odbc_pconnect()

Syntax

```
int odbc_pconnect (string dsn, string user,
string password [, int cursor_type])
```

Description

The odbc_pconnect() function, which is available with PHP 3.0.6 and higher, establishes a persistent connection to an ODBC data source. The return value is a connection ID on success, and FALSE otherwise. The optional parameter cursor_type can take the values SQL_CUR_USE_IF_NEEDED, SQL_CUR_USE_ODBC, SQL_CUR_USE_DRIVER, and SQL_CUR_DEFAULT. The cursor_type parameter is not normally needed, but can be useful for resolving ODBC driver-related problems. Using SQL_CUR_USE_ODBC will often correct the issue. The connection will remain even after a script's processing is complete. If a persistent connection already exists that was created with the same arguments, that connection ID will be returned instead of creating a new one.

odbc_prepare()

Syntax

```
int odbc_prepare (int connection_id, string query_string )
```

Description

The odbc_prepare() function, which is available from PHP 3.0.6 and higher, prepares the *query_string* SQL statement for execution and returns an ODBC result identifier if successful. The result identifier is used when executing the statement.

odbc_num_rows()

Syntax

```
int odbc_num_rows (int result_id)
```

Description

The odbc_num_rows() function, which is available with PHP 3.0.6 and higher, is used to return the number of rows in an ODBC result set referenced by a *result_id*. For insert, update, and delete statements, the return value is the number of rows affected; for a select statement, the return value is the number of rows available in the result set. Note that this function returns -1 for many drivers when used with the result set of a select statement.

odbc_result()

Syntax

```
string odbc_result (int result_id, mixed field)
```

Description

The odbc_result() function, which is available with PHP 3.0.6 and higher, returns the contents of the field in the *result_id* result set, at the *field* position. The *field* parameter can be either an integer representing the column number (1 based), or a string with the name of the column. The return value will be FALSE if the column name or number is invalid.

odbc_result_all()

Syntax

```
int odbc_result_all (int result_id [, string format])
```

Description

The odbc_result_all() function, which is available with PHP 3.0.6 and higher, returns all the rows in the result set referenced by the result_id parameter, in a formatted HTML table. The optional format parameter represents any additional formatting that should be used with the table, such as borders or shading.

odbc_rollback()

Syntax

```
int odbc_rollback (int connection_id)
```

Description

The odbc_rollback() function, which is available with PHP 3.0.6 and higher, rolls back all pending transactions that are tied to the connection_id. The return value is TRUE on success and FALSE otherwise.

odbc_setoption()

Syntax

```
int odbc_setoption (int id, int function, int option, int param)
```

Description

The odbc_setoption() function, which is available with PHP 3.0.6 and higher, is used to modify the options for a result set or connection. The options and results of this function vary with ODBC drivers, so an ODBC programmer's reference should be consulted before using this function. The id parameter represents either the result ID or the connection ID to which you want to apply the parameters. The function parameter represents the ODBC function to use, where 0 is SQLSetConnectOption() and 1 is SQLSetStmtOption(). The option and param parameters represent the option and the value you want to set.

Oracle

The following functions enable you to access data stored in an Oracle database with interface libraries prior to OCI8. If you need more recent library support, you should use the OCI functions in the next section. The following example opens the users table and retrieves user123's password from the user table:

```
<?

$oracle_db = ora_logon("username@mytnsname","password");
ora_parse (1,"select password from user where username=user123",0);
ora_exec(1);
ora_fetch(1);
echo ora_getcolumn (1,"password");
ora_close(1);
ora_logoff ($oracle_db);
?>
```

ora_bind()

Syntax

```
int ora_bind (int cursor, string PHP_variable_name,
string SQL_parameter_name, int length, [, int type])
```

Description

The ora_bind() function, which is available with PHP 3.0 and higher, binds the PHP_variable_name to the SQL_parameter_name, which must be in the form ':name'. The optional type parameter is used to indicate how the SQL parameter will be used. A value of 0 (which is the default) indicates in/out. A value of 1 represents in and 2 represents out. With PHP 3.0.1 and higher, you may also use the constant values ORA_BIND_INOUT, ORA_BIND_IN, and ORA_BIND_OUT instead. This function must be called after ora_parse() and before ora_exec().

ora_close()

Syntax

```
int ora_close (int cursor)
```

Description

The ora_close() function, which is available with PHP 3.0 and higher, is used to close the *cursor*. The return value is TRUE for success and FALSE otherwise. This function is used in tandem with ora_close().

ora_columnname()

Syntax

```
string ora_columnname (int cursor, int column)
```

Description

The ora_columnname() function, which is available with PHP 3.0 and higher, returns the name of the column in the *cursor* at the *column* position. Note that the name is returned in all uppercase letters.

ora_columntype()

Syntax

```
string ora_columntype (int cursor, int column)
```

Description

The ora_columntype() function, which is available with PHP 3.0 and higher, returns the column type for the *column* in *cursor*. The possible return values are VARCHAR2, VARCHAR, CHAR, NUMBER, LONG, LONG RAW, ROWID, DATE, and CURSOR.

ora_commit()

Syntax

```
int ora_commit (int conn)
```

Description

The ora_commit() function, which is available with PHP 3.0 and higher, commits the transaction associated with the *conn* connection. A transaction begins at the start of a connection, or since the last commit or rollback, or when autocommit is turned off.

ora_commitoff()

Syntax

```
int ora_commitoff (int conn)
```

Description

The `ora_commitoff()` function, which is available with PHP 3.0 and higher, disables autocommit for connection indicated by the *conn* parameter.

ora_commiton()

Syntax

```
int ora_commiton (int conn)
```

Description

The `ora_commiton()` function, which is available with PHP 3.0 and higher, enables autocommit for connection indicated by the *conn* parameter.

ora_error()

Syntax

```
string ora_error (int cursor_or_connection)
```

Description

The `ora_error()` function, which is available with PHP 3.0 and higher, returns an error message that was generated on the *connection* or *cursor*. The format of the message is *XXX-NNNN*, where *XXX* represents the origin of the error and *NNNN* represents the error itself. For information on the error message, see Oracle's oerr ora command.

ora_errorcode()

Syntax

```
int ora_errorcode (int cursor_or_connection)
```

Description

The ora_errorcode() function, which is available with PHP 3.0 and higher, returns the numeric error code generated for the last statement executed with the given *cursor* or *connection*.

ora_exec()

Syntax

```
int ora_exec (int cursor)
```

Description

The ora_exec() function, which is available with PHP 3.0 and higher, executes a parsed statement against the specified *cursor*.

ora_fetch()

Syntax

```
int ora_fetch (int cursor)
```

Description

The ora_fetch() function, which is available with PHP 3.0 and higher, fetches a row of data from the given *cursor*. The return value is TRUE on success and FALSE otherwise.

ora_getcolumn()

Syntax

```
mixed ora_getcolumn (int cursor, mixed column)
```

Description

The ora_getcolumn() function, which is available with PHP 3.0 and higher, returns the data at the *column* position in the specified *cursor*. The return value will be FALSE if an error occurred or if other non-error conditions occurred, such as no data (NULL) or an empty string is found.

ora_logoff()

Syntax

```
int ora_logoff (int connection)
```

Description

The ora_logoff() function, which is available with PHP 3.0 and higher, closes the connection referenced by the connection parameter. The return value is TRUE on success and FALSE otherwise. The function will also effectively log out the user if that is the user's only connection.

ora_logon()

Syntax

```
int ora_logon (string user, string password)
```

Description

The ora_logon() function, which is available with PHP 3.0 and higher, creates a connection to an Oracle database with the given username and password. To include the TNS name, append @<TNSNAME> to the user name. The return value is a connection index or FALSE on failure. If using non-ASCII characters, be sure to set NLS_LANG in your environment.

ora_open()

Syntax

```
int ora_open (int connection)
```

Description

The ora_open() function, which is available with PHP 3.0 and higher, opens a cursor for the specified connection. The return value is a cursor index or FALSE on failure.

ora_parse()

Syntax

```
int ora_parse (int cursor_ind, string sql_statement, int defer)
```

Description

The ora_parse() function, which is available with PHP 3.0 and higher, parses the SQL statement or PL/SQL block referenced by the *sql_statement* parameter, and associates it with the cursor specified by the *cursor_ind* parameter. The return value is TRUE on success and FALSE otherwise.

ora_rollback()

Syntax

```
int ora_rollback (int connection)
```

Description

The ora_rollback() function, which is available with PHP 3.0 and higher, rolls back the transaction associated with the *connection*. The return value is TRUE on success and FALSE otherwise.

Oracle 8

The following functions enable you to access an Oracle 7 or 8 database by using the Oracle 8 interface library. These functions offer additional functionality not found in the standard Oracle extensions, including the binding of local and global variables to Oracle placeholders, along with full support for LOB, FILE, and ROWIDs.

ocidefinebyname()

Syntax

```
int ocidefinebyname (int stmt, string column-name,
mixed &variable, [, int type])
```

Description

The ocidefinebyname() function, which was added in PHP 3.0.7 and PHP 4.0, fetches columns into the user-defined variables. Note that the *column-name* parameter should be in uppercase, and that if you define a variable that doesn't exist in your statement, no error will be given.

ocibindbyname()

Syntax

```
int ocibindbyname (int stmt, string ph_name,
mixed &variable, int length, [,int type])
```

Description

The `ocibindbyname()` function, which was added in PHP 3.0.7 and PHP 4.0, binds the PHP variable indicated by the *&variable* parameter to the placeholder *ph_name* for the given SQL *stmt*. The *length* parameter is used to indicate the maximum length for the bind, whereas a -1 value causes the length to be set to *&variable*'s max length. The optional *type* parameter sets the descriptor to use and can take the values OCI_B_FILE (binary file), OCI_B_CFILE (character file), OCI_B_CLOB (character LOB), OCI_B_BLOB (binary LOB), and OCI_B_ROWID (ROWID). Whether the variable is input or output is determined at runtime.

ocilogon()

Syntax

```
int ocilogon (string username ,string password [string db ])
```

Description

The `ocilogon()` function, which is available in PHP 3.0.7 and higher, returns a connection identifier that is used as a handle for most other Oracle functions. The optional *db* parameter is used to identify either the name of the local Oracle instance you want to connect to, or an entry found in the tnsnames.ora file. If no *db* parameter is specified, PHP uses the ORACLE_SID or TWO_TASK environment variable to determine the database to which it should connect. Note that connections are shared at the page level when using this function, which means that commits and rollbacks apply to all transactions associated with the page, even if they exist in separate connections.

ociplogon()

Syntax

```
int ociplogon (string username, string password [, string db])
```

Description

The `ociplogon()` function, which is available in PHP 3.0.8 and higher, acts the same as the `ocilogon()` function except that a persistent connection is established, which is not destroyed at the end of script's processing.

ocinlogon()

Syntax

```
int ocinlogon (string username, string password [,string db])
```

Description

The `ocinlogon()` function, which is available in PHP 3.0.8 and higher, establishes a new connection to an Oracle database and logs on. The optional *db* parameter is used to identify either the name of the local Oracle instance you want to connect to, or an entry found in the tnsnames.ora file. If no *db* parameter is specified, PHP uses the `ORACLE_SID` or `TWO_TASK` environment variables to determine the database to which it should connect. This function forces a new connection to be established instead of sharing an existing connection if possible. Any commits and rollbacks performed on this connection are not shared with the page's other connections, unlike the `ocilogon()` function.

ocilogoff()

Syntax

```
int ocilogoff (int connection)
```

Description

The `ocilogoff()` function, which is available in PHP 3.0.4 and higher, destroys the *connection* indicated and frees any associated resources.

ociexecute()

Syntax

```
int ociexecute (int statement [, int mode])
```

Description

The `ociexecute()` function, which is available in PHP 3.0.4 and higher, executes a previously parsed statement. The optional *mode* parameter can be used to specify the execution mode; the default is `OCI_COMMIT_ON_SUCCESS`. If you don't want statements to commit automatically, you should use `OCI_DEFAULT` for your mode.

ocicommit()

Syntax

```
int ocicommit (int connection)
```

Description

The `ocicommit()` function, which is available in PHP 3.0.7 and higher, commits any pending transactions associated with the given *connection*.

ocirollback()

Syntax

```
int ocirollback (int connection)
```

Description

The `ocirollback()` function, which is available in PHP 3.0.7 and higher, rolls back the last committed transaction associated with the given *connection*.

ocinewdescriptor()

Syntax

```
string ocinewdescriptor (int connection, [, int type])
```

Description

The `ocinewdescriptor()` function, which is available in PHP 3.0.7 and higher, allocates storage for descriptors or LOB objects. The optional *type* parameter can have the value `OCI_D_FILE`, `OCI_D_LOB`, or `OCI_D_ROWID`. For LOB descriptors, the load, save, and savefile methods are associated with the descriptor, but for BFILE, only the load method exists.

ocirowcount()

Syntax

```
int ocirowcount (int statement)
```

Description

The ocirowcount() function, which is available in PHP 3.0.7 and higher, returns the number of rows affected for an update, insert, or delete statement. This function will not tell you the number of rows returned from a select statement.

ocinumcols()

Syntax

```
int ocinumcols (int stmt)
```

Description

The ocinumcols() function, which is available in PHP 3.0.4 and higher, returns the number of columns in a statement.

ociresult()

Syntax

```
mixed ociresult (int statement, mixed column)
```

Description

The ociresult() function, which is available in PHP 3.0.7 and higher, returns the data from the given column in the given statement. The return value is a string except for the abstract data types such as ROWID, LOB, and FILE.

ocifetch()

Syntax

```
int ocifetch (int statement)
```

Description

The ocifetch() function, which is available in PHP 3.0.7 and higher, fetches the next row of the result set identified by the *statement* parameter into the internal result buffer.

ocifetchinto()

Syntax

```
int ocifetchinto (int stmt, array &result [, int mode])
```

Description

The ocifetchinto() function, which is available in PHP 3.0.7 and higher, fetches the next row from the result set indicated by *stmt* into the *&result* array. The default behavior is for *&result* to be a 1-based array with all non-NULL columns as values. The optional *mode* parameter is used to change this behavior. The options are

- OCI_ASSOC—Return an associative array

- OCI_NUM—Return a numbered array starting with 1 (default)

- OCI_RETURN_NULLS—Return the NULL columns as well

- OCI_RETURN_LOBS—Return the value of a LOB instead of its descriptor

Note that these flags may be added together for combined behavior.

ocifetchstatement()

Syntax

```
int ocifetchstatement (int stmt, array &variable)
```

Description

The ocifetchstatement() function, which is available in PHP 3.0.7 and higher, fetches all the rows of the result set indicated by the *stmt* parameter into the *&variable* array.

ocicolumnisnull()

Syntax

```
int ocicolumnisnull (int stmt, mixed column)
```

Description

The ocicolumnisnull() function, which is available in PHP 3.0.4 and higher, returns TRUE if the *column* indicated in the result set *stmt* contains a NULL value. The *column* parameter can be either the 1-based column number or the column name.

ocicolumnsize()

Syntax

```
int ocicolumnsize (int stmt,mixed column)
```

Description

The ocicolumnsize() function, which is available in PHP 3.0.7 and higher, returns the size of the *column* in the result set *stmt*. The *column* parameter can be either the 1-based column number or the column name.

ociserverversion()

Syntax

```
string ociserverversion (int conn)
```

Description

The ociserverversion() function, which is available in PHP 3.0.4 and higher, returns a string containing information about which version of the Oracle server is running. *conn* is a valid connection to the server.

ocistatementtype()

Syntax

```
string ocistatementtype (int stmt)
```

Description

The ocistatementtype() function, which is available in PHP 3.0.7 and higher, returns the type of the result set *stmt*, which can be one of the following values: SELECT, UPDATE, DELETE, INSERT, CREATE, DROP, ALTER, BEGIN, DECLARE, or UNKNOWN.

ocinewcursor()

Syntax

```
int ocinewcursor (int conn)
```

Description

The ocinewcursor() function, which is available in PHP 3.0.8 and higher, allocates a new statement handle for the connection specified by the *conn* parameter. This function is used to bind reference cursors.

ocifreestatement()

Syntax

```
int ocifreestatement (int stmt)
```

Description

The ocifreestatement() function, which is available in PHP 3.0.7 and higher, frees all resources associated with the result set indicated by the *stmt* parameter.

ocifreecursor()

Syntax

```
int ocifreecursor (int stmt)
```

Description

The ocifreecursor() function, which is available in PHP 3.0.7 and higher, frees all resources associated with the cursor referenced by the *stmt* parameter.

ocicolumnname()

Syntax

```
string ocicolumnname (int stmt, int col)
```

Description

The `ocicolumnname()` function, which is available in PHP 3.0.4 and higher, returns the name of the column indicated by the `col` parameter in the result set `stmt`. The `col` parameter should be the 1-based column number for the statement.

ocicolumntype()

Syntax

```
mixed ocicolumntype (int stmt, int col)
```

Description

The `ocicolumntype()` function, which is available in PHP 3.0.4 and higher, returns the data type of the column indicated by the `col` parameter in the result set referenced by the `stmt` parameter, where `col` is the 1-based number of the column in the result set.

ociparse()

Syntax

```
int ociparse (int conn, string query)
```

Description

The `ociparse()` function, which is available in PHP 3.0.7 and higher, parses the referenced `query` for the given connection `conn`. The return value is a statement identifier for a valid query or FALSE otherwise. The `query` parameter can be any valid SQL statement.

ocierror()

Syntax

```
array ocierror ([int stmt | conn | global)
```

Description

The `ocierror()` function, which is available in PHP 3.0.7 and higher, returns the last error for the parameter specified and FALSE if no error occurred. If no parameter is specified, the last error encountered is returned. The return value is an associative array with the *code* key representing the Oracle error code and the value is the Oracle error string.

ociinternaldebug()

Syntax

```
void ociinternaldebug (int onoff)
```

Description

The `ociinternaldebug()` function, which was added in PHP 3.0.4 and PHP 4.0, toggles the internal debug output. The default is off (0).

PostgreSQL

The PostgreSQL functions enable you to access data in a Postgres database. More information can be found at http://www.PostgreSQL.org.

pg_close()

Syntax

```
bool pg_close (int connection)
```

Description

The `pg_close()` function, which is available in PHP 3.0 and higher, closes the referenced *connection* and returns TRUE on success and FALSE otherwise. This is not normally used because the connection is automatically closed at the end of a script's processing.

pg_cmdtuples()

Syntax

```
int pg_cmdtuples (int result_id)
```

Description

The pg_cmdtuples() function, which is available in PHP 3.0 and higher, returns the number of tuples (instances) affected by an insert, update, or delete query.

pg_connect()

Syntax

```
int pg_connect (string host, string port,
string options, string tty, string dbname)
```

Description

The pg_connect() function, which is available in PHP 3.0 and higher, establishes a connection to a PostgreSQL server and returns the connection index on success and FALSE otherwise. Each parameter should be a quoted string with options and tty being optional parameters.

pg_dbname()

Syntax

```
string pg_dbname (int connection)
```

Description

The pg_dbname() function, which is available in PHP 3.0 and higher, returns the name of the database for the given connection or FALSE if the connection is not valid.

pg_errormessage()

Syntax

```
string pg_errormessage (int connection)
```

Description

The `pg_errormessage()` function, which is available in PHP 3.0 and higher, returns a string containing the last error message generated on the given *connection*.

pg_exec()

Syntax

```
int pg_exec (int connection , string query)
```

Description

The `pg_exec()` function, which is available in PHP 3.0 and higher, executes the *query* utilizing the given *connection* and returns an index to the result set or FALSE on error.

pg_fetch_array()

Syntax

```
array pg_fetch_array (int result , int row [,int result_type])
```

Description

The `pg_fetch_array()` function, which is available in PHP 3.0.1 and higher, returns an array for the fetched *row* in the *result* set. The optional *result_type* parameter can take the following values: PGSQL_ASSOC, PGSQL_NUM, and PGSQL_BOTH. The returned array has the data in both indexed and associate formats with the column names as keys.

pg_fetch_object()

Syntax

```
object pg_fetch_object (int result , int row [, int result_type ])
```

Description

The `pg_fetch_object()` function, which is available in PHP 3.0.1 and higher, returns an object containing the data from the fetched row, with the fields accessible by name only. The optional *result_type* parameter can take the values PGSQL_ASSOC, PGSQL_NUM, and PGSQL_BOTH.

pg_fetch_row()

Syntax

```
array pg_fetch_row (int result, int row)
```

Description

The pg_fetch_row() function, which is available in PHP 3.0.1 and higher, returns a zero-based array containing the data in the *result* set at the indicated *row*.

pg_fieldisnull()

Syntax

```
int pg_fieldisnull (int result_id, int row, mixed, field)
```

Description

The pg_fieldisnull() function, which is available in PHP 3.0 and higher, returns TRUE if the *field* in the *row* for the referenced *result_id* is NULL and FALSE otherwise. The *field* parameter can be the zero-based column number of the column name.

pg_fieldname()

Syntax

```
string pg_fieldname (int result_id , int field_number)
```

Description

The pg_fieldname() function, which is available in PHP 3.0 and higher, returns the name of the field at the position *field_number* in the result set referenced by the *result_id* parameter. Note that field numbering starts at 0.

pg_fieldnum()

Syntax

```
int pg_fieldnum (int result_id, string field_name)
```

Description

The `pg_fieldnum()` function, which is available in PHP 3.0 and higher, returns the number of the given *field_name* in the result set identified by the *result_id* parameter.

pg_fieldprtlen()

Syntax

```
int pg_fieldprtlen (int result_id , int row_number, string field_name)
```

Description

The `pg_fieldprtlen()` function, which is available in PHP 3.0 and higher, returns the actual printed character length of a field referenced by the *field_name* parameter at the *row_number* in the result set referenced by the *result_id* parameter.

pg_fieldsize()

Syntax

```
int pg_fieldsize (int result_id, int field_number)
```

Description

The `pg_fieldsize()` function, which is available in PHP 3.0 and higher, returns the internal storage size of the field indicated by the *field_number* parameter in the result set referenced by the *result_id* parameter.

pg_fieldtype()

Syntax

```
string pg_fieldtype (int result_id, int field_number)
```

Description

The `pg_fieldtype()` function, which is available in PHP 3.0 and higher, returns a string with the type name of the *field_number* in the given *result_id* set. Note that *field_numbering* starts at 0.

pg_freeresult()

Syntax

```
int pg_freeresult (int result_id)
```

Description

The pg_freeresult() function, which is available in PHP 3.0 and higher, frees all resources associated with the *result_id* result set.

pg_getlastoid()

Syntax

```
int pg_getlastoid (int result_id)
```

Description

The pg_getlastoid() function, which is available in PHP 3.0 and higher, returns the oid assigned to an inserted tuple if the result identifier is used from the last command sent via pg_exec() and it was an insert statement. The return value will be FALSE if there was an error or if the last command sent via pg_exec() was not an insert statement.

pg_host()

Syntax

```
string pg_host (int connection_id)
```

Description

The pg_host() function, which is available in PHP 3.0 and higher, returns the name of the host associated with the given *connection_id*.

pg_loclose()

Syntax

```
void pg_loclose (int fd)
```

Description

The `pg_loclose()` function, which is available in PHP 3.0 and higher, closes the large object referenced by the *fd* parameter.

pg_locreate()

Syntax

```
int pg_locreate (int conn)
```

Description

The `pg_locreate()` function, which is available in PHP 3.0 and higher, creates an inversion large object and returns its oid.

pg_loopen()

Syntax

```
int pg_loopen (int conn, int objoid, string mode)
```

Description

The `pg_loopen()` function, which is available in PHP 3.0 and higher, opens a large object and returns a file descriptor for it. The *mode* parameter can take the value `'r'`, `'w'`, or `'rw'` for read, write, or read and write, respectively.

pg_loread()

Syntax

```
string pg_loread (int fd, int len)
```

Description

The `pg_loread()` function, which is available in PHP 3.0 and higher, reads the large object referenced by the *fd* parameter up to *len* bytes.

pg_loreadall()

Syntax

```
void pg_loreadall (int fd)
```

Description

The pg_loreadall() function, which is available in PHP 3.0 and higher, reads an entire large object referenced by the *fd* parameter and returns its contents directly to the browser. This is often used for sound or image data.

pg_lounlink()

Syntax

```
void pg_lounlink (int conn, int lobjid)
```

Description

The pg_lounlink() function, which is available in PHP 3.0 and higher, deletes the large object referenced by the *lobjid* parameter.

pg_lowrite()

Syntax

```
int pg_lowrite (int fd, string buf)
```

Description

The pg_lowrite() function, which is available in PHP 3.0 and higher, attempts to write the *buf* to the large object and returns the number of bytes written or FALSE if an error occurs.

pg_numfields()

Syntax

```
int pg_numfields (int result_id)
```

Description

The pg_numfields() function, which is available in PHP 3.0 and higher, returns the number of fields in the result set referenced by the *result_id* parameter and returns FALSE on error.

pg_numrows()

Syntax

```
int pg_numrows (int result_id)
```

Description

The pg_numrows() function, which is available in PHP 3.0 and higher, returns the number of rows in the result set referenced by the *result_id* parameter and returns FALSE on failure.

pg_options()

Syntax

```
string pg_options(int connection_id)
```

Description

The pg_options() function, which is available in PHP 3.0 and higher, returns a string containing the options for the given *connection_id*.

pg_pconnect()

Syntax

```
int pg_pconnect (string host, string port,
string options, string tty, string dbname)
```

Description

The pg_pconnect() function, which is available in PHP 3.0 and higher, opens a persistent connection to a PostgreSQL database and returns the connection index on success, and FALSE otherwise. A persistent connection is not destroyed when a script completes its processing.

pg_port()

Syntax

```
int pg_port (int connection_id)
```

Description

The pg_port() function, which is available in PHP 3.0 and higher, returns the port used for the given *connection_id*.

pg_result()

Syntax

```
mixed pg_result (int result_id, int row_number ,mixed fieldname)
```

Description

The pg_result() function, which is available in PHP 3.0 and higher, returns data from the result set identified by the *result_id* parameter at the location referenced by *row_number* and *fieldname*. For *fieldname*, you may use the name or the zero-based column number.

pg_tty()

Syntax

```
string pg_tty (int connection_id)
```

Description

The pg_tty() function, which is available in PHP 3.0 and higher, returns the tty associated with the given *connection_id*.

Sybase

The Sybase functions enable you to access data in a Sybase database. More information can by found at http://www.Sybase.com. The following example opens a connection to the users database and retrieves user123's password from the user table:

```
<?

$sybase_db = sybase_connect("users","username","password");
$sybase_result_id =
sybase_query ("select password from user where username='user123'",$sybase_db)
```

```
$sybase_row = sybase_fetch_row ($sybase_result_id);
echo $sybase_row[0];
sybase_close ($sybase_db);
?>
```

sybase_affected_rows()

Syntax

```
int sybase_affected_rows ([int link_identifier])
```

Description

The sybase_affected_rows() function, which is available in PHP 3.0.6 and higher, returns the number of rows affected by the last insert, update, or delete statement performed using the connection specified by the `link_identifier`. The function is not useful for select statements because it reports only the number of rows modified by a statement. The sybase_num_rows() function should be used to examine the results of a select statement.

sybase_close()

Syntax

```
int sybase_close (int link_identifier)
```

Description

The sybase_close() function, which is available in PHP 3.0 and higher, closes the link referenced by the `link_identifier` and returns TRUE on success and FALSE otherwise. This function isn't normally used because connections are automatically closed at the end of a script's processing.

sybase_connect()

Syntax

```
int sybase_connect (string servername , string username , string password)
```

Description

The sybase_connect() function, which was added in PHP 3.0.7 and PHP 4.0, tries to establish a connection to a Sybase server and return a link identifier. If a connection already exists, its link identifier will be returned instead. The connection lasts until sybase_close() is called or the script finishes processing.

sybase_data_seek()

Syntax

int sybase_data_seek (int *result_identifier,* int *row_number*)

Description

The sybase_data_seek() function, which is available in PHP 3.0 and higher, moves the internal row pointer for the result set indicated by the *result_identifier* to the corresponding *row_number*. This causes the next call to sybase_fetch_row() to use this *row_number* if none is specified.

sybase_fetch_array()

Syntax

int sybase_fetch_array (int *result*)

Description

The sybase_fetch_array() function, which is available in PHP 3.0 and higher, returns an array that corresponds to the row fetched from the *result* set. Data in the return array is available by both numerical and associative indices.

sybase_fetch_field()

Syntax

object sybase_fetch_field (int *result,* int *field_offset*)

Description

The sybase_fetch_field() function, which was added in PHP 3.0.7 and PHP 4.0, returns an object containing properties of the field referenced in the *result* set at the *field_offset* or the next field if no offset is specified. The properties of the return object are name, column_source, max_length, and numeric (1 if TRUE).

sybase_fetch_object()

Syntax

```
int sybase_fetch_object (int result)
```

Description

The `sybase_fetch_object()` function, which is available in PHP 3.0 and higher, returns an object that contains data from the fetched row with the data accessible using the field names.

sybase_fetch_row()

Syntax

```
array sybase_fetch_row (int result)
```

Description

The `sybase_fetch_row()` function, which is available in PHP 3.0 and higher, returns a zero-based array containing one row of data from the `result` set.

sybase_field_seek()

Syntax

```
int Sybase_field_seek (int result ,int field_offset)
```

Description

The `sybase_field_seek()` function, which is available in PHP 3.0 and higher, seeks to the specified `field_offset` in the `result` set.

sybase_free_result()

Syntax

```
int sybase_free_result (int result)
```

Description

The `sybase_free_result()` function, which is available in PHP 3.0 and higher, frees all resources associated with the `result` set.

sybase_num_fields()

Syntax

```
int sybase_num_fields (int result)
```

Description

The sybase_num_fields() function, which is available in PHP 3.0 and higher, returns the number of fields in the result set.

sybase_num_rows()

Syntax

```
Sybase_num_rows (string result)
```

Description

The sybase_num_rows() function, which is available in PHP 3.0 and higher, returns the number of rows in a result set and is typically used with a select statement.

sybase_pconnect()

Syntax

```
int sybase_pconnect (string servername, string username, string password)
```

Description

The sybase_pconnect() function, which is available in PHP 3.0 and higher, is similar to sybase_connect() except that the connection isn't terminated at the end of a script's processing.

sybase_query()

Syntax

```
int sybase_query (string query, int link_identifier)
```

Description

The sybase_query() function, which is available in PHP 3.0 and higher, sends the *query* to the database using the *link_identifier* connection. If no link exists, the function will try to establish a connection as though sybase_connect() were called.

sybase_result()

Syntax

```
int sybase_result (int result, int row, mixed field)
```

Description

The sybase_result() function, which is available with PHP 3.0 and higher, returns the contents of the cell located at the *field* and *row* in the *result* set. The *field* parameter can be the name (use alias column name if aliased), offset, or table name dot field name (*tablename.fieldname*).

sybase_select_db()

Syntax

```
int sybase_select_db (sting database_name , int link_identifier)
```

Description

The sybase_select_db() function, which is available in PHP 3.0 and higher, sets the current active database for the given *link_identifier* to the given *database_name*. If no connection is given, the last opened one will be used; if none exists, an attempt to establish one will be made.

CHAPTER 11

Utility Extensions

Within the PHP programming languages you will find many different utility extensions. These extensions represent some of the more useful shrink-wrapped functions of the language itself. They include the following:

- Calendar
- Compression
- Date and time
- Encryption
- GNU recode
- Image
- Regular expression

Calendar

This set of calendar functions represents items from both the MCAL (Modular Calendar Access Library) module and built-in functionality within PHP.

MCAL

The MCAL set of functions operates in very much the same manner as the IMAP functions. You open a stream to a particular calendar and then perform operations on it. To use these functions, you need to download the MCAL library from `http://mcal.chek.com`, compile and install it, and compile PHP with the `--with-mcal` option.

> **Note**
> The functions in this set were added in PHP 3.0.13 unless otherwise stated.

The functions in the MCAL library use some predefined constants. These are shown in Table 11.1.

Table 11.1 *Constants Used in the MCAL Library*

Type	Constant
Day of Week	MCAL_SUNDAY
	MCAL_MONDAY
	MCAL_TUESDAY
	MCAL_WEDNESDAY
	MCAL_THURSDAY
	MCAL_FRIDAY
	MCAL_SATURDAY
Monthly	MCAL_JANUARY
	MCAL_FEBRUARY
	MCAL_MARCH
	MCAL_APRIL
	MCAL_MAY
	MCAL_JUNE
	MCAL_JULY
	MCAL_AUGUST
	MCAL_SEPTEMBER
	MCAL_OCTOBER
	MCAL_NOVEMBER
	MCAL_DECEMBER

Table 11.1 *(continued)*

Type	Constant
Reoccurrence	MCAL_RECUR_NONE
	MCAL_RECUR_DAILY
	MCAL_RECUR_WEEKLY
	MCAL_RECUR_MONTHLY_MDAY
	MCAL_RECUR_MONTHLY_WDAY
	MCAL_RECUR_YEARLY

mcal_append_event()

Syntax

int mcal_append_event (int *mcal_stream*)

Description

The mcal_append_event() function, which was added in PHP 4, enables you to store a new event in the MCAL calendar. If successful, the function returns the ID of the new event.

mcal_close()

Syntax

int mcal_close (int *mcal_stream*, int *flags*)

Description

The mcal_close() function, which was added in PHP 3.0.13, closes a previously opened *mcal_stream*.

mcal_date_compare()

Syntax

int mcal_date_compare (int *1st_yr*, int *1st_month*, int *1st_day*, int *2nd_yr*,
    int *2nd_month*, int *2nd_day*)

Description

The `mcal_date_compare()` function, which was added in PHP 3.0.13, is used to compare the *1st* set of dates against the *2nd* set. Table 11.2 shows the possible return values.

Table 11.2   *Return Values for the* `mcal_date_compare()` *Function*

Returns	Meaning
<0	*1st < 2nd*
0	*1st == 2nd*
>0	*1st > 2nd*

mcal_create_calendar()

Syntax

```
int mcal_create_calendar(string calendar)
```

Description

The `mcal_create_calendar()` function creates a new calendar named *calendar*.

mcal_date_valid()

Syntax

```
int mcal_date_valid (int year, int month, int day)
```

Description

The `mcal_date_valid()` function, which was added in PHP 3.0.13, checks whether the date passed is a valid date. If it is, the function returns 1; otherwise, it returns 0.

mcal_day_of_week()

Syntax

```
int mcal_day_of_week(int year, int month, int date)
```

Description

The mcal_day_of_week() function, which was added in PHP 3.0.13, returns the day of the week for the given *month/date/year* passed.

mcal_day_of_year()

Syntax

```
int mcal_day_of_year(int year, int month, int date)
```

Description

The mcal_day_of_year() function returns the day of the year for the given *month/date/year* passed.

mcal_days_in_month()

Syntax

```
int mcal_days_in_month(int month, int year)
```

Description

The mcal_days_in_month() function returns the number of days in the *month* and *year* passed. The *year* is needed to accommodate leap year instances.

mcal_delete_event()

Syntax

```
int mcal_delete_event (int mcal_stream [, int id])
```

Description

The mcal_delete_event() function deletes the event specified by the optional *id* passed; otherwise, it deletes the current event connected to by the *mcal_stream*. This function returns 1 if successful.

mcal_delete_calendar()

Syntax

```
int mcal_delete_calendar(string calendar)
```

Description

The `mcal_delete_calendar()` function deletes the specified MCAL *calendar*.

mcal_event_add_attribute()

Syntax

```
mcal_event_add_attribute(int mcal_stream, string attribute, string value)
```

Description

The `mcal_event_add_attribute()` function, which was added in PHP 3.0.15, adds *attribute* to the *mcal_stream*'s global event structure. This *attribute* is assigned *value*.

mcal_event_init()

Syntax

```
int mcal_event_init (int mcal_stream)
```

Description

The `mcal_event_init()` function initializes the *mcal_stream*'s global event structure, which sets all values to 0.

mcal_event_set_alarm()

Syntax

```
int mcal_event_set_alarm(int mcal_stream, int alarm)
```

Description

The `mcal_event_set_alarm()` function sets the *mcal_stream*'s global event structure's alarm to *alarm* minutes before the event.

mcal_event_set_category()

Syntax

```
int mcal_event_set_category (int mcal_stream, string category)
```

Description

The mcal_event_set_category() function sets the mcal_stream's global event structure's category. This function returns 1 if successful.

mcal_event_set_class()

Syntax

```
int mcal_event_set_class(int mcal_stream, int class)
```

Description

The mcal_event_set_class() function sets the mcal_stream's global event structure's class. This function returns 1 if successful.

mcal_event_set_description()

Syntax

```
int mcal_event_set_description (int mcal_stream, string description)
```

Description

The mcal_event_set_description() function sets the mcal_stream's global event structure's description. This function returns 1 if successful.

mcal_event_set_end()

Syntax

```
int mcal_event_set_end(int mcal_stream, int year, int month [, int date
    [, int hour [, int minutes [, int seconds]]]])
```

Description

The `mcal_event_set_end()` function sets the *mcal_stream*'s global event structure's end date and time to the passed values. This includes the *month* and *year*, as well as an optional *date*, *hour*, *minute*, and *seconds*. This function returns 1 if successful.

mcal_event_set_start()

Syntax

```
int mcal_event_set_start(int mcal_stream, int year, int month [, int date
   [, int hour [, int min [,int sec]]]])
```

Description

The `mcal_event_set_start()` function sets the *mcal_stream*'s global event structure's start date and time to the passed values. This includes the *month* and *year*, as well as an optional *date*, *hour*, *minute*, and *seconds*. This function returns 1 if successful.

mcal_event_set_title()

Syntax

```
int mcal_event_set_title (int mcal_stream, string title)
```

Description

The `mcal_event_set_title()` function sets the *mcal_stream*'s global event structure's *title*. This function returns 1 if successful.

mcal_event_set_recur_daily()

Syntax

```
int mcal_event_set_recur_daily(int mcal_stream, int year, int month, int date,
   int interval)
```

Description

The `mcal_event_set_recur_daily()` function sets the *mcal_stream*'s global event structure's reoccurrence to a daily *interval* ending on *month/date/year*.

mcal_event_set_recur_monthly_mday()

Syntax

```
\int mcal_event_set_recur_monthly_mday(int mcal_stream, int year, int month,
    int day, int interval)
```

Description

The `mcal_event_set_recur_monthly_mday()` function sets the *mcal_stream*'s global event structure's reoccurrence to a monthly-by-month *interval* ending on *month/date/year*.

mcal_event_set_recur_monthly_wday()

Syntax

```
int mcal_event_set_recur_monthly_wday(int mcal_stream, int year, int month,
    int day, int interval)
```

Description

The `mcal_event_set_recur_monthly_wday()` function sets the *mcal_stream*'s global event structure's reoccurrence to a monthly-by-week *interval* ending on *month/date/year*.

mcal_event_set_recur_none()

Syntax

```
int mcal_event_set_recur_none(int mcal_stream)
```

Description

The `mcal_event_set_recur_none()` function, which was added in PHP 3.0.15, sets the *mcal_stream*'s global event structure's reoccurrence to no reoccurrence.

mcal_event_set_recur_weekly()

Syntax

```
int mcal_event_set_recur_weekly(int mcal_stream, int year, int month, int date,
    int interval, int weekdays)
```

Description

The mcal_event_set_recur_weekly() function sets the *mcal_stream*'s global event structure's reoccurrence to a weekly *interval*, including only the passed *weekdays*, ending on *month/date/year*.

mcal_event_set_recur_yearly()

Syntax

```
int mcal_event_set_recur_yearly(int mcal_stream, int year, int month,
    int date, int interval)
```

Description

The mcal_event_set_recur_yearly() function sets the *mcal_stream*'s global event structure's reoccurrence to a monthly *interval*, ending on *month/date/year*.

mcal_expunge()

Syntax

```
int mcal_expunge(int mcal_stream)
```

Description

The mcal_expunge() function deletes all events that have been previously marked for deletion.

mcal_fetch_current_stream_event()

Syntax

```
int mcal_fetch_current_stream_event(int mcal_stream)
```

Description

The mcal_fetch_current_stream_event() function returns an object of the current *mcal_stream* and its event structure. This object includes the properties in Table 11.3.

Table 11.3 *Properties of the Returned Object*

Property	Description
alarm	This is the number of minutes before the event to send an alarm or reminder.
category	This is the category string of the event.
description	This is the description string of the event.
end	This is an object containing a date/time entry.
id	This integer is the ID of that event.
public	This is a 1 if the event is public, 0 if it is private.
recur_data	This is the recurrence data.
recur_enddate	This is the recurrence end date, in date/time format.
recur_interval	This is the recurrence interval.
recur_type	This is the recurrence type.
start	This is an object containing a date/time entry.
title	This is the title string of the event.

The date/time entries are also objects. These objects contain the properties shown in Table 11.4.

Table 11.4 *Properties of the Returned Date/Time Objects*

Property	Description
alarm	The number of minutes before an event to send out an alarm.
hour	The numeric hour.
mday	The numeric day of the month.
min	The numeric minute.
month	The numeric month.
sec	The numeric second.
year	The numeric year.

mcal_fetch_event()

Syntax

```
object mcal_fetch_event (int mcal_stream, int id [, int flags])
```

Description

The `mcal_fetch_event()` function returns an object of the event at *mcal_stream* specified by *id* and its event structure. This object includes the properties in Table 11.5.

Table 11.5   *Properties of the Returned Object*

Property	Description
alarm	This is the number of minutes before the event to send an alarm or reminder.
category	This is the category string of the event.
description	This is the description string of the event.
end	This is an object containing a date/time entry.
id	This integer is the ID of that event.
public	This is a 1 if the event is public; 0 if the event is private.
recur_data	This is the recurrence data.
recur_enddate	This is the recurrence end date, in date/time format.
recur_interval	This is the recurrence interval.
recur_type	This is the recurrence type.
start	This is an object containing a date/time entry.
title	This is the title string of the event.

The date/time entries are also objects. These objects contain the properties shown in Table 11.6.

Table 11.6   *Properties of the Returned Date/Time Objects*

Property	Description
alarm	The number of minutes before an event to send out an alarm
hour	The numeric hour
mday	The numeric day of the month
min	The numeric minute
month	The numeric month
sec	The numeric second
year	The numeric year

mcal_is_leap_year()

Syntax

```
int mcal_is_leap_year(int year)
```

Description

The mcal_is_leap_year() function returns 1 if the *year* is a leap year.

mcal_list_alarms()

Syntax

```
array mcal_list_alarms (int mcal_stream [, int begin_year
    [, int begin_month [, int begin_day [,int end_year [, int end_month
    [, int end_day]]]]]])
```

Description

The mcal_list_alarms() function returns an array of IDs that have alarms that fall within the passed *begin* and *end* dates. If no dates are passed, the function uses the start and end dates in the global event structure.

mcal_list_events()

Syntax

```
array mcal_list_events (int mcal_stream, object begin_date [, object end_date])
```

Description

The mcal_list_events() function returns an array of IDs that fall within the passed *begin* and *end* dates. If no dates are passed, the function uses the start and end dates in the global event structure. As for the *date* entries, they are objects. These objects contain the properties shown in Table 11.7.

Table 11.7   *Properties of the Returned Date/Time Objects*

Property	Description
alarm	The number of minutes before an event to send out an alarm
hour	The numeric hour
mday	The numeric day of month
min	The numeric minute
month	The numeric month
sec	The numeric second
year	The numeric year

mcal_next_recurrence()

Syntax

```
object mcal_next_recurrence(int mcal_stream, int week_start, array id)
```

Description

The mcal_next_recurrence() function returns a date and time object that contains information about the next time an event, contained in the *id* array, is supposed to occur. You must pass the *week_start* property to signify the day on which you consider the week to start.

The returned object contains the properties shown in Table 11.8.

Table 11.8   *Properties of the Returned Date/Time Objects*

Property	Description
alarm	The number of minutes before an event to send out an alarm
hour	The numeric hour
mday	The numeric day of the month
min	The numeric minute
month	The numeric month
sec	The numeric second
year	The numeric year

mcal_open()

Syntax

```
int mcal_open (string calendar, string username, string password, int options)
```

Description

The mcal_open() function creates an open stream, or handler, to calendar. It accesses calendar using the specified username and password. You can also pass any additional options as needed. The stream's internal event structure is also initialized.

mcal_popen()

Syntax

```
int mcal_popen (string calendar, string username, string password, int options)
```

Description

The mcal_popen() function creates a persistent stream, or handler, to calendar. It accesses calendar by using the specified username and password. You can also pass any additional options as needed. The stream's internal event structure is also initialized.

mcal_rename_calendar()

Syntax

```
int mcal_rename_calendar(string old_name, string new_name)
```

Description

The mcal_rename_calendar() function renames the old_name calendar to new_name.

mcal_reopen()

Syntax

```
int mcal_reopen (string calendar, int options)
```

Description

The mcal_reopen() function, using a previously opened stream, opens a new *calendar* and passes it any necessary *options*.

mcal_snooze()

Syntax

```
int mcal_snooze (int id)
```

Description

The mcal_snooze() function turns off the alarm event for the specified event *id*.

mcal_store_event()

Syntax

```
int mcal_store_event (int mcal_stream)
```

Description

The mcal_store_event() function stores any previously modified information about the event connected to by *mcal_stream*. The function returns 1 if successful, and 0 otherwise.

mcal_time_valid()

Syntax

```
int mcal_time_valid(int hour, int minutes, int seconds)
```

Description

The mcal_time_valid() function returns 1 if the *hour*, *minutes*, and *seconds* passed represent a valid time.

Miscellaneous

This set of miscellaneous calendar functions enables you to change between calendar formats. It is based on the Julian day count standard, which applies the Julian calendar back to approximately 4713 B.C. You must compile in the Calendar extension for this set of functions to work.

easter_date()

Syntax

```
int easter_date(int year)
```

Description

The easter_date() function, which was added in PHP 3.0.9, returns the UNIX-formatted date for midnight on Easter of the specified year.

```
echo date ("M-d-Y", easter_date(2001));  // returns Apr-15-2001
```

easter_days()

Syntax

```
int easter_days([int year])
```

Description

The easter_days() function, which was added in PHP 3.0.9, returns the number of days since March 21 on which Easter falls for the passed year. If year is left off, the current year is assumed.

frenchtojd()

Syntax

```
int frenchtojd(int month, int date, int year)
```

Description

The frenchtojd() function converts a date, specified by month/date/year, from the French Republican calendar to a Julian day count. This converts dates only in years 1 through 14, which are the Gregorian dates from September 22, 1792 through September 22, 1806.

gregoriantojd()

Syntax

```
int gregoriantojd(int month, int date, int year)
```

Description

The gregoriantojd() function converts a date, specified by *month/date/year*, from the Gregorian calendar to a Julian day count. This converts dates only from the Gregorian calendar 4714 B.C. to 9999 A.D.

jddayofweek()

Syntax

```
mixed jddayofweek(int julian_date, int mode)
```

Description

The jddayofweek() function returns the Julian day count day of week, given the *julian_date*. Depending on the *mode* passed, this returns either an integer or string value. Possible *mode* values are shown in Table 11.9.

Table 11.9   mode *Values*

Mode	Description
0	Returns the day number as an integer. For example, 0 is Sunday, 1 is Monday, and 2 is Tuesday.
1	Returns a string containing the day of week, such as Monday, Tuesday, or Wednesday.
2	Returns a string containing the abbreviated day of week, such as Mon, Tues, or Wed.

jdmonthname()

Syntax

```
string jdmonthname(int julian_date, int mode)
```

Description

The `jdmonthname()` function takes a *julian_date*, and based on the *mode*, returns the name of the month in which the date falls. Possible *mode* values are shown in Table 11.10.

Table 11.10 mode *Values*

Mode	Description
0	Gregorian—abbreviated
1	Gregorian
2	Julian—abbreviated
3	Julian
4	Jewish
5	French Republican

jdtofrench()

Syntax

```
string jdtofrench(int month, int date int year)
```

Description

The `jdtofrench()` function converts a Julian day count date, defined by *month*, *date*, and *year*, to the French Republican calendar.

jdtogregorian()

Syntax

```
string jdtogregorian(int julian_date)
```

Description

The `jdtogregorian()` function converts a *julian_date* to a Gregorian date in the format of month/day/year.

jdtojewish()

Syntax

```
string jdtojewish(int julian_date)
```

Description

The jdtojewish() function converts a *julian_date* to a Jewish calendar date.

jdtojulian()

Syntax

```
string jdtojulian(int julian_date)
```

Description

The jdtojulian() function formats a *julian_date* to that of month/day/year.

jdtounix()

Syntax

```
int jdtounix(int julian_date)
```

Description

The jdtounix() function, which was added in PHP 4, returns a UNIX-formatted date stamp of the passed *julian_date*. If the date falls outside of the UNIX supported range (1970 to 2037), 0 is returned.

jewishtojd()

Syntax

```
int jewishtojd(int month, int day, int year)
```

Description

The jewishtojd() function converts a date in the Jewish calendar, defined by *month*, *date*, and *year*, to Julian date count.

juliantojd()

Syntax

```
int juliantojd(int month, int day, int year)
```

Description

The `juliantojd()` function converts a Julian calendar date, defined by *month*, *date*, and *year*, to Julian day count.

unixtojd()

Syntax

```
int unixtojd([int time_stamp])
```

Description

The `unixtojd()` function, which was added in PHP 4, converts a UNIX *time_stamp* to Julian date count.

Compression

The set of compression functions uses functions of the zlib, which was written by Jean-loup Gailly and Mark Adler. The compression functions allow your script to read and write gzip (.gz) compressed files. You must have zlib version 1.0.9 or greater to use this module.

gzclose()

Syntax

```
int gzclose(int gz_pointer)
```

Description

The `gzclose()` function closes an opened *gz_pointer*, or file, that was previously opened using `gzopen()`. If the function is successful, 1 is returned.

gzcompress()

Syntax

```
string gzcompress(string data [, int level])
```

Description

The gzcompress() function, which was added in PHP 4.0.1, returns a compressed file containing *data*. The *level* of compression can also be passed to this function, where it is a number from 1 to 9, with 9 asking for maximum compression.

gzeof()

Syntax

```
int gzeof(int gz_pointer)
```

Description

The gzeof() function returns 1 if the *gz_pointer* is at the end of the file (EOF) or on error.

gzfile()

Syntax

```
array gzfile(string gz_file [, int include_path])
```

Description

The gzfile() function, which operates like readgzfile() except that it returns an array, returns the contents of a *gz_file*. If the optional *include_path* is set to 1, PHP will look for the *gz_file* in the include_path, as specified by the php.ini file.

gzgetc()

Syntax

```
string gzgetc(int gz_pointer)
```

Description

The gzgetc() function returns a single, uncompressed character from the file pointed to by *gz_pointer*. If the file is at the end (EOF), FALSE is returned.

gzgets()

Syntax

```
string gzgets(int gz_pointer, int length)
```

Description

The gzgets() function returns a single, uncompressed line from the file pointed to by *gz_pointer*. It stops when it hits a newline character or the end of file (EOF) marker. If the EOF is hit, FALSE is returned.

gzgetss()

Syntax

```
string gzgetss(int gz_pointer, int length [, string allowable_tags])
```

Description

The gzgetss() function returns uncompressed *length* number of characters from *gz_pointer*, and removes any HTML or PHP tags. After PHP 3.0.13, an optional *allowable_tags* parameter has been added to specify HTML or PHP tags that you want to leave in. If the EOF is hit, FALSE is returned.

gzopen()

Syntax

```
int gzopen(string gz_file, string mode [, int include_path])
```

Description

The gzopen() function attempts to open *gz_file* and return a file pointer for later operations. If you have *include_path* set to 1, PHP will look for the *gz_file* in the include_path specified in the php.ini file. The *mode* parameter tells the function how to open the file. This can be any of the items listed in Table 11.11.

Table 11.11   *Various Modes in Which a gz File Can Be Opened*

Mode	Description
r	Read
w	Write
1-9	Compression level
f	Filtered data (strategy)
h	Huffman only compression

gzpassthru()

Syntax

```
int gzpassthru (int gz_pointer)
```

Description

The gzpassthru() function returns all remaining data located at the *gz_pointer* that has not been retrieved. This stops only at the end of file (EOF) marker.

gzputs()

Syntax

```
int gzputs(int gz_pointer, string string [, int length])
```

Description

The gzputs() function is an alias to the gzwrite() function, where it writes *string* until *length* to the file located at *gz_pointer*.

> **Note**
> If the optional *length* argument is passed, the magic_quotes_runtime configuration option in the php.ini file is ignored.

gzread()

Syntax

```
string gzread(int gz_pointer, int length)
```

Description

The gzread() function reads and returns until *length* is reached in the uncompressed *gz_pointer* file.

gzrewind()

Syntax

```
int gzrewind (int gz_pointer)
```

Description

The gzrewind() function resets *gz_pointer* to the beginning of the gz file. If an error occurs, 0 is returned.

gzseek()

Syntax

```
int gzseek(int gz_pointer, int offset)
```

Description

The gzseek() function sets the current pointer inside the gz file to *offset* bytes from its current location. Do note that if the file is opened for reading only, this operation can be very slow. Additionally, if the file is opened for writing, you can seek only in a forward direction.

gztell()

Syntax

```
int gztell(int gz_pointer)
```

Description

The gztell() function returns the current position of the internal pointer to the *gz_pointer* file.

gzuncompress()

Syntax

```
string gzuncompress(string data [, int level])
```

Description

The gzuncompress() function, which was added in PHP 4.0.1, takes the *data* compressed by the gzcompress() function and returns up to *length* of that data in an uncompressed format.

gzwrite()

Syntax

```
int gzwrite(int gz_pointer, string string [, int length])
```

Description

The gzwrite() function is the same as the gzputs() function; it writes *string* up to *length* to the file located at *gz_pointer*.

> **Note**
> If the optional *length* argument is passed, the magic_quotes_runtime configuration option in the php.ini file will be ignored.

readgzfile()

Syntax

```
int readgzfile(string gz_file [, int include_path])
```

Description

The readgzfile() function reads *gz_file*, decompresses it, and sends it to standard output (STDOUT). If you specify *include_path* to equal to 1, PHP looks for *gz_file* in the include_path directory, which is set in the php.ini file.

Date and Time

The date and time functions within PHP enable you to obtain and format time and date stamps for your scripts. There are also functions that enable you to validate specific styles of time formats.

checkdate()

Syntax

```
int checkdate(int month, int date, int year)
```

Description

The checkdate() function validates the Gregorian date/time passed, which is represented by the month, date, and year parameters. If the date is valid, 1 is returned. Do note that the following rules apply to these parameters:

- *month*—Must be between 1 and 12.

- *date*—Must be within the allowed number of days for the given month. Leap years are taken into consideration.

- *year*—Must be between 1 and 32767.

date()

Syntax

```
string date(string format [, int time_stamp])
```

Description

The date() function returns a string of the *time_stamp*, according to the *format* passed. Table 11.12 has the possible values for *format*.

Table 11.12   *Possible* format *Values*

Value	Description
a	"am" or "pm"
A	"AM" or "PM"
B	Swatch Internet time

Table 11.12   *(continued)*

Value	Description
d	2-digit day of the month
D	3-letter abbreviated day of the week
F	Complete month; for example, October
g	1 or 2-digit, 12-hour format
G	1 or 2-digit, 24-hour format
h	2-digit, 12-hour format
H	2-digit, 24-hour format
i	2-digit number of minutes
I	1 if daylight saving time; otherwise, 0
j	1- or 2-digit day of the month
l	Complete day of the week; for example, Friday
L	1 if current year is leap year; otherwise, 0
m	2-digit month
M	3-letter abbreviated month
n	1- or 2-digit month
s	2-digit number of seconds
S	2-character English ordinal suffix; for example, th or nd
t	Number of days in the given month, which range from 28 to 31
T	3-letter time zone setting
U	Number of seconds since the start of the UNIX epoch
w	1-digit day of the week, starting with 0 indicating Sunday
Y	4-digit year
y	2-digit year
z	1- to 3-digit day of the year, which ranges from 0 to 366 during leap year
Z	Time zone offset in seconds, which ranges from -43200 to 43200

getdate()

Syntax

```
array getdate(int time_stamp)
```

Description

The getdate() function takes the *time_stamp* passed and returns an associative array ("key" with an associated value) of the information contained in *time_stamp*. Table 11.13 shows the contents of this array and their description.

Table 11.13   *Contents of Returned Array*

Key	Description of Value
hours	Hour
mday	Day of the month
minutes	Minute
mon	Numeric month
month	Month; for example, January
seconds	Second
wday	Numeric day of the week
yday	Numeric day of the year
year	Numeric year
weekday	Day of the week; for example, Friday

gettimeofday()

Syntax

```
array gettimeofday()
```

Description

The gettimeofday() function, which was added in PHP 3.0.7, returns an associative array ("key" with an associated value) of the results from calling the gettimeofday(2) system call. Table 11.14 has the contents of this array and their description.

Table 11.14   *Contents of Returned Array*

Key	Description of Value
dsttime	Type of daylight saving time correction
minuteswest	Minutes west of Greenwich
sec	Seconds
usec	Microseconds

The type of daylight saving time correction is contained in Table 11.15.

Table 11.15   *Type of Daylight Saving Time Correction*

Return Value	Type
0	Not on
1	USA
2	Australian
3	Western European
4	Middle European
5	Eastern European
6	Canada
7	Great Britain and Eire
8	Rumania
9	Turkey
10	Australian (with shift in 1986)

gmdate()

Syntax

```
string gmdate(string format, int time_stamp)
```

Description

The `gmdate()` function returns a string of the *time_stamp*, formatted to Greenwich mean time (GMT) and according to the *format* passed. Table 11.16 has the possible values for *format*.

Table 11.16   *Possible* format *Values*

Value	Description
a	"am" or "pm"
A	"AM" or "PM"
B	Swatch Internet time
d	2-digit day of the month
D	3-letter abbreviated day of the week
F	Complete month; for example, October

Table 11.16 *(continued)*

Value	Description
g	1- or 2-digit, 12-hour format
G	1- or 2-digit, 24-hour format
h	2-digit, 12-hour format
H	2-digit, 24-hour format
i	2-digit number of minutes
I	1 if daylight saving time; otherwise, 0
j	1- or 2-digit day of the month
l	Complete day of the week; for example, Friday
L	1 if current year is leap year; otherwise, 0
m	2-digit month
M	3-letter abbreviated month
n	1- or 2-digit month
s	2-digit number of seconds
S	2-character English ordinal suffix, as in th or nd
t	Number of days in the given month, which range from 28 to 31
T	3-letter time zone setting
U	Number of seconds since the start of the UNIX epoch
w	1-digit day of the week, starting with 0 indicating Sunday
Y	4-digit year
y	2-digit year
z	1- to 3-digit day of the year, which ranges from 0 to 366 during leap year
Z	Time zone offset in seconds, which ranges from -43200 to 43200

gmmktime()

Syntax

```
int gmmktime(int hour, int minute, int second, int month, int day, int year
   [, int is_dst])
```

Description

The gmmktime() function returns a UNIX timestamp according to the *hour*, *minute*, *second*, *month*, *day*, and *year* passed, which are in Greenwich mean time (GMT). This represents the number of seconds between the start of the UNIX epoch (January 1, 1970) and the time specified. The optional *is_dst* parameter, which was added in PHP 3.0.10, should be set to 1 if it is currently daylight saving time.

gmstrftime()

Syntax

```
string gmstrftime(string format, int time_stamp)
```

Description

The `gmstrftime()` function, which was added in PHP 3.0.12, returns a string, according to the *format* specified, which is in Greenwich mean time (GMT), of *time_stamp*. If *time_stamp* is not passed, the current time is used. Table 11.17 contains the available formatting options.

Table 11.17 *Formatting Options*

Option	Description
%a	Abbreviated weekday name
%A	Full weekday name
%b	Abbreviated month name
%B	Full month name
%c	Preferred date and time format
%C	2-digit century number
%d	2-digit day of the month
%D	Same as %m/%d/%y
%e	1- or 2-digit day of the month
%h	Same as %b
%H	2-digit hour using a 24-hour clock
%I	2-digit hour using a 12-hour clock
%j	3-digit day of the year
%m	1- or 2-digit month
%M	Minute
%n	Newline character
%p	'am' or 'pm' depending on given time
%r	Time in a.m. and p.m. notation

Table 11.17 *(continued)*

Option	Description
%R	Time in 24-hour notation
%S	Second
%t	Tab character
%T	Current time, equal to %H:%M:%S
%u	1-digit weekday with 1 representing Monday and 7 representing Sunday
%U	Week number of the current year, starting with the first Sunday of the year as the first day of the first week in counting
%V	2-digit ISO 8601:1988 week number of the current year, where the first week has at least four days in the year, and with Monday as the first day of the week
%W	Week number of the current year, starting with the first Monday as the first day of the first week
%w	1-digit day of the week with Sunday being 0
%x	Preferred date representation without the time
%X	Preferred time representation without the date
%y	2-digit year without a century
%Y	Year including the century
%Z	Time zone or name or abbreviation
%%	% character

localtime()

Syntax

```
array localtime([int time_stamp [, boolean is_associative]])
```

Description

The localtime() function, which was added in PHP 4, returns an array of the local time, or of *time_stamp* if this optional parameter is passed. If the *is_associative* parameter is 1, the array returned is an associative array ("key" with an associated value). Otherwise, it is your normal zero-based index array. The contents of the associative array are shown in Table 11.18.

Table 11.18   *Contents of Returned Array*

Key	Description of Value
tm_hour	Hour
tm_mday	Day of the month
tm_min	Minute
tm_mon	Month of the year
tm_isdst	Whether daylight saving time is in effect
tm_sec	Second
tm_wday	Numeric day of the week
tm_yday	Numeric day of the year
tm_year	Numeric year

microtime()

Syntax

```
string microtime();
```

Description

The microtime() function returns the string "msec *seconds*" where *seconds* is the number of seconds since the UNIX epoch began (0:00:00 January 1, 1970 GMT), and *msec* is the microseconds part.

> **Note**
> This function is available only on systems that support the gettimeofday() system call.

mktime()

Syntax

```
int mktime(int hour, int minute, int second, int month, int day, int year
    [, int is_dst])
```

Description

The mktime() function returns a UNIX timestamp according to the *hour*, *minute*, *second*, *month*, *day*, and *year* passed. This represents the number of seconds between the start of the UNIX epoch (January 1, 1970) and the time specified. The optional *is_dst* parameter, which was added in PHP 3.0.10, should be set to 1 if it is currently daylight saving time.

strftime()

Syntax

```
string strftime(string format [, int time_stamp])
```

Description

The strftime() function returns a string, according to the *format* specified, of *time_stamp*. If *time_stamp* is not passed, the current time is used. Table 11.19 contains the various formatting options you have.

Table 11.19   *Formatting Options*

Option	Description
%a	Abbreviated weekday name
%A	Full weekday name
%b	Abbreviated month name
%B	Full month name
%c	Preferred date and time format
%C	2-digit century number
%d	2-digit day of the month
%D	Same as %m/%d/%y
%e	1- or 2-digit day of the month
%h	Same as %b
%H	2-digit hour using a 24-hour clock
%I	2-digit hour using a 12-hour clock
%j	3-digit day of the year
%m	1- or 2-digit month
%M	Minute
%n	Newline character
%p	'am' or 'pm' depending on given time
%r	Time in a.m. and p.m. notation
%R	Time in 24-hour notation

Table 11.19   *(continued)*

Option	Description
%S	Second
%t	Tab character
%T	Current time, equal to %H:%M:%S
%u	1-digit weekday with 1 representing Monday and 7 representing Sunday
%U	Week number of the current year, starting with the first Sunday of the year as the first day of the first week in counting
%V	2-digit ISO 8601:1988 week number of the current year, where the first week has at least four days in the year, and with Monday as the first day of the week
%W	Week number of the current year, starting with the first Monday as the first day of the first week
%w	1-digit day of the week with Sunday being 0
%x	Preferred date representation without the time
%X	Preferred time representation without the date
%y	2-digit year without a century
%Y	Year including the century
%Z	Time zone or name or abbreviation
%%	% character

strtotime()

Syntax

```
int strtotime(mixed date_time )
```

Description

The strtotime() function, which was added in PHP 3.0.12, will parse almost any *date_time* string you can pass it in the English language and will return an UNIX timestamp version. You can also pass items such as the string "now" to get the current time, or "+1 day" to get a time/date stamp for tomorrow at the same time.

time()

Syntax

```
int time()
```

Description

The `time()` function returns the current time, in the number of seconds since the start of UNIX epoch, which is January 1, 1970 00:00:00 GMT.

Encryption

The encryption set of functions actually works by using mcrypt. To use this set of functions, you must first download libmcrypt from `ftp://argeas.cs-net.gr/pub/unix/mcrypt` and compile it with the `--disable-posix-threads` option. Then you need to compile PHP with the `--with-mcrypt` parameter. The library itself supports the following methods of encryption:

- DES
- 3-WAY
- Blowfish
- GOST in CBC, OFB, CFB, and ECB cipher modes
- IDEA
- RC2 in CBC, OFB, CFB, and ECB cipher modes
- RC6
- SAFER-SK128
- SAFER-SK64
- TEA
- TripleDES
- TWOFISH

If you downloaded a version of mcrypt greater than 2.4.x, you have access to the following block algorithms:

- CAST
- LOKI97
- RIJNDAEL
- SAFERPLUS
- SERPENT

Additionally, you have access to the following stream ciphers with the mcrypt library:

- ENIGMA
- nOFB (2.4.x or greater)
- PANAMA
- RC4
- WAKE

> **Note**
> The functions in this section were added in PHP 3.0.8 and PHP 4.0.2. So that you can differentiate, we have included a note in the description if the entry was added in 4.0.2.

mcrypt_cbc()

Syntax

```
string mcrypt_cbc(int cipher, string key, string data, int mode
    [, string init_vector])
```

(when linked against libmcrypt 2.2.x)

```
string mcrypt_cbc(string cipher, string key, string data, int mode
    [, string init_vector])
```

(when linked against libmcrypt 2.4.x)

Description

The mcrypt_cbc() function will encrypt or decrypt the *data* with *cipher* and *key* in CBC cipher mode. *cipher* is passed in the form of MCRYPT_*name* where *name* is the name of the cipher used. The determination of encrypting or decrypting the data is done by looking at the *mode*, which can be MCRYPT_ENCRYPT or MCRYPT_DECRYPT. The optional *init_vector* parameter is the initialization vector.

mcrypt_cfb()

Syntax

```
string mcrypt_cfb (int cipher, string key, string data, int mode,
    string init_vector)
```

(when linked against libmcrypt 2.2.x)

```
string mcrypt_cfb (string cipher, string key, string data, int mode
    [, string init_vector])
```

(when linked against libmcrypt 2.4.x)

Description

The mcrypt_cfb() function will encrypt or decrypt the *data* with *cipher* and *key* in CFB cipher mode. *cipher* is passed in the form of MCRYPT_*name* where *name* is the name of the cipher used. The determination of encrypting or decrypting the data is done by looking at the *mode*, which can be MCRYPT_ENCRYPT or MCRYPT_DECRYPT. The optional *init_vector* parameter is the initialization vector.

mcrypt_create_iv()

Syntax

```
string mcrypt_create_iv(int size, int source)
```

Description

The mcrypt_create_iv() function creates an initialization vector of *size* and of *source*. The *source* can be one of the items in Table 11.20.

Table 11.20   *Possible* source *Values*

Source	Description
MCRYPT_DEV_RANDOM	Read data from /dev/random.
MCRYPT_DEV_URANDOM	Read data from /dev/urandom.
MCRYPT_RAND	System random number generator. Make sure to call srand() before to initialize the random number generator.

mcrypt_ecb()

Syntax

```
string mcrypt_ecb(int cipher, string key, string data, int mode)
```

(when linked against libmcrypt 2.2.x)

```
string mcrypt_ecb(string cipher, string key, string data, int mode
   [, string init_vector])
```

(when linked against libmcrypt 2.4.x)

Description

The mcrypt_ecb() function will encrypt or decrypt the *data* with *cipher* and *key* in ECB cipher mode. *cipher* is passed in the form of MCRYPT_*name* where *name* is the name of the cipher used. The determination of encrypting or decrypting the data is done by looking at the *mode*, which can be MCRYPT_ENCRYPT or MCRYPT_DECRYPT. The optional *init_vector* parameter is the initialization vector.

mcrypt_enc_get_algorithms_name()

Syntax

```
int mcrypt_enc_get_algorithms_name(resource encrypt_descriptor)
```

Description

The mcrypt_enc_get_algorithms_name() function, which was added in PHP 4.0.2, returns the name of the currently opened algorithm.

mcrypt_enc_get_block_size()

Syntax

```
int mcrypt_enc_get_block_size(resource encrypt_descriptor)
```

Description

The `mcrypt_enc_get_block_size()` function, which was added in PHP 4.0.2, returns the block size, in bytes, of the algorithm specified by *encrypt_descriptor*.

mcrypt_enc_get_iv_size()

Syntax

```
int mcrypt_enc_get_iv_size(resource encrypt_descriptor)
```

Description

The `mcrypt_enc_get_iv_size()` function, which was added in PHP 4.0.2, returns the size, in bytes, of the initialization vector of the algorithm specified by *encrypt_descriptor*. This should work in CBC, CFB, and OFB modes, and in some algorithms it also works in stream mode. If the initialization vector is ignored in the algorithm, the function returns 0.

mcrypt_enc_get_key_size()

Syntax

```
int mcrypt_enc_get_key_size(resource encrypt_descriptor)
```

Description

The `mcrypt_enc_get_key_size()` function, which was added in PHP 4.0.2, returns the maximum key size, in bytes, of the algorithm referenced by *encrypt_descriptor*.

mcrypt_enc_get_modes_name()

Syntax

```
int mcrypt_enc_get_modes_name(resource encrypt_descriptor)
```

Description

The mcrypt_enc_get_modes_name() function, which was added in PHP 4.0.2, returns the name of the opened *encrypt_descriptor*.

mcrypt_enc_get_supported_key_sizes()

Syntax

```
int mcrypt_enc_get_supported_key_sizes(resource encrypt_descriptor)
```

Description

The mcrypt_enc_get_supported_key_sizes() function, which was added in PHP 4.0.2, returns an array with the supported key sizes of *encrypt_descriptor*.

mcrypt_enc_is_block_algorithm()

Syntax

```
int mcrypt_enc_is_block_algorithm(resource encrypt_descriptor)
```

Description

The mcrypt_enc_is_block_algorithm() function, which was added in PHP 4.0.2, returns 1 if the algorithm specified by *encrypt_descriptor* is a block algorithm. If it is a stream algorithm, 0 is returned.

mcrypt_enc_is_block_algorithm_mode()

Syntax

```
int mcrypt_enc_is_block_algorithm_mode(resource encrypt_descriptor)
```

Description

The mcrypt_enc_is_block_algorithm_mode() function, which was added in PHP 4.0.2, returns 1 if the mode attached to *encrypt_descriptor* is for use with block algorithms, such as CBC, CFB, and OFB. Otherwise, the function returns 0 for stream.

mcrypt_enc_is_block_mode()

Syntax

```
int mcrypt_enc_is_block_mode(resource encrypt_descriptor)
```

Description

The mcrypt_enc_is_block_mode() function, which was added in PHP 4.0.2, returns 1 if the mode attached to *encrypt_descriptor* outputs blocks of bytes, as with CBC, CFB, and OFB. Otherwise, the function returns 0 for non-block byte output.

mcrypt_enc_self_test()

Syntax

```
int mcrypt_enc_self_test(resource encrypt_descriptor)
```

Description

The mcrypt_enc_self_test() function, which was added in PHP 4.0.2, runs a self test on the algorithm specified by *encrypt_descriptor*. It returns 1 if the test is successful or 0 otherwise.

mcrypt_encrypt()

Syntax

```
string mcrypt_encrypt(string cipher, string key, string data, string mode
    [, string init_vector])
```

Description

The mcrypt_encrypt() function, which was added in PHP 4.0.2, encrypts the *data* with *cipher* and *key* in the specified *cipher* mode. *cipher* is passed in the form of MCRYPT_*name* where *name* is the name of the cipher used. The *mode* is one of the MCRYPT_MODE_*name* constants (ECB, CBC, CFB, OFB, NOFB, or STREAM) and it determines the mode of the encryption. The optional *init_vector* parameter is the initialization vector for CBC, CFB, OFB modes, and in some algorithms, for STREAM mode.

> **Note**
> If the *data* is not of the appropriate block size, it is padded with \0. Additionally, if the
> *intt_vector* parameter is not passed, it is assumed to be all \0.

mcrypt_decrypt()

Syntax

```
string mcrypt_decrypt(string cipher, string key, string data, string mode
   [, string init_vector])
```

Description

The mcrypt_decrypt() function, which was added in PHP 4.0.2, will decrypt the *data*
with *cipher* and *key* in the specified *cipher* mode. *cipher* is passed in the form of
MCRYPT_*name* where *name* is the name of the cipher used. The *mode* is one of the
MCRYPT_MODE_*name* constants (ECB, CBC, CFB, OFB, NOFB, or STREAM) and it determines the
mode of the encryption. The optional *init_vector* parameter is the initialization
vector for CBC, CFB, OFB modes, and in some algorithms, for STREAM mode.

> **Note**
> If the *data* is not of the appropriate block size, it is padded with \0. Additionally, if the
> *init_vector* parameter is not passed, it is also assumed to be all \0.

mcrypt_generic()

Syntax

```
int mcrypt_generic(resource encrypt_descriptor, string data)
```

Description

The mcrypt_generic() function, which was added in PHP 4.0.2, will encrypt *data*. If
the data is not of the appropriate block size, the returned data will be padded with \0.

mcrypt_generic_end()

Syntax

```
boolean mcrypt_generic_end(resource encrypt_descriptor)
```

Description

The mcrypt_generic_end() function, which was added in PHP 4.0.2, ends the encryption specified by *encrypt_descriptor*. The function returns TRUE on success, and FALSE otherwise.

mcrypt_generic_init()

Syntax

```
int mcrypt_generic_init(resource encrypt_descriptor, string key,
    string init_vector)
```

Description

The mcrypt_generic_init() function, which was added in PHP 4.0.2, initializes all buffers needed for encryption including the *encrypt_descriptor*, *key*, and *init_vector*. The *init_vector* normally should have the size of the algorithm's block size, which you can obtain by calling mcrypt_enc_get_iv_size(). This option is ignored in ECB mode, but must exist in CFB, CBC, STREAM, NOFB, and OFB modes.

mcrypt_get_block_size()

Syntax

```
int mcrypt_get_block_size(int cipher)
```

Description

The mcrypt_get_block_size() function returns the block size, in bytes, of the specified *cipher*. The *cipher* parameter is one of the MCRYPT_*name* constants.

mcrypt_get_cipher_name()

Syntax

```
string mcrypt_get_cipher_name(int cipher)
```

(when linked against libmcrypt 2.2.x)

```
string mcrypt_get_cipher_name(string cipher)
```

(when linked against libmcrypt 2.4.x)

Description

The mcrypt_get_cipher_name() function returns the name of the specified *cipher*, which is the cipher number when linked against the 2.2.x library and the actual name when linked against the 2.4.x library. This function will return false if the name does not exist.

mcrypt_get_key_size()

Syntax

```
int mcrypt_get_key_size(int cipher)
```

Description

The mcrypt_get_key_size() function returns the key size, in bytes, of the specified *cipher*. The *cipher* parameter is one of the MCRYPT_*name* constants.

mcrypt_get_iv_size()

Syntax

```
int mcrypt_get_iv_size(string cipher, string mode)
```

Description

The mcrypt_get_iv_size() function, which was added in PHP 4.0.2, returns the size of the initialization vector that is associated with the *cipher/mode* combination. The *cipher* parameter is one of the MCRYPT_*name* constants and *mode* is one of the MCRYPT_MODE_*name* constants (ECB, CBC, CFB, OFB, NOFB, or STREAM).

mcrypt_list_algorithms()

Syntax

```
array mcrypt_list_algorithms([string algorithm_dir])
```

Description

The mcrypt_list_algorithms() function, which was added in PHP 4.0.2, returns an array of all support algorithms. The optional *algorithm_dir* parameter is a directory that specifies where all algorithms are located. If this is not passed, PHP uses the mcrypt.algorithms_dir setting in the php.ini file.

mcrypt_list_modes()

Syntax

```
array mcrypt_list_modes([string modes_dir])
```

Description

The mcrypt_list_modes() function, which was added in PHP 4.0.2, returns an array of all support modes. The optional *modes_dir* parameter is a directory that specifies where all modes are located. If this is not passed, PHP uses the mcrypt.modes_dir setting in the php.ini file.

mcrypt_module_get_algo_block_size()

Syntax

```
int mcrypt_module_get_algo_block_size(string algorithm [, string modes_dir])
```

Description

The mcrypt_module_get_algo_block_size() function, which was added in PHP 4.0.2, returns the block size, in bytes, of the *algorithm* specified. The optional *modes_dir* parameter is a directory that specifies where all modes are located. If this is not passed, PHP uses the mcrypt.modes_dir setting in the php.ini file.

mcrypt_module_get_algo_key_size()

Syntax

```
int mcrypt_module_get_algo_key_size(string algorithm [, string modes_dir])
```

Description

The mcrypt_module_get_algo_key_size() function, which was added in PHP 4.0.2, returns the maximum key size, in bytes, of the *algorithm* specified. The optional *modes_dir* parameter is a directory that specifies where all modes are located.

mcrypt_module_get_algo_supported_key_sizes()

Syntax

```
array mcrypt_module_get_algo_supported_key_sizes(string algorithm
    [, string modes_dir])
```

Description

The mcrypt_module_get_algo_supported_key_sizes() function, which was added in PHP 4.0.2, returns an array of the supported key sizes of the *algorithm* specified. The optional *modes_dir* parameter is a directory that specifies where all modes are located.

mcrypt_module_is_block_algorithm()

Syntax

```
boolean mcrypt_module_is_block_algorithm (string algorithm
    [, string algorithm_dir])
```

Description

The mcrypt_module_is_block_algorithm() function, which was added in PHP 4.0.2, checks whether the specified *algorithm* is a block algorithm. It returns TRUE for a block algorithm, and FALSE for a stream algorithm. The optional *algorithm_dir* parameter is a directory that specifies where all algorithms are located.

mcrypt_module_is_block_algorithm_mode()

Syntax

```
boolean mcrypt_module_is_block_algorithm_mode(string mode [, string modes_dir])
```

Description

The mcrypt_module_is_block_algorithm_mode() function, which was added in PHP 4.0.2, checks whether the specified *mode* is used with block algorithms. The function returns TRUE if the mode is used with block algorithms and FALSE if it is not. The optional *modes_dir* parameter is a directory that specifies where all modes are located.

mcrypt_module_is_block_mode()

Syntax

```
boolean mcrypt_module_is_block _mode(string mode [, string modes_dir])
```

Description

The mcrypt_module_is_block _mode() function, which was added in PHP 4.0.2, checks whether the specified *mode* outputs blocks of bytes. The function returns

TRUE if so and FALSE if the mode just outputs bytes. The optional *modes_dir* parameter is a directory that specifies where all modes are located.

mcrypt_module_open()

Syntax

```
resource mcrypt_module_open(string algorithm, string algorithm_dir,
    string mode, string mode_dir)
```

Description

The mcrypt_module_open() function, which was added in PHP 4.0.2, opens the module of the *algorithm* and the *mode* to be used. The name of the *algorithm* is specified in the algorithm itself or is represented using one of the MCRYPT_*name* constants. The *mode_dir* parameter is a directory that specifies where all modes are located, and the *algorithm_dir* parameter is a directory that specifies where all algorithms are located. The function itself returns an encryption descriptor.

mcrypt_module_self_test()

Syntax

```
boolean mcrypt_module_self_test(string algorithm [, string algorithm_dir])
```

Description

The mcrypt_module_self_test() function, which was added in PHP 4.0.2, runs a self test on the *algorithm* specified. The *algorithm_dir* parameter is a directory that specifies where all algorithms are located.

mcrypt_ofb()

Syntax

```
string mcrypt_ofb(int cipher, string key, string data, int mode,
    string init_vector)
```

(when linked against libmcrypt 2.2.x)

```
string mcrypt_ofb(string cipher, string key, string data, int mode
    [, string init_vector])
```

(when linked against libmcrypt 2.4.x)

Description

The mdecrypt_ofb() function encrypts or decrypts the *data* with *cipher* and *key* in OFB cipher mode. *cipher* is passed in the form of MCRYPT_*name* where *name* is the name of the cipher used. The determination of encrypting or decrypting the data is done by looking at the *mode*, which can be MCRYPT_ENCRYPT or MCRYPT_DECRYPT. The optional *init_vector* parameter is the initialization vector.

mdecrypt_generic()

Syntax

```
int mdecrypt_generic(resource encrypt_descriptor, string data)
```

Description

The mdecrypt_generic() function, which was added in PHP 4.0.2, decrypts the *data* pointed to by the *encrypt_descriptor*.

GNU Recode

The GNU Recode set of functions actually works by using GNU Recode 3.5 or higher. The group can understand and produce approximately 150 different character sets. With this vast range of functionality, it can convert almost any set of characters between any of the 150 sets. Most RFC 1345 character sets are supported in the library.

To use this set of functions, you must compile PHP with the --with-recode parameter.

> **Note**
> The functions in this set were added in PHP 3.0.13 unless otherwise stated.

recode()

Syntax

```
boolean recode(string request, string string)
```

Description

The recode() function, which was added in PHP 4, is an alias for the recode_string() function. Please see that entry for more information.

recode_file()

Syntax

```
boolean recode_file(int input, int output)
```

Description

The recode_file() function recodes the *input* file into the *output* file and returns TRUE if successful, or FALSE otherwise.

recode_string()

Syntax

```
string recode_string(string request, string string)
```

Description

The recode_string() function recodes the *string* according to the *request*. Check the GNU Recode library for more information on the types of *request*.

Image

The set of image functions enable you to return the size of the following types of images:

- JPEG—You will need to download and install jpeg-6b from ftp://ftp.uu.net/graphics/jpeg, and compile gd to make use of jpeg-6b for this functionality. You will also have to compile PHP with --with-jpeg-dir=/<*path_to_*>/jpeg-6b.

- GIF—For this format, you first will have to install the GD library from http://www.boutell.com/gd. Versions older than gd-1.6 will support GIF format images.

- PNG—For this format, you first will have to install the GD library from `http://www.boutell.com/gd`. Versions newer than gd-1.6 will support PNG format images.

- SWF

Finally, you can add support for Type 1 fonts by installing t1lib, which you can download from `ftp://ftp.neuroinformatik.ruhr-uni-bochum.de/pub/software/t1lib`. After t1lib is downloaded, you must compile PHP with the `--with-t1lib=/<path_to_>/t1lib` option.

getimagesize()

Syntax

```
array getimagesize(string filename [, array imageinfo])
```

Description

The `getimagesize()` function will return the size of any GIF, JPG, PNG, or SWF image, and return that information along with the file type. This information is contained in the array and contains a height/width text string that can be used inside a normal HTML <img> tag.

The array itself contains the following four elements:

- 0—Width of the image in pixels

- 1—Height of the image in pixels

- 2—Flag indicating the type of the image, which is one of these: 1 = GIF, 2 = JPG, 3 = PNG, 4 = SWF

- 3—Text string with the correct "height=X width=X" string that can be used directly in an <img> tag

imagearc()

Syntax

```
int imagearc(int image, int center_x, int center_y, int width, int height,
    int start, int end, int color)
```

Description

The imagearc() function draws an ellipse centered at *center_x* and *center_y* in *image*. The *height* and *width* of the ellipse are passed, as well as the *start* and *end* degree points. You can also specify the *color*.

imagechar()

Syntax

```
int imagechar(int image, int font, int x, int y, string character, int color)
```

Description

The imagechar() function draws a *character* located at *x* and *y* in *image*. The *font* size is passed, as well as the *color*.

imagecharup()

Syntax

```
int imagecharup(int image, int font, int x, int y, string character,
    int color)
```

Description

The imagecharup() function draws a *character* vertically (pointing up) located at *x* and *y* in *image*. The *font* size is passed, as well as the *color*.

imagecolorallocate()

Syntax

```
int imagecolorallocate(int image, int red, int green, int blue)
```

Description

The imagecolorallocate() function returns the color identifier for the passed *red*, *green*, and *blue* (RGB) parameters. The *image* is the return value of the imagecreate() function.

imagecolordeallocate()

Syntax

```
int imagecolordeallocate(int image, int variable)
```

Description

The imagecolordeallocate() function, which was added in PHP 3.0.6, deallocates a color in *image* that was previously defined in *variable* by calling the imagecolorallocate() function.

imagecolorat()

Syntax

```
int imagecolorat(int image, int x, int y)
```

Description

The imagecolorat() function returns the index number of the color located at *x* and *y*.

imagecolorclosest()

Syntax

```
int imagecolorclosest(int image, int red, int green, int blue)
```

Description

The imagecolorclosest() function returns the index number of the color closest to the *red*, *green*, and *blue* (RGB) values passed.

imagecolorexact()

Syntax

```
int imagecolorexact(int image, int red, int green, int blue)
```

Description

The imagecolorexact() function returns the index number of the color specified by the passed *red*, *green*, and *blue* (RGB) values. If there is no color at that location, -1 is returned.

imagecolorresolve()

Syntax

```
int imagecolorresolve(int image, int red, int green, int blue)
```

Description

The imagecolorresolve() function, which was added in PHP 3.0.2, returns the index number of the color specified by the passed *red*, *green*, and *blue* (RGB) values, or the color closest to that value.

imagegammacorrect()

Syntax

```
int imagegammacorrect(int image, double input_gamma, double output_gamma)
```

Description

The imagegammacorrect() function, which was added in PHP 3.0.13, applies the gamma correction to the *image* based on the *input_gamma* and *output_gamma*.

imagecolorset()

Syntax

```
boolean imagecolorset(int image, int index, int red, int green, int blue)
```

Description

The imagecolorset() function sets the color located at the *index* number passed to the specified *red*, *green*, and *blue* (RGB) values for the *image*.

imagecolorsforindex()

Syntax

```
array imagecolorsforindex(int image, int index)
```

Description

The `imagecolorsforindex()` function returns an associative array ("key" with an associated value) where the keys are red, green, and blue, and the values are their respective values at the *index* position in the *image*.

imagecolorstotal()

Syntax

```
int imagecolorstotal(int image)
```

Description

The `imagecolorstotal()` function returns the total number of colors in the palette of the *image* passed.

imagecolortransparent()

Syntax

```
int imagecolortransparent(int image [, int color])
```

Description

The `imagecolortransparent()` function defines the *color* passed as transparent in the *image*.

imagecopy()

Syntax

```
int imagecopy(int destination_image, int source_image, int destination_x,
    int destination_y, int source_x, int source_y, int source_width,
    int source_height)
```

Description

The `imagecopy()` function, which was added in PHP 3.0.6, copies the part of the *source_image*, starting at the *source_x* and *source_y* point and constrained by the *source_width* and *source_height* to the *destination_image*. The copied portion is placed on this image, starting at the *destination_x* and *destination_y* location.

imagecopyresized()

Syntax

```
int imagecopyresized(int destination_image, int source_image,
    int destination_x, int destination_y int source_x, int source_y,
    int destination_width, int destination_height, int source_width,
    int source_height)
```

Description

The `imagecopyresized()` function copies the part of the *source_image*, starting at the *source_x* and *source_y* point and constrained by the *source_width* and *source_height* to the *destination_image*. The copied portion is placed on this image starting at the *destination_x* and *destination_y* location, and stretched to the *destination_width* and *destination_height* parameters.

imagecreate()

Syntax

```
int imagecreate(int width, int height)
```

Description

The `imagecreate()` function returns a blank image identifier of the size defined by the *width* and *height* parameters.

imagecreatefromgif()

Syntax

```
int imagecreatefromgif(string location)
```

Description

The `imagecreatefromgif()` function returns an image identifier for the GIF image at *location*, which can be a filename or URL. If the process fails, the function returns an error message. To avoid this, you can use the following type of code in which you create an image if the one you seek is not there:

```
$image = imagecreatefromgif("myimage.gif");
if(!$image){ // check for error
   $image = imagecreate(1, 1); // create blank image
   $background = imagecolorallocate($image, 0, 0, 0); // white
   imagefill($image, 0, 0, $background); // create white image
   }
return $image;
```

imagecreatefromjpeg()

Syntax

```
int imagecreatefromjpeg(string location)
```

Description

The `imagecreatefromjpeg()` function returns an image identifier for the JPEG image at *location*, which can be a filename or URL. If the process fails, the function returns an error message. To avoid this, you can use the following type of code in which you create an image if the one you seek is not there:

```
$image = imagecreatefromjpeg("myimage.jpg");
if(!$image){ // check for error
   $image = imagecreate(1, 1); // create blank image
   $background = imagecolorallocate($image, 0, 0, 0); // white
   imagefill($image, 0, 0, $background); // create white image
   }
return $image;
```

imagecreatefrompng()

Syntax

```
int imagecreatefrompng(string location)
```

Description

The imagecreatefrompng() function, which was added in PHP 3.0.13, returns an image identifier for the PNG image at *location*, which can be a filename or URL. If the process fails, the function returns an error message. To avoid this, you can use the following type of code in which you create an image if the one you seek is not there:

```
$image = imagecreatefrompng("myimage.png");
if(!$image){ // check for error
  $image = imagecreate(1, 1); // create blank image
  $background = imagecolorallocate($image, 0, 0, 0); // white
  imagefill($image, 0, 0, $background); // create white image
  }
return $image;
```

imagedashedline()

Syntax

int imagedashedline(int *image*, int *x_1*, int *y_1*, int *x_2*, int *y_2*, int *color*)

Description

The imagedashedline() function draws a dashed *color* line from x_1, y_1 to x_2, y_2 on *image*.

imagedestroy()

Syntax

int imagedestroy(int *image*)

Description

The imagedestroy() function frees any memory (destroys in the PHP runtime) associated with *image*.

imagefill()

Syntax

int imagefill(int *image*, int *x*, int *y*, int *color*)

Description

The `imagefill()` function fills *image* with *color* starting at *x* and *y* and continuing for the rest of the image.

imagefilledpolygon()

Syntax

```
int imagefilledpolygon(int image, array points, int num_points, int color)
```

Description

The `imagefilledpolygon()` function fills the location defined by *points* and *num_points* of the *image* with a polygon of *color*. The *points* parameter is an array containing the polygon's vertices (that is, `points[0]` = x0, `points[1]` = y0, `points[2]` = x1, `points[3]` = y1, and so on) and *num_points* is the total number of vertices.

imagefilledrectangle()

Syntax

```
int imagefilledrectangle(int image, int x_1, int y_1, int x_2, int y_2,
    int color)
```

Description

The `imagefilledrectangle()` function fills a rectangle in *image* with *color* starting at *x_1* and *y_1* and continuing to *x_2* and *y_2*.

imagefilltoborder()

Syntax

```
int imagefilltoborder(int image, int x, int y, int border_color, int color)
```

Description

The `imagefilltoborder()` function fills *image*, starting at *x* and *y*, with *color* and continues until it hits *border_color*.

imagefontheight()

Syntax

```
int imagefontheight(int font)
```

Description

The `imagefontheight()` function returns the pixel height of a character in *font*.

imagefontwidth()

Syntax

```
int imagefontwidth(int font)
```

Description

The `imagefontwidth()` function returns the pixel width of a character in *font*.

imagegif()

Syntax

```
int imagegif(int image [, string filename])
```

Description

The `imagegif()` function creates a GIF87a image referenced by *image*. The optional *filename* enables you to save the file to disk if you do not want to send it out directly in a stream to the browser. If you do want to do this, you must set the content-type HTTP header directive to `image/gif` by using the `header()` function.

imagepng()

Syntax

```
int imagepng(int image [, string filename])
```

Description

The `imagepng()` function, which was added in PHP 3.0.13, creates a PNG image referenced by *image*. The optional *filename* enables you to save the file to disk if you do not want to send it out directly in a stream to the browser. If you do want to do this, you must set the content-type HTTP header directive to image/png by using the header() function.

imagejpeg()

Syntax

```
int imagejpeg(int image [, string filename [, int quality]])
```

Description

The imagejpeg() function creates a JPEG image referenced by *image*. The optional *filename* enables you to save the file to disk if you do not want to send it out directly in a stream to the browser. If you do want to do this, you must set the content-type HTTP header directive to image/jpeg by using the header() function. Optionally, you can specify a value from 0 to 100 for the *quality* parameter.

imageinterlace()

Syntax

```
int imageinterlace(int image [, int interlace])
```

Description

The imageinterlace() function turns the interlace bit on or off in *image*. The function toggles the bit unless you use the optional *interlace* parameter, which when set equal to 1 turns on the bit, and when set to 0 turns off the bit.

imageline()

Syntax

```
int imageline(int image, int x_1, int y_1, int x_2, int y_2, int color)
```

Description

The imageline() function draws a *color* line from *x_1, y_1* to *x_2, y_2* on *image*.

imageloadfont()

Syntax

```
int imageloadfont(string font)
```

Description

The imageloadfont() function loads a user-defined, bitmap font. The function returns an identifier that is always greater than 5 so that it does not conflict with the built-in fonts. Because the format is binary and architecture dependent, you should generate the font files on the same type of CPU as the machine on which you are running PHP.

imagepolygon()

Syntax

```
int imagepolygon(int image, array points, int num_points, int color)
```

Description

The imagepolygon() function creates a polygon, of color, defined by points and num_points in the image. The points parameter is an array containing the polygon's vertices (that is, points[0] = x0, points[1] = y0, points[2] = x1, points[3] = y1, and so on) and num_points is the total number of vertices.

imagepsbbox()

Syntax

```
array imagepsbbox(string text, int font, int size [, int space
    [, int character_space [, float angle]]])
```

Description

The imagepsbbox() function, which was added in PHP 3.0.9, gives the bounding box of a text rectangle using a PostScript Type 1 font. The optional space parameter enables you to define the size of a space, and character_space enables you to define the space between characters.

> **Note**
> Because the box is using information available from character metrics, you might want to
> specify an *angle* of 1 for what would normally be 0.

The array that is returned contains the items listed in Table 11.21.

Table 11.21   *Contents of the Returned Array*

Indexed Array Position	Description
0	Lower left x-coordinate
1	Lower left y-coordinate
2	Upper right x-coordinate
3	Upper right y-coordinate

imagepsencodefont()

Syntax

```
int imagepsencodefont(string encoding_file)
```

Description

The imagepsencodefont() function, which was added in PHP 3.0.9, changes the
character encoding vector of a font to *encoding_file*. Rather than calling this file,
which is often used when you are creating text in a language other than English, you
can set the ps.default_encoding directive in the php.ini file to the appropriate
encoding font.

imagepsfreefont()

Syntax

```
imagepsfreefont(int font_index)
```

Description

The imagepsfreefont() function, which was added in PHP 3.0.9, frees any memory
(destroys) used by a PostScript Type 1 font.

imagepsloadfont()

Syntax

```
int imagepsloadfont(string font)
```

Description

The imagepsloadfont() function, which was added in PHP 3.0.9, loads the PostScript Type 1 font. If there was an error, it will be returned and printed to you.

imagepsextendfont()

Syntax

```
boolean imagepsextendfont(int font, double extend_or_condense)
```

Description

The imagepsextendfont() function, which was added in PHP 3.0.9, enables you to extend or condense the font by providing a larger or smaller number in the extend_or_condense parameter.

imagepsslantfont()

Syntax

```
boolean imagepsslantfont(int font, double slant)
```

Description

The imagepsslantfont() function, which was added in PHP 3.0.9, slants a particular font.

imagepstext()

Syntax

```
array imagepstext(int image, string text, int font, int size, int foreground,
    int background, int x, int y [, int space [, int character_space [, float
    angle [, int antialias]]]])
```

Description

The `imagepstext()` function, which was added in PHP 3.0.9, draws a *text* string over an *image* using PostScript Type 1 *font* that is proportioned by *size*. The *foreground* parameter contains the color you want to use for this text, and the *background* parameter contains the background color. The drawing itself starts at the specified *x* and *y* location.

The optional *space* parameter enables you to define the size of a space, and the *character_space* enables you to define the space between characters. The *antialias* setting enables you to control the number of colors that will be used to antialias the text. This value can be between 4–16.

Note
Because the string is using information available from character metrics, you might want to specify an *angle* of 1 for what would normally be 0.

The array that is returned contains the items listed in Table 11.22.

Table 11.22   Contents of the Returned Array

Indexed Array Position	Description
0	Lower left x-coordinate
1	Lower left y-coordinate
2	Upper right x-coordinate
3	Upper right y-coordinate

imagerectangle()

Syntax

```
int imagerectangle(int image, int x_1, int y_1, int x_2, int y_2, int color)
```

Description

The `imagerectangle()` function draws a rectangle with *color* in *image* that starts at *x_1* and *y_1* and ends at *x_2* and *y_2*.

imagesetpixel()

Syntax

```
int imagesetpixel(int image, int x, int y, int color)
```

Description

The imagesetpixel() function draws a single pixel with *color* in *image* that starts at *x_1* and *y_1* and ends at *x_2* and *y_2*.

imagestring()

Syntax

```
int imagestring(int image, int font, int x, int y, string text, int color)
```

Description

The imagestring() function draws *text* in *image* with *color* in a horizontal manner. It starts at the *x* and *y* position defined and is in *font*.

imagestringup()

Syntax

```
int imagestringup(int image, int font, int x, int y, string text, int color)
```

Description

The imagestringup() function draws *text* in *image* with *color* in a vertical (pointing up) manner. It starts at the *x* and *y* position defined and is in *font*.

imagesx()

Syntax

```
int imagesx(int image)
```

Description

The imagesx() function returns the width of the *image*.

imagesy()

Syntax

```
int imagesy(int image)
```

Description

The imagesy() function returns the height of the *image*.

imagettfbbox()

Syntax

```
array imagettfbbox(int size, int angle, string font, string text)
```

Description

The imagettfbbox() function, which was added in PHP 3.0.1, calculates, based on the *size*, *angle*, and *font*, and returns the bounding box in pixels for a TrueType *text*. The *font* parameter can either be a filename or a URL. The contents of the array returned can be seen in Table 11.23.

Table 11.23　*Contents of the Returned Array*

Indexed Array Position	Description
0	Lower-left corner, x-coordinate
1	Lower-left corner, y-coordinate
2	Lower-right corner, x-coordinate
3	Lower-right corner, y-coordinate
4	Upper-right corner, x-coordinate
5	Upper-right corner, y-coordinate
6	Upper-left corner, x-coordinate
7	Upper-left corner, y-coordinate

imagettftext()

Syntax

```
array imagettftext(int image, int size, int angle, int x, int y, int color,
    string font, string text)
```

Description

The `imagettftext()` function writes, based on the *size*, *angle*, and *font*, a TrueType *text* to *image*. The *font* parameter can either be a filename or a URL. It starts at the *x* and *y* position.

imagetypes()

Syntax

```
int imagetypes();
```

Description

The `imagetypes()` function, which was added in PHP 4.0.2, returns the image formats supported by your build of PHP. The following items represent what can be returned:

- `IMG_GIF`
- `IMG_JPG`
- `IMG_PNG`
- `IMG_WBMP`

Regular Expressions

Having the ability to effectively parse text for characters and phrases of various formats is an extremely powerful thing. The modules discussed in this section describe the regular expression functions available in PHP. The discussion is broken into "Native PHP" and "Perl Semantics" sections.

Native PHP

These sets of functions are for performing regular expression pattern matching in PHP. Unlike the items listed in the "Perl Semantics" section of this chapter, these functions represent semantics and syntax that are native to PHP.

ereg()

Syntax

```
int ereg(string pattern, mixed string [, array matches])
```

Description

The ereg() function searches *string* for any items that match the *pattern*. If the optional *matches* array variable is passed, the results are stored in that array. Otherwise, the function returns 1 if a match was found, and 0 if not. The only difference between this and the eregi() function is that this function does not ignore alphabetic case.

ereg_replace()

Syntax

```
string ereg_replace(string pattern, mixed replacement, mixed string)
```

Description

The ereg_replace() function searches *string* for *pattern* and replaces it with *replacement*. If successful, the modified string is returned.

eregi()

Syntax

```
int eregi(string pattern, string string [, array regs])
```

Description

The eregi() function searches *string* for any items that match the *pattern*. If the optional *matches* array variable is passed, the results are stored in that array. Otherwise, it returns 1 if a match was found, and 0 if not. The only difference between this and the ereg() function is that this function ignores alphabetic case.

eregi_replace()

Syntax

```
string eregi_replace(string pattern, string replacement, string string)
```

Description

The eregi_replace() function searches *string* for *pattern* and replaces it with *replacement*. If successful, the modified string is returned. The only difference between this and the eregi_replace() function is that this function ignores alphabetic case.

split()

Syntax

```
array split(string pattern, mixed string [, int limit])
```

Description

The split() function searches *string* and splits it into individual elements, each stored in the returned array, based on the *pattern*. You can limit the number of items stored in the array by using the optional *limit* parameter. The only difference between this and the spliti() function is that this function does not ignore alphabetic case.

spliti()

Syntax

```
array split(string pattern, mixed string [, int limit])
```

Description

The spliti() function, which was added in PHP 4.0.1, searches *string* and splits it into individual elements, each stored in the returned array, based on the *pattern*. You can limit the number of items stored in the array using the optional *limit* parameter. The only difference between this and the split() function is that this function ignores alphabetic case.

sql_regcase()

Syntax

```
string sql_regcase(string string)
```

Description

The sql_regcase() function takes a *string* and returns a new string that contains the uppercase and lowercase equivalents of the characters in the *string*, each contained in its own set of brackets.

```
echo sql_regcase ("Hello World"); // [Hh][Ee][Ll][Ll][][Ww][Oo][Rr][Ll][Dd]
```

Perl Semantics

These sets of functions are for performing regular expression pattern matching. However, their syntax resembles that of the Perl programming language's regular expression syntax.

> **Note**
> The functions contained in this set were added in PHP 3.0.9 unless otherwise specified.

preg_match()

Syntax

```
int preg_match(string pattern, mixed string [, array matches])
```

Description

The preg_match() function searches *string* for any items that match the *pattern*. If the optional *matches* array variable is passed, the results are stored in that array. Otherwise, it returns 1 if a match was found, and 0 if not.

```
preg_match ("/ll/", "Hello ,World!."); // returns 1
```

preg_match_all()

Syntax

```
int preg_match_all(string pattern, mixed subject, array matches [, int order])
```

Description

The preg_match_all() function searches *string* for any items that match the *pattern* and stores the results in the *matches* array. If the optional parameter is passed, the storing of the matched values are in *order*, which can be one of the items listed in Table 11.24:

Table 11.24   *Values for the* order *Parameter*

Value	Description
PREG_PATTERN_ORDER	Orders results so that $matches[0] is an array of full pattern matches, whereas $matches[1] is an array of strings matched by the first parenthesized subpattern.
PREG_SET_ORDER	Orders results so that $matches[0] is an array of the first set of matches, and $matches[1] is the second set.

preg_replace()

Syntax

```
mixed preg_replace(string pattern, mixed replacement, mixed string
    [, int limit])
```

Description

The preg_replace() function searches *string* for matches of *pattern*, and replaces them with *replacement*. The optional *limit* parameter can limit the number of matches you want to make.

preg_split()

Syntax

```
array preg_split(string pattern, mixed string [, int limit [, int flag]])
```

Description

The preg_split() function returns an array of substrings or *string* that have been split by *pattern* and stored into individual array entries. The optional *limit* parameter can limit the number of matches you want to make. If the optional *flag*—which can only be PREG_SPLIT_NO_EMPTY—is passed, only non-empty pieces are returned.

preg_quote()

Syntax

```
string preg_quote(mixed string [, string delimiter])
```

Description

The preg_quote() function escapes any special characters in the *string* provided. A *delimiter* will also be escaped if it is provided. These can be any of the following:

- \
- *
- [
-]
- (
- {
- =
- <
- |

- +
- ?
- ^
- $
-)
- }
- !
- >
- :

preg_grep()

Syntax

```
array preg_grep(string pattern, array input)
```

Description

The preg_grep() function, which was added in PHP 4, returns an array of elements from the *input* array that match the *pattern* specified.

CHAPTER 12

PHP Compilation Options

This chapter describes the options that are available to the user when compiling PHP on a UNIX platform. These options enable and disable certain functionality and add external libraries to the core PHP binary. These options are made available to PHP through the configuration process prior to compilation. For instance, a configuration line might be

```
./configure --with-apache=/usr/lib/apache --with-
pgsql=shared
```

This chapter describes the syntax and parameters around each of these compile-time options.

These options are divided into two separate groups: the `enable`, `disable`, and `help` group and the `with` group.

Enable, Disable, and Help

This group of options enables and disables functionality within PHP. These options are not set by using on or off parameters, but rather they are turned on or off based solely on the command. This group also includes an official description of the `--help` command.

disable-short-tags

Syntax

```
--disable-short-tags
```

Description

This option disables PHP's capability to use the abbreviated scripting tags. The short tags look like this: <? .. ?>. If you disable this option, the only PHP script tag that will be recognized is the <?PHP .. ?> tag. Short tags must be disabled for PHP to work with XML.

disable-syntax-hl

Syntax

```
--disable-syntax-hl
```

Description

This option turns off syntax highlighting.

disable-unified-odbc

Syntax

```
--disable-unified-odbc
```

Description

This option disables the Unified ODBC module. The Unified ODBC module provides a common interface to ODBC. This option is necessary only if you are using one of the following options: --with-iodbc, --with-solid, --with-ibm-db2, --with-adabas, --with-velocis, or --with-custom-odbc.

enable-bcmath

Syntax

```
--enable-bcmath
```

Description

This option enables the bc math functions in PHP. The bc math functions provide access to arbitrary-precision math functions. Chapter 5, "PHP Language Extensions," describes these functions in detail.

enable-c9x-inline

Syntax

```
--enable-c9x-inline
```

Description

This option enables support for the C9x compiler standard. The PHP support site recommends that you enable this option if you encounter undefined references to i_zend_is_true and other symbols.

enable-debug

Syntax

```
--enable-debug
```

Description

This option enables extra debugging information. This makes it possible to gather more detailed information when there are problems with PHP. (Note that this doesn't have anything to do with debugging facilities or information available to PHP scripts.)

enable-debugger

Syntax

```
--enable-debugger
```

Description

This option enables the internal PHP debugger. At the time of this writing, the internal debugger was still under development.

enable-discard-path

Syntax

```
--enable-discard-path
```

Description

This option allows the PHP CGI binary to run in a directory other than the normal cgi-bin directory. When this option is used, people will not be able to get around the .htaccess security.

enable-force-cgi-redirect

Syntax

```
--enable-force-cgi-redirect
```

Description

This option enables the security check for internal server redirects. This option should be enabled if you are running the PHP as a CGI on the Apache Web server.

This option ensures that the PHP CGI cannot be used to circumvent normal Web server authentication. If this option is not enabled, httpd authentication can be bypassed, which can create a serious security hole.

enable-magic-quotes

Syntax

```
--enable-magic-quotes
```

Description

This option enables magic quotes.

enable-safe-mode

Syntax

```
--enable-safe-mode
```

Description

This option enables PHP to run in safe mode. Safe mode enables a higher security level and restricts some of the operations that PHP can perform. Some of these restrictions include restricted file access and user type security checks.

enable-sysvsem

Syntax

```
--enable-sysvsem
```

Description

This option enables support for System V semaphores. If you are using shared memory or semaphores, this option must be enabled. See Chapter 9, "System Extensions," for more information about semaphores and shared memory.

enable-sysvshm

Syntax

```
--enable-sysvshm
```

Description

This option enables support for System V shared memory. If you are using shared memory or semaphores, this option must be enabled. See Chapter 9 for more information about semaphores and shared memory.

enable-track-vars

Syntax

```
--enable-track-vars
```

Description

This option enables the PHP track variables feature. This feature enables PHP to keep track of where HTTP GET/POST/cookie variables come from in the arrays HTTP_GET_VARS, HTTP_POST_VARS, and HTTP_COOKIE_VARS, respectively.

enable-url-includes

Syntax

```
--enable-url-includes
```

Description

This option makes it possible to run PHP scripts on other HTTP or FTP servers by using the PHP `include()` function. See also the `include_path` option in the configuration file.

help

Syntax

```
--help
```

Description

This option displays all the configuration options and a short description of each one.

With

The second group of useful options is the `with` set. These options often describe only the default setting, and then allow the option to be enabled or disabled through the use of the .ini file. These options often include a directory that is defined by the *DIR* keyword. The *DIR* tells the compiler where to find the libraries or the configuration that is defined by the `with` command.

with-adabas

Syntax

```
--with-adabas=DIR
```

Description

This option enables Adabas D support. The *DIR* parameter points to the Adabas D install directory. The *DIR* parameter defaults to `/usr/local/adabasd`.

with-apache

Syntax

```
--with-apache=DIR
```

Description

This option enables PHP to work with the Apache Web server. The *DIR* parameter points to the Apache base directory.

with-config-file-path

Syntax

```
--with-config-file-path=DIR
```

Description

This option tells PHP where to look for the configuration file on initialization. The *DIR* parameter points to the directory where the php.ini file resides.

with-custom-odbc

Syntax

```
--with-custom-odbc=DIR
```

Description

This option tells PHP where to find a custom ODBC library. The *DIR* option defines the base directory and defaults to /usr/local.

with-dbase

Syntax

```
--with-dbase
```

Description

This option enables dBASE support. dBASE is included with PHP by default, therefore no external libraries are required and no directory is defined.

with-exec-dir

Syntax

```
--with-exec-dir=DIR
```

Description

This option allows the execution of PHP scripts in the directory defined by `DIR` only when PHP is running in safe mode. The `DIR` parameter is `/usr/local/bin` by default.

with-fhttpd

Syntax

```
--with-fhttpd=DIR
```

Description

This option enables you to build PHP as an fhttpd module. The `DIR` option defines the fhttpd source base directory and defaults to `/usr/local/src/fhttpd`. The fhttpd module gives better performance, more control, and remote execution capability.

with-filepro

Syntax

```
--with-filepro
```

Description

This option enables FilePro support. This library is bundled with PHP and therefore needs no `DIR` parameter to define the directory.

with-iodbc

Syntax

```
--with-iodbc=DIR
```

Description

This option enables PHP to use iODBC support. This is an ODBC driver manager that runs under many different versions of UNIX. The `DIR` parameter points to the iODBC installation directory and defaults to `/usr/local`.

with-ldap

Syntax

`--with-ldap=DIR`

Description

This option includes Lightweight Directory Access Protocol (LDAP) support. The `DIR` parameter is the LDAP base install directory and defaults to `/usr/local/ldap`.

with-mcrypt

Syntax

`--with-mcrypt=DIR`

Description

This option includes support for the mcrypt library. The `DIR` option for this command is optional and defines the mcrypt base install directory.

with-msql

Syntax

`--with-msql=DIR`

Description

This option enables mSQL support in PHP. The `DIR` parameter specifies the mSQL install directory and defaults to `/usr/local`.

with-mysql

Syntax

`--with-mysql=DIR`

Description

This option enables MySQL support in PHP. The `DIR` parameter specifies the MySQL install directory and defaults to `/usr/local`.

with-openlink

Syntax

```
--with-openlink=DIR
```

Description

This option includes OpenLink ODBC support. The `DIR` parameter points to the OpenLink ODBC installation directory and defaults to `/usr/local/openlink`.

with-oracle

Syntax

```
--with-oracle=DIR
```

Description

This option includes Oracle support. The `DIR` parameter points to the `ORACLE_HOME` directory.

with-pgsql

Syntax

```
--with-pgsql=DIR
```

Description

This option includes PostgreSQL support. The `DIR` parameter is the PostgreSQL base install directory and defaults to `/usr/local/pgsql`.

with-solid

Syntax

```
--with-solid=DIR
```

Description

This option includes Solid support. The *DIR* parameter points to the Solid install directory and defaults to /usr/local/solid.

with-sybase

Syntax

```
--with-sybase=DIR
```

Description

This option includes Sybase support. The *DIR* parameter points to the Sybase install directory and defaults to /home/sybase.

with-sybase-ct

Syntax

```
--with-sybase-ct=DIR
```

Description

This option includes Sybase-CT support. The *DIR* parameter is the Sybase-CT install directory and defaults to /home/sybase.

with-system-regex

Syntax

```
--with-system-regex
```

Description

This option uses the system's regular expression library rather than one that is included in the PHP installation. Enable this if the system's library provides special features you need.

with-velocis

Syntax

```
--with-velocis=DIR
```

Description

This option includes Velocis support. The `DIR` parameter points to the Velocis install directory and defaults to `/usr/local/velocis`.

with-xml

Syntax

```
--with-xml
```

Description

This option includes support for a nonvalidating XML parser. Support for this function is included in the PHP distribution.

CHAPTER 13

PHP Directives

This chapter outlines the many configurable options that you can set to affect the behavior of the PHP scripting engine. These options, which are referred to as *directives*, can be found in the php.ini or php3.ini file and also in the Apache Web server's configuration and .htaccess files when used as an Apache module. The location of the php.ini file where most of the directives are found is dependent on the operating system you are using. The syntax for a directive is *name=value*, and it is important to note that the directive names are case sensitive. Note that for Boolean values, '1','True', 'Yes', and 'On' are equivalent values. Also '0','False','No', and 'Off' are equivalent. A value of 'none' (without quotes) should be used to indicate an empty string. Last, you can use phpinfo() to view all settings and get_cfg_var() to view an individual setting.

General

The following directives are used to affect the overall behavior of the PHP engine.

asp_tags

Syntax

```
asp_tags boolean
```

Description

The `asp_tags` directive allows you to indicate PHP code in a source file by wrapping the code in Active Server Pages–style HTML tags. ASP code is indicated by the `<%` and `%>` tags. The default tags (`<?PHP` and `?>`) are still available. The ASP language shortcut for printing variable contents (`<%=$variable %>`) is also supported when this option is set. The default value for this directive is `Off`. The following sets of code generate the equivalent output when `asp_tags` is turned `On`.

```
<?PHP $text = "Hello World!";
echo $text; ?>
```

and

```
<% $text = "Hello World!"; %>
<%=$text%>
```

auto_append_file

Syntax

```
auto_append_file string
```

Description

The `auto_append_file` directive indicates which file should be parsed after the main file is processed. The effective result is as though the file were called with an `include()` function; therefore, the `include_path` setting is used. To disable this feature, set the option to none. This option is useful for displaying copyright information and other details you might need at the end of each Web page. The default value is none.

auto_prepend_file

Syntax

```
auto_prepend_file string
```

Description

The `auto_prepend_file` directive indicates which file should be parsed before the source file is processed. The effective result is as though the file were called with the `include()` function; therefore, the `include_path` setting is used. To disable this feature, set the option to none. This option is useful for titles and other content that is used at the beginning of each Web page. The default value is none.

cgi_ext

Syntax

```
cgi_ext string
```

Description

The cgi_ext directive is not yet implemented.

display_errors

Syntax

```
display_errors boolean
```

Description

The display_errors directive is used to indicate whether PHP error messages should be returned within the output HTML. The error messages are generally used only during debugging. In production environments, a "friendly" error should be returned to the user. The default value is On.

doc_root

Syntax

```
doc_root string
```

Description

The doc_root directive is used in conjunction with safe_mode to allow PHP to access files only from this directory. This provides an additional layer of security. The default value is none.

error_log

Syntax

```
error_log string
```

Description

The error_log directive specifies the name of the file in which any errors that occur during processing should be logged. A value of syslog indicates that the system logger mechanism is used instead of a file. For UNIX systems, this is the syslog file referred to as output option 3, where standard out is (1) and standard error is (2). On Windows NT and Windows 2000, this information is logged by the Event Log System. The default value is none.

error_reporting

Syntax

```
error_reporting integer
```

Description

The error_reporting directive indicates which level of error messages should be reported. The options include

1 for normal errors

2 for normal warnings

4 for parser errors

8 for noncritical, style-related warnings

These options can be added together to provide combinations of the reporting levels. For instance, the default value of 7 indicates levels $1 + 2 + 4 = 7$.

open_basedir

Syntax

```
open_basedir string
```

Description

The open_basedir directive limits which files can be opened from a PHP script to those in the specified directory tree. The common methods for opening a file that this will affect are fopen and gzopen. Symbolic links are resolved by PHP so that you can't circumvent this security level. To specify multiple directories, separate the values with semicolons in Windows and colons otherwise (similar to the PATH environment variable). A "." indicates that files can be accessed from the same directory from which the script is running. The default for this directive is to allow files from any location to be opened.

gpc_order

Syntax

```
gpc_order string
```

Description

The gpc_order directive sets the order of GET/POST/COOKIE variable parsing. Note that this function has been deprecated in favor of variable_order. When PHP reads an incoming request, it automatically analyzes the request and identifies variables and their values, making them available for script access. This setting specifies the order in which the request is analyzed. The order indicates which option will take precedence when the same variable name appears more than once. The options to the right have a higher precedence than those to the left. For example, a gpc_order of PC tells PHP to ignore the GET variables and that variables from the COOKIE value have precedence over POST values. The default value is GPC.

ignore_user_abort

Syntax

```
ignore_user_abort boolean
```

Description

The ignore_user_abort directive specifies whether a script should run to completion if the connection with the user is lost. The default is on, which indicates that a script should always finish running. Note that you will likely want to ensure that this value is set to On if your script is performing a transactional operation.

include_path

Syntax

```
include_path string
```

Description

The `include_path` directive indicates which directories should be searched when an included file is specified. The syntax for this setting mimics the operating system's PATH environment variable, where a semicolon separates multiple paths in Windows and a colon in UNIX. The default for this option is the current directory (only). Here is a UNIX example:

```
include_path_= /usr/local/apache/htdocs:/home/user1
```

isapi_ext

Syntax

```
isapi_ext string
```

Description

The `isapi_ext` directive is not yet implemented.

log_errors

Syntax

```
log_errors boolean
```

Description

The `log_errors` directive indicates whether error messages should be logged to the Web server's error log. The actual details of this error log depend on the Web server that is being used with PHP. The default value is Off.

magic_quotes_gpc

Syntax

```
magic_quotes_gpc boolean
```

Description

The `magic_quotes_gpc` directive sets whether single quotes, double quotes, NULLs, and backslashes are automatically escaped with a backslash when processing the GET/POST/COOKIE values for variables. The similar option, `magic_quotes_sybase`, indicates that a single quote should be escaped with another single quote instead of a backslash. The default value is On.

magic_quotes_runtime

Syntax

```
magic_quotes_runtime boolean
```

Description

The magic_quotes_runtime directive indicates that when data or text is returned from an external datasource, all quotes will be escaped with a backslash. If magic_quotes_sybase is also on, an occurrence of a single quote will be escaped with a second single quote instead of a backslash. The default value is Off.

magic_quotes_sybase

Syntax

```
magic_quotes_sybase boolean
```

Description

The magic_quotes_sybase directive is used in conjunction with the magic_quotes_runtime and magic_quotes_gpc options to indicate that a single quote should be escaped with another single quote instead of a backslash. The default value is Off.

max_execution_time

Syntax

```
max_execution_time integer
```

Description

The max_execution_time directive indicates how much time, in seconds, a single script is allowed to execute before terminating. The default is thirty seconds.

memory_limit

Syntax

```
memory_limit integer
```

Description

The `memory_limit` directive specifies the maximum amount of memory in bytes, that one executing script can allocate. The default value is `8388608` or 8MB.

nsapi_ext

Syntax

```
nsapi_ext string
```

Description

`nsapi_ext` is not yet implemented.

short_open_tag

Syntax

```
short_open_tag boolean
```

Description

The `short_open_tag` directive indicates whether the short form (<? and ?>) for PHP tags is allowed. XML requires that the long form (<?php and ?>) of the tags be used. The default value is `On`.

sql.safe_mode

Syntax

```
sql.safe_mode boolean
```

Description

The `sql.safe_mode` directive indicates that any username and password information given as part of a connection string should be ignored. This is an added layer of security, and prevents someone from trying to guess a username/password combination.

track_errors

Syntax

```
track_errors boolean
```

Description

The `track_errors` directive causes the last error message generated to be available in the global variable `$php_errormsg`. The default value is `Off`.

track_vars

Syntax

```
track_vars boolean
```

Description

The `track_vars` directive indicates whether variables from the GET, POST, and COOKIE portions of a request should be accessible through the global associative arrays `$HTTP_GET_VARS`, `$HTTP_POST_VARS`, and `$HTTP_COOKIE_VARS`, respectively. With PHP 4.0.3, `track_vars` is always on.

upload_tmp_dir

Syntax

```
upload_tmp_dir string
```

Description

The `upload_tmp_dir` configuration setting indicates the directory into which any files uploaded by a user should be placed. The user PHP is running under must have write permissions to this directory. The system default will be used if none is specified.

```
upload_tmp_dir = /usr/uploads
```

user_dir

Syntax

```
user_dir string
```

Description

The `user_dir` configuration setting indicates the base name used for a user's home directory. For example, a value of `"/home"` tells PHP to look in `/home/~username` for a person's PHP files. The default value is none.

variable_order

Syntax

```
variable_order string
```

Description

The variable_order directive sets the order of GET/POST/COOKIE variable parsing. Note that this function replaces the gpc_order directive, which has been deprecated. When PHP reads an incoming request, it automatically analyzes the request and identifies variables and their values, making them available for script access. This setting specifies the order in which the request is analyzed. The order indicates which option will take precedence when the same variable name appears more than once. The options to the right have a higher precedence than those options to the left. For example, a variable_order of PC tells PHP to ignore the GET variables and that variables from the COOKIE value have precedence over POST values. The default value is GPC.

warn_plus_overloading

Syntax

```
warn_plus_overloading boolean
```

Description

The warn_plus_overloading directive is used to indicate whether a warning message should be generated when the parser encounters string concatenation done with a plus (+) sign instead of the . operator, which is the preferred method for concatenating strings. The default value is Off.

Extension Loading

PHP allows for the specification of additional libraries whose functions will be available from PHP scripts.

enable_dl

Syntax

```
enable_dl boolean
```

Description

The `enable_dl` directive applies only to the Apache module for PHP. It is used to turn on or off dynamic loading of PHP extensions at the virtual server or virtual directory level. Dynamic loading is accomplished by using the `dl()` function. This directive defaults to `True` except when running in safe mode where dynamic loading cannot be used.

extension_dir

Syntax

```
extension_dir string
```

Description

The `extension_dir` directive specifies the directory in which the PHP engine should look for dynamically loadable libraries.

Syntax

```
extension string
```

extension

The `extension` directive specifies which dynamically loadable extensions should be loaded by the PHP engine upon startup. Here are some Windows examples:

```
;Windows Extensions
extension=php_mysql.dll
extension=php_nsmail.dll
extension=php_calendar.dll
```

Browser Compatibility

PHP allows for the capabilities of different browsers to be stored in a file typically known as the browscaps.ini. This file enables you to adjust your script's execution and output based on the feature set of the browser making the request.

browscap

Syntax

```
browscap string
```

Description

The browscap directive specifies the name of the file that should be used for determining a particular browser's capabilities based on its agent string. The get_browser() function is used to retrieve values from the browscap file.

Mail

PHP can be configured to interface with a mail system. The mail system needs to support the SMTP protocol to work with PHP.

SMTP

Syntax

```
SMTP string
```

Description

The SMTP directive specifies the host (either IP address or hostname) through which Windows should route mail when the mail() function is utilized. This function is used only with Windows. The default is localhost.

sendmail_from

Syntax

```
sendmail_from string
```

Description

The sendmail_from directive specifies the sender's name for mail sent using the mail() function and works only with Windows. The default is me@localhost.com.

sendmail_path

Syntax

```
sendmail_path string
```

Description

The `sendmail_path` directive specifies the location of the sendmail program on UNIX systems, which is typically /usr/sbin/sendmail or /usr/lib/sendmail. This directive is set during the configure step of building PHP as a default, but can be altered. If the mail program you are using supports a sendmail type reference, it can be utilized using this directive. You may also supply arguments with the path and the default value is `sendmail - t`.

Database

PHP has separate but similar configuration file directives for each database version that it supports.

MySQL

mysql.allow_persistent

Syntax

```
mysql.allow_persistent boolean
```

Description

The `mysql.allow_persistent` directive specifies whether persistent connections should be used with MySQL databases. Persistent connections typically improve overall performance and should be used when possible, but are not available when PHP is run as a CGI program. The default value is `On`.

mysql.default_host

Syntax

```
mysql.default_host string
```

Description

The `mysql.default_host` directive specifies the hostname to which connections should be made if a hostname is not specified in the connection string. The default value is `none`.

mysql.default_user

Syntax

```
mysql.default_user string
```

Description

The mysql.default_user directive specifies the username that a connection should use if one is not defined in the connection string. The default value is none.

mysql.default_password

Syntax

```
mysql.default_password string
```

Description

The mysql.default_password directive specifies the password that a connection should use if one is not defined in the connection string. The default value is none.

mysql.max_persistent

Syntax

```
mysql.max_persistent integer
```

Description

The mysql.max_persistent directive specifies the maximum allowable number of persistent connections per process when connecting to a MySQL database. The default value is -1, which indicates unlimited.

mysql.max_links

Syntax

```
mysql.max_links integer
```

Description

The `mysql.max_links` directive specifies the total number of connections that a single process can have, including both persistent and nonpersistent connections. The default value is -1, which indicates unlimited.

mSQL

msql.allow_persistent

Syntax

```
msql.allow_persistent boolean
```

Description

The `msql.allow_persistent` directive specifies whether persistent mSQL connections should be used. Persistent connections typically improve overall performance and should be used when possible, but are not available when PHP is run as a CGI program. The default value is On.

msql.max_persistent

Syntax

```
msql.max_persistent integer
```

Description

The `msql.max_persistent` directive specifies the maximum number of persistent connections allowed per process. The default value is -1, which indicates unlimited.

msql.max_links

Syntax

```
msql.max_links integer
```

Description

The `msql.max_links` directive specifies the total number of connections allowed per process. This includes both persistent and nonpersistent connections. The default value is -1, which indicates unlimited.

Postgres

pgsql.allow_persistent

Syntax

```
pgsql.allow_persistent boolean
```

Description

The `pgsql.allow_persistent` directive specifies whether persistent connections should be used when connecting to a Postgres database. Persistent connections typically improve overall performance and should be used when possible, but are not available when PHP is run as a CGI program. The default value is `On`.

pgsql.max_persistent

Syntax

```
pgsql.max_persistent integer
```

Description

The `pgsql.max_persistent` directive specifies the maximum number of persistent connections allowed per process. The default value is `-1`, which indicates unlimited.

pgsql.max_links

Syntax

```
pgsql.max_links integer
```

Description

The `pgsql.max_links` directive specifies the maximum number of connections allowed per process. This includes both persistent and nonpersistent connections. The default value is `-1`, which indicates unlimited.

Sybase

sybase.allow_persistent

Syntax

```
sybase.allow_persistent boolean
```

Description

The `sybase.allow_persistent` directive specifies whether persistent connections should be used when connecting to a Sybase database. The default value is `On`.

sybase.max_persistent

Syntax

```
sybase.max_persistent integer
```

Description

The `sybase.max_persistent` directive specifies the maximum number of persistent connections per process. Persistent connections typically improve overall performance and should be used when possible, but are not available when PHP is run as a CGI program. The default value is `-1`, which indicates unlimited.

sybase.max_links

Syntax

```
sybase.max_links integer
```

Description

The `sybase.max_links` directive specifies the total number of connections allowed per process. This includes both persistent and nonpersistent connections. The default value is `-1`, which indicates unlimited.

Sybase-CT

sybct.allow_persistent

Syntax

```
sybct.allow_persistent boolean
```

Description

The `sybct.allow_persistent` directive specifies whether persistent connections should be used when connecting to a Sybase-CT database. Persistent connections typically improve overall performance and should be used when possible, but are not available when PHP is run as a CGI program. The default value is `On`.

sybct.max_persistent

Syntax

```
sybct.max_persistent integer
```

Description

The `sybct.max_persistent` directive specifies the maximum number of persistent connections per process. The default value is -1, which indicates unlimited.

sybct.max_links

Syntax

```
sybct.max_links integer
```

Description

The `sybct.max_links` directive specifies the total number of connections allowed per process. This includes both persistent and nonpersistent connections. The default value is -1, which indicates unlimited.

sybct.min_server_severity

Syntax

```
sybct.min_server_severity integer
```

Description

The sybct.min_server_severity directive determines the minimum level of server messages that will be reported as warnings. The level defaults to 10, which includes errors that are of information severity or greater.

sybct.min_client_severity

Syntax

sybct.min_client_severity integer

Description

The sybct.min_client_severity directive sets the minimum level of client library messages that should be reported. The default value of 10 effectively disables reporting.

sybct.login_timeout

Syntax

sybct.login_timeout integer

Description

The sybct.login_timeout directive specifies how long a script should wait for connection to the database. The default value is one minute. If the timeout occurs after your script max_execution_time has been reached, you will not be able to act on this event.

sybct.timeout

Syntax

sybct.timeout integer

Description

The sybct.timeout directive specifies how long the script should wait for a select_db or query operation to return before indicating failure. The default timeout is no limit. If the timeout occurs after your script has reached the max_execution_time, you will not be able to act on this event.

sybct.hostname

Syntax

```
sybct.hostname string
```

Description

The sybct.hostname directive specifies the hostname from which you claim to be connecting. This information is visible using the sp_who() command in Sybase. The default value is none.

Informix

ifx.allow_persistent

Syntax

```
ifx.allow_persistent boolean
```

Description

The ifx.allow_persistent directive specifies whether persistent connections should be used with an Informix database. Persistent connections typically improve overall performance and should be used when possible, but are not available when PHP is run as a CGI program. The default value is On.

ifx.max_persistent

Syntax

```
ifx.max_persistent integer
```

Description

The ifx.max_persistent directive specifies the maximum number of persistent connections available per process. The default value is -1, which indicates unlimited.

ifx.max_links

Syntax

```
ifx.max_links integer
```

Description

The `ifx.max_links` directive specifies the total number of connections available per process. This includes both persistent and nonpersistent connections. The default value is -1, which indicates unlimited.

ifx.default_host

Syntax

```
ifx.default_host string
```

Description

The `ifx.default_host` directive indicates which hostname should be used to connect if none is provided in the connection string. The default value is none.

ifx.default_user

Syntax

```
ifx.default_user string
```

Description

The `ifx.default_user` directive indicates which user should be used to connect if none is provided in the connection string. The default value is none.

ifx.default_password

Syntax

```
ifx.default_password string
```

Description

The `ifx.default_password` directive indicates which password should be used to connect if none is provided in the connection string. The default value is none.

ifx.blobinfile

Syntax

```
ifx.blobinfile boolean
```

Description

The `ifx.blobinfile` directive specifies whether blob (binary large object) column data should be returned in memory or in a file. The default value is `Off`.

ifx.textasvarchar

Syntax

```
ifx.textasvarchar boolean
```

Description

The `ifx.textasvarchar` directive specifies whether text large object columns should be returned as normal strings (true) or as blob ID parameters (false). You can override the setting by using the `ifx_textasvarchar()` function. The default value is `Off`.

ifx.byteasvarchar

Syntax

```
ifx.bytesasvarchar boolean
```

Description

The `ifx.bytesasvarchar` directive specifies whether byte large object columns should be returned as normal strings (true) or as blob ID parameters (false). You can override the setting by using the `ifx_textasvarchar()` function. The default value is `Off`.

ifx.charasvarchar

Syntax

```
ifx.charasvarchar boolean
```

Description

The `ifx.charasvarchar` directive specifies whether white space should be removed (trimmed) from CHAR column data when returned. For example, if the data is stored as `"   some_data   "`, it will be returned as `"some_data"` when this directive is turned on. The default value is `Off`.

ifx.nullformat

Syntax

```
ifx.nullformat boolean
```

Description

The `ifx.nullformat` directive specifies how you would like empty values to be returned. Use true for the literal string `"NULL"` and false for the empty string `""`. This can be overridden by using the `ifx_nullformat()` function at runtime. The default value is `Off`.

Unified ODBC

uodbc.default_db

Syntax

```
uodbc.default_db string
```

Description

The `uodbc.default_db` directive specifies the name of the database when none is specified in the `odbc_connect()` or `odbc_pconnect()` function.

uodbc.default_user

Syntax

```
uodbc.default_user string
```

Description

The `uodbc.default_user` directive specifies which user to use when connecting to the database if none is specified in the `odbc_connect()` or `odbc_pconnect()` function. The default value is `none`.

uodbc.default_pw

Syntax

```
uodbc.default_pw string
```

Description

The uodbc.default_pw directive specifies which password to use when connecting to the database if none is specified in the odbc_connect() or odbc_pconnect() function. The default value is none.

uodbc.allow_persistent

Syntax

```
uodbc.allow_persistent boolean
```

Description

The uodbc.allow_persistent directive specifies whether persistent connections should be used when connecting to the database. Persistent connections typically improve overall performance and should be used when possible, but are not available when PHP is run as a CGI program. The default value is On.

uodbc.max_persistent

Syntax

```
uodbc.max_persistent integer
```

Description

The uodbc.max_persistent directive specifies the total number of persistent connections allowed per process. The default value is -1, which indicates unlimited.

uodbc.max_links

Syntax

```
uodbc.max_links integer
```

Description

The uodbc.max_links directive specifies the total number of connections allowed per process. This includes both persistent and nonpersistent connections. The default value is -1, which indicates unlimited.

BC Math

BC Math is the PHP library that enables you to perform arbitrary precision mathematics in your scripts. Arbitrary precision mathematics enables you to specify the number of digits after the decimal point in a number that should be used in calculations.

bcmath.scale

Syntax

```
bcmath.scale integer
```

Description

The `bcmath.scale` directive specifies the number of digits to the right of the decimal point to be considered and used in the result when doing BC Math calculations. For example, if `bcmath.scale` is set to 2, `bcadd (2.002,2.002)` results in `4.00`.

Debugger

The debugging method for PHP consists of specifying a hostname and port of a process that is listening for error messages sent from the PHP engine.

debugger.host

Syntax

```
debugger.host string
```

Description

The `debugger.host` directive specifies the DNS name or IP address of the host that is running the debugger. The default value is `localhost`.

debugger.port

Syntax

```
debugger.port string
```

Description

The `debugger.port` directive specifies the port on which the debugger is running. The default value is `7869`.

debugger.enabled

Syntax

```
debugger.enabled boolean
```

Description

The `debugger.enabled` directive specifies whether the debugger is On or Off. The default value is `Off`.

Safe Mode

The safe mode option in PHP allows control of which files can be accessed from a script using functions that access the file system, such as `include()`, `fopen()`, `readfile()`, and so on. The restriction is as follows: A file can be accessed either if it is owned by the same user ID as the script that is trying to access it, or if the file is in a directory to which the user of the running script has access.

safe_mode

Syntax

```
safe_mode boolean
```

Description

The `safe_mode` directive specifies whether `safe_mode` is enabled or disabled. The default value is `Off`.

safe_mode_exec_dir

Syntax

```
safe_mode_exec_dir string
```

Description

The `safe_mode_exec_dir` directive specifies the location of programs that are allowed to execute when running under safe mode. The `system()` function and other functions that execute system programs are covered by this directive. The default value is `none`.

Apache

Certain PHP directives can be set from within the Apache configuration files.

php_value

Syntax

```
php_value name value
```

Description

The `php_value` directive enables you to specify a PHP variable from an Apache config-uration file. The `php_admin_value` directive has more power, but is limited to being used only in the httpd.conf file.

php_flag

Syntax

```
php_flag name on | off
```

Description

The `php_flag` directive is used within an Apache configuration file to specify a PHP value as either `On` or `Off`. The `php_admin_flag` directive has more power, but is limited to being used only in the httpd.conf file.

php_admin_value

Syntax

```
php_admin_value name value
```

Description

The php_admin_value directive sets the value of a PHP variable from within an Apache configuration file. This directive can be used only from server-wide Apache configuration settings and cannot be used from the .htaccess files. This directive is capable of modifying the value of any PHP directive.

php_admin_flag

Syntax

```
php_admin_flag name  off | on
```

Description

The php_admin_flag directive sets the Boolean value of a PHP variable from within an Apache configuration file. This directive can be used only from server-wide Apache configuration settings and cannot be used from the .htaccess files. This directive is capable of modifying the value of any PHP directive.

engine

Syntax

```
engine boolean
```

Description

The engine directive is valid only when running PHP as an Apache module. It is used to turn on and off PHP parsing for individual directories or virtual servers. This setting is used in Apache's httpd.conf file.

Index

Symbols

A

F

G

H

N

Y-Z